Contemporary Treatment of Adult Male Sex Offenders

Mark S. Carich and Martin C. Calder

Russell House Publishing

First published in 2003 by:
Russell House Publishing Ltd.
4 St George's House
Uplyme Road
Lyme Regis
Dorset DT7 3LS

Tel: 01297-443948
Fax: 01297-442722
e-mail: help@russellhouse.co.uk
www.russellhouse.co.uk

British Library Cataloguing-in-publication Data:
A catalogue record for this book is available from the British Library.

ISBN: 1-903855-19-5

Typeset by TW Typesetting, Plymouth, Devon

Printed and bound in Great Britain by Antony Rowe Ltd., Chippenham ,Wiltshire

Russell House Publishing
is a group of social work, probation, education and
youth and community work practitioners and
academics working in collaboration with a professional
publishing team.
Our aim is to work closely with the field to produce
innovative and valuable materials to help managers,
trainers, practitioners and students.
We are keen to receive feedback on publications and
new ideas for future projects.

This book is dedicated to the significant people in my life.
First, to my immediate family, my wife Audrey, and daughters
Andrea and Cassie who have allowed me to pursue my interests.
Second, to my father Dr Peter A. Carich, to whom I have always
looked up to, deeply respected and learned the determination to
follow through with completing goals, and to my mother Mary Carich
who has always encouraged me. Third, to my mentors throughout
the years, Dr Harold Mosak of the Adler School in Chicago
and Dr Rolf Gordhamer of Texas Tech University

Mark S. Carich

To Janet, Stacey and Emma: who make life worth living.
To Callum Martin and Luke Santiago: so near yet so far.

Martin C. Calder

Contents

About the Authors

Mark S. Carich Ph.D. is co-ordinator of the Sexually Dangerous Persons Program with Illinois Corrections at Big Muddy River Correctional Center. He is on both the teaching and the dissertation faculties of the Alder School of Professional Psychology in Chicago. Dr Carich has written extensively around issues relating to the management of sex offenders. Dr Carich can be contacted on *MCarich@aol.com*

Martin C. Calder MA, CQSW is a Child Protection Co-ordinator with City of Salford Community and Social Services Directorate. He has written extensively on different aspects of child sexual abuse in order to collate and make available diverse and previously inaccessible materials for frontline staff. In doing so, he is attempting to narrow the gap between offender sophistication and professional capability. He is available for consultancy and training and can be contacted at *martinccalder@aol.com*

Introduction

The authors first united to address the need for accessible materials for busy frontline practitioners in 1999 and have collaborated since. This has proven useful since they bring a wealth of varied experience to their writing. Mark S. Carich operates within the criminal justice system in the United States whilst Martin C. Calder operates within the child protection system within the United Kingdom.

The idea for this book stemmed from the rapid changes taking place within the sex offender treatment system, many of which are universally experienced, and the need for generic frontline staff to keep up. The primary audience is thus workers who need to have a good preliminary introduction to the relevant issues and operational materials available to them. It does also contain some nuggets of innovative work for specialist workers in this area. These derive from clinical experience and this is essential at a time when we appear to be driven almost exclusively by a 'what works' agenda.

We hope that we have assembled a useful handbook for workers to begin to get a grasp of the key issues facing individuals and the field as a whole in treating adult male sex offenders.

Mark S. Carich and Martin C. Calder
December 2002

Chapter One

An Introduction to Adult Male Sex Offenders and Their Treatment

The sex offender treatment industry has grown significantly over the last decade as a response to public and professional pressure. This has been accompanied by a number of theoretical and practice developments, needed to tackle such a difficult target population. This book identifies the key components of sex offender treatment, exploring the key elements of each and making practical suggestions on how to approach the areas in practice. The synthesis of diverse information will allow the professional to discover:

- That sex offenders are treatable.
- That many professionals are equipped to undertake this work, given the space and guidance.
- How the initial and comprehensive assessments link with treatment work.
- Strategies for conducting the work.
- A framework for ordering the work.
- How to explore programme integrity and treatment effectiveness.
- How to assess future risks.

Sexual offending is a complex, often multi-determined problem (ATSA, 1997; Calder, 1999). It follows therefore that contemporary sex offender treatment is complex, requiring a variety of approaches and methods. Before we explore the approaches and methods associated with sex offender treatment, we feel that it is important to provide some guidance in this chapter around understanding the sex offender as this provides an essential building block to understanding sex offender treatment and management.

Understanding sexual offences and offenders

Definitions are important for several reasons: if they are too narrow, they restrict our understanding, figures of incidence and prevalence, as well as our intervention threshold (Calder, 1999). Conversely, if they are too broad, they are all embracing and can detract from focusing on the highest risk cases.

Sexual offending or aggression is a type of paraphilia. The term paraphilia simply means 'substitute love'. It has been defined as a deviant sexual activity outside the (culturally defined) 'norms' (Laws and O'Donohue, 1997); and as 'an erotic sexual condition of being recurrently responsive to, and obsessively dependent on, an unusual, personally or socially acceptable social stimulus, perceptual or in fantasy, in order to have a state of erotic arousal initiated or maintained, and in order to achieve or maintain orgasm (Money, 1986). While some sex offenders have multiple paraphilias (averaging 3-4) (Marshall and Eccles, 1991) not all inappropriate sexual behaviour can be characterised as a paraphilia. Indeed, isolated acts can be precipitated by mental problems, illness, or loneliness (Becker and Kaplan, 1988).

There are many types of sex offenders and offences (Carich and Adkerson, 1995) and include:

- exhibitionism (exposing their genitals)
- voyeurism: (observing others without their knowledge or consent)
- obscene phone calls
- frotteurism or fondling/unwarranted sexual touch or rubbing, i.e.
  - breast fondling
  - genital fondling
  - fondling on genitals during the offence etc.
- dry intercourse
- perform/receive vaginal intercourse
- perform/receive anal intercourse
- penetration with an object
- sexual behaviour involving unwarranted urination or defecation
- physical violence
- sadism (inflict physical pain)
- masochism (receive physical pain)
- mutilation
- bestiality
- public masturbation
- rape
- cross dressing
- photographing others
- being photographed
- paedophilia (sex of any type with children)
- use of pornography
- any type of fetish involving sexual assault
- stalking

- acquaintance rape
- stranger rape
- date rape
- marital rape
- unwarranted sexual sadism
- attempted rape
- adult rape/physical force
- adult rape/verbal coercion
- sexual attempted murder
- sexual murder
- serial sexual murder
- necrophilia (sex with the dead)

There is a wide range of paraphilias beyond the scope of this book, each requiring a clearly unique treatment approach. Laws and O'Donohue (1997) have edited a useful book that explores the detail of each paraphilia and the recommended treatment approaches.

Towards a definition of sexual abuse

Given that child sexual abuse is a complex and multi-determined problem, it can be viewed from a wide range of perspectives. This is reflected in the number and variance of definitions. It is generally accepted to be any form of non-consenting interpersonal sexual behaviour that poses some risk of harm to the other individual (Groth and Oliveri, 1989). It is usually defined according to several key elements:

- The betrayal of trust and responsibility.
- The abuse of power.
- The inability of children to consent.
- The violation of another's rights.
  (extended from MacLeod and Saraga, 1988).

The problem for professionals is that there are too many different definitions and this makes it very difficult for them when they are trying to understand the problem. It also makes it very difficult when they try to interpret the findings of any 'comparative' research. We will try to make several points around the three key elements above by selecting a number of high profile definitions of sexual abuse. For example, Schechter and Roberge (1976) defined sexual abuse as:

> ... *the involvement of dependent, developmentally immature children and adolescents in [sexual] activities they do not truly comprehend, to which they are unable to give informed consent, or that violate the social taboos of family roles.*

The last part of this definition is unnecessary for extra-familial abuse. This definition is general enough to allow the worker discretion in each individual case. The strength of this definition is that it talks about informed consent. Consent is agreement based on the knowledge of the full consequences. It is difficult to accept that children are capable of giving informed consent to sex with adults. In situations where they are threatened or fear being threatened, they may 'consent', but it is not freely given and is certainly not informed in the sense that they are unaware of the significance of their actions. There is a need to differentiate between true consent and legal consent as there can be consent to an unlawful sexual act, thus leaving legal/true consent in conflict. As such, true consent refers to 'being informed, not forced, in an equal relationship, without financial or other inducements, and free of any pressure to comply' (Calder, 1999).

Many of the terms here require definition in their own right. For example, 'dependent', 'developmentally immature', 'do not truly comprehend', etc. This definition also does not include any explicit breakdown of contact and non-contact abuse, which is unfortunate as it does not capture the range of abuses perpetrated against children. The range of sexual behaviours that constitute child sexual abuse is an integral part of any definition, as it acts as a boundary between acceptable and unacceptable behaviours (Calder, 1997; 2001). It also does not allow for the severity of the abuse to be assessed, whereas other writers, such as Russell (1983) have. She offered three categories of abuse in terms of its severity: very serious (e.g. vaginal intercourse or oral sex), serious (e.g. genital fondling or digital penetration), and least serious (e.g. intentional sexual touching of clothed breasts or genitals). This allows some gradient for the abuse to be considered. Table 1.1 overleaf provides some details of contact versus non-contact offences.

The definition is useful in that it allows for culturally relative considerations, although it does not embrace the destructiveness to the victim of the abuse, even where the offender has been seductive rather than forceful. It also does not acknowledge that the harm caused is not always predictable to an outsider, as there is not always a direct correlation between the severity of the abuse and the ensuing harm. What some may consider 'minor' abuse may have devastating and traumatic consequences for the victim. Tower (1989) advised us to consider the following variables in assessing the degree of

Table 1.1: Types of contact vs non-contact offences.

Non-contact offences	Contact offences
Obscene phone calling	Physical sexual harassment
Stalking	Fondling (frottage)
Peeping (voyeurism)	Paedophilia (sex with children)
Flashing (exhibitionism)	Date rape
Verbal sexual harassment	Sadistic rape
Unwarranted computer sex	Marital rape
Photography	Bestiality
Pornography	Sexual attempted murder
Mail/computer sex	Sexual murder
	Serial sexual murder
	Necrophilia (sex with the dead)

trauma to a child: the type of abuse; the identity of the perpetrator; the duration of the abuse; the extent of the abuse; the age at which the child was abused; the first reactions of significant others at disclosure; the point at which the abuse was disclosed; and the personality structure of the victim.

Another useful definition of sexual abuse is that of Suzanne Sgroi as it emphasises the power relationship between the perpetrator and the child and points to the fact that the child has had no choice in the matter:

> *Child sexual abuse is a sexual act imposed on a child who lacks emotional, maturational, and cognitive development. The ability to lure a child into a sexual relationship is based upon the all-powerful and dominant position of the adult or older adolescent perpetrator, which is in sharp contrast to the child's age, dependency and subordinate position. Authority and power enable the perpetrator, implicitly or directly, to coerce the child into sexual compliance.*
>
> (Sgroi, 1982)

Baker and Duncan (1985) offered us a definition focusing on the aims of the perpetrator:

> *A child ... is usually sexually abused when another person who is sexually mature involves the child in any activity which the other person expects to lead to their sexual arousal. This might involve intercourse, touching, exposure of the sexual organs, showing pornographic material or talking about sex in an erotic way.*

If we are to ever agree a definition of child sexual abuse, there are certain key issues that would need to be embraced and agreement reached. They might include:

The range of sexual acts
Elliott et al. (1995) found that all the offenders in their sample indecently assaulted their victims,

sometimes in more than one way. 72% of them reported that this included masturbating the child and being masturbated by the child. 31% engaged in mutual oral sex and 57% attempted or actually engaged in full sexual intercourse, either vaginal or anal. 8% murdered or attempted to murder the child victim during or after the sexual assault. 85% committed the sexual acts with one victim at a time although the remaining 5% had multiple victims present. 93% acted alone.

The first abusive action often involved one or two immediate sexual acts, such as sexual touching or genital kissing, whilst others desensitised the child by asking them to do something that would help the offender, such as undressing. The majority of offenders carefully tested the child's reaction to sex, by bringing up sexual matters or having sexual materials around, or by subtly increasing sexual touching. This 'normalised' sexual setting could be achieved by using sexually explicit videos, or magazines, or sexualised talking.

Waterhouse et al. (1993) reported that most sexual abuse was severe. In 40% of cases children were subjected to sexual manipulation of their genitals either beneath or above their clothing, vaginal intercourse occurred in 20% of cases, whilst 4% of the sample were subjected to oral sex, 4% to sodomy, and 5% to non-contact abuse.

Age differences
The key issue here is the equality of the relationship. Any factor which makes a relationship unequal creates a power imbalance – which can occur through differences in age, size, levels of sexual knowledge or understanding, or developmental level. Elliott et al. (1995) found that the child victim ranged

from 1-18 years. The mean age of the youngest victims was 8.5 years: the mean age of the eldest victims was 13 years. 6.6% also assaulted victims aged 19–45; one offender abused a 65 year old victim (583-4).

Researchers usually include an age differential between abuser and victim of five years or more (Watkins and Bentovim, 1992, 198). The narrower the age difference, the more difficult the judgement becomes. For example, the issue of informed consent usually runs into some trouble when we talk about 15 and 16 year olds (Trowell, 1991, 85), although the offender cannot argue with figures of 13% of girls abused being under six, and 60% of girls sexually abused being under 12 when first abused (Elliott, 1986). Despite this evidence, there are those who believe that the child plays a role in their own abuse (West, 1986), regardless of the age or power imbalance.

Coercion

Location of offence
Elliott et al. (1995) found that offenders often used more than one location to abuse children. 61% reported abusing in their own home compared to 49% in the victim's home. 44% reported abusing in public places such as toilets or parks, compared to 13% in the homes of friends, 6% in the vicinity of the offender's home and 4% in the car. It is highly significant that 48% of the offenders isolated their victims through baby-sitting.

Strategies used

- Offering to play games, teach them a sport or play a musical instrument.
- Giving bribes, taking them on outings, or giving them a lift home.
- Using affection, understanding and love.
- Telling stories involving lies, magic or treasure hunts.
- Asking a child for help.

(Elliott et al., 1995)

They found that 84% used a strategy that had been previously successful compared to 16% who adapted theirs over time. 30% replayed their own experiences, whilst 14% were influenced through pornography, television, films and the media.

Offenders can use one or a combination of methods to secure a child's compliance. Elliott et al. found that 19% used physical force with a child, 44% used coercion and persuasion, and 46% used bribery and gifts in exchange for sexual touches. 39% were prepared to use threats or violence to control a resisting child. 61% used passive methods of control such as stopping the abuse and then coercing and persuading once again. 33% specifically told the child not to tell compared to 24% who used threats of dire consequences, whilst 24% used anger and the threat of physical force, and 20% threatened the loss of love or said the child was to blame. 61% were 'very worried' about the child disclosing.

The Waterhouse research reported on a wide range of means sex offenders used to procure sex from naïve children. Actual physical coercion and force was used in some 20% of cases, verbal inducements or bribes in 14%, and coercion by verbal threats of violence in 6% of cases. Margolin (1992) shattered the myth of the friendly and 'gentle' grandfather approaches reported earlier by Goodwin et al. (1983), finding evidence of explicit threats and overt physical coercion (740). Conte et al. (1989) also noted that verbal threats are based on an understanding of the child and what will be an effective threat against them. Conte et al. found that those relatively non-violent sex offenders in their sample had employed a range of coercive behaviours, e.g. conditioning through the use of reward and punishment, and letting the child view violence towards their mother (299). Furniss (1991) noted that the offender will deliberately induce sexual arousal in the child which can lead to loyalty from their victims.

Relationships
The context of the relationship in which the sexual behaviour occurs defines the harmful or abusive or illegal nature of the act (Ryan et al., 1990). Russell (1988) differentiated intra- and extra-familial abuse as follows. She defined extra-familial child sexual abuse as 'one or more unwanted sexual experiences with persons unrelated by blood or marriage, ranging from petting (touching of breasts or genitals or attempts at such touching) to rape, before the victim turned 14 years of age, and completed or attempted forcible rape experiences from the ages of 14 to 17 years (inclusive).' She defined intra-familial child sexual abuse as 'any kind of exploitive sexual contact that occurred between relatives, no matter how distant the relationship, before the victim turned 18 years old.

Experiences involving sexual contact with a relative that were wanted and with a peer were regarded as non-exploitive, for example, sex play between cousins or siblings of approximately the same ages. An age difference of less than five years was the criterion for a peer relationship' (22).

Sexual offences are often perpetrated by someone very familiar to the victim. Elliott et al. (1995) found that 46% of the sex offenders felt that a 'special relationship' with the child was vital. They found that 66% knew their victims. Most sex offenders can be divided into three groups based on their relationship with the victim: family members, friends or acquaintances, and strangers:

- **Family members**: Waterhouse et al. (1993) found that 40% of offenders were related to the victim. In their earlier research, Waterhouse and Carnie (1992) found that the offender was the natural father in 31% of cases, step-fathers in 21% of cases, and co-habitees in 11% of cases. Kelly et al. (1991) found that close relatives (father-figures, siblings, grandfathers, uncles and aunts) offended in 14% of cases, compared to 68% perpetrated by distant relatives, known adults and peers. Oates (1990) found that in 75% of cases the offender was known to the child and vice-versa. In 50% of the cases, the offender was a member of the child's own family, whilst 50% were trusted friends who had access to the children.
- **Friends or acquaintances**: Elliott et al. (1995) found that 66% of offenders knew their victims through their families, friends or acquaintances, e.g., babysitting. Waterhouse et al. (1993) found that 60% of the sex offenders in their sample were not biologically related to their victim, and
- **Strangers**: The range of offenders unknown to the child pre-abuse ranges from 18% (Kelly et al., 1991) through 25% (Oates, 1990) to one-third (Elliott et al., 1995).

Consent

Consent implies full knowledge, understanding and choice. Consent as agreement should include all of the following: understanding what is proposed based on age, maturity, developmental level, functioning and experience; knowledge of societal standards of what is being proposed; awareness of potential consequences and alternatives; assumption that

agreement or disagreement will be respected equally; voluntary decision; and mental competence (The National Task Force, 1993, 8–9). This is different from compliance. Freeman-Longo and Blanchard (1998, 36) state that 'compliance is the act or process of going along with or giving in to another desire, demand or proposal and may occur under psychological pressure or duress . . . may indicate lack of knowledge of consequences, rather than clear and informed agreement.'

The child's specific vulnerability

Summit (1990) addressed himself to the various aspects of intrinsic, specific vulnerability of children in this equation. He argued that we can only comprehend the child's abject helplessness to deal with sexual assault as we come to see our own determined avoidance on this issue. The following factors highlight the child's specific vulnerabilities:

Children are perfect victims: if only by virtue of size and power. They are not allowed to challenge the demands of responsible adults. To the naïve adult, they cannot imagine that a child would not resist and would not tell, nor imagine the extraordinary gulf of power that a large person imposes on a child. To reverse this, we ' . . . need to risk painful empathy with the uniquely powerless position of the child as sex object . . .' (61). Until people can make transitions, they are 'one-down to all offenders', who know already that they can overpower the child and the trusting adult.

Children are totally dependent: on adults, without whom they cannot survive. They will therefore protect their access to the victim at any price, adapting tenaciously to any mysterious conditions that adults impose on that access. Secrecy is paradoxical to our habitual trust that a child would confide their deepest concerns to a loving parent. Children may assume that mothers should know everything and, therefore must know and not care. They may then become discredited by the child due to their ineffectual protection. The intruder, having broken the rules and got away with it, assumes a kind of divine authority, and the child becomes fearfully dependent on the offender's instructions. Where the child's need for love, attention, approval and affection are thwarted at home, they search for them elsewhere. Once abused, they may fall into the trap of believing the abuse is the only reliable anchor. We should not feel that sexual abuse of children only occurs in dysfunctional families, as many children across all types and classes of family feel alienated in their family settings.

Children are vulnerable through their intrinsic naïvety: Their need to be taught renders them vulnerable to abuse and to a position of irrelevance, as if their ideas and feelings do not count. A victimised child is therefore in no position to teach us that we must suspect someone that we know to be trustworthy. Any detraction from this is viewed as dangerous to adult authority and may lead to mockery by their peers. Thus the child who discloses child sexual abuse infects the listener with a peculiar helplessness, with the ultimate threat of being disgraced.

Children are vulnerable through their imagination: They translate reality into playful games and fantasies. We often discredit unwelcome complaints despite research that shows that children tend to be accurate witnesses (Goodman et al., 1987). If they found the abuse painful to remember, they will dissociate themselves as a defence. The more severe the abuse, the most effective dissociation will occur. As a perpetrator, many will learn to manipulate dissociation, in the knowledge that the more severe the invasion, the more immune they may become from detection.

Children are vulnerable because they are sexual: As they may have a physical response to the abuse, e.g. reflex erection, even though they may not like the abuse itself. Many can become confused by this, and may feel more guilty about it. It is a maxim amongst sex offenders that a boy will never tell if he has been stimulated to erection. They glory in the illusion that sex with children is both natural and healthy.

Children are vulnerable because of their innocence and may become vulnerable as a result of their resemblance to the offender's particular obsession: Where the child prototype is considered to fit a specific gender, age, shape and colour.

Offenders also have a tendency to target vulnerable children, e.g. handicapped, those with a physical or learning difficulty (Craft, 1992, iii) those in poor parenting situations and disorganised families, those previously victims to sexual abuse (Miller, 1978), as well as children who are not assertive or outgoing, and who are trusting or withdrawn (Renvoize, 1993, 109). Sanderson pointed out that the abuser can almost instinctively pick out vulnerable

children, whilst ignoring those who might resist (44).

Conte et al. (1989) interviewed a sample of adult sex offenders who claimed a special ability to identify such vulnerable children, and to manipulate this vulnerability as a means of sexually using them. Vulnerability was defined in terms of children's status (e.g. living in a divorced home or being young), and in terms of emotional or psychological state (e.g. a needy child, a depressed or unhappy child). Regardless of their current targeting, we all need to acknowledge that **all** children have inherent vulnerabilities. The protection of children needs to include a strategy for making children less vulnerable, recognising that all the factors remain weighted on the side of the adult, e.g. superior knowledge level and skill which will not easily be overcome by children.

Elliott et al. (1995) found the following selection characteristics used by sex offenders:

- 42% felt the child had to be pretty.
- 27% cited the way the child dressed was important.
- 18% reported being young or small was significant for them.
- 13% focused on innocent or trusting children.
- 49% reported an attraction to those who lacked confidence or had low self-esteem.

It is clear therefore that a sexually aggressive act or sexual offence is defined as a sexual behaviour (of some type) that violates another person's rights.

Towards a definition of sexual offenders

There are also as many definitions of sex offenders as there are individuals doing the defining. Schwartz (1995) noted that the definition of sex offenders is shaped largely by the sexual mores of the times. An act may be defined as a sex crime depending on the degree of consent of the partner, their age, kinship, sex, the nature of the act, the offender's intention, or the setting. A behaviour that in itself may be considered perfectly normal can become a serious criminal offence if it violates any of the above qualifiers.

Sexual offenders do not neatly fit into categories, and thus a continuum of behaviours is a preferred method of definition. Many feminists see sexual offending behaviour along a continuum of 'normal' male behaviour, with such offending representing one of the most

Figure 1.1: A continuum of sexual behaviours.

Consenting – sexual activities	**Paraphiliac –** behaviour that doesn't harm others	**Sexual harassment –** behaviour that harms others	**Prostitution –** sexual assault	**Paraphiliac –** murder	**Sex crimes –**	**Rape**

This continuum derives from work with adult victims of sexual abuse. This continuum ranges from consenting sexual activities to sexual offences and ultimately rape and murder. Consenting sexual activities have no negative experiences (i.e., nude dancing, consenting telephone sex, pornography, etc.). The next category involves sexual behaviour with unanticipated negative experiences (i.e., triggers traumatic experiences). This continuum moves through illegal consenting sexual behaviours to sexual crimes. The second continuum (below) relates to hands-on and hands-off sexual offences:

Covert offences (non-physical contact)						**Overt offences** (physical contact)
(Hands off _____					_____	**Hands on)**
verbal sexual harrassment	non contact, non consensual (peeping/ flashing)	sexual contact without sadism (date rape, paedophilia) sexual (contact) harassment	physically (sadistic) rape	sexual murder		serial sexual murder

extreme consequences of the socialisation of boys and men. Sexual offending is seen as a means of assuring them of their male identity as well as serving as a method of social control via the maintenance of unequal gender relations (Calder, 1999).

The term 'offending' is a legal concept that refers to any sexual behaviour prohibited by law. Whilst this term implies that a criminal conviction will have been secured, it is widely recognised that many sexual assaults remain unreported, and many of these that are do not secure a successful criminal outcome. Just because allegations from a child are believed, this does not equate with legal proof that abuse has taken place. Only 2% of allegations are found to be untrue (Jones, 1985), whilst close to one-third of allegations are falsely retracted (Sahd, 1980). Additional factors that inhibit successful criminal outcomes include a lack of corroborative evidence, the age of the child and the stress of participating in any criminal forum. In the UK, convicted sex offenders whose victims are children under 18 years assume the 'Schedule One' status for life.

As such, it is widely accepted that a broader definition of sexual offending through a continuum is needed to embrace all the behaviours that result in sexual abuse.

A continuum of sexual offending

Freeman-Longo and Blanchard (1998) proposed a useful continuum of sexual behaviours (see Figure 1.1).

Typologies of sex offenders

Sex offenders are an extremely heterogeneous group that cannot be characterised by single motivational or aetiological factors. This has not prevented various attempts being made to create typological frameworks, which aim to split this broad group into more homogeneous sub-groups. Typologies or categories of offenders are based on a number of variables: victim type, victim selection, arousal, criminal characteristics, social skills, lifestyle, personality characteristics, motivation, type of offences, and situation. Categories are arbitrarily selected based on the above characteristics.

Classical typologies

The current typologies according to the DSMIV (for details see Chapter 2) involve non-contact offences (i.e., voyeurism or peeping, exhibitionism or flashing) and contact offences (i.e. frottage or fondling, sadism, adult sexual abuse and paedophilia). Paedophilia is defined as 'adults whose preferred or exclusive method of achieving sexual excitement is the act of fantasy in engaging in sexual activity with pre-pubescent children (generally aged 13 and under). The difference in age between the adult (who must be at least 16 years of age) and the pre-pubescent child is at least five years. For late adolescents with this disorder, no precise age difference is specified' (Becker and Kaplan, 1988). The strong attraction to children is usually for at least a six month period. The DSMIV does not include other factors to help differentiate between offenders in the above categories.

The following are some examples of sex offender typologies:

Regressed and fixated offenders

Regressed offenders do not have a lengthy history of offending, but offend later in life. They are now viewed as situational offenders. These offenders have a conventional lifestyle and appropriate age relationships prior to the offence. Characteristics include:

- Their primary sexual orientation is to their own age mates.
- They become sexually interested in children only in adulthood.
- Their sexual attraction to children is usually precipitated by stress.
- Their involvement with children is frequently on an occasional basis.
- Their first sexual offence is more likely to be impulsive than premeditated.
- They regress to involvement with children as a result of conflicts in their adult relationships; they treat the child as a substitute for an adult, and in incest situations, they totally abandon their parental role.
- Their primary sexual interest is in girls.
- Their sexual contact with children co-occurs with their sexual relationships with adults, and they are usually married or in long-term cohabitating relationships with women.
- The consumption of alcohol is quite often associated with their sexual offences.
- They have more traditional lifestyles than the fixated offenders, although their peer relationships are often undeveloped.
- Their sexual offences constitute a 'maladaptive attempt to cope with specific life, stresses'.

(Groth, 1982)

Fixated offenders are long-term chronic offenders. They have a lifestyle of offending. Their characteristics include (Groth, 1982, 217):

- Their primary sexual orientation is to children.
- Their sexual interest in children emerges at the onset of adolescence.
- Their sexual attraction to children is not precipitated by stress.
- Their sexual orientation to children is persistent and involves compulsive behaviour.
- Their sexual offences tend to be premeditated.
- They identify closely with the victim and may behave on the same level as children, or they may play a parental role toward the child.
- Their primary sexual interest is in boys.
- They rarely have sexual contacts with age mates, and tend to be 'single or in a marriage of convenience'.
- They usually have no history of alcohol or other drug abuse.
- They are immature, and suffer from 'poor socio-sexual peer relationships'.
- Their sexual offences constitute a 'maladaptive resolution of life issues'.

According to Groth, fixated offenders who are sexually attracted to pre-adolescent children are technically described as paedophile, while those who are sexually attracted to adolescent children are hebephiles (1982, 216). Hebophiles are those who find themselves sexually attracted to young teenagers or adolescents. It is a term rarely used today.

Groth goes on to outline three classical types of rapists:

1. **Anger rape** – 'Anger rape is intended to hurt, debase and express contempt for the victim and is marked by gratuitous violence. The act is not sexually satisfying for the rapist, who often views any type of sexuality as offensive and thus an appropriate weapon.'
2. **Power rape** – 'Power rape serves as a means of exercising dominance, mastery, strength, authority, and control over the victim. There is little need for excessive physical force.'
3. **Sadistic rape** – 'Sadistic rape represents the most severe pathologies as well as the most dangerous type of assault. The ritual of torturing the victim and the perception of suffering and degradation becomes eroticised, and as the assailant's arousal

builds, so may the violence of his acts, progressing in some cases to lust murder.'

Rapists may also be classified by either taking advantage of an opportunity with little planning (situational) or by carefully planned, stalking behaviours.

Preferential and situational sexual offenders

Freeman-Longo and Blanchard (1998) distinguish between preferential and situational sexual offenders.

Preferential offenders are the chronic offenders who prefer child sexual relationships and peer age. These are the paedophilas, who are highly aroused to children. Much of their lives are centred around searching for victims and molesting children. Extroverted molesters have social skills to seduce their victims while introverted offenders do not. Preferential offenders are usually chronic long-term offenders. These individuals develop lifestyles in which offending is a predominant theme.

Situational child offenders are similar to regressed offenders (Freeman-Longo and Blanchard, 1998). These offenders have normal conventional social and sexual development over the years. They prefer and usually have age-appropriate peers. Later in life, they sexually focus on children. This is triggered by stress, interpersonal tension and conflicts, and inability to cope with life. Situational offenders do not have chronic patterns of offending.

Another typology used by the FBI and other law enforcement agencies was developed by Lanning (1992) to help law enforcement officials track and apprehend sex offenders, who are child molesters and/or kidnappers. He subdivided situational and preferential offenders as outlined in Table 1.2 overleaf.

MTC typologies

Knight and Prentky (1990) have developed an elaborate taxonomy involving two Axis': Axis 1 and Axis 2. Axis 1 involves sexual deviance, while Axis 2 involves social competence. They have developed two taxonomics: one for rapists and the second for child molesters. Although quite complicated, it does add a unique dimension on social competence. A brief synopsis of the different types is provided in Table 1.4.

Figures 1.2 and 1.3 offer a useful guide to the scoring process.

Figure 1.4 provides a useful diagrammatic view of how the typology is scored.

Typologies: an integrative model

Campbell, Carich and Burgener (2000) developed a five factor typology to encapsulate those described here.

Type 1: Regressed offender

- Low risk to re-offend by actuarial measure
- Primarily incest offender
- Short offending history (time span and frequency)
- Few victims (1-2 victims)
- Preference for appropriate consenting sex

Type 2: Situational/opportunity to offend

- Low-moderate risk to re-offend by actuarial measure
- Sporadic/occasional victims (2-4 victims)
- Takes advantage of situation to offend
- No serious Axis I and II problems
- Preference toward opposite sex victim
- Moderate offending history

Type 3: Chronic offender

- High risk to re-offend by actuarial measure
- Strong deviant arousal patterns
- Negative lifestyle
- Personality disorder
- Preference toward same sex

Type 4: Extreme hard core

- Extreme high risk to re-offend by actuarial measure
- Low motivation for change
- High psychopathy index
- Long history of offending
- Diverse victim pattern
- Large numbers of victims

Type 5: Mentally disturbed offender

- Serious Axis 1 diagnosis
- Organic brain damage
- Mentally retarded or developmentally disabled

Whilst such typologies played a vitally important part in forging an understanding of why people offend sexually, the more understanding they allowed us to gain has relegated them to being too limited and restrictive.

Table 1.2: FBI/law enforcement typologies.

Situational Types

A. Regressed:
1. Low self-esteem
2. Poor coping skills
3. Uses children as sexual substitutes
4. Victim criteria is based on availability
5. Will coerce victim into sex
6. May or may not collect pornography (child/adult), if so will usually make it homemade)

B. Morally Indiscriminate:
1. Seems to be a growing category
2. Has a general pattern of abusive behaviour
3. Abuses wife and friends
4. Lies, cheats and steals whenever he/she thinks they can get away with it
5. Has a 'why not' attitude
6. Selects victims based on vulnerability and availability
7. Acts on urge, for example a child is there, so he acts out
8. Tends to be impulsive person
9. Lacks conscience
10. Victims may be strangers
11. Collects detective magazines or adult porn (S and M)
12. May collect child porn especially pubescent children
13. Tends to lure, force, or manipulate victims

C. Sexually Indiscriminate:
1. A sexual experimenter, will try anything sexual
2. Has no real sexual preference for children
3. Boredom with sex
4. Could be their own children
5. Provide children to other adults via sex groups, swapping, etc.
6. Clearly defined S and M sexual preference
7. Large collections of adult pornography
8. May have some child pornography

D. Inadequate:
1. Seems to be a social misfit
2. May have mental retardation or psychosis
3. May be a shy teenager with no friends
4. Mostly harmless but can kill
5. Children are not viewed as threatening
6. Motives seem to be curiosity and insecurity
7. Eccentric personality disorders

8. Possible senility
9. May still live with parents
10. Tends to be a build up of impulses
11. Appears to be a loner
12. Has difficulty expressing anger and can be explosive
13. May be into sexual torture, in conjunction with anger
14. Victims may be elderly
15. Low social competence
16. Selects vulnerable victims
17. May select or substitute adult victims even though he fears adults

Preferential Types

A. Seducer:
1. Dates with gifts, attention and affection
2. Seduces over a period of time
3. Lowers sexual inhibitions
4. Has multiple victims simultaneously
5. Sex rings
6. Ability to identify with children
7. Knows how to listen to children
8. Knows how to communicate well with children
9. Will use adult status and authority
10. Emphasises secrecy
11. May use violence and threats

B. Introverted:
1. Has preference to children, but lacks the interpersonal skills to seduce
2. Uses minimal amount of verbal communication
3. Hangs around playgrounds and parks
4. May expose himself as a precursor
5. May make obscene telephone calls
6. May marry a woman with children, to access the children
7. Has predictable selection of children
8. May use a child prostitute

C. Sadistic:
1. Sexual preference for children
2. Sexual arousal involves inflicting pain or suffering (distress of the victim)
3. Uses lures or force
4. More likely to abduct, kidnap or kill
5. There does not appear to be a large number, maybe less than 5% of all sexual offenders

What are the characteristics of sexual offenders?

It is impossible to effectively intervene in a process that you do not fully understand. This section attempts to describe what we know about how offenders operate. This can be useful to both the workers and the offenders themselves, as the latter are unlikely to change if they do not understand why or in what ways success may be found.

What is consistently clear is that sex offenders do not present as remarkably different from others with social, personal or behavioural

Table 1.3: MTC: R3-9 Factor typology of rapist.

Type 1:   Opportunistic/high social competence – impulsive, unplanned, but socially competent, controlled by environmental factors.

Type 2:   Opportunistic/low social competence – impulsive, unplanned, lacks social skills or competence, controlled by environmental factors.

Type 3:   Pervasively angry – undifferentiated anger or chronically angry, in which rage is not sexualized.

Type 4:   Sexual sadistic/overt type – poor differentiation between sexual and aggressive drives/erotic and destructive thoughts and/or fantasies, in which this type are belligerent, uses physically damaging behaviour and greater planning in offences.

Type 5:   Sexual sadistic/high social competence/muted type – same as Type 4 except that sadistic behaviour is expressed symbolically or through covert fantasies, lifestyle impulsivity, with social skills.

Type 6:   Sexual non-sadistic/high social competency – this type includes the following characteristics: sexual fantasies are devoid of the synergistic (fused) relation between sex and aggression; less interpersonal aggression in both sexual and non-sexual contexts; core feelings of inadequacy regarding sexuality, masculinity, etc. with high level of social adequacy.

Type 7:   Sexual non-sadistic/low social competency – this is the same as Type 6 except for the level of social skills.

Type 8:   Vindictive low social competency type – patterns reflect targeting of women as the exclusive focus on anger, marked with degrading comments, humiliation, etc. including verbal abuse to brutal murders, lack of social skills.

Type 9:   Vindictive moderate social competence – the same as type 8 except the level of social competence.

Table 1.4: MTC: CM3 – Typologies of child molesters.

The authors use a two axis system with four types on Axis 1 and six types on Axis 2 (see below for descriptions). Since every offender is classified on both levels there are 24 possible combinations. Axis 1 assesses the paedophilic interest, while Axis 2 assesses social competence.

Axis 1

Type 0:   High fixation/low social competence: high level of paedophilic arousal with low social competence.

Type 1:   High fixation/high social competence: high level of arousal with high social skills.

Type 2:   Low fixation/low social competence: low levels of arousal with inadequate social skills.

Type 3:   Low fixation/high social competence: low levels of arousal and high levels of skills.

Axis 2

Type 1:   High amount of contact time with children, but the relationships are non-sexual and non-orgasmic.

Type 2:   High amount of contact time with children, but the relationship is narcissistic and lacks meaning and orgasmic behaviours.

Type 3:   Low amount of contact with children/low physical injury/non-sadistic: low level of contact with children, lacks physical injury and cruelty.

Type 4:   Low amount of contact with children/low physical injury/sadistic: lacks multiple contextual relationships (other than sexual) with children, does not inflict physical injury, but can be verbally sadistic and may engage in bondage, urination, spanking etc. Sadism in this context is sexualised aggression.

Type 5:   Low amount of contact/high physical injury/non-sadistic: lack of multi-contextual non-sexual relationships with children, high on physical injury, but non-sadistic.

Type 6:   Low amount of contact/high physical injury/sadistic: lack of multiple contextual sexual relationships with children, high level of physical injury and very sadistic (enjoys inflicting pain).

difficulties, except in the nature of their offending, rendering detection remarkably difficult (Calder, 1999). We know that as many as 90% of sexual crimes go unreported, thus leaving us to construct our knowledge base from a relatively small sample of the offending population. Many sex offenders present as outwardly respectable men who don't resemble 'monsters'. Indeed, 'monsters' don't get near children – 'nice men' do. Most research tells us that offenders function as 'normal' and heterosexual members of society, often in

Figure 1.2: Primary motivation.

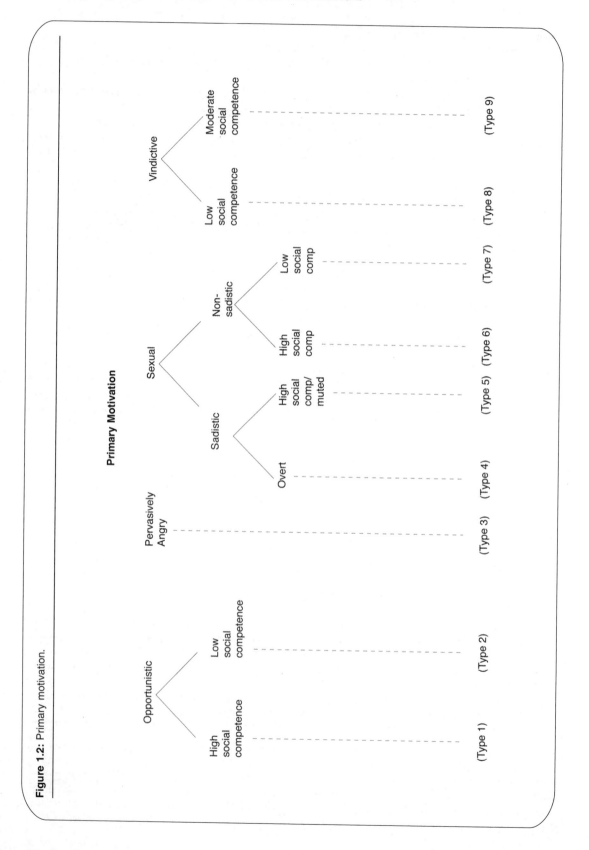

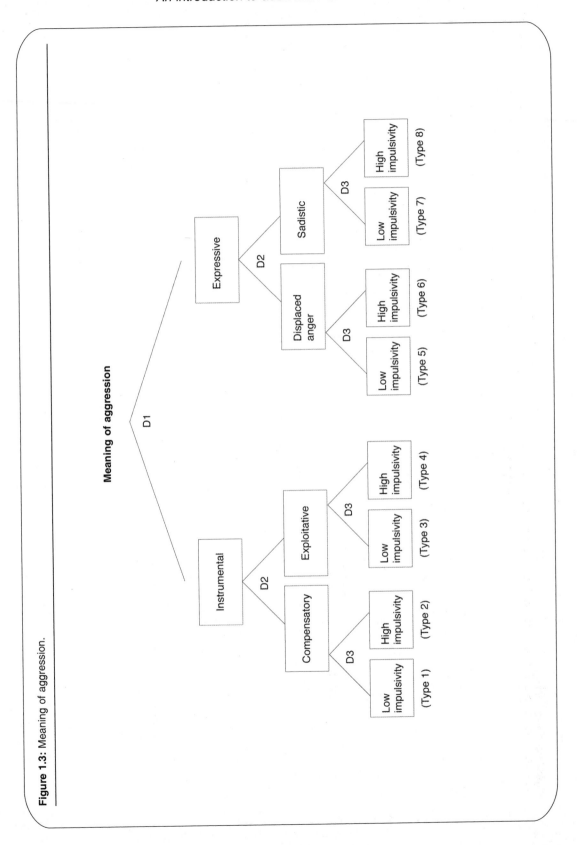

Figure 1.3: Meaning of aggression.

Figure 1.4: Degree of fixation.

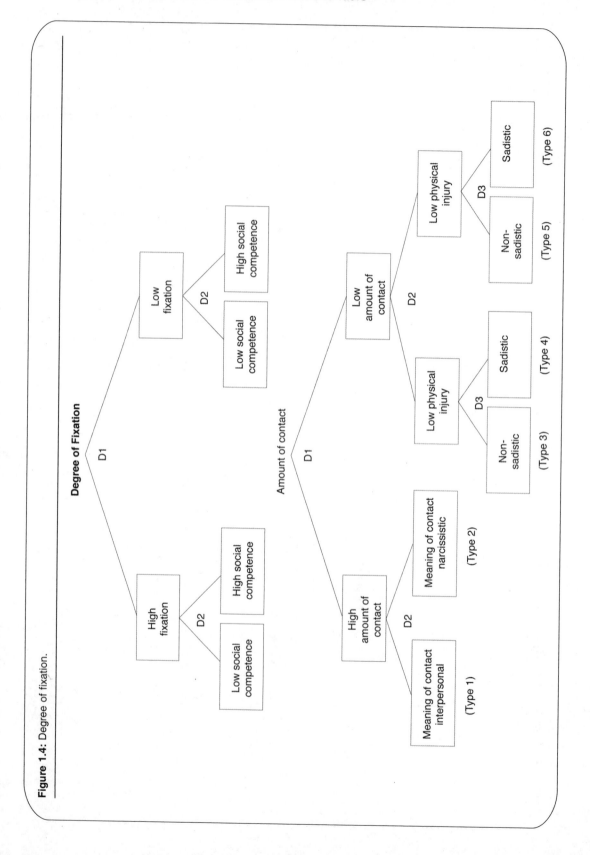

mature and stable relationships. They usually have the same emotional and psychological profile as people who do not abuse.

Sex offenders are thus an extremely heterogeneous group that cannot be characterised by single motivational or aetiological factors, but this has not halted numerous attempts to create typological frameworks, which aim to split this broad group into more homogeneous sub-groups (see following section). In doing so, there is often an acknowledgement that sexual offending behaviour is varied, complex, and multiply determined. The aim for workers in the process of their initial and then comprehensive assessment is to identify the specific factors pertinent to the offender in question (see chapter two for details), as this is a preface to constructing an individually tailored treatment and relapse prevention package.

Just as there are many different kinds of sex offender, so it is important to have a range of potential theories. These theories attempt to order the presenting characteristics of many sex offenders. Knowledge is an essential source for workers endeavouring to counter offender power: we need to ensure the offender is only one and not two or more steps ahead of us.

Calder (1999) provided us with an excellent overview of the theory on adult sex offenders and Calder (2001) provided an overview of the theory governing children and young people who sexually abuse. The following is a brief overview of several commonly used integrative theories for understanding sexual offending behaviour.

The cycle of offending (Wolf)

Steven Wolf (1984) provided a theory of the cycle of offending which links factors known frequently to occur in the lives of individuals identified as sexually deviant. His paper builds on earlier research to suggest a comprehensive model to explain (in part) the development and maintenance of sexually deviant orientations. Wolf's cycle of offending can be expressed as follows:

This addiction cycle charts the entry level then all the points the offender must go through in order to sexually offend, and then rationalise and continue their behaviour. The entry point of poor self-image is often related to their early life experiences and to a general dissatisfaction with their life. Indeed, offenders frequently present with a significantly disturbed developmental history; early feelings of emotional and social isolation, often combined with physical and sexual abuse, which leads them to distort cognitively about themselves, others and the

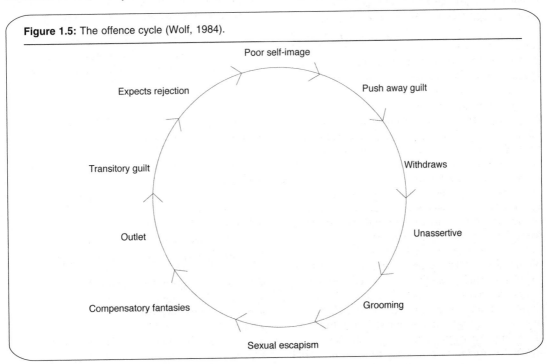

Figure 1.5: The offence cycle (Wolf, 1984).

Poor self-image

Expects rejection

Push away guilt

Withdraws

Transitory guilt

Unassertive

Outlet

Compensatory fantasies

Grooming

Sexual escapism

way in which the world operates. They often present in a state of 'victim posture'. They expect rejection, so they withdraw. They compensate through needs fulfilment fantasies, which often have a sexual dimension or tone. This 'escape to sexuality' can be understood as a learned coping mechanism, which develops fairly early in life out of a realisation that sexual gratification is a way of displacing other more painful feelings. These belief systems form the beginning components of the 'offence cycle' as the offender develops a habit of using fantasy in order to manage emotional needs unmet because of a lack of connection with others. These fantasies serve as a cognitive rehearsal for deviant behaviour and may include aspirations of wealth, power, control and revenge. The escape to fantasy places the offender in control and they then start targeting victims that match their deviant sexual interest. Indeed, if the offender fixes their fantasy on a specific behaviour or individual it will increase the need for, or attraction to, that behaviour or individual. The result is that the fantasy begins to 'groom' the environment, as the offender rehearses sexual behaviours and this reinforces their belief that the primary goal of sexual relations is to feel better about themselves. Behaviourally, compulsive masturbation often follows, as does the incorporation to their fantasy of rationalisation and justification. Although guilt and embarrassment follow (particularly relating to the possibility of being caught), it is quickly pushed away, and this is symptomatic of their general inability to take responsibility for themselves. They externalise responsibility and often promise never to do it again, although we need to note that they rarely learn from their mistakes. Since the offender has not really changed and been unsuccessful in applying discontinuation strategies they are again at step one and the whole process begins anew.

It is clear from the thoroughness of this cycle, that it forms the basis of the 'relapse prevention' model utilised in most sex offender treatment (described further in Chapter 8).

Many offenders engage in both offence-specific and global cognitive distortions to support their sexually abusive behaviour. A cognitive distortion is any type of 'dysfunctional' perception, thought, belief, automatic thought (spontaneous thought), thought process, pattern, etc. that enables, facilitates, supports, and leads to 'dysfunctional'

deviant, inappropriate behaviour. A brief list of 'common' themes of distortions are provided below:

1. Denial – Not admitting to or leaving out information.
2. Lying – Deliberately distorting, twisting, or leaving out information.
3. Justifying – Making behaviours okay.
4. Minimising – Making things smaller or less significant.
5. Entitlement – Unrealistic expectations to get or have something.
6. Power Games – Controlling others.
7. Depersonalise – Dehumanising/ de-individualising another by changing their identity or who they represent, to fit one's needs. They symbolically represent some other figure.
8. Poor Me – Self-pity, feeling sorry for one's self.
9. Extremes – Either/or thinking and behaving, drastic, overly excessive.
10. Apathy – Don't care attitude.
11. Rationalising – Logical justifications for deviant behaviour.
12. Blame – Placing responsibility for one's behaviour onto someone else.
13. Victim Stancing – Acting like a victim by feeling sorry for one's self.
14. Fairness Fallacy – Life 'should' be fair all the time and how awful it is when it is not.

For a more detailed list of distortions, see Chapter 5 on cognitive restructuring. Typical justifications used by offenders might include:

- I enjoyed it
- To feel better in general
- I don't care
- To escape problems
- I got away with it
- To prove manhood
- I deserve it
- To gain love
- I didn't use force
- No one will find out
- They enjoyed it
- It won't happen again
- It happened to me
- I deserve to get what I want
- I didn't hurt them
- No one cares anyway
- I can't stop
- It was pleasurable
- He or she wanted it

- This is the last time
- No one got hurt
- She wanted it
- Last time
- Not hurting anyone
- I deserved it (entitlement)
- Can't stop (no control/powerless)
- Sexual education/teaching
- Life is arbitrary and 'shit happens'
- He enjoyed it
- It was pleasurable
- I don't get caught
- Apology (false)
- Call Rape Hot Line
- Their/her choice (typically may occur when two victims are involved in which one of the two may have to choose which one is going to be raped)
- We love each other (phony love)
- No force 'they volunteered'
- She owed it to me
- They approached me so they must have wanted it
- I showed my wife that I can have sex (getting even)
- Someone victimised me, I didn't get hurt
- I gave them stuff, so it is okay
- I didn't hurt her
- Someone did it to me so I'll do it to them

What is important is that we use the cycle to help the offender acknowledge the structure of their offending behaviour, rather than making all offenders 'fit' into the cycle. We know that many offenders do not neatly fit into this cycle as they do not need to feel low to start the process of offending thoughts and behaviours. In fact, there is much currency in the assertion that the anger cycle is more appropriate in exploring triggers to this kind of behaviour.

Various cycles of offending behaviour (Eldridge)

Eldridge (1998) developed the work of Wolf by introducing the concepts of the 'continuous cycle', the 'inhibited cycle' and the 'short-circuit cycle'. These cycles focus on the particular route an offender will take after the commission of the offence. A brief overview of each cycle is provided below, but the detail can be located in Eldridge (1998).

The continuous cycle
In this cycle, an offender will retrace each of the stages of the cycle, selecting a new victim each time. This is perhaps most common in the case of an offender with an indecent exposure pattern, where, having sexually offended, he will repeat the pattern in its entirety.

The inhibited cycle
In this cycle, the offender becomes blocked or inhibited following the commission of an offence and may stop for a period of time. In time, the offender finds a way to overcome these inhibitors and progress through the various stages of his cycle in order to commit another offence. Typically, this cycle relates to an offender who selects a new victim each time he offends, where he returns to general illegal sexual fantasy before choosing the next victim.

The short-circuit cycle
In this cycle, the offender does not become inhibited following the commission of the offence, but rather returns to the cycle at the point of fantasy rehearsal and speeds up. In this case, the offender continues to abuse either the same child or in a similar manner. This cycle is typical where the offender is abusing a child in the family or within a context where he will have contact with the child.

Mark Carich has developed a series of cycles with a differing number of stages that will be explored in detail in chapter four.

An integrated theory of child sexual abuse (Finkelhor)

Finkelhor (1984) developed a multi-factor model to explain child sexual abuse by integrating a variety of single factor theories. It incorporates characteristics of the offender, disinhibitors, the environment and the victim (see Figure 1.6 overleaf). It operates at a high level of generality, thus allowing its use across a wide range of sexual offenders, whilst also encouraging analysis of the relative significance of the different factors in individual cases. It allows individual cases to be examined in detail, moving an offender on from asserting that his behaviour 'just happened' to an understanding of the thoughts, feelings and conscious manipulation of people and events which he undertook before the offence could take place. It thus emphasises that sexual abuse only takes place if the offender already has sexual feelings towards the child, and this firmly locates responsibility with the offender. Finkelhor's

Figure 1.6: Preconditions of sexual abuse (Finkelhor, 1984).

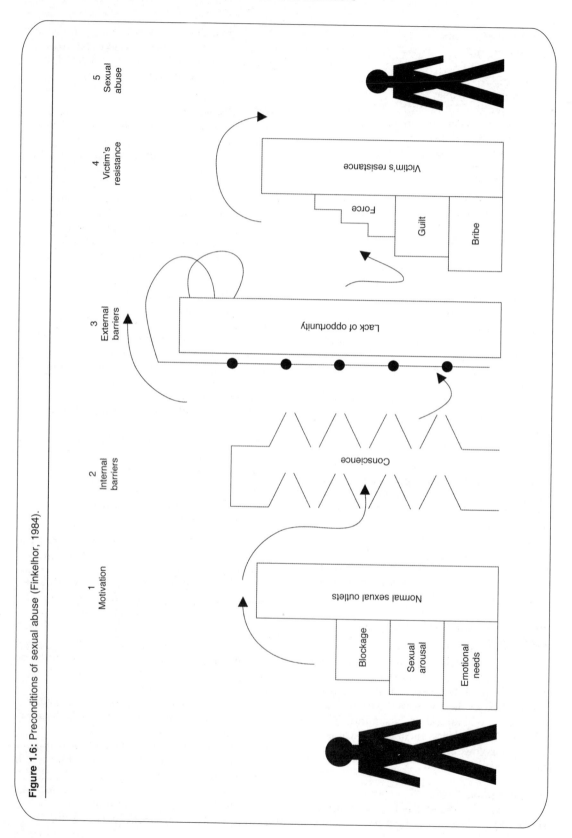

model accounts for both familial and extra-familial child sexual abuse.

Finkelhor argues that all the known factors contributing to child sexual abuse can be grouped into four pre-conditions, which need to be met prior to the instigation of child sexual abuse. The four pre-conditions are: *Motivation*: The potential offender needs to have some motivation to sexually abuse a child. Thus, he will need to find children erotically and sexually desirable. *Internal inhibitions*: The potential offender must overcome internal inhibitions that may act against his motivation to sexually abuse. *External inhibitions*: The potential offender also has to overcome external obstacles and inhibitions prior to sexually abusing the child. *Resistance*: Finally, the potential offender has to overcome the child's possible resistance to being sexually abused.

All four preconditions have to be fulfilled, in a logical, sequential order, for the abuse to commence. The presence of only one condition, such as a lack of maternal protection, social isolation or emotional deprivation is not sufficient to explain abuse.

1. Motivation to sexually abuse

Finkelhor argues that there are three functional components subsumed under the motivation to sexually abuse children:

- *Emotional congruence* in which sexual contact with a child satisfies profound emotional needs.
- *Sexual arousal* in which the child represents the source of sexual gratification for the abuser.
- *Blockage* when alternative sources of sexual gratification are not available or are less satisfying.

As these components are not actual preconditions, not all three need to be present for sexual abuse to occur. They are however important in explaining the variety of motivations' offenders may have for sexually abusing children. The three components explain not only the instance of offenders who aren't sexually motivated but enjoy degrading victims by wielding power, but also the paedophile, and the sexually motivated offender who looks towards children for variety, even though he has access to other sources of sexual gratification. In some instances elements from all three components may be present to account for whether the motivation is strong and persistent, weak and episodic, or whether the focus is primarily on girls or boys, or both.

Common motivations include:
1. seeks attention
2. power and control
3. rebellion of any sort
4. retaliation/revenge
5. to feel better about self
6. compensation from organ inferiority
7. acceptance
8. approval
9. acknowledgement
10. general forms of compensation
11. compensation from inferiority
12. ego boosters
13. to fulfil needs
14. solutions to problems
15. venting/expressing anger
16. an expression of 'love'
17. expecting/receiving 'love'
18. seeking validation of self
19. to avoid responsibility
20. stress reduction
21. ways of coping with life
22. to boost self esteem
23. some level of sexual gratification
24. to compensate from inadequacy
25. to compensate from loneliness
26. an expression of hatred
27. to enhance self image
28. to enhance self-concept
29. an addictive high
30. superiority

These issues or motives can be encompassed by four basic motivations: (1) attention; (2) power and control; (3) revenge (striking back), and (4) inadequacy. It is speculated that the offender's interpretation of various perceived life events occurring during critical developmental periods, are entrenched in the brain. At some time, the offender was exposed to deviant behaviour and derived satisfaction from engaging in deviant behaviour. The exposure was either observed, participated in or self-generated. Carich (1995) has outlined the following typology of causative developmental events (called contributing factors):

Types of developmental experiences

A. General themes (ongoing situations, i.e., relationships).
B. Specific events (specific life events, incidents or experiences).

C. Initial sensitising events through deviancy.
   – Direct exposure – direct involvement with deviancy or directly eroticised by involvement of some sexual behaviour.
   – Indirect exposure – indirect disposer or involvement such as participant observer.
   – Self generated events that are generated at random.

It is proposed that lifestyles emerge from these central core issues. These are not excuses for the offender.

2. Overcoming internal inhibitors

To sexually abuse, the offender needs not only to be motivated but also to be able to overcome his internal inhibitions against acting on his motivation. No matter how strong the sexual interest in children might be, if the offender is inhibited by taboos then he will not abuse. Arguably, most people do have some inhibitions towards sexually abusing children.

Dis-inhibition is not a source of motivation, it merely releases the motivation. Thus an individual who has no inhibitions against child sexual abuse, but who is not motivated, will not abuse. The second precondition aims to isolate the factors that account for how inhibitions are overcome and whether they are temporary or not. The element of dis-inhibition is an integral part of understanding child sexual abuse.

3. Overcoming external inhibitors

While preconditions one and two account for the offender's behaviour, preconditions three and four consider the environment outside the offender and child which control whether and whom he abuses. External inhibitors that may restrain the offender's actions include family constellation, neighbours, peers, and societal sanctions, as well as the level of supervision that a child receives.

Although a child cannot be supervised constantly, a lack of supervision has been shown in the clinical literature to be a contributing factor to sexual abuse, as has physical proximity and opportunity. External inhibitions against committing child sexual abuse may easily be overcome if the offender is left alone with a child who is not supervised.

4. Overcoming the resistance of the child

Offenders may sense which children are good potential targets, who can be intimidated, and can be exhorted to keep a secret. Offenders report that they can almost instinctively pick out a vulnerable child on whom to focus their sexual attentions, while ignoring those who might resist. Frequently these children may not even be aware that they are being sexually approached, or indeed resisting such advances.

Some of the risk factors that inhibit the capacity to resist include emotional insecurity and neediness, lack of physical affection, lack of friends, lack of support and interest from parents, age, naïvety, and lack of information. Knowing which factors make children vulnerable is essential in formulating prevention programmes. Isolating behaviours that continue a risk, while emphasising those that enhance resistance or avoidance, can empower children to protect themselves. This is not to say that children who are not vulnerable do not get abused. Many children may be forced or coerced despite displaying resistance or avoidance behaviours. In such instances the factors overcoming a child's resistance has nothing to do with the child, or the child's relationship with the offender, but is the result of force, threat or violence. No matter how much resistance is manifested by the child, this may not necessarily prevent abuse.

The spiral of sexual abuse (Sullivan)

Joe Sullivan (2002) has developed a very useful spiral model of sexual abuse that builds upon the work of Wolf and Finkelhor (see Figure 1.7).

This model is an open-ended conceptual framework which allows for the illustration of the evolutionary nature of a pattern of offending (from motivation to sexually offend to a sexual offence). From this point the spiral will develop in any number of ways depending on the behaviour of the offender, the victim and others who might protect the victim. There is also scope for including other stages such as 'targeting', 're-grooming' and repeating stages, placing them in the order which best fits the individual pattern of the offender. It can also be used to focus on a part or phase of the overall offending pattern. It applies to all forms of abuse and is applicable to both male and female offenders. Workers can work with offenders on phases of their spiral, which may relate to a specific victim and/or set of offences and later combine these with other phases of their offending pattern to produce a complete spiral which can be as long as necessary to illustrate all the different phases of offending in the perpetrator's life.

Figure 1.7: The spiral of sexual abuse (Sullivan, 2002).

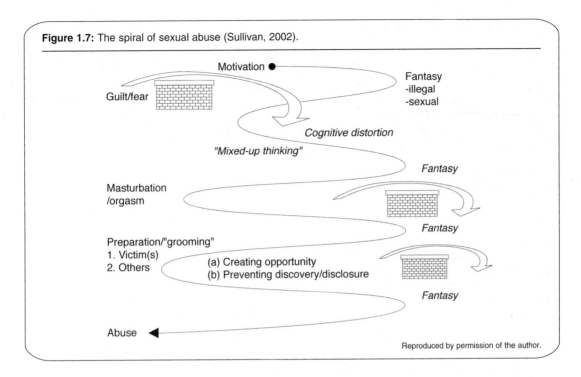

Reproduced by permission of the author.

Many of the distinct stages of the spiral have been sufficiently explained earlier, but a couple of points can usefully be made here.

'The brick wall': Having thought or fantasised about an illegal sexual act for the first time, most potential offenders will experience what they might refer to as guilt. On exploration, it often emerges that the feeling was in fact one of fear, arising out of the likely consequences if they were to get caught. This guilt or fear acts like a barrier or 'the brick wall', making a return to the illegal fantasy more difficult. For some people, this may be as far as they are able to progress as they may not be able to find a way past the guilt or fear and back into the fantasy. For others, they use cognitive distortions to provide themselves with the necessary permission to engage in a behaviour that is known to be wrong. This allows the offender to successfully overcome the guilt or fear and their return to fantasy facilitated. There remains the potential for other 'brick walls' to block progress although these walls become progressively smaller and the distorted thinking to overcome the blocks will have become more refined, that the spiral often continues unabated.

Preparation/'grooming': Although the offender's arousal driven by the desire to act out their fantasy is often present, they also know that they may be caught. The creation of

opportunities to offend thus represents another stage in the spiral as the offender explores means of avoiding discovery or disclosure on the part of the victim. This is referred to as the 'grooming phase' and usually involves two groups: the victim and the people who may protect the victim. The grooming tactics will vary depending on the context within which they are abusing and will often be modified and adapted as the process develops.

Sex offender lifestyle behaviours

The focus of sex offender treatment is shifting to embrace the social dimensions of their behaviour that are believed central to the origins of the offending behaviour (Calder, 1999). Carich and Adkerson (1995) have developed some useful material in relation to sex offender lifestyle behaviours. Lifestyle behaviours are chronic and recursive patterns of behaviour or tendencies. It is the style in which one acts or behaves, thinks, feels, and perceives. It is the rules which one follows: these are personality characteristics. There are several basic assumptions:

- Lifestyle behaviours are chronic patterns of behaviour: that is recursively connected thinking, feeling, overt activities, physiological responses, social behaviours, etc.

- Not all offenders have all of these characteristics.
- Behaviours occur in degrees of intensity with different offenders.
- Behaviours are interconnected together following the principles of holism (i.e. the whole is greater than the sum or its parts).
- Many behaviours are related to the assault cycle and state dependent memory learning and behaviour systems.
- Lifestyle behaviours are purposeful in nature.
- This is a holistic approach.

Categories of lifestyle behaviours

There are five basic lifestyle behaviours that are found in sex offenders: antisocial, narcissistic, schizoid, passive-aggressive and borderline. Dissociative behaviours were added as many offenders dissociate to some degree. These are described below.

Antisocial

1. exploitation (taking advantage of others)
2. victimising (verbally hurt others physically)
3. sadistic/evil/cruelty (enjoys physically hurting others)
4. lies (denies, twists/distorts information)
5. manipulates (uses other people as pawns)
6. cheats (acts dishonestly)
7. sneaky
8. slick/conning in a way that looks good
9. lacks victim empathy (compassion for victim)
10. lacks remorse (guilt, feels bad)
11. holds dirty little secrets
12. mistrust (I don't trust)
13. presents a false image/front ('phoney')
14. difficulty with loyalty
15. tends to be reckless
16. unstable work history
17. breaks institutional and/or society's rules
18. breaks group rules

Narcissistic

1. unwarranted entitlement ('I want what I want when I want it')
2. self-centredness ('I'm out for myself')
3. grandiose (exaggerated expectations/fantasies)
4. me first attitude
5. know it all attitudes
6. unrealistic expectations (overly high)
7. inflated ego (exaggerated self importance)
8. superior attitude ('I'm better')
9. reacts strongly to criticism with rage/anger
10. brags and exaggerates abilities

Borderline

1. dependency (needy, cling to others, insecure)
2. moodiness
3. over controlling/domineering (controls others)
4. possessive
5. jealous
6. seeks immediate gratification (satisfy needs, asap)
7. over-attachment (clings to others)
8. enmeshed boundaries (no sense of individual identity and smothers others)
9. fearful of rejection
10. going to extremes (either/or thinking/absolute thinking
11. fearful of rejection (abandonment)
12. deep feelings of inadequacy/inferiority

Schizoidal

1. flat affect (I don't show/express feelings)
2. stuff feelings (I keep feelings shut down)
3. dissociates feelings (unaware of feelings)
4. lack social skills (trouble communicating with others)
5. apathy (I don't care attitude)
6. alienates/isolates (distance from others)
7. lacks functional healthy relationships
8. superficial relationships (relationships are shallow, phoney, lack depth insignificant conversation)
9. withdraws from appropriate adult relationships
10. feels threatened (insecure) from others
11. remains emotionally uninvolved within interpersonal relationships
12. guarded (defensive, not open, closed up)

Passive-aggressive

1. creates obstacles for others
2. expresses anger indirectly
3. feels continuously put down
4. provides resistance (usually covertly, criticised under the table)
5. reacts with anger when criticised

Dissociative

1. fixation of attention
2. total concentration

3. inner (internal) focusing of attention/highly focused
4. fantasy – sensory visualisation or imagery (pretending)
5. high intensity of focus
6. oblivious to external surroundings
7. possible regression (trance like)
8. trance state of awareness
9. out of body experiences or hidden observer phenomena
10. possible catalepsy or rigidity in behaviour
11. ecstatic emotional states similar to euphoria
12. depersonalisation (i.e., people are objects, detachment) (Vetter, 1990)
13. detachment at cognitive and emotional levels
14. behavioural indicators: change in psychological response (heart rate, blood pressure, respiration, swallowing, muscular activity, etc.), glassy eyes, possible ideodynamic signaling processes, staring off into space, etc.
15. dream state/daydreaming (Vetter, 1990)
16. altered state of awareness/and heightened sense of awareness and sensory perception
17. unconscious processes, along with conscious processes
18. state dependent memory learning and behaviour systems (i.e., context specific)
19. high level involvement with right hemispheric functioning
20. offending states tend to be triggered by stimuli indicated by cues
21. disinhibitors are suspended at least temporarily
22. offending patterns or states can be internally/externally interrupted or terminated
23. there seems to be an internal switch box that the offender uses to turn on the offending mode state
24. sensory modes seem to be in tune with specific types of sensory experiences
25. anesthesia-numbering effect
26. flashbacks

*Note: This part of the list is based on clinical observation, unless indicated by reference (Carich, 1994).

*Numbers 27–44 are taken from Dolan's (1991) work with sexual abuse victims and applies to offenders and also Harold Vetter's sexual killer research as indicated by the reference (Vetter, 1990).

27. amnesia
28. numbing-unfeeling
29. spacing out
30. de-realisation (feeling of one's surroundings not real) (Vetter, 1990)
31. out of body experiences
32. general disengagement from one's environment into a state of detached observation (hidden observer phenomena)
33. memory lapses
34. flat affect
35. lapse in verbal response time, as if one is off somewhere else
36. perceptual distortion
37. hypnotic states
38. splitting off (Vetter, (1990)
39. de-compartmentalising (Vetter, 1990)
40. ego state behaviour (Vetter, 1990)
41. spontaneous utterances (Vetter, 1990)
42. psychopathic glibness (Vetter, 1990)
43. absence of guilt (Vetter, 1990)
44. somatic dementia (words have/do not have acceptable meanings) (Vetter, 1990)

Hypnotic behaviours are naturalistic behaviours stemming from right hemispheric functioning. They often involve: disassociation, intense focusing/concentration/inner-absorption/fixed attention and often immobilised behaviour. A hypnotic state is considered an altered state.

By definition, a sexual offence is a violation of another's rights, which makes it an antisocial behaviour. During the offending process, the offender is self-centred and feeling entitled. This does not mean all offenders have antisocial and narcissistic personality disorders. The harder core offenders have more antisocial/narcissistic characteristics along with the others. Again, lesser hard core offenders do not have these features or at least they are not strongly entrenched.

Many hard core offenders have difficulty expressing emotions, except perhaps anger. They appear to be very schizoidal in nature. That is, flat affect, isolated, lonely, alienated, etc. An interesting clinical observation is that once an offender begins to develop appropriate relationships, the borderline characteristic seems to emerge. The level and type of borderline feature depends on the amount and degree of resources the offender has.

Offenders appear very dissociative in nature. Many spend a large amount of time fantasising and highly focused on sexual deviancy. Many describe their offences as trauma like behaviours. In general, there are varying degrees of detachment.

Challenging myths and stereotypes

These models do help us challenge and dispel myths held by workers and the general public alike. Figure 1.8 overleaf addresses certain myths by providing some answers:

Assumptions when approaching work with adult male sex offenders

It is considered appropriate and necessary for workers to make assumptions about sex offenders based on a combination of research findings and practice wisdom. These may include:

- Assume the offender's actions were premeditated – it is rarely a spontaneous crime, and develops through a process of establishing and normalising need.
- Assume the offender's role was active and conscious. Offending is a choice at all levels of awareness including conscious, subconscious and unconscious (Carich, 1997). Even those with a history of being sexually abused themselves have to make some choices about the re-enactment of their abuse (Hackett, 2002). All offenders are thus fully accountable and responsible for their behaviours. There are no acceptable excuses.
- Assume that they rehearsed the offence in fantasy. Offending is rooted in a bed of cognitive distortions or thinking errors (Murphy and Carich, 2001).
- Assume that the decision to offend is propelled by the various psychological and emotional needs that are fused with sex offending (Mussack and Carich, 2001).
- Assume they targeted their victim.
- Assume that they groomed the environment – using seductive techniques, which surprise many workers as to why children ever tell.
- Assume that their offending is repetitive (offender's rarely commit 'one-off' offences). Time does not heal sex offenders. Assume therefore that recovery is a lifelong process (Carich, 1999) and requires a holistic approach to treatment.
- Assume that offenders have multiple patterns, offences and victim types (Carich, 1997).
- Assume that an addictive cycle of behaviour has developed.
- Assume that offending is supported by the dysfunctional lifestyle behaviours (i.e. antisocial, narcissistic), although these will vary in both intensity and strength of pattern (Carich, 1997).

- Assume they will seek support for their rationalisations from peers, family, victims and professionals, yet assume the rationalisations and excuses may not be what they actually believe – although it is easy to persuade oneself of the truth of one's own rationalisations (MacLeod and Saraga, 1991, 38).
- Assume their motivation to adhere to the assessment and the treatment process will fluctuate.
- Assume they have a long-term risk of re-offending. There is no cure, but there is the potential for the offender to learn to reduce deviant sexual arousal and learn alternative behaviours (Carich, 1997). The latter is the offender's primary treatment goal.
- Assume that they will be sexually aroused when they commit their offences (Abel et al., 1981), and that there is a far more fundamental sexual component to their offending pattern (Morrison, 1989, 11).
- Assume that for every piece of information they reveal, the question arises as to what information they have thereby decided to conceal (Wyre, 1989).
- Assume that their version of events is incorrect and incomplete (Moore, 1990, 21).
- Assume that their apparent normality is their most striking diagnostic characteristic (Lewis Herman, 1990, 180).
- Assume they will analyse and feed the needs/wants of the worker (Prendergast, 1991, 115).
- Assume they know their actions are wrong because they persuade, coerce or threaten children into secrecy (MacLeod and Saraga, 1991, 8).
- Assume they will attempt to manipulate and deceive those making the assessment (Bernard and Bernard, 1984).
- Assume they have a vested interest in silencing their victims and partners (Kelly and Radford, 1990/1, 40).
- Assume they will portray the child as being responsible for all the above (Abel et al., 1984).
- Assume they will deny all the above (adapted from Calder, 1999).

We need to make assumptions as we trust people too much and often expect too much from them. We need to be curious, think the unthinkable, imagine the unimaginable, and we might sometimes get close to the truth. Wyre

Figure 1.8: Challenging myths and stereotypes.

Myths	Facts
Rapists are healthy, lusty young men, sowing wild oats. Rape is a crime of passion.	Rape is always a sign of weakness, indicating a need to exert power and control over someone else, an unhealthy willingness to ignore another person's wishes. Rape is not an expression of sexual desire; it is an act of sexual violence. It's about the desire for power and domination. Rapists purposely use forced sex to humiliate and degrade victims. Rapists can be of any age.
Women really want to be raped. After the initial shock, they enjoy being sexual with a powerful man. Some women act seductive and alluring to provoke rapists.	Being raped is universally traumatic, one of the worst events that a person can experience. Why would anyone, woman or man, want to be raped? Anyone who thinks women want to be raped is wrong. Rapists are usually desperate, angry, insecure men . . . Most rapists select their victims because they are available or vulnerable, not because of the way they dress.
Pornography causes rapes.	Pornography does not cause rapes. Men choose to rape. Those who think of women as sexual objects are more likely to use pornography which keeps alive the myths about rape and fuels violent fantasies. Rapists may use pornography to help them plan their attacks or to help them get and keep an erection.
Rapists rape attractive women who are drunk in bars.	Rapists rape anyone anywhere. Most rapes occur in the victim's home.
Rapes occur in the summer when people are wearing fewer clothes.	Rapes occur every time of day and night, summer, autumn, winter and spring.
Rapist are mostly accused falsely by women or girls who went along and regretted it later.	Rapists blame the victim to avoid taking responsibility for their crimes. Some victims may comply with the rapist's demands because they are in fear for their lives. Compliance is not consent.
Rapists are just men who were being sexual with a woman, but after the woman turned him on, she wanted to stop. She deserved what she got.	Appropriate sex stops if and when **either** partner becomes uncomfortable with what is happening. Everyone has the right to stop sex at any point. No one deserves to have his or her body violated. No one deserves to be raped.
A woman can stop a rape if she really wants to.	Some women do stop rapes by resisting, running, using self-defence skills, or figuring out how to get help or get away. Most victims are afraid of being killed or maimed during a rape. Rapists use weapons, violence and threats to force their victims, and are usually larger and stronger. Rapists choose situations where the victims will be vulnerable. Rapists are always responsible for their actions. Rape will stop when rapists stop raping; victims cannot stop rape.
All sex offenders are male.	Sex offenders can be either male or female.
White, middle-class people of average or above-average intellectual abilities do not commit sexual offences.	Sex offenders come from all races, socioeconomic classes and levels of intellect.
The offender does not know his victims.	Offenders are frequently known to their victims as trusted people, such as family members, neighbours, or babysitters.
Sexual offences are exclusively motivated by sexual needs.	Sexual assaults are not primarily sexually motivated behaviours.
Sexual offences are a result of sudden, uncontrollable urges.	Sexual offences are planned actions. Offenders purposely select victims and circumstances in which to offend.
Sexual offending can be treated by addressing other problems.	Adolescent sex offenders require sex offender-specific treatment to address the thinking errors, deviant arousal patterns, and values that maintain offending behaviours.

Figure 1.8: *Continued.*

Myths	Facts
Sexual assault does not happen very often.	Studies show that about one out of every four girls and one out of every eight boys will be sexually assaulted prior to reaching age 18.
A person who does nothing to resist is not really being sexually abused.	Fear of death, threat of violence, aggression, coercion, bribery and intimidation are all means of making victims go along even though they do not all include direct violence.
If a person was really abused then he/she would report it right away.	Many victims of sexual abuse are too frightened or embarrassed to tell someone.
Mothers and fathers always know if the other parent is being sexually abusive towards someone in the family.	The offender who sexually abuses others in the family uses a lot of secrecy to stop others from knowing about the abuse. For a full description of this issue, the reader is referred to Calder et al. (2001).

Material adapted from Freeman-Longo, Bays and Bear (1996); Perry and Orchard (1992); and Loss, Ross and Richardson (1988).

(1989) warns us that we are taking men down roads that they do not want to go, and we do so by using a certain tone of voice and level of assumption. We must believe that this behaviour is addictive. As such, we cannot accept that it is a one-off as we assume that it is deliberate. It did not 'just happen' as it is 'in character' – even though they will argue that it is not. They will re-interpret the behaviour of the victim to excuse and justify, and this will be accompanied by minimisation, normalisation, justification, and projection. We need to assume that there are clear patterns of behaviour in sexual offending and that we can identify that pattern of behaviour (Wyre, 1990, 11). He highlighted the level of risk posed by offenders who claim that something 'just happened'. Here, the fact that he has done it once does not bode well as he might just 'do it' again. Wyre (1990b) suggested that if assumptions have to be used at all, then it is probably more appropriate to operate by the most unlikely of alternatives (9).

These assumptions are the building blocks from which we need to build a picture of their offending history and profile. Presumption is legitimate, but persecution is not.

An overview of contemporary adult male sex offender treatment

Contemporary sex offender treatment has been defined as those 'techniques designed to assist sexual abusers in maintaining control of their sexual deviance throughout their lifetime by reducing and managing their sexually abusive behaviour. Treatment intervention is focused on assisting the individual to accept responsibility, increase recognition, institute change and manage sexually deviant thoughts, attitudes and behaviours.' (ATSA, 1997, 17).

Contemporary treatment can be characterised by several key aspects:
1. The emphasis on group therapy as the primary mode of treatment, with individual support (i.e., arousal control).
2. The Cognitive-Behavioural approach predominates, focusing on patterns of thinking and behaviour. The focus is on three primary areas: on changing thoughts and behaviours; on cognitive mediators; and on antecedents and consequences (i.e., the events preceding the offences along with the consequences).
3. The primary focus on sexual deviancy and related issues.
4. The necessity of adopting a holistic view or framework (Longo, 2002). This incorporates all experiential domains: cognitive, affective, behavioural, social or interpersonal, contextual, bio-physiological and spiritual and different types/levels of learning. This allows the workers flexibility in maintaining the use of a variety of interventions.
5. The emphasis on skill development with therapeutic process.
6. The need to tightly structure the treatment process according to the individual circumstances.
7. An emphasis on workers controlling the treatment process.

Table 1.5: Differences.

Sex offender specific	Non-sex offender specific
1. Limited confidentiality	1. High level of confidentiality
2. Limited trust and continuous scepticism	2. Trust the client
3. Focus on sexual deviancy	3. Focus on other problems
4. NO CURE (no permanent abstinence)	4. Views a cure
5. Structured and more direct (rules, boundaries)	5. Less structure/direct-flexible
6. Emphasis on responsibility/accountability	6. May or may not emphasise it
7. Induces pain (initially and throughout at some level)	7. Takes pain away
8. Group is the primary mode of treatment	8. May use group, individual.
9. Workers maintain control	9. Client/worker are seen as equals
10. More confrontation oriented	10. Less confrontational
11. Cognitive-behavioural (experiential) approach	11. May or may not be
12. Society is the client	12. Client is the client

Differences between sex offender and non-sex offender treatment

Table 1.5 above outlines some of the principal differences in the treatment of sex offenders and non-sex offenders.

Similarities

These may be universal principles.

1. Respect and viewing the client as a person.
2. Eliciting cooperation at some level.
3. Developing a therapeutic rapport or some type of psychological contact.
4. Flexibility to use a variety of interventions towards therapeutic goals.
5. The Cybernetic systems view that to induce change by supporting patterns of stability.
6. Respecting and recognising individual uniqueness (there may be common themes, patterns, etc., but there are individual differences).

Some of the most significant differences centre around: confidentiality, trust, power and control and the client. Given that there is no magical cure or permanent abstinence from offending, the sex offender specialists are more sceptical and less trusting of offenders than other workers. Their focus is on the prevention of future victims rather than offender therapy. A relapse equals a human victim, besides the offender. In these circumstances, confidentiality is limited to help offset the secrecy engendered in the offender's modus operandi and to help prevent the offender from using secrecy to manipulate the system.

Sex offender treatment is offence-specific. The focus is on sexual deviancy and the private logic that has enabled the offender to act in a sexually

deviant manner. Sexual behaviour and fantasy is usually not a primary focus of therapy with persons who have not sexually offended.

Sex offender treatment is a more directive-structured approach in which confrontation is frequently used and control issues are a focus of treatment. Confrontation compels offenders to become more and more aware of their own private logic and the distortions they have used to enhance false senses of self-esteem. Given the issues of boundary violations and power-control inherently involved in sexual aggression, offender treatment has to be more structured and directive, with staff in control. Specific rules are established with consequences for violations. Rule infractions and boundary intrusions are directly addressed. Thus, the worker tends to be more confrontational and he or she maintains control, especially in the early stages of treatment.

Confrontation refers to the fact that offenders are held accountable. Clinical experience indicates that nondirective Rogerian approaches are not effective with high-risk sex offenders. Directive and confrontive approaches work best. Indirect tactics or techniques can be effectively integrated into a directive context, as the worker maintains control of treatment. When the treatment is not structured, offenders will try and assume control. Any compliance and cooperation are elicited within a context of the therapist's control and direction.

Another critical difference in offender treatment is the initial induction of pain by inducing victim empathy and remorse in conjunction with issues of accountability and responsibility. The offender's realisation at both intellectual and emotional levels of the impact of his or her offending behaviour on others hurts as the offender identifies the pain of the victim. In essence, the offender learns to feel bad for violating his or her victim.

It is important to respect the offender as a unique individual with problems (Marshall, 1996). Freeman-Longo and Blanchard (1998) advocate a non-punitive approach based on respect and empathy. Although shaming, punitive, and hot-seat approaches were extensively used in the past, these were considered ineffective due to the fact that the offender's inferiority feelings were being fed, leading to additional acting out to demonstrate power in an anti-social manner. Cooperation from the client is essential to any attempt to facilitate change. The worker can gain cooperation by communicating his or her respect to the client and by developing rapport within the therapeutic relationship. Honesty, consistency, and firm boundaries increase the likelihood of developing cooperation (Carich, Newbauer and Stone, 2001).

In Table 1.5, several 'universal similarities' were provided. Offenders need to be respected and treated as unique individuals with problems (Marshall, 1996). If workers view them as monsters, a victimising treatment will follow. The old confrontation approaches are now outdated: more compassionate (motivational) approaches are in vogue (see Mann, 1996). Compassion is tempered with a firm 'hand'. Firmness is mixed with compassion (not sympathy) to gain cooperation and compliance. Rapport or psychological contact is critical. Observing for clinical experiences shows the significance of developing a rapport.

The goals and values of sex offender treatment

The International Association for the Treatment of Sexual Offenders (IATSO) was founded on 24 March 1998 and is committed to the promotion of research of, and treatment, for sexual offenders throughout the world. It has noted that as we gain a better understanding of the sex offender and develop better treatment techniques, public policy around the world encourages more punishing laws and less support for treatment. However, we know that punishment and incarceration does relatively little to stem the tide of rising sexual violence and this predominant view is not supported by scientific evidence. As such, societies must face

a very pragmatic decision: will it support therapeutic rehabilitation for individuals who have committed sexual crimes or will it succumb to public pressures to build more prisons and dole out longer sentences for their crimes? IATSO has the following goals and values:

1. Furthering the knowledge about the nature of sexual offenders and sexual offences and the improvement of treatment methods.
2. Supporting the development and improvement of effective sexual offender treatment.
3. Committed to scientifically evaluating therapeutic methods and to periodically revise and disseminate the standards of care for the treatment of sexual offenders (see below)*.
4. Committed to scientifically evaluating studies of treatment effectiveness of sex offenders.
5. Believes that sex offender treatment and research is enhanced through international communications and exchange of ideas, research and treatment methods.
6. Believes that sex offender treatment will result in the reduction of the incidence of sexual offences.
7. Believes that punishment alone for sexual crimes is an inadequate deterrent for sexual crimes.
8. Believes that sex offender recidivism is reduced best by the treatment of the sex offender.
9. Believes that sex offender treatment is a basic human right.
10. Believes that freedom from sexual aggression and sexual abuse is a basic human right.

(Coleman and Miner, 2001)

*The standards of care for the treatment of adult sex offenders (Coleman et al., 1996) set out some minimum standards of professional competence that include the possession of an academic degree in behavioural science or medicine; they should have clinical training and experience in the diagnosis and treatment of a range of psychiatric and psychological conditions and also specialised training and experience in the assessment and treatment of paraphilic and sexual offender problems.

Eligibility for treatment

Treatment should be based on the needs of each offender as determined by a comprehensive assessment of them within their particular family situation. A number of factors are key in determining offender suitability for treatment. Most treatment programmes require that the offender must acknowledge that he committed the sexual abuse and take responsibility for his behaviour. Realistically, many offenders still have a long way to go at the end of the assessment, but they must have shown some commitment and movement in the right direction if they are to benefit further from treatment. We also need to note that some dimensions of denial (such as admission with justification) are less responsive to intervention, often entrenching the denial further. In order to benefit from treatment, the offender must acknowledge that their behaviour has been harmful to the victims; they must consider their offending behaviour a problem that they want to stop, and that they have expressed a desire to change; they must be willing to enter into and participate in treatment, and they must be prepared to comply with any conditions relating to the management of the risks they pose. Simply being in treatment should help reduce the risks.

There will be some offenders who meet the above eligibility criteria, but whose offences are so serious that they need to be incarcerated. In general terms, the offender eligible for community treatment is the individual who has an overall pro-social lifestyle; one who has demonstrated the capacity to follow through on tasks; who has relationships in the community; and who has no history of pronounced physical violence (Wolf et al., 1988).

One of the aims of the assessment is to gate-keep treatment, which is lengthy (12–36 months) and should arguably be reserved for cases where some success is anticipated. Yet we need to target the high-risk groups where the cost of not intervening substantially is ongoing, arguably escalating patterns of offending as they get older. This may not do wonders for the success rates for treatment, but it has to be cost-effective in the community (Breiling, 1994).

It is impossible however to pretend that resources are not scarce and that performance accountability is not upon us. Better identification and selective targeting of high-risk offenders is critical to ensure the most cost-effective allocation of resources and the best hope of a positive impact on reduced rates of reconviction. Our view is that every sex offender has to be considered eligible for treatment as the costs of not offering it to them are evident in the longer-term. If choices have to be made on the basis of resources, we should opt to treat the high-risk groups, whilst using a legal mandate to determine a safe and appropriate placement, and supervised contact with children. High-risk men remain more difficult to treat than low-risk men (Friendship, Mann and Beech, submitted). There is a body of evidence that says that the recidivism rate of low-risk offenders subject to intensive supervision may be increased (Lauen, 1997).

Workers need to be aware that whatever the locally agreed criteria are for accessing treatment, it is futile to make a treatment recommendation when we are not in a position to offer any input, or where the quality of the treatment programme is questionable. Neither should we duck the need to make a 'no-treatment' recommendation where it is absolutely necessary, as inappropriate treatment recommendations are harmful to both the offender and to society. Frances, Clarkin, and Perry (1984) suggested the following benefits that may follow from a no-treatment decision:

● Avoiding a semblance of treatment when no effective treatment exists.
● Delaying treatment until a more appropriate time.
● Protecting the offender and the workers from wasting time, effort and money.

Mayer (1988) argued that some sex offenders do have a very poor prognosis and remain a high risk, regardless of what the workers might like to try to achieve. She set out numerous factors which contribute to poor-risk candidates for treatment. They included: the use of force or violence during the offences; they have a prior criminal record; they present with bizarre rituals associated with the offences; they chronically use alcohol or drugs; they sexually abused very young children; there is evidence of severe mental health problems; a history of severe childhood abuse; low IQ/capacity for insights; and chronic stressors in the environment.

It is important that we are clear on the difference between risk control (constraints placed on the offender to ensure they remain crime free when under supervision) and risk reduction (the effort to achieve a permanent reduction in the offender's likelihood of re-offending).

Treating sex offenders in denial: a crucial consideration

The issue of whether to allow sex offenders in denial into treatment is a crucial and contentious issue. Ethically, there is an argument against allowing them access whilst in denial, particularly as this can be misleading to the courts and others. It also appears unfair to allocate some of the precious places in treatment to those who claim they are innocent. If the denier is to remain in the community, we have to consider whether they will be accepted by the community and, if rejected, how this will affect their chances of relapse. The alternative view is that there is such a broad range of denial, with a clear starting point, that we should allow them access to treatment in order to facilitate some positive movement. This group does pose such a high risk for re-offending that they should be offered priority treatment places so they do not cause continued harm to others and themselves. Unfortunately, even where treatment is mandated, there is no guarantee that the offender will be engaged in the process of change.

Given that denial is central to most cases of sexual abuse, we have learned to develop some strategies for confronting these defences and assisting the offender to participate fully in any treatment programme. There needs to be time-limited focus on challenging denial in the first stages of treatment, and the offender can be very responsive to the recognition that they are viewed as 'whole' people and the focus is not simply on their sexual offences in isolation. The reader is referred to Schlank and Shaw (1996, 1997) for discussions of how to treat sex offenders in denial. Brake and Shannon (1997) explored the concept of using a pre-treatment phase to increase admission in sex offenders. They reminded us that, as denial is not static, a 'snapshot assessment' of denial can be inaccurate. When was it done (at one week, a month, etc.?) and by whom (police officers, psychologists, courts, etc.?). They argue that a programme for 'deniers' offers the advantage of being able to evaluate the offender over time and deal with the range of their oppositional behaviour as it arises. Such a programme acknowledges that treatment requires a gradual, incremental approach, allowing for a systematic approach from the workers. Their pre-treatment programme aims to lessen denial so the offender can become eligible for the broader treatment regime. The programme consists of six stages: containment (to de-escalate and contain power struggles); symptom relief (which allows the offender to shift from their defence mechanisms which entrench rather than resolve their despair); reframe denial (by exploring with them the protective function served by denial); reframe accountability (so they may become ready to risk abandoning old defensive manoeuvres and accept increasing accountability and pro-social behaviour); enhance empathy (as the offender begins to accept increasing personal responsibility for his behaviour, he can begin to recognise the pain of others and identify it as his own); and successive approximation of confrontation (where they may now be ready to accept gradual confrontation of his behaviour). Using this approach, the authors have found a significant reduction in denial in 58% of offenders.

They argue that an accurate assessment of denial should take into account the full range of the offender's resistance and defensiveness, both conscious and unconscious. Offenders who deny some aspect of the offence or who minimise and justify their behaviour are less amenable to change than other groups of deniers, as they become more entrenched in their resistance.

For a multi-dimensional typology of sex offender denial, the reader is referred to Calder (1999).

Steen (1996) explored the issue of treating those in denial about their abusive behaviour. Effective treatment should always be more than them taking responsibility for their abuse. We need to remember that many do accept responsibility but then go on to re-offend. There are other types of things the offender must learn and internalise before they are capable of abstaining from offending. Whether or not they admit to their offence, they are still able to absorb the material and can gain much in the way of:

- Better choices – learning to look at the consequences of acts and making conscious decisions rather than just acting on impulses.
- Increased self-esteem – if feelings of self worth are increased through positive experiences, the person would not want to do anything bad and will self monitor.
- Getting in touch with own and others' feelings – increased self understanding and

empathy minimises the need to act out inappropriately and helps them see what effect their actions would have on a potential victim before they act.

- Sexual understanding – learning to differentiate between sex and affection so that they can maintain appropriate boundaries.
- Social skills development – learning how to relate appropriately to age-mates so it will not be necessary to get social support needs met improperly or with improper-aged persons.
- Improved communication – increasing abilities to communicate needs and feelings appropriately so he/she will not express them in an inappropriate sexual or other anti-social manner.
- Arousal reconditioning and delay of satisfaction – offenders can learn to fantasise about appropriate sex objects, change deviant sexual arousal patterns, delay gratification of impulses by learning and assimilating various techniques so they are less likely to re-offend.
- Offence chain intervention – offenders can learn relapse prevention techniques including appropriate coping strategies or re-accusation as the end point.
- Offence cycle intervention – this can apply in the same way as the offence chain in relapse prevention.
- Problem-solving – everyone can increase these skills, which in turn increase available coping skills for all activities when stress or gratification needs are present . . . and many other things to learn.

Contemporary treatment and Adlerian connections

When treating sex offenders, Adler (1934) identified the importance of inferiority and superiority dynamics and social connectedness. Although Adler is not often given credit by the leading authorities in the sex offender treatment field, themes involving Adler's theory, philosophy and therapy are apparent in contemporary treatment.

Prior to the 1970s, individually orientated psychodynamic therapy was the primary mode of treatment for sexual offenders. In general, such therapy proved ineffective with moderate to high risk offenders (Carich and Mussack, 2001). In the 1970s, behaviour modification and behavioural therapy became the treatment of choice. However, the outcome results with these approaches were poor (Quinsey and Marshall,

1983). In the late 1970s and 1980s, both group and cognitive therapies became popular with therapists who worked with sexual offenders. Initially, group work was modelled after the Synanon drug treatment approach (Baker and Price, 1997). Soon therapists began using Yochelson and Samenow's (1976, 1977; Samenow, 1984) cognitive thinking error approach within a group format. Still, therapists realised that behavioural techniques were useful in arousal control. As the cognitive behavioural therapies emerged, they were applied to sex offenders in a group context. Cognitive behavioural approaches solidified with the application of relapse prevention strategies to sex offenders. Thus, contemporary sex offender treatment has evolved into a cognitive behavioural approach that entails a holistic view of targeting specific patterns of thinking and behaviour (Carich, Newbauer and Stone, 2001).

Contextual parameters of contemporary sex offender treatment

- Maintain the focus on the primary goals: **No more victims; reduce deviant arousal; and change any supporting lifestyle behavioural patterns.**
- Utilise empathy with firmness.
- Maintain control of the treatment. The worker needs to maintain the structure and control without abusing the power inherent in their role. It is essential that power is kept or maintained by the offenders' treatment staff given the authority, power and control issues. Part of the structure for achieving this objective is by maintaining control of the therapeutic process, centreing around cognitive and interpersonal restructuring, arousal control and cycle intervention. The therapeutic structure centres around a cognitive educational learning or skill developmental process and an affective experiential process. Both go hand in hand and compliment each other to optimise the results. The structure also consists of focusing on offence specific issues first and then related trauma issues. This avoids victim stancing and self-pity.
- The focus is on working on sex offenders specific issues first (i.e. offence disclosure/honesty, deviant fantasies, assault cycle, offence-related cognitive distortions, arousal control, etc.) and then related issues

(i.e., interpersonal issues, attachment/relational issues, various needs/core issues and beliefs, skills, social skills, global cognitive distortions, lifestyle behavioural patterns, offender trauma, etc.). It is important to start with offending and offender-specific issues rather than offender trauma issues (because of the potential of falling into the 'self-pity' trap). However, there is work emerging that suggests some offenders are unable to deal with their behaviour without having first successfully explored their own abuse (Calder, 2001). Hackett (2002) offered us a very useful summary of the issues raised in this area as well as a suggested framework for operational use that addresses both and links them so the offender can see how they have made some choices in the transition from abused to abuser.

- Avoid 'self-pity' traps.
- Link all offender behaviours/traumas to the promotion of victim empathy.
- Avoid enabling deviancy.
- Structure the treatment, by being directive when necessary, holding to rules.
- Emphasise insight with behavioural change or change in all of the experiential domains or dimensions (i.e. cognitive emotional, social, etc.)
- Utilise the offender's behaviour towards treatment goals.
- Limited self-disclosure (as offenders may use it against workers and it could distract them from the agreed goals).
- Emphasise both the process and skill development.
- As workers, maintain a high level of confidence (see later section for cues on this point).
- Develop and maintain a rapport or psychological contact.
- Use both psych-educational and experiential processes.
- Group therapy is the primary mode of treatment.
- A confrontational approach at some level is necessary, although we should always allow ourselves the flexibility to utilise a variety of interventions.
- The contemporary therapeutic framework consists of a cognitive-behavioural (experiential) mode. This is flexible to use a variety of strategies and techniques.
- Emphasise responsibility and accountability; choice; skill development; cognitive restructuring; social restructuring; arousal control; core issue/offender trauma resolution; assault cycle intervention; lifestyle/behavioural characteristics; a 'no cure' attitude, with an emphasis on control and management, through relapse prevention.
- Initially induce pain (not their behaviour/rules) instead of being 'warm' in our approach.
- The primary goal is to protect society, not to rehabilitate the offender.
- Do **not** allow offenders to victimise anyone, including the workers.

The aims of treatment

If the assessment of sex offenders is aimed at risk management, then the goal of assessment is to identify the factors related to the risk for sexual offending, and the goal of treatment is to change these risk factors amenable to change. Other aims may include:

- To help them control their actions in a way that avoids, or lessens, the risk of further abuse/developing relapse prevention skills and establishing supervision conditions.
- Accepting responsibility and modifying cognitive distortions.
- Developing victim empathy.
- Controlling sexual arousal.
- To lengthen the time between the abusive incidents.
- To reduce the seriousness of the abusive incidents.
- To encourage pro-social interactions by the offender/improving social competence.
- To strengthen the family unit by focussing on healthier, interactional communication patterns.
- To decrease the pathology by creating healthier family dynamics (adapted from Griggs and Bold, 1995).

Sex offender treatment aims to reduce the possibility of future sex offending from the level it would have maintained without treatment and each treatment programme is based upon the nature of the offending and the circumstances of the offender.

Characteristics of adequate treatment

The following list provides an overview of some of the agreed characteristics of sex offender treatment:

- provides much more structure
- less nurturing
- emphasises society and offender as a client
- fair but firm
- stresses victim empathy/victim impact
- emphasises 'no cure'
- uses cognitive restructuring
- uses relapse prevention as a central part of the intervention
- consistently sceptical
- authoritarian
- emphasises personal responsibility
- stresses the assault cycle
- directive
- emphasises supervision/monitoring
- continuously hits offender specific issues. Offender specific treatment addresses the following issues:
  - sexual aggression
  - victimology
  - victim impact
  - responsibility
  - violence related issues
  - deviant fantasies
  - deviant behaviour management
  - victim empathy
  - interpersonal relationships
  - relapse prevention
  - assault cycle-behaviour
  - case reviews
- checks deviant fantasies
- monitors deviant arousal
- willingness to help revoke parole
- doesn't personalise
- doesn't maintain secrecy with offender

Key treatment processes

Treatment processes are the proceedings, actions or series of actions that bring about a particular required change. Carich(1998) and Carich, Newhauer and Stone (2001) have outlined seven key treatment processes that usually occur in contemporary treatment. They are:

1. cognitive restructuring
2. social restructuring
3. arousal control
4. skill development
5. cycle intervention
6. clinical core issue resolution
7. lifestyle characteristics/behavioural change

We will now explore each of these processes individually.

1. **Cognitive restructuring** refers to changing the offender's belief systems, beliefs, types of thought processes, perceptions, attitudes, frame of references, world views, etc. Cognitions at both levels of the offence-specific distortions and global distorted cognitions are altered. Supporting victimising cognitions are changed and replaced with appropriate thoughts. Dysfunctional core beliefs and cognitions that promote maladaptive behaviours and emotions are targeted. This includes both supporting offence-specific distortions and global distortions. Most 'core beliefs are developed early in life and are influenced by messages received from parents, other influential people and (interpretations from) major life events' (ATSA, 1997, 23). Core beliefs influence decisions and attitudes. People's frame of references and/or world views are based on beliefs and belief systems. These are belief patterns that reflect one's fundamental beliefs about self and the world. Restructuring refers to identifying both offence-specific and global distortions. Once distortions are identified, they are challenged and replaced with appropriate functional beliefs.

2. **Social restructuring** refers to the process designed to generate changes in the structure of the offender's interpersonal relationships. This includes developing empathy as a child and victim empathy at both intellectual and emotional levels. The offender learns specific social skills and relationship skills. The entire social context is restructured. This involves working on various interpersonal issues (i.e., power, control, jealousy, alienating, possessiveness, etc.).

3. **Arousal control** refers to the management of deviant arousal. Deviant arousal can be seen as sexual attraction to inappropriate stimuli. It also refers to internal responses (both sexual at both emotional and physiological levels) to deviant stimuli generated internally and/or externally. Controlling arousal refers to the lowering or decreasing and/or managing of the offender's deviant responses and behaviour. More specifically, deviant arousal is decreased, while appropriate arousal is increased. The offender reduces offending arousal patterns and learns to live without them. Typically, methods of arousal control are used when the offender experiences high frequency or levels of

deviant fantasies, urges and 20% of full erection. Arousal control techniques are conditioning or behavioural interventions. ATSA recommends the following: odour aversion (pairing of noxious odours with deviant behaviour); verbal satiation (offender verbalises deviant fantasy nonstop for 10 to 20 minutes several times per week); masturbation satiation (offender masturbates past ejaculation during refraction (ATSA, 1997, 81). In essence, deviant arousal is decreased, while appropriate arousal increased.

4. **Skill development** refers to the offender learning specific coping skills, social skills, arousal (management) control skills, interventions, stress management, anger management, etc. Research indicates that many offenders have varying degrees of deficits in basic social and interpersonal skills. Specific skills include: personal hygiene, social isolation versus belonging, communication skills, assertiveness, anger management, stress management, interpersonal skills of developing and maintaining relationships within and outside of the family unit (ATSA, 1997). Offenders vary on their levels and types of skills.

5. **Cycle intervention** Sex offender treatment often involves and centres around the assault cycle or patterns of offending. Offenders learn how to recognise their cycles of abuse and risky situations. This encompasses the 'relapse prevention' approaches, strategies and tactics. Offenders learn their cues, triggers, cycles, cycle-behaviours and specific interventions or ways to diffuse their cycles.

6. **Clinical core issue resolution** It was mentioned earlier in the chapter that offending is multi-determined. Offending involves more than sexual gratification that stems from core issues linked to current/past interpretations or perceptions of key development events. These may be traumatic in nature. Offenders typically have many related issues. They are identified and resolved at differing levels.

7. **Lifestyle characteristics/behavioural change** Earlier in this chapter, offender lifestyle characteristics and patterns were discussed. The primary clusters of patterns include: antisocial, narcissistic, schizoid and borderline. The offender changing involves addressing their deviant inappropriate lifestyle behaviours. Offenders change patterns of lying, victimising, self-centredness, entitlement, alienation, withdrawal, and patterns of instability. Appropriate behavioural patterns are learned.

ATSA (1997; 2001) set out some additional considerations:

Relapse prevention: Relapse prevention (RP) approaches provide a set of methods to enable the offender to maintain abstinence and avoid relapse. RP is a cognitive-behavioural multi-model approach that enables the offender to identify cycle behaviour offence chains, risk factors (triggers), cues, pattern enablers, and develop some specific coping strategies or interventions. RP is best viewed as a self-management approach.

Victim awareness and empathy: One of the disinhibitors for offenders is the lack of empathy and remorse (ATSA, 1997). Although scientific research is unclear as to the necessity and reality of victim empathy, most clinicians agree that it is a necessary component of any treatment programme. Awareness, knowledge and insight of victim impact information is necessary for the offender to counter distorted thinking that supports their offending. Identifying victim harm leads to remorse (the painful regret of violating another individual). For the most effective results, it is suggested that victim empathy needs to occur at an emotional level.

Developing healthy relationships: Related to social competency skills include developing interpersonal relationships. This includes: sex education, dating, poor intimacy skills, social anxiety, sexual dysfunction, confidence in relationships (ATSA 1997). This model of achieving and maintaining healthy relationships based on respect, compassion, compatibility, mutual interests and affection.

Couple and parent therapy: Couple therapy is necessary when the offender's significant other is still involved to help monitor short and long term gains by the offender (ATSA, 1997). For those who offended within the family, reunification of the couple is necessary to help successful reunification of the family unit.

Pharmacological agents: Treatment through medications does not apply to all offenders. Anti-androgens, anti-depressants and other pharmacological agents may provide sex offenders greater control over excessive fantasies and compulsive behaviour (ATSA,

1997). For highly compulsive offenders, anti-depressants based on re-uptake inhibitors seem to be effective in reducing the obsessive-compulsive behaviour. Specialised medications may be selected for those individuals who are highly compulsive, extreme high risk, and who have history of treatment failure.

Follow-up treatment: Aftercare is a considerable continued element for the treatment of the sex offenders. Aftercare or follow-up treatment increases the likelihood that treatment gains are maintained and that the offender continues successful application of self-management skills. Aftercare treatment also involves some form of support. Typically, aftercare involves a progressive de-escalation of treatment contacts. For offenders coming from a residential setting, aftercare involves some type of extreme supervision.

Key components of sex offender treatment

A component is defined in this context as a part of the structure in a programme. There are a number of components in contemporary sex offender treatment. Each builds on the other, starting with assessment to aftercare. A summary of the 11 component parts and elements of ideal contemporary treatment include:

- Assessment and treatment planning.
- Offence-specific disclosure.
- Identify assault cycle and initial arousal control.
- Offence-specific cognitive restructuring.
- Initiate victim empathy.
- Skill development and the development of skill deficits.
- Identify and work through offender trauma and related core issues.
- Arousal control.
- Relapse prevention.
- Aftercare preparation.
- Continued support and treatment.

Carich (1998) offered us the following guidelines as to what elements might be addressed within each component part:

Assessment and treatment planning:
- Basic historical data collection; skill assessment.
- Offence/assault data and dynamics; pathology assessment.

- Victimology; identify issues.
- Non-historical or process data; treatment plan.
- Victim/assault profiles; risk assessment (static/dynamic factors).
- Social history and issues; cognitive distortions.

Offence-specific disclosure responsibility:
- Victim/assault profiles; initially defuse deviant arousal.
- Explore documented and non-recorded offences.
- Promote honesty and no secrets.
- Promote responsibility and accountability.
- Identify patterns and dynamics.

Identify assault cycle and initiate arousal control:
- Identify specific cognitive-behaviour chains, offence patterns, assault cycle, offending modes, etc.
- Develop early interventions to defuse arousal.
- Select relevant models.
- Develop a generic overall pattern of the cycle: (1) pre-assault, (2) assault, (3) post-assault cycle.
- Cycles are identified by: review and analysis of offences, and inserting data into cycle model.
- Arousal during this process is challenged and crushed.

Offence-specific cognitive restructuring:
- Identify and challenge specific distortions supporting offences and other deviant behaviours.
- Change or restructure distorted thinking to appropriate thinking.
- Emphasise accountability and responsibility.

Initiate victim empathy (VE) and remorse:
- Educational approach.
- Experiential approach.
- Key components: emotional recognition, victim harm recognition, responsibility, perspective taking, emotional expression.
- VE is the compassionate understanding of the victims pain, trauma and impact of offending.
- Remorse is the painful regret (feeling bad or guilt) of violating another person.
- VE is initiated early in treatment and continued throughout the treatment.

Skill development and the development of skill deficits:
- Developing social skills:
  - eye contact
  - 'I' messages
  - listening skills
  - paraphrasing
  - active listening
  - summarising
  - confrontational skills
  - conflict resolution tactics
  - conversational skills
  - emotional recognition
  - anger management
- Interpersonal issues or dynamics:
  - jealousy
  - power/control
  - boundaries
  - possessiveness
  - alienation/isolation
  - dependency
  - intimacy
  - attachment issues
  - enmeshed boundaries
- General coping skills:
  - anger and stress management
  - introduction to RP (after a solid foundation of empathy)
  - RET, or cognitive restructuring skills
  - social skills
  - life history
  - victim empathy
  - assault cycle
  - emotional recognition
  - life skills
  - coping skills
  - arousal interventions

Identify and work through offender trauma and related core issues:
   All offender trauma/core issue work is linked to victim empathy and appropriate remorse:
- Identify core issues stemming from developmental life experiences (i.e., core issues on key offender's perceptions and interpretations of specific life experiences).
- Emphasise offender responsibility.
- Develop insight into dynamics and issues.
- Access traumatic memories.
- Change offender reactions (responses) to memories (i.e., restructure supporting belief systems and emotional patterns).
- Emphasis is on action, that is change in all experiential modes (remember, insight is nice, but action is required).

Arousal control:
- Identify specific sexual arousal interests or deviant arousal.
- Target deviant arousal.
- Utilise various behavioural arousal interventions (i.e., aversive conditioning, minimal arousal conditioning, boredom therapy, verbal and masturbating satiation, covert sensitising, olfactory aversion therapy, etc.).
- Collapse deviant arousal with aversive stimulus and/or response.
- Re-condition appropriate arousal patterns.
- Increase and promote appropriate arousal.

Relapse prevention:
- RP is the fundamental set of skills to maintain recovery and aftercare preparation.
- Identify offence-specific cognitive-behavioural chains/dynamics and cycles or offending modes.
- Identify risk factors/triggers (stimulus events) and cues (warnings/signals).
- Develop and implement specific intervention skills.
- Program in or learn specific and general coping strategies (i.e. interventions).
- Develop specific relapse prevention plans.

Aftercare preparation:
- Most offenders, especially hard-core and chronic offenders, need after-care programming or continued care. The skills and changes learned in treatment need to be supported after the intensive treatment has ended.
- Recovery and risk assessment.
- Continue to refine RP skills.
- Develop conditions of aftercare release or plans, including supervision, treatment, placement, support systems and other components.

Continued support and treatment:
- Utilise internal monitoring supervision systems.
- Utilise external supervision systems (these may be formal or informal peer group support).
- Continue treatment (i.e., RP skills, further issue resolution, interpersonal development, support systems, etc.).
- Develop and attend specific support groups (i.e., AA, NA etc.).

Key elements of sex offender treatment

Elements are defined as a fundamental part of the whole treatment package. They include:

Basic sex offender-specific (community/outpatient) treatment

- Offence disclosure.
- Identifying and restructuring offence-specific cognitive distortions.
- Assault cycle and relapse prevention/intervention skills.
- Arousal control.
- Victim awareness and empathy.

Basic residential sex-offender specific treatment

1. *Offence disclosure and personal responsibility:*
   - denial and responsibility issues
   - disclosing offence
2. *Offence-specific cognitive restructuring:*
   - identify cognitive distortions
   - restructure distortions
3. *Assault cycle and intervention:*
   - identify offending patterns/processes
   - cognitive restructuring of global and offence-specific distortions
   - arousal control
   - social/interpersonal restructuring
   - interventions and coping skills
4. *Victim empathy:*
   - offence-specific cognitive restructuring
   - arousal control through victim empathy/cognitive restructuring
   - social skills-empathy specific
   - affective expression with perspective taking
5. *Arousal control:*
   - identify and reduce deviant arousal patterns
   - develop appropriate patterns
6. *Clinical/core issue resolution:*
   - identify and resolve any key issues
   - cognitive emotional restructuring
   - identify and change lifestyle behaviours
7. *Social skills and interpersonal restructuring:*
   - develop social skills
   - develop relationships
   - resolve interpersonal issues
8. *Lifestyle restructuring:*
   - identify and restructure dysfunctional lifestyle behaviours (antisocial, narcissistic, schizoid and borderline)

These elements can be condenswed into 5 basic tracks or components of treatment: 1 core issues/psychotherapy group, 2. victim empathy track, 3 psycho-educational skill, 4 cycle/RP skills, 5 arousal control.

Calder (1999) set out a complimentary package from which to draw from when individualising treatment programmes for sex offenders. This included:

- acceptance of responsibility
- confronting denial
- victim awareness and increased victim empathy
- full understanding of their abusive cycle
- full understanding of their targeting and grooming behaviours
- fantasy work – fully exploring their distorted thought processes
- decreasing cognitive distortions
- decreasing deviant arousal
- sexuality and perception
- sex and relationship education
- communications skills
- personal and social skills/increased social competency
- anger management
- assertiveness training
- reinforcement of internal and external inhibitors
- addressing family dynamics
- identifying risk factors
- where appropriate, addressing their own experiences of being abused
- work with the family
- identification of a relapse prevention programme

Any treatment programme, regardless of its theoretical base, can only stand a chance of being successful if it is both flexible as well as being rigorously and properly implemented. Treatment programmes should be individualised, planned, implemented and fully evaluated by fully trained staff, under supervision.

Treatment integrity

A lack of confidence in treatment is more likely to result in 'treatment drift', such that treatment is poorly delivered and lacks integrity. Any treatment programme, regardless of its theoretical base, can only stand a chance of being successful if it is rigorously and properly implemented. As such, all treatment programmes should be individualised, planned, implemented and fully evaluated by fully trained staff, under supervision.

Most treatment providers who work with sex offenders do so in the belief that it may enable them to refrain from further victimisations. Society tends to support treatment for this population principally because sex offenders are repetitive and because there is a prevailing belief that specialised treatment might enable sex offenders to refrain from further abuse of innocent women and children. However, the use of confrontational techniques clearly raises some issues to outside observers about the ethics of such an approach. This would be compounded if those workers adopting this approach did not believe the offender capable of change. Any hostility toward sex offenders can lead to workers denigrating the offender rather than fostering change in beliefs and behaviours. If treatment providers fail to respect the human dignity of clients, the likelihood of significant change is greatly diminished. Workers must ensure that society's anger at sex offenders does not exert a negative influence on their professional conduct (Pithers, 1997).

The meta-analyses strongly suggest that the high effect programmes have high 'treatment integrity'. The integrity principle is concerned with the management structures and practices required for the effective delivery of offender treatment. In practice, integrity encompasses the design of the treatment but, crucially, is also concerned with the implementation and maintenance of treatment. The need for treatment integrity makes many demands on organisations providing a treatment service: the need for integrity demands that management must address the training and supervision of the staff conducting the treatment; the need for integrity demands that those individuals responsible for the management and supervision of treatment are involved in all the operational phases of the programme; the need for integrity demands the assurance of quality; and the need for integrity demands that evaluation is an essential component of treatment so that failing programmes can be rescued (Hollin, 1999). Calder (1999b) developed a framework for organisations at a local level to embrace such concepts that has been widely used to encourage integrity of response (see Calder, 2001b; 2002d).

The sequencing of treatment programmes and Adlerian therapy

Adler is the father of cognitive-behavioural approaches and thus reference to Adlerian therapy is important in considering sex offender treatment.

Sex offender treatment programmes can be sequenced in certain ways to maximise outcomes. The components set out above can be arranged in a certain order to maximise each component. Each component can be built upon each other. Some component themes run continuously throughout the course of treatment. For example, assault cycle and intervention, victim empathy, social and cognitive restructuring, skill development, and arousal control are ongoing themes. Some components can be started at the same time, assuming one's programme has multiple types of groups.

The first two stages of Adlerian therapy – building rapport and investigating – are crucial. Blanchard (1995) emphasised the necessity of a therapeutic relationship in sex offender treatment. The second stage, investigation, allows the worker and the offender to identify lifestyle and personality characteristics and the level and type of sexual deviancy. The identification of specific sexual interest is important so they can be specifically targeted in treatment. The third Adlerian stage of therapy, insight, takes on a different connotation with regard to sex offenders. Insight is important in offence disclosure and identified victimology or offending history; identified distorted private logic; assault cycle; victim impact awareness; identifying deviant arousal; and risk factors (Calder, 1999). There is less emphasis placed on understanding specific offender traumas and motivational factors or the teleology of offending than in taking action or preventing re-offence. The fourth counselling stage is re-orientation or the action stage. Behavioural change is necessary to prevent sexual aggression. The elements discussed in the insight stage are transformed into action. For example, the offender needs to understand the impact of offending and to develop victim empathy and remorse. Not only do offenders need to identify and understand their cycles and accompanying risk factors, but they also need to develop specific skills to defuse or interrupt and cope with risk factors (Carich and Stone, 1996; Carich, Gray, Rombouts, Stone and Pithers, 2001). The critical elements and components of basic offender specific treatment can best be summarised as follows: relationship development and establishment of boundaries; offence disclosure; identifying offence-specific cognitive distortions (and restructuring private logic); initiating arousal control while identifying the assault cycle; developing victim empathy and remorse; arousal control intervention; social skills and skill development; resolving developmental-motivational core issues (or aetiological and teleological factors); developing adequate relapse prevention or intervention skills; and aftercare programming (Carich, Newbauer and Stone, 2001).

Treatment goals are derived from these elements. For details of possible programme sequences see Figures 1.9 and 1.10 overleaf.

Treatment planning

Green (1995) defines a responsible treatment plan as 'a remediation plan that, based on the sex offender's identified resources, problems, needs, and/or deficiencies, uses the most effective, appropriate, and available treatment methods to achieve the offender's treatment goals'. Such a plan also has the advantage of showing those involved with the offender what treatment has been offered as well as seeing their response to treatment. A comprehensive treatment plan identifies issues that are yet to be addressed or resolved. Accountability and professional quality assurance standards can be enhanced by an established treatment planning and documentation process. It invites the worker to continuously think about needs and objectives as well as providing the offender with an opportunity to trace their progress on each objective throughout the period of treatment. Reviews of progress should be taking place three-monthly, or as the need dictates, especially if the offender is not responding to the work.

Treatment planning is critical to contemporary treatment. It involves identifying the following elements:

- treatment goals
- specific objectives
- a plan of strategies and interventions
- expected outcomes
- time-frames of initiating and completion
- actual outcome

These combined increase the likelihood of a thorough treatment plan (Metzger and Carich, 1999).

Adult sex offenders are a heterogeneous group with varied treatment needs. Effective treatment planning requires an understanding of the overall personality and environmental context in which the sexually abusive behaviour occurred. Treatment plans need to address all the emotional and behavioural needs of the offender, not just their psychosexual problems. Adequate treatment planning involves assessing the degree of pathology and the resources that a sex offender has. For example, one offender may have a brief victimology and social skills, whereas another extensive history of sexual deviancy and a lack of social skills. Goals, strategies, and interventions need to be tailor made to fit the offender's needs.

Inadequate treatment planning or a lack of understanding about sex offenders can result in a mistaken judgement by workers that an offender has successfully completed treatment and is safe to live in the community. Reinforcement of offenders' denial or minimisation problems is often the result of such misunderstanding. Whilst planning is often viewed as a luxury, it is an essential foundation for quality treatment. 'Comprehensive treatment planning for sex offenders is a complex process requiring staff who understand the key components of such treatment and who have an organised process to systematically deliver the core treatment methodologies' (Green, 1995).

Treatment outcome and treatment planning are linked: poor and unclear planning and goals correlate with poor and unsafe outcomes. The workers need to translate the aims of treatment into measurable goals and an explicit plan. They must be specific to the individual case, and must include dates for review and revision as new information or changing circumstances present themselves.

Treatment goals

Treatment outcome and treatment planning are linked: poor and unclear planning and goals correlate with poor and unsafe outcomes. The workers need to translate the aims of treatment into measurable goals and an explicit plan. They must be specific to the individual case, and must include dates for review and revision as new information or changing circumstances present themselves. Carich and Adkerson (1995) set out 12 common sex offender treatment goals:

- Acknowledge and accept personal responsibility for complete sexual assault history.
- Improve understanding of human sexuality, including normal sexual development and functioning, reproduction, and sexual health.

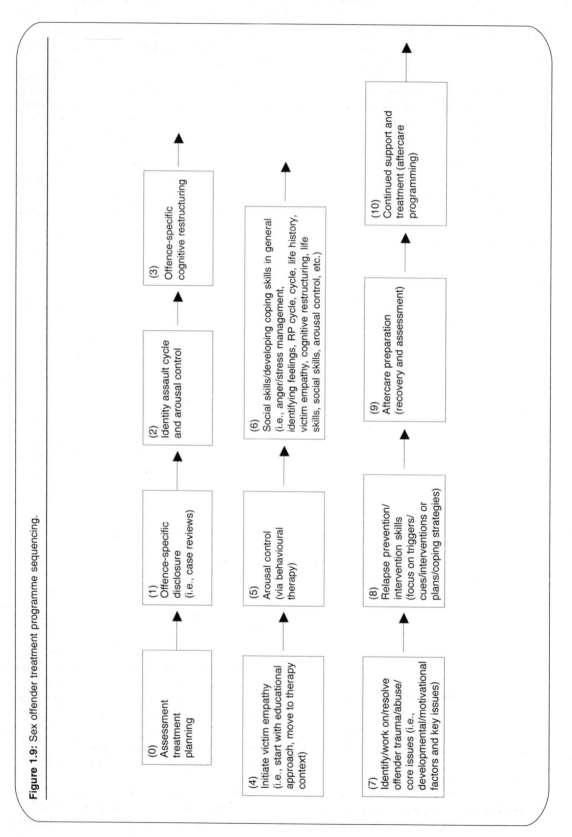

Figure 1.9: Sex offender treatment programme sequencing.

(0) Assessment treatment planning

(1) Offence-specific disclosure (i.e., case reviews)

(2) Identity assault cycle and arousal control

(3) Offence-specific cognitive restructuring

(4) Initiate victim empathy (i.e., start with educational approach, move to therapy context)

(5) Arousal control (via behavioural therapy)

(6) Social skills/developing coping skills in general (i.e., anger/stress management, identifying feelings, RP cycle, cycle, life history, victim empathy, cognitive restructuring, life skills, social skills, arousal control, etc.)

(7) Identify/work on/resolve offender trauma/abuse/core issues (i.e., developmental/motivational factors and key issues)

(8) Relapse prevention/intervention skills (focus on triggers/cues/interventions or plans/coping strategies)

(9) Aftercare preparation (recovery and assessment)

(10) Continued support and treatment (aftercare programming)

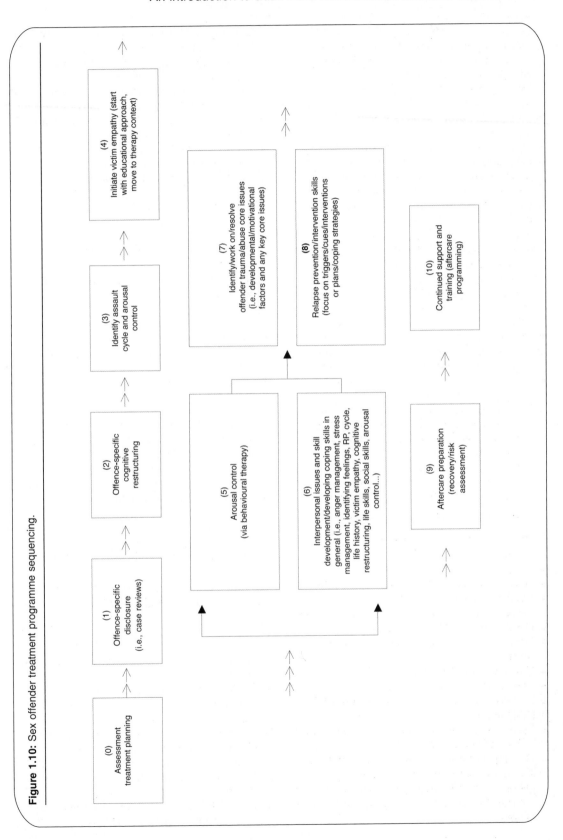

Figure 1.10: Sex offender treatment programme sequencing.

- Develop an understanding of how sexual assault negatively impacts the victim (short and long-term harm/risks) and develop empathy for own victim(s).
- Develop social and relationship skills to improve ability to meet social/sexual needs through appropriate relationships with age-mates.
- Separate anger, power, and other motivational issues from sexual behaviour. Improve anger management skills and remediate other motivations as needed.
- Clarify sexual arousal patterns and utilise modification techniques as appropriate.
- Clarify personal sexual offence cycle, include thoughts, feelings, behaviours and situations preceding offence. Demonstrate ability to recognise recurring aspects of the cycle.
- Actively change the distorted thinking and lifestyle supports of the sexual offence behaviour.
- Develop realistic, achievable intervention plans for each step in the sexual assault cycle. Demonstrate ability to intervene in cycle.
- Develop motivation and commitment to recovery and to remaining offence-free.
- Inform significant others completely and honestly about offending problem and seek support in offence abstinence from appropriate sources.
- Explore unresolved issues from personal victimisation, sexual or other, and work toward healing (57).

Carich (1997) extended this further:

- Develop victim empathy at both emotional and intellectual levels.
- Develop remorse.
- Develop the general notion of social interest.
- Resolve various issues within relationships such as possessiveness, jealousy, over-attachment, etc.
- Develop social skills.
- Develop an appropriate sense of power and control.
- Develop a number of functional relationships.
- Clarify one's sexual identity.
- Identify and change dysfunctional lifestyle behaviours.
- Resolve issues with emotional alienation and isolation from others.
- Develop an understanding at both intellectual and emotional levels of one's developmental history, and in particular to those events that are transformed into the various motivational factors.

- Develop an understanding of the motivations involved in sexual offending, in other words, the emotional satisfaction gained in sexual aggression.
- Develop skills to learn to manage one's deviant behaviour. Develop relapse intervention skills.
- Resolve various developmental motivational dynamics to a less intense level.
- Express appropriate affect.
- Develop stress management skills.
- Develop an appropriate sense of self-worth.
- Identify and change cognitive distortions or dysfunctional thinking.
- Identify and change disowning behaviours.

Within these goals are various objectives.

Attitude, responsibility and motivational level toward recovery

Objectives:

- Attendance at sessions.
- To actively participate in the programme of work.
- To develop internal motivation towards recovery.
- To develop a commitment towards treatment.
- Complete task assignments (compliance).
- Initiate or maintain journal or log.
- Outline life history and/or autobiography.
- Complete life history and/or autobiography.
- Identify offence-specific cognitive distortions.
- To accept responsibility for offences.
- Restructure offence distortions.
- Identify global distortions.
- Restructure global distortions.
- To develop responsibility for their behaviour.

Offender shows social interest in general care, concern, victim empathy and remorse

Objectives:

- To develop a general care and concern for others, by consistently expressing concern for others.
- To develop global empathy in general by consistently expressing understanding of others.
- To develop empathy at intellectual levels for victims i.e. can cognitively express understanding of others.
- To develop victim empathy for their specific victims at an intellectual level.
- To develop victim empathy for their victims at an emotional level as defined by emotional

recognition, victim harm recognition, assuming responsibility, perspective taking and emotional expression.
- To develop remorse (consistently expresses guilt or painful regret for violating victims).
- To express empathy (consistently using perspective-taking skills).

Offender develops appropriate social relationships and skills

Objectives:

- To learn specific social skills:
  - respect
  - 'I' messages
  - eye contact
  - active listening skills
  - initiating conversations
  - maintaining conversations
  - terminating conversations
  - conflict resolution/compromising skills
  - paraphrasing skills
  - summarising skills
- To identify and resolve specific interpersonal issues:
  - power/control
  - possessiveness
  - jealousy
  - enmeshed boundaries
  - isolation/alienation
  - rejection
  - dependency
  - unstable relationships
- To learn effective expression skills:
  - identify feelings
  - access and express feelings
- To develop appropriate close intimate relationships without sexual connotations:
  - engage in interpersonal relationships
  - develop appropriate relationships

Offender understands assault cycle concept and identifies his assault cycle

Objectives

- Understands the assault cycle.
- Applies the assault cycle concept.
- Identifies his assault cycle (3, 4 and 6-stage cycles) (see Chapter 4 for further details).

Offender displays target specific lifestyle characteristics

Objectives

- Antisocial behavioural characteristics/ patterns:

- exploitation (takes advantage of others)
- lies (purposefully and wholly untruthful statements) or distorts information (through omission, adding facts or embellishments)
- deceives others (deliberate concealing/ hiding the truth; intentionally misleading; secretive)
- current display of destructive and sadistic behaviour or cruelty
- Narcissistic behavioural characteristics/ patterns that need changing:
  - attitude of superiority
  - brags, exaggerates and exhibits grandiose behaviours
  - exaggerated sense of self-importance
  - distorted sense of entitlement, unrealistic expectations and demands
  - self-centred (out for self)
- Borderline behavioural characteristics/ patterns that need changing:
  - seeks immediate gratification and/or impulse control (especially in sexual behaviour and substance abuse)
  - repeated suicidal ideation/threats/ gestures/attempts
  - emotionally unstable (marked intense moodiness with mood shifts)

Offender displays insight into developmental/motivational dynamics and includes sexual identity issues

Objectives:

- Identify key developmental events (perceptions) that contribute to sex offending dynamics and increase autonomy/ independence lifestyle.
- Identify key motivational factors.
- Resolve key changing one's perceptions of those developmental events and/or traumas.
- Identify sexual identity issues.
- Resolve any key motivational dynamics or core issues that feed the offending process. Specifics include insecurity, rejection/ acceptance, abandonment, manhood issues, inferiority, low self-worth etc.

Offender will control his deviant behaviour

Objectives:

- Assess and identify deviant arousal patterns.
- Track deviant urges/fantasies (self-report).
- Reduce deviant sexual arousal patterns.
- Develop self-management arousal control skills.

- Develop appropriate arousal/fantasies.
- Reduce excessive masturbation.
- Eliminate self-abusive sexual behaviour.

Reduce and manage offender's psychopatholgy

Objectives:

- Identify any psychopathology.
- Resolve any/or reduce specified pathologies identified.

Offender will develop and understand relapse intervention model, process and skills

Objectives:

- Understand relapse prevention/intervention models and related concepts.
- Identify assault cycle/relapse process.
- Identify triggers/risk factors (high/low).
- Identify relapse cues.
- Identifying dysfunctional coping patterns (maladaptive coping response) and/or automatic relapse intervention responses.
- Develop functional coping (adaptive coping response).
- Identify lapse behaviours.

Offender will develop appropriate self-structure, self-esteem, self-image, self-confidence, self-worth and self-control based on non-deviant/victimising behaviours

Objectives:

- Identify patterns of dynamics ('old me' identities) involving poor self-concept constructs including worth, image, inferiority, esteem, confidence, security etc. That leads to compensation via offending.
- Identify underlying perceptions and related core issues and related core beliefs of 'old me' pattern.
- Defuse dysfunctional patterns of 'old me' via cognitive restructuring and cognitive behavioural experiential approaches.
- Develop an appropriate worth and self-concept or self-structure.

MacHovec (1994) argued that two major treatment goals should be included in treatment planning: normalisation and re-socialisation. Normalisation is intra-personal because it involves a thorough understanding of societal, community, and family values, lawful behaviour, and appropriate sexual outlet. It requires exploring and processing what is, and is not, normal behaviour and the self-concept including role identity, sexual preference, and self-esteem to restore personality function and continue normative development. Re-socialisation is interpersonal because it educates the offender in appropriate social and socio-sexual interaction in society, the home and community.

What do sex offenders want from sex offender treatment and what do they say about the process?

Langevin et al. (1988) reported on what treatment sex offenders wanted. Less than half actually desired any treatment at all. The preferred therapies were individual psychotherapy, social skills training and group therapy. The most frequently used therapy (aversion therapy) was among the most unacceptable, along with castration, sex drive reducing drug therapy and paradoxically group therapy. Male workers were preferred more than twice as much as female workers. Sex offenders saw interpersonal relations and a lack of social skills as their major problems. Overall, the results suggested that there is a considerable disparity between workers' application of treatment and the offenders' perceptions of their own needs. This has very clear implications in terms of agreeing a treatment programme and objectives as well as motivating the offender to change (Calder, 2002). Simkins et al. (1990) explored characteristics of sex offenders and their response to treatment. They found that offenders from higher socioeconomic classes show better treatment progress than those in the lower socioeconomic strata (possibly due to greater social competence, better verbal skills, better education, greater ability to provide the desired answers, etc.); they found that denial of their behaviour was a major impediment; those who had a sexually conservative orientation progressed more slowly than those whose sexual views were more liberal; and those offenders who had been victimised during their own childhood responded more rapidly than offenders with no such history.

Martin (1997) identified the journey through sex offender treatment, charting the triumphs and challenges facing the offenders. She identified five themes that stood out in their journey:

- Contending with the rough spots: where the offender faced a number of personal challenges that tested their strength and ability to persevere. Many said they found it hard sticking with the journey as they were continually being faced with challenges such as feeling forced to stay on track, getting the lay of the land, and resisting the journey.
- Feeling supported by others: they described their journey as leading to an increased knowledge of self and others and a powerful sense of feeling understood, supported and cared for by others.
- Working hard to stay on track: this was when the offenders were going through 'rough spots' and may well be resisting treatment and other times when they invested a lot of energy into staying on track and moving forward. During the times when they felt they were on track and working hard, it was evident that they had made a decision to take action, they were working hard, and were engaged in a process of new understandings.
- Being transformed by the journey: many described feeling a 'whole new person' entering a 'new life' when they left treatment. Most described feeling a better person than before.
- After the journey: the real work: although graduating from the treatment programme was a time of celebration, it was only the start of the change process and the real task of reorganising their lives and implementing new behaviours lay ahead. Their new world has many uncertainties and often lacks the same restrictions or structure.

Treatment effectiveness: What works or nothing works?

There is an unprecedented demand for knowledge and information concerning the efficacy of sex offender treatment. This is fuelled in part by belt-tightening budgets, widely publicised unfavourable media and other reports on outcomes of programmes, and the politicising of treatment of criminal behaviours in general, but especially of sexually aggressive behaviours (see Freeman-Longo and Knopp, 1992 for further details). Freeman-Longo and Knopp (1992) have noted that basing evaluations of treatment programme on 'success' rates is further complicated by the methodological shortcomings of virtually all published studies on sex offender recidivism

(such as Furby et al., 1989). As such, at the time of their article, no reliable body of longitudinal outcome data existed. They argued that in fact such information was not necessary as treatment is the most desirable, cost effective and safest long-range option available as a response to sex offending behaviour.

Calder (2002) has explored the difficult issues surrounding the determination of whether an intervention is successful or not. Hill (1999) noted that effectiveness generally refers to the extent to which goals are achieved and can be attributed to the programme itself. Goals normally involve some kind of change or improvement, such as new learning, more control over life circumstances, altered behaviour, fewer stresses or greater self-esteem. Thus two key elements are involved: assessing that change has occurred and establishing that the change would not have occurred anyway. It is often important to know whether a particular service made a difference compared with none or an alternative. Effectiveness thus differs from satisfaction with a service, although that may be a significant component in judging effectiveness. It is also important to look at all the effects not only those that were wished or anticipated. As we know from certain kinds of medication, it can be important to assess whether side effects outweigh the benefits in relation to the illness or condition. Interventions tend to have unintended consequences which need to be considered alongside the planned outcomes.

Hollin (1999) provided an excellent meta-analysis of 'what works' in offender treatment programmes.

Green (1995b) has explored issues of programme evaluation. He believes that it has to be an integral part of sex offender treatment as there is still a need for scientifically collected information regarding the efficacy of sex offender treatment, in terms of recidivism and behaviour change. At this time, it has not been established which treatment works best with what type of offender. This is problematic when opponents of treatment express concern at an inability to draw any firm conclusions on the overall effect of rehabilitative programmes (Gendreau and Andrews, 1990). This is even more problematic when they ask what works, for whom, under what conditions? Programme evaluation should elicit feedback on which type of treatment is most effective with what type of offender and at what cost, as well as to what degree the programme is achieving success in accomplishing its established goals and objectives. At the present time, methods of determining effectiveness of treatment methodologies have lagged behind other areas of development (such as risk assessment). However, the advent of meta-analyses and its application to the offender treatment literature has precipitated a major re-assessment of the 'nothing works' position. Hollin (1999) provided us with the following components of effective treatment programmes:

- Indiscriminate targeting of treatment programmes is counterproductive in reducing recidivism: medium to high risk offenders should be selected and programmes should focus on criminogenic targets.
- The type of treatment programme is important, with stronger evidence for structured behavioural and multi-modal approaches than for less-focused approaches.
- The most successful studies, while behavioural in nature, include a cognitive component to focus on attitudes and beliefs.
- Treatment programmes should be designed to engage high levels of offender responsivity.
- Treatment programmes conducted in the community have a stronger effect than residential programmes. While the latter can be effective, they should be linked structurally with community-based interventions.
- The most effective programmes have high treatment integrity in that they are carried out by trained staff and the treatment initiators are involved in all the operational phases of the treatment programmes.

Andrews and Bonta (1994) formulated the risk principle for effective programme delivery. The risk principle states that an important predictor of success is that offenders assessed as medium to high risk of recidivism (by criminal history or a standardised measure) should be selected for intensive treatment programmes. Effective risk assessment will allow accurate matching of the client group with the consequent level of delivery of the programme. These authors also offered the responsivity principle in referring to the need to deliver programmes in a style that will engage offenders. Some offenders will not have a high degree of verbal ability, high levels of personal insight, a willingness to engage in treatment work, display an aptitude to learn effectively from discussion, or have the same social and cultural backgrounds. Thus, treatment design

should actively seek to address these issues by engaging offenders at a level that is consistent with their individual ability and learning style. In practice, this may mean a very active style of delivery, with a predominance of role play and other active exercises.

One intriguing finding from the emerging meta-analyses is that treatment appears to be most effective with high-risk offenders (Lipsey, 1992).

Unlike outcome assessments for many psychological disorders (such as depression) the criteria for evaluating whether an individual sex offender has benefited from treatment must be indirect. The strongest outcome criterion for successful sex offender treatment is reduced sexual re-offending, and is the preferred outcome criterion in group outcome studies that follow the sex offender for several years. This direct measure, however, cannot be used for sexual offenders because sex offences are relatively infrequent, kept secret by the offender, and have devastating consequences for the victims (see Calder et al., 2001 for a detailed review). Recidivism also cannot be used as an outcome criterion for incarcerated offenders since they lack the opportunity to re-offend. Consequently, individual assessments of sex offenders must rely on indirect risk indicators, recognising that specific risk factors may be quite different for different offenders (Hanson, Cox and Woszcyna, 1991).

Freeman-Longo and Knopp (1992) argue that programme evaluation should be divided into two categories: process evaluation and outcome evaluation. Process evaluation is the measurement of a client's progress as he advances through the treatment process. Although a poor measure of programme success, failure or effectiveness, sex offender recidivism is generally the bottom-line used. This should not be used as the sole measure as relapse is ultimately a **choice** on the part of the offender and not necessarily a result of the adequacy of treatment delivery. Outcome evaluation is the measurement of overall programme effectiveness in treating sex offenders.

There have been some evaluation studies that have attempted to examine the effectiveness of treatment. In the UK, Barker and Morgan (1993) published a survey of the provision of community-based treatment programmes for sex offenders provided by the Probation Services in England, Wales and the Channel

Islands. Whilst they did discover some useful information (such as the lack of managerial support for the work; inadequate resourcing; and most offenders received 50 hours of intervention), there was a dearth of follow-up information and no attempt to monitor or evaluate the effectiveness of the work being done. Procter and Flaxington (1996) repeated this survey, finding that the number of groups had doubled, the duration of treatment had risen to 81 hours, and many programmes had started to evaluate their effectiveness. A series of further studies were then commissioned by the Home Office to undertake an evaluation of the effectiveness of treatment in prisons. One such study, the STEP (Sex Offender Treatment Evaluation Project) attempted to:

- Describe the developmental and presenting characteristics of sex offenders undergoing therapy in a number of representative treatment programmes conducted by probation services in England.
- Evaluate the extent to which these treatment programmes were successful in treating offence-specific and personality problems in treatment.
- Provide a framework for the long-term examination of the relationship between change achieved after treatment and recidivism (Beckett et al., 1994).

This was one of a series of evaluation studies carried out by the STEP team (see also Beech, Fisher, Beckett and Fordham, 1998). In assessing the extent to which treatment had been effective with individual offenders, the level of pre-treatment deviancy was taken into account. Highly deviant offenders had to make substantial changes to show treatment effect, whereas less deviant offenders needed to change relatively less. Treatment effectiveness was measured using a battery of psychological tests that measured the areas covered in treatment programmes. Overall, the results revealed that:

- More than half of the total sample showed a treatment effect. Such individuals had profiles indistinguishable from the non-offending sample on most of the assessment measures at post-test.
- All of the programmes were found to have a significant effect on offenders' willingness to admit to their offences and sexual problems

and the programmes significantly reduced the extent to which offenders justified their offending. They also reduced offenders' distorted thinking about children and sexuality.

- Short-term programmes (about 60 hours of therapy) appeared to have a good overall success rate (59%). However, the result was likely to be due to the fact that most of the offenders in these programmes could be considered 'low deviancy'. They had no success with highly deviant men.
- Two-thirds of the offenders who attended the specialist facility at the Gracewell Clinic and received an average of 462 hours of group therapy showed significant treatment effect. Such therapy with serious offenders was found to be related to a greater admittance of offending behaviours and improvements in self-esteem, assertiveness, and intimacy skills. Improvements in these areas may be an important factor in reducing the risk of reconviction because if offenders do not have the appropriate skills and self-confidence to form effective relationships with adults, they may continue to seek intimacy with underage and inappropriate partners (Marshall, 1989).

Marshall, Anderson and Champagne (1999) obtained information on 12 sexual offender treatment programmes, each of which was able to compare the participants with a reasonably well matched group of untreated offenders. All these studies accessed official recidivism data over a satisfactory period of time. Four of the reports found no value for treatment whereas the other eight demonstrated a statistically significant treatment effect. These results are encouraging and are consistent with the meta-analytic studies of treatment effects conducted by Alexander (1999), Hall (1995) and Hanson and Bussiere (1998). Each of these meta-analyses revealed positive, although not always remarkable, effects for treatment. The more sophisticated the outcome studies have become, the stronger the evidence that sexual offenders can be treated effectively. There is some emerging evidence that treatment has been effective even for the highest risk offenders (Looman et al., 1999).

Most of the research focuses on the type of treatment approach adopted and the characteristics of sex offenders who benefit from treatment, rather than on group processes (Beech and Fordham, 1997). The general conclusions from the available research shows that comprehensive cognitive-behavioural programmes work best, that treatment was most effective with child molesters and exhibitionists, and that rapists showed little or no improvement during treatment (Marshall, Ward, Jones, Johnston and Barbaree, 1991). Stephenson (1991) reported on a comparison between eight community based groupwork programmes and found that only one was successful in reducing recidivism. This group was found to be better managed than the other programmes; those involved in running the group kept accurate records, and the workers prepared a comprehensive pre-treatment plan, did not tolerate denial, and were tough-minded in their approach but were respected by their clients. In the less successful programmes, the offenders' behaviour was often disruptive and considerable hostility was expressed towards some workers.

Many factors clearly influence treatment outcome: such as the amount of treatment, the level of post-treatment support, the level of sexual and social problems before treatment, and the acquisition and employment of an effective relapse prevention plan. However, Beech and Fordham (1997) also found that group climate has an important influence on the quality and impact of treatment for sex offenders.

Hanson et al. (2002) produced a meta-analytic review of the effectiveness of psychological treatment for sex offenders by summarising data from 43 studies embracing 9000 offenders. They found that:

- The sex offender recidivism rate was lower for treatment groups (12.3%) than the comparison groups (16.8%) and for general recidivism (27.9% treatment compared to 39.2% in the comparison group).
- CBT and systemic approaches were associated with reductions in both sexual recidivism (from 17.4 to 9.9%) and general recidivism (from 51 to 32%).
- Older forms of treatment (operating prior to 1980) appeared to have little effect.

This study offers a cautious optimism for modern sex offender treatment programmes (SOTP) for high-risk offenders. In the case of low-risk sex offenders the beneficial value of SOTP hasn't and perhaps cannot be demonstrated because of the difficulty in improving the low base rate for recidivism.

Print (2000) has pointed to the following issues to enhance the effectiveness of our intervention:

- Interventions should be ecologically orientated, promoting systemic change and multi-modal – employing a variety of methods e.g. individual, family and groupwork.
- Interventions should promote skill development, behavioural and attitudinal change.
- Programmes should be structured to address factors that contribute to the maintenance of all forms of criminal/anti-social behaviour.
- Treatment for more problematic and deviant clients requires significant intensity and duration.
- Programmes should actively involve families and carers.
- The design of interventions should be informed by those factors seen to promote resilience and positive outcomes for young people.
- Services need to consider how to engage non-co-operative parents and poorly motivated clients.
- More effective programmes are characterised by high treatment integrity.

Marshall and Serran (2000) explored how to improve the effectiveness of sex offender treatment. They point out that treatment programmes are still in their infancy and sexual offender treatment has only recently emerged as a separate clinical focus. More effective treatment will result as we begin to identify the full range of problems experienced by sex offenders, as well as the type of treatment required by different types of offenders. Marshall, Fernandez, Hudson and Ward (1998) produced a book on how to adapt cognitive-behavioural programmes for imprisoned sex offenders, psychiatrically disturbed offenders, community-based clients, culturally diverse groups, a range of distinct client groups and offenders with disabilities. With the advent of empirical research, we have to be optimistic that the application of this to the development of treatment programmes will improve the outcomes.

One of the most neglected areas of treatment relates to the process as the focus has long been on the procedures that produce changes aimed for in treatment with these offenders. Some workers have pointed to the centrality of the rker style and the client's response (such as Barnard et al., 1989). Marshall (1996) discussed three possible general styles that sex offender workers may adopt. He pointed out that the strongly confrontational style is likely to decrease the client's self-confidence, which in turn impedes therapeutic change. It also fails to model empathy. At the other end of the continuum is where the worker colludes with the offender, failing to challenge any of his statements. He suggested that supportively and firmly challenging the offenders, providing encouragement for progress, being expressively empathic when appropriate, and explicitly enhancing the offender's self-esteem, is the ideal therapeutic style.

Recommendations to workers

Mussack and Carich (2001) produced a useful list for workers to consider when undertaking sex offender treatment work. They included:

- Know your material and the client.
- Focus on strengths as well as problems (explored in detail in Calder, 1999 and 2002b).
- Emphasise what over why: since the origins of their behaviour are often multiple and complicated and are rarely fully understood.
- Join thoughts and behaviours with feelings: as the offender's misattribution and misidentification of both their own affective states and the emotional experiences of victims are intrinsic components of many sexual assaults.
- Focus initially on facts and behaviours over words: offenders prevent being overwhelmed by negative emotional states through employing cognitive distortions. The worker will often find a discrepancy between what the offender says and what they observe. By providing consistent feedback of a factual nature the offender can begin the development of cognitive dissonance, the presence of two competing ways of understanding the same event, within the offender. This can provide opportunities to address the required areas of change.
- Depersonalise interactions: to reduce the chances of the offender successfully distracting the worker from their task.
- Reinforce new learning with repetition.
- Use examples and specifics.
- Use presumptive questioning (see section on assumptions earlier in this chapter).
- Maintain clear therapeutic boundaries (p6-8).

Summary

As a specialised discipline, sex offender discipline is comparatively young. As such the development of the work is dynamic at the same time as being vulnerable to attack. What this chapter and the remainder of the book will confirm is that most programmes include a variety of assessment and treatment techniques, although there is often a tendency to include cognitive-behavioural techniques and relapse prevention. We believe that although treatment is costly the decision not to treat can be more costly emotionally and psychologically for the offender, for the victims and the future victims, and for society. The benefits of treating sex offenders are numerous: it helps the offender to manage his behaviour; it encourages the reporting of sexual abuse; it contributes to our understanding of sexual abuse; and most importantly, it prevents the creation of new victims (Freeman-Longo and Knopp, 1992).

References

Abel G G, Becker J V, Cunningham-Rathner J, Kaplan M and Reich, J (1984) *The Treatment of Sex Offenders*. NY: SBC-TM.

Abel G G, Becker J V, Murphy N and Flanagan B (1981) Identifying Dangerous Child Molesters. In Stuart R B (Ed.) *Violent Behaviour: Social Learning Approaches to Prediction, Management and Treatment*. NY: Brunner-Mazel, 116–37.

Adler A (1934) Sexual Perversion. *Individual Psychology Pamphlets*. 13: 25–36.

Alexander M A (1999) Sexual Offender Treatment Efficacy Revisited. *Sexual Abuse: A Journal of Research and Treatment*. 11: 101–16.

Andrews D A and Bonta J (1994) *The Psychology of Criminal Conduct*. Cincinnati, OH: Anderson Publishing Co.

ATSA (1997) *Ethical Standards and Principles for the Management of Sexual Abusers*. Beaverton, OR: ATSA.

Baker A W and Duncan S F (1985) Child Sexual Abuse: A Study of Prevalence in Great Britain. *Child Abuse and Neglect*. 9: 457–76.

Baker D and Price S (1997) Developing Therapeutic Communities for Sex Offenders. In Schwartz B K and Cellini H R (Eds.) *The Sex Offender: New Insights, Treatment Innovations and Legal Developments*. Kingston, NJ: Civic Research Institute, 19–31.

Barker M and Beech A R (1993) *Sex Offenders: A Framework for The Evaluation of*

Community-Based Treatment. London: Home Office Publications Unit.

Barker M and Morgan R (1993) *Sex Offenders: A Framework of Community-Based Treatment*. London: Home Office Publications Unit.

Barnard G W, Fuller A K, Robbins L and Shaw T (1989) *The Child Molester: An Integrated Approach to Evaluation and Treatment*. NY: Brunner/Mazel.

Becker J V and Kaplan M S (1988) The Assessment and Treatment of Adolescent Sexual Offenders. *Advances in Behavioural Assessment of Children and Families*. 4: 97–118.

Beckett R C, Beech A R, Fisher D and Fordham A S (1994) *Community-Based Treatment for Sexual Offenders: An Evaluation of Seven Treatment Programmes*. London: Home Office Publications Unit.

Beech A and Fordham A S (1997) Therapeutic Climate of Sexual Offender Treatment Programs. *Sexual Abuse: A Journal of Research and Treatment*. 9: 3, 219–37.

Beech A R et al. (1998) A Psychometric Typology of Child Abusers. *International Journal of Offender Therapy and Comparative Criminology*. 42: 319–49.

Bernard J and Bernard M (1984) The Abusive Male Seeks Treatment: Jekyll and Hyde. *Family Relations*. 33: 543–7.

Blanchard G T (1996) *The Difficult Connection: The Therapeutic Relationship in Sex Offender Treatment*. Brandon, VT: Safer Society Press.

Brake S C and Shannon D (1997) Using Pre-Treatment to Increase Admission in Sex Offenders. In Schwartz B K and Cellini H R (Eds.) *The Sex Offender: New Insights, Treatment Innovations and Legal Developments*. Kingston, NJ: Civic Research Institute.

Breiling J (1994) Paper Presented at The 10th National Training Conference of The National Adolescent Perpetrator Network. Denver, Colorado, February 1994.

Calder M C (1997) *Juveniles and Children Who Sexually Abuse: A Guide to Risk Assessment*. Lyme Regis, Dorset: Russell House Publishing.

Calder M C (1999) *Assessing Risk in Adult Males Who Sexually Abuse Children: A Practitioner's Guide*. Lyme Regis, Dorset: Russell House Publishing.

Calder M C (1999b) A Conceptual Framework for Managing Young People Who Sexually Abuse: Towards A Consortium Approach. In Calder M C (Ed.) *Working With Young People Who Sexually Abuse: New Pieces of The Jigsaw Puzzle*. Lyme Regis, Dorset: Russell House Publishing, 109–50.

Calder M C (2001) *Juveniles and Children Who Sexually Abuse: Frameworks for Assessment*. (2nd edn). Lyme Regis, Dorset: Russell House Publishing.

Calder M C (2001b) Child Prostitution: Developing Effective Protocols. *Child Care in Practice*. 7: 2, 98–115.

Calder M C (2002b) A Framework for Conducting Risk Assessments. *Child Care in Practice*. 8: 1, 1–18.

Calder M C (2002d) *Children Affected by Domestic Violence: Generating A Framework for Effective Inter-Agency Responses*. Presentation to A Nexus Conference 'Not in Front of Children: Responding to Conflict at All Ends of the Spectrum', TUC Congress Centre, London, 27th June, 2002.

Calder M C (Ed.) (2002) *Young People Who Sexually Abuse: Building the Evidence-Base for Your Practice*. Lyme Regis, Dorset: Russell House Publishing.

Campbell T, Carich M S and Burgener J (2000) *5-Factor Typology of Sex Offenders*. Unpublished Handout.

Carich M S (1995) The Use of RI/RP in Sex Offender Treatment – Part IV: Overview of The RI Model. *The Post* 2: 3, 3–9.

Carich M S (1997) *Sex Offender Treatment and Overview: Training for The Mental Health Professional*. Springfield, Illinois: Illinois Department of Corrections.

Carich M S (1998) *Developing A Contemporary Context for Treatment*. Paper Presented at IDOC Sex Offender Training, Joilet, Illinois, 26th June 1998.

Carich M S (1999a) Evaluation of Recovery: 15 Common Factors or Elements. In Calder M C *Assessing Risk in Adult Males Who Sexually Abuse Children*. Lyme Regis, Dorset: Russell House Publishing, 279–81.

Carich M S and Adkerson D L (1995) *Adult Sexual Offender Assessment Packet*. Brandon, VT: Safer Society Press.

Carich M S and Stone M (1996) *The Sex Offender Relapse Prevention Workbook*. Chicago: Adler School of Professional Psychology.

Carich M S, Baig M and Harper J (2002) A Brief Review of Contemporary Sex Offender Treatment. *The Forensic Therapist*. 1: 6–11.

Carich M S, Gray A, Rombouts S, Stone M and Pithers W D (2001) Relapse Prevention and The Sexual Assault Cycle. In Carich M S and Mussack S E (Eds.) *Handbook for Sexual Abuser*

Assessment and Treatment. Brandon, VT: Safer Society Press.

Carich M S, Newbauer J F and Stone M H (2001) Sexual Offenders and Contemporary Treatments. *The Journal of Individual Psychology*. 57: 1, 3–17.

Coleman E and Miner M (2000) Introduction: Promoting Sexual Offender Treatment Around The World. *Journal of Psychology and Human Sexuality*. 11: 3, 1–10.

Coleman E, Dwyer S M, Abel G, Berner W, Breiling J, Hindman J, Honey-Knopp F, Langevin R and Phafflin F (1996) Standards of Care for The Treatment of Adult Sex Offenders. *Journal of Offender Rehabilitation*. 22: 5–11.

Conte J R, Wolf S and Smith T (1989) What Sexual Offenders Tell Us About Prevention. *Child Abuse and Neglect*. 13: 293–301.

Craft A (1992) Remedies for Difficulties. *Inside Supplement*. 25.6.92, Iii–Iv.

Doren D (2002) *Evaluating Sex Offenders: A Manual for Civil Commitments and Beyond*. Thousand Oaks, CA: Sage Publications.

Eldridge H (1998) *Therapist's Guide for Maintaining Change*. London: Sage Publications.

Elliott M (1986) *Keeping Safe: A Practice Guide to Talking to Children*. London: NVCO/Bedford Press.

Elliott M, Browne K and Kilkoyne J (1995) Child Sexual Abuse Prevention: What Offenders Tell Us. *Child Abuse and Neglect*. 19: 5, 579–94.

English K (1998) The Containment Approach: An Aggressive Strategy for the Community Management of Sex Offenders. *Psychology, Public Policy and Law*. 4 (1/2): 218–35.

Finkelhor D (1984) *Child Sexual Abuse: Theory and Research*. NY: The Free Press.

Frances A, Clarkin J and Perry S (1984) *Differential Therapeutics in Psychiatry*. NY: Brunner/Mazel.

Freeman-Longo R, Bays L and Bear E (1996) *Empathy and Compassionate Action Issues and Exercises: A Guided Workbook for Clients in Treatment*. Brandon, VT: Safer Society Press.

Freeman-Longo R E and Blanchard G T (1998) *Sexual Abuse in America: Epidemic of The 21st Century*. Brandon, VT: Safer Society Press.

Freeman-Longo R E and Knopp F H (1992) State-Of-The-Art Sex Offender Treatment: Outcome and Issues. *Annals of Sex Research*. 5: 141–60.

Furby L, Weinrott M R and Blackshaw L (1989) Sex Offender Recidivism: A Review. *Psychological Bulletin*. 10: 1, 3–30.

Furniss T (1991) *The Multi-Professional Handbook of Child Sexual Abuse*. London: Routledge.

Gendreau P and Andrews D A (1990) What The Meta-Analyses of the Offender Treatment Literature Tell Us About 'What Works'. *Canadian Journal of Criminology*. 32: 173–84.

Goodman G S (1984) The Child Witness. *Journal of Social Issues*. 40: 2 Summer.

Goodwin J, Cormier L and Owen J (1983) Grandfather-Grand-Daughter Incest: A Tri-Generational View. *Child Abuse and Neglect*. 7: 163–70.

Green (1995) Comprehensive Treatment Planning for Sex Offenders. In Schwartz B K and Cellini H R (Eds.) *The Sex Offender: Correction, Treatment and Legal Practice*. Kingston, NJ: Civic Research Institute.

Green R (1995b) Sex Offender Treatment Program Evaluation. In Schwartz B K and Cellini H R (Eds.) *The Sex Offender: Correction, Treatment and Legal Practice*. Kingston, NJ: Civic Research Institute.

Griggs D R and Bold A (1995) Parallel Treatment of Parents of Abuse-Reactive Children. In Hunter M (Ed.) *Child Survivors and Perpetrators of Sexual Abuse: Treatment Innovations*. Thousand Oaks, Ca; Sage, 147–65.

Grossman L (1985) Research Directions in the Evaluation and Treatment of Sex Offenders: An Analysis. *Behavioral Sciences*. 3 (4): 421–40.

Grossman L, Martis B and Fichtner C (1999) Are Sex Offenders Treatable? A Research Overview. *Psychiatric Services*. 50 (3): 349–61.

Groth A N and Oliveri F J (1989) Understanding Sexual Abuse Offence Behaviour and Differentiating Among Sexual Abusers: Basic Conceptual Issues. In Sgroi S M (Ed.) *Vulnerable Populations (Volume 2)*. Lexington: D C Health, 309–27.

Groth N (1982) The Incest Offender. In Sgroi S M (Ed.) *Handbook of Clinical Intervention in Child Sexual Abuse*. Lexington, MA: Lexington Books.

Hackett S (2002) Abused and Abusing: Work With Young People Who Have A Dual Sexual Abuse Experience. In Calder M C (Ed.) *Young People Who Sexually Abuse: Building The Evidence-Base for Your Practice*. Lyme Regis, Dorset: Russell House Publishing, 203–17.

Hall G C N (1995) Sexual Offender Recidivism Revisited: A Meta-Analysis of Treatment Studies. *Journal of Consulting and Clinical Psychology*. 63: 82–9.

Hanson R K (2000) *Risk Assessment*. Beaverton, Oregon: ATSA.

Hanson R K (2002) Introduction to The Special Section on Dynamic Risk Assessment With Sex Offenders. *Sexual Abuse: A Journal of Research and Treatment.* 14: 2, 99–101.

Hanson R K and Bussiere M T (1998) Predicting Relapse: A Meta-Analysis of Sexual Offender Recidivism Studies. *Journal of Consulting and Clinical Psychology.* 66: 348–62.

Hanson R K, Cox B and Woszcyna C (1991) Assessing Treatment Outcome for Sexual Offenders. *Annals of Sex Research.* 4: 177–208.

Hill M (1996) Effective Professional Intervention in Children's Lives. In Hill M (Ed.) *Effective Ways of Working With Children and Their Families.* London: Jessica Kingsley.

Hollin C R (1995) The Meaning and Implications of 'Programme Integrity'. In Mcguire J (Ed.) *What Works: Effective Methods to Reduce Re-Offending.* Chichester: John Wiley and Sons, 195–208.

Hollin C R (1999) Treatment Programs for Offenders: Meta-Analysis, 'What Works?' and Beyond. *International Journal of Law and Psychiatry.* 22: 361–72.

Jones D (1985) *False Reports of Sexual Abuse: Do Children Lie?* Paper Presented at The 7th National Conference on Child Abuse and Neglect. Chicago: November.

Kelly L and Radford J (1990/1) 'Nothing Really Happened'! The Validations of Women's Experiences of Sexual Violence. *Critical Social Policy.* 30: 39–53.

Kelly L, Regan L and Burton S (1991) *An Exploratory Study of The Prevalence of Sexual Abuse in A Sample of 16–21 Year Olds.* London: Child Abuse Studies Unit.

Knight R A and Prentky R B (1990) Classifying Sexual Offenders: The Development and Corroboration of Taxonomic Models. In Marshall W L, Laws D R and Barbaree H (Eds.) *Handbook of Sexual Assault.* NY: Plenum Press, 23–54.

Langevin R, Wright P and Handy L (1988) What Treatment Do Sex Offenders' Want? *Annals of Sex Research.* 1: 363–85.

Lanning, K V (1992). *Child Molesters: A Behavioral Analysis for Law Enforcement Officers Investigating Cases of Child Sexual Exploitation.* Arlington, VA: National Center for Missing Children.

Lauen R J (1997) *Positive Approaches to Corrections: Research, Policy and Practice.* Maryland: American Correctional Association.

Laws D R and O'Donohue W (Eds.) (1997) *Sexual Deviance: Theory, Assessment and Treatment.* NY: Guilford Press.

Lewis-Herman J (1990) Sex Offenders: A Feminist Perspective. In Marshall W L, Laws D R and Barbaree H E (Eds.) *Handbook of Sexual Assault.* NY: Plenum Press, 177–93.

Lipsey M W (1992) Juvenile Delinquency Treatment: A Meta-Analytic Enquiry Into The Variability of Effects. In Cook T D, Hoper H, Cordray D S, Hartmann H, Hedges L V, Light R J, Louis T A and Mosteller F (Eds.) *Meta-Analysis for Explanation: A Casebook.* NY: Russell Sage Foundation, 83–127.

Looman J, Abracen J and Nicholaichuk T (1999) *Recidivism Among Treated Sexual Offenders and Matched Controls.* Unpublished.

Loss P, Ross J E and Richardson J (1988) *Psycho-Educational Curriculum for Adolescent Sex Offenders.* New London, Conneticut: Loss and Ross.

Macovec F (1994) A Systemic Approach to Sex Offender Therapy: Diagnosis, Treatment and Risk Assessment. *Psychotherapy in Private Practice.* 13: 2, 93–108.

Macleod M and Saraga M (1988) Challenging The Orthodoxy: Towards A Feminist Theory of Practice. *Feminist Review.* 28: 16–55.

Macleod M and Saraga M (1991) Clearing A Path Through The Undergrowth: A Feminist Reading of Recent Literature on Child Sexual Abuse. In Carter P, Jeffs T and Smith M K (Eds.) *Social Work and Social Welfare.* Milton Keynes: Open University Press, 30–45.

Mann R (Ed.) (1996) *Motivational Interviewing With Sex Offenders: A Practice Manual.* Hull: Bluemoon Corporate Services.

Margolin L (1992) Sexual Abuse by Grandparents. *Child Abuse and Neglect.* 16: 735–41.

Marshall W L (1993) The Role of Attachment, Intimacy, and Loneliness in The Aetiology and Maintenance of Sexual Offending. *Sexual and Marital Therapy.* 8: 109–21.

Marshall W L (1989) Intimacy, Loneliness and Sexual Offending. *Behavioural Research and Therapy.* 17: 491–503.

Marshall W L (1996) Assessment, Treatment and Theorizing About Sex Offenders: Development Over The Past 20 Years and Future Directions. *Criminal Justice and Behaviour.* 23: 1, 162–99.

Marshall W L (1999) Current Status of North American Assessment and Treatment Programs for Sexual Offenders. *Journal of Interpersonal Violence.* 14 (3): 221–39.

Marshall W L and Eccles A (1991) Issues in Clinical Practice With Sex Offenders. *Journal of Interpersonal Violence.* 6: 68–93.

Marshall W L and Serran G A (2000) Improving The Effectiveness of Sexual Offender Treatment. *Trauma, Violence and Abuse.* 1: 3, 203–22.

Marshall W L, Anderson D and Champagne F (1996) Self-Esteem and Its Relationship to Sexual Offending. *Psychology, Crime and The Law.* 3: 81–106.

Marshall W L, Anderson D and Fernandez Y M (1999) *Cognitive Behavioural Treatment of Sexual Offenders.* Chichester: John Wiley and Sons.

Marshall W L, Ward T, Jones R, Johnston P and Barbaree H E (1991) An Optimistic Evaluation of Treatment Outcome With Sex Offenders. *Violence Update.* 1: 8–11.

Marshall W L, Barbaree H E and Fernandez (1995) Some Aspects of the Social Incompetence in Sex Offenders. *Sexual Abuse: A Journal of Research and Treatment.* 7: 113–27.

Martin S (1997) Sex Offender Treatment: An Uphill Struggle. *Journal of Child and Youth Care.* 11: 1, 27–42.

Mayer A (1988) *Sex Offenders: Approaches to Understanding and Management.* Holmes Beach, FI: Learning Publications, Inc.

Metzger C and Carich M S (1999) Eleven Point Comprehensive Sex Offender Treatment Plan. In Calder M C (Ed.) *Assessing Risk in Adult Males Who Sexually Abuse Children.* Lyme Regis, Dorset: Russell House Publishing, 293–311.

Miller J (1978) Recidivism Among Sexual Assault Victims. *Journal of Social Issues.* 39: 2, 139–52.

Money J (1986) *Lovemaps: Clinical Concepts of Sexual Health and Pathology Paraphilia and Gender Transposition in Childhood, Adolescence and Maturity.* NY: Irvington Publishers.

Moore J (1990) Confronting The Perpetrator. *Community Care,* 12.4.90, 20–1.

Morrison T (1989) Treating The Untreatable? Groupwork With Intra-Familial Sex Offenders. In NSPCC Occasional Paper 2, 'The Treatment of Child Sexual Abuse.' London NSPCC, 6–13.

Murphy W D and Carich M S (2001) Cognitive Distortions and Restructuring in Sexual Abuser Treatment. In Carich M S and Mussack S E (Eds.) *Handbook for Sexual Abuser Assessment and Treatment.* Brandon, VT: Safer Society Press, 65–75.

Mussack S E and Carich M S (2001) Sexual Abuser Evaluation. In Carich M S and Mussack S E (Eds.) *Handbook for Sexual Abuser Assessment and Treatment.* Brandon, VT: Safer Society Press, 11–29.

National Task Force (1993) The Revised Report From The National Task Force on Juvenile Sexual Offending. *Juvenile and Family Court Journal.* 44: 4, 1–121.

Oates R K (Ed.) (1990) *Understanding and Managing Child Sexual Abuse.* Marrickville: Harcourt. Brace Jovanovich.

Perry G P and Orchard J (1992) *Assessment and Treatment of Adolescent Sex Offenders.* Sarasota, FL.: Professional Resource Press.

Pithers W D (1997) Maintaining Treatment Integrity With Sexual Abusers. *Criminal Justice and Behaviour.* 24: 1, 34–51.

Prendergast W E (1991) *Treating Sex Offenders in Correctional Institutions and Outpatient Clinics: A Guide to Clinical Practice.* NY: Haworth Press.

Print B (2000) *Model of Treatment and Intervention With Young People Who Sexually Abuse.* Presentation to The Positive Outcomes Conference, Manchester Airport, 11th–13th July 2000.

Proctor E and Flaxington F (1996) *Community Based Interventions With Sex Offenders Organised by The Probation Service: A Survey of Current Practice* (Report for ACOP Work With Sex Offenders Committee). England: Probation Service.

Quinsey V L and Marshall W L (1983) Procedures for Reducing Inappropriate Sexual Arousal. In Greer J G and Stuart R I (Eds.) *The Sexual Aggressor.* NY: Van Nostrand Reinhold, 267–89.

Quinsey V L, Harris G T, Rice M E and Cormier C A (1998) *Violent Offenders: Appraising and Managing Risk.* Washington, DC: American Psychological Association

Renvoize J (1993) *Innocence Destroyed: A Study of Child Sexual Abuse.* London: Routledge.

Russell D E H (1983) The Incidence and Prevalence of Intra-Familial and Extra-Familial Sexual Abuse of Female Children. *Child Abuse and Neglect.* 7: 133–46.

Russell D E H (1988) The Incidence and Prevalence of Intra-Familial Sexual Abuse of Female Children. In Walker L E (Ed) *Handbook on Sexual Abuse of Children: Assessment and Treatment Issues.* NY: Springer Publishing Co, 19–36.

Ryan G D, Metzner J C and Krugman R D (1990) When The Abuser Is A Child. In Oates R K (Ed.), Op Cit, 258–73.

Sahd D (1980) Psychological Assessment of Sexually Abusing Families and Treatment Implications. In Holder W (Ed.) *Sexual Abuse of Children: Implications for Treatment.* Englewood, Co: American Humane Association.

Samenow S E (1984) *Inside The Criminal Mind.* NY: Times Books.

Sanderson C (1990) *Counselling Adult Survivors of Child Sexual Abuse.* London: Jessica Kingsley.

Schechter M D and Roberge L (1976) Sexual Exploration. In Helfer R E and Kempe C H (Eds.) *Child Abuse and Neglect: The Family and The Community.* Cambridge, Mass: Ballinger, 129.

Schlank A M and Shaw T (1996) Treating Sexual Offenders Who Deny Their Guilt: A Pilot Study. *Sexual Abuse: A Journal of Research and Treatment.* 8: 1, 17–23.

Schlank A M and Shaw T (1997) Treating Sexual Offenders Who Deny: A Review. In Schwartz B K and Cellini H R (Eds.) *The Sex Offender: New Insights, Treatment Innovations and Legal Developments.* Kingston, NJ: Civic Research Institute.

Schwartz B K (1995) Group Therapy. In Schwartz B K and Cellini H R (Eds.) *The Sex Offender: Corrections, Treatment and Legal Practice.* Kingston, NJ: Civic Research Institute, 14–15.

Schwartz B F (1995) Theories of Sexual Offenders. In Schwartz B K and Cellini H R (Eds.) *The Sex Offender: Corrections, Treatment and Legal Practice.* Kingston, NJ: Civic Research Institute, Inc.

Sgroi S M (Ed.) (1982) *Handbook of Clinical Intervention in Child Sexual Abuse.* Lexington, Mass: Lexington Books.

Simkins L, Ward W, Bowman S and Rinck C M (1990) Characteristics Predictive of Child Sex Abusers' Response to Treatment: An Exploratory Study. *Journal of Psychology and Human Sexuality.* 3: 1, 19–55.

Steen C (1996) Treating The Denying Sex Offender. *California Coalition on Sexual Offending Newsletter.* 2: 3–5.

Stephenson M (1991) A Summary of An Evaluation of The Community Sex Offender Program in The Pacific Region. *Forum on Corrections Research.* 3: 25–30.

Sullivan J (2002) The Spiral of Sexual Abuse: A Conceptual Framework for Understanding and Illustrating The Evolution of Sexually Abusive Behaviour. *NOTA NEWS.* 41, April, 17–21.

Summit R C (1990) The Specific Vulnerability of Children. In Oates R K (Ed.) *Understanding and Managing Child Sexual Abuse.* Marrickville: Harcourt Brace Jovanovich, 59–74.

Tower C C (1989) *Understanding Child Abuse and Neglect.* Boston: Allyn and Bacon.

Trowell J (1991) Teaching About Child Sexual Abuse. In Pietroni M (Ed.) *Right or Privilege? Post-Qualifying Training for Social Workers, With Special Reference to Child Care.* London: CCETSW.

Vetter H (1990) Dissociation, Psychopathy and The Serial Murderer. In Egger S A (Ed.) *Serial Murderer: An Elusive Phenomena.* NY: Praeger.

Waterhouse L and Carnie J (1992) Assessing Child Protection Risk. *British Journal of Social Work.* 22: 47–60.

Waterhouse L, Carnie J and Dobash R (1993) The Abuser Under The Microscope. *Community Care,* 24.6.93, 24.

Watkins B and Bentovim A (1992) The Sexual Abuse of Male Children and Adolescents: A Review of Current Research. *Journal of Child Psychiatry.* 33: 1, 197–248.

West D J (1986) The Victim's Contribution to Sexual Offences. In Hopkins J (Ed.) *Perspectives on Rape and Sexual Assault.* London: Harper and Row, 1–14.

Wolf S (1984) *A Multi-Factor Model of Deviant Sexuality.* Paper at 3rd International Conference on Victimology. Lisbon, Portugal, November, 1984.

Wolf S C, Conte J R and Engel-Meinig G M (1988) Assessment and Treatment of Sex Offenders in a Community Setting. In Walker L E A (Ed.) *Handbook of Sexual Abuse of Children.* NY: Springer, 365–83.

Wood R, Grossman L and Fichtner C (2000) Psychological, Assessment, Treatment and Outcome with Sex Offenders. *Behavioral Science and the Law.* 18: 23–41.

Wyre R (1989) *Workshop for Post-Qualifying Diploma in Child Protection.* University of Lancaster.

Wyre R (1990) *Working With Sexual Abuse.* Presentation to Conference on Working With The Sex Offender. London: Regents College, 29.3.90.

Wyre R (1990b) Sex Abuse 'Addictive'. *Social Work Today.* 29.3.90, 9.

Yochelson S and Samenow S E (1976) *The Criminal Personality: Volume 1: A Profile for Change.* NY: Jason Aronson.

Yochelson S and Samenow S E (1977) *The Criminal Personality: Volume 2: The Change Process.* NY: Jason Aronson.

Chapter Two

Assessments of Sex Offenders: Suggested Frameworks and Strategies for Operational Use

In this chapter, we will provide an overview of the different types of assessment; set out the principal goals of assessment, and look at the differences between sex offender assessment and more traditional assessment approaches. The process of assessment is an attempt to:

- Comprehend the key elements in the problem situation.
- Understand the meaning of the problem to the client in their situation.
- Use all of the client's understanding.
- Direct all of the professional knowledge to identify what needs to change, before
- Planning how these desired changes may be effected (Calder, 1999).

The process is as crucial as the content. The test of a good assessment is the contribution it makes to satisfactory problem resolution and in guiding any client and worker action. Assessment is the systematic collection of information to try and inform the decision-making processes linked to the risks associated with abusive behaviour, whether there is a need for further work, and what form this should take. It can also be used to assess the client's motivation and capacity for change (Calder, 1999).

Sex offender assessment is the evaluation of an individual in order to make several decisions that might include: disposition of the case (i.e., level of dangerousness) diagnostic purposes (type of offender, etc.) eligibility for treatment/capacity for change as well as the ongoing evaluation of progress in treatment.

The aims of the offender assessment

- To provide an assessment of various problems involved in the offending, besides sexual deviancy (specific issues, lifestyle behaviour and mental health status).
- To help them identify some of the factors that led to their offending via the process of targeting, grooming, fantasising, masturbating, abusing regretting and rationalising.
- To establish the degree of accepted responsibility for the abuse by the offender. In

particular, we need to assess just how close a match we achieve between victim account and offender admission.
- To explore any reasons for being unable to assume responsibility for the offending.
- To explore the potential for future abuse.
- To determine if the client is, indeed, an offender.
- Occasionally, workers are asked to assist the court in a determination of guilt or innocence. It is not the assessors' role to make this judgement. They can only offer an opinion based on the known dimensions of the problem – unless the offender openly admits the offence.
- To explore the degree of reluctance to change their attitudes and behaviour/to establish their motivation and capability to change. For example, the re-use of certain tasks and questionnaires is a useful gauge of change.
- To look at their attitude towards the victim and their understanding of the harm they have caused to them.
- To assess the specific risks (short and long-term) posed to the children, and in which situations such risk becomes more or less acute. These are best 'guess-timates', as no instrumentation is specific and absolute. This may involve recommendations on where they live and contact issues. Retaining the offender in the community needs to consider such issues as the number of victims, the compulsiveness of the behaviour, violence in the offence, and an offenders' general criminal history.
- To provide data to help develop a tailor-made treatment plan.
- To develop an understanding of their attitude towards their own sexuality, and that towards women and children, and
- To assess the viability of, and necessity for, longer-term treatment and/or management, and what forms they may take. The offenders need for, interest in, and potential performance in treatment are important factors in these considerations (adapted from Calder, 1999).

Principles in sex offender assessment

- Treat the client with respect, as a unique individual.
- Differentiate the offender's self-worth as a person from their deviant behaviour. Remember attitudes are projected onto the client at both conscious and unconscious levels.
- Maintain control of the interview.
- Remember they may have multiple offences and victim types.
- Offenders tend to deny/distance reality.
- Utilise both patterns of stability and change dynamics. Stability is the dynamic patterns of maintaining change (i.e., security, comfort). Change is a difference, initiated by assessment questions.
- Utilisation Principle – The principle of utilising any interventions (ethically) and/or behaviour to elicit targeted responses. Thus, the client's responses can be used to elicit specified responses.
- Collect the facts prior to the interview via reports, other interviews, etc. Do your homework and be prepared.
- Guessing Principle – Avoid telling the offender all the information that you know. This places the offender in a position to guess what information you know and don't know. (You may get more sincere and spontaneous responses).
- Look for patterns of behaviour, or sequences of behaviour that logically relate. Look for tendencies (Carich and Adkerson, 1995).

Steps in assessment

Phase 1 – Pre-interview data collection
Step 1
File review data

Phase 2 – Interviews
Step 2
Confidentiality waivers/purpose of interview
Step 3
Self-administered tests: offence specific/non-specific
Step 4
Establish rapport (via empathy, respect for and with the offender's position)
Step 5
Basic non-offending (personal-social biographical) history data
Step 6
Sexual history data

Step 7
Offending history data (the 9-factor assault profile)
Step 8
Review of index offences
Step 9
Work through denial issues
Step 10
Compare offender's stories with other sources of data
Step 11
Testing that is administered to offender
Step 12
Assessment of needs/risk factors/problem or issues/profile/skills/resources: treatment planning
Step 13
Risk assessment

Phase 3 – Post-interview outcome phase
Step 14
Determination of outcome: recommendations.

Differences between sex offender and general assessments

Sex offender assessment is different from traditional assessment approaches in a number of ways that are set out below:

General	Sex offender
shared control	authoritarian
supportive	confrontational
permissive	limit-setting
more non-directive	more directive
client-defined goals	society-defined goals
accepting/trusting	suspicious/suspect
facilitate relaxation	utilise anxiety
confidential	waived confidentiality
voluntary	forced
less sceptical	more sceptical

Historically, the evaluation of sex offenders has been more confrontative, directive and authoritarian-oriented than general evaluations. Such an approach has been unsuccessful and has often led to client denial becoming more entrenched. If the interviewer is humiliating and degrading, the offender will withdraw. In more recent times, there has been a major shift towards more motivational approaches to engage the offender in becoming more motivated to address the behaviour of concern. We have realised that if the worker does not have a rapport with the offender, then the chances are slimmer to elicit cooperation and information. Sex offenders need to be shown respect, and empathy (not sympathy or pity) to develop a rapport (Blanchard, 1996). Sex offender assessment professionals are always sceptical and suspicious of what the sex offender says, particularly since the consequences of admission are often multiple and enduring, and this is compounded where workers are reliant only on offender self-report. A balance of respect, empathy along with scepticism, firmness, directiveness is necessary. Whatever approach is adopted, workers need to guard against enabling the offender. We will now consider issues relating to the interviewing of sex offenders.

Interviewing issues to consider

Engaging the offender in the assessment work

This is a crucial area that is often overlooked in child protection work, yet it can be essential to the outcome of any assessment work. Most clients are involuntary and this leaves an uphill challenge for the workers whose initial task is to convert them to accept the planned work. Many offenders have grown up permeated with denial and projection of responsibility and these are likely to become more entrenched in the face of immediate confrontation. It is clear, therefore, some degree of flexibility and creativity will be needed from the workers when attempting to engage the resistant client. In order to start the process, workers do need to consider where the offender is starting from, as there is frequently a discrepancy between professional and offender starting points, which contribute to the problem, rather than serving to address and resolve it (see the model of change set out later).

Workers clearly need to reserve the right to use authority and statutory powers where necessary, but only to the extent that it provides a mandate for the work. Punishment is not a feature that encourages offender co-operation, although workers may become tempted to adopt such an approach where the offender is denying in the face of overwhelming evidence to the contrary, and where the denial serves little purpose. Any partnership between a worker and an offender is also acutely difficult where the details of the crime are very clear and graphic, as the worker may wish to adopt a punitive, non-therapeutic approach. Workers new to the work do need to guard against falling for the diversionary tactics employed by the offender, and often his family.

The engagement triangle (Calder)

It is important that there is a context to the interviewing process. Calder (2002) has set out

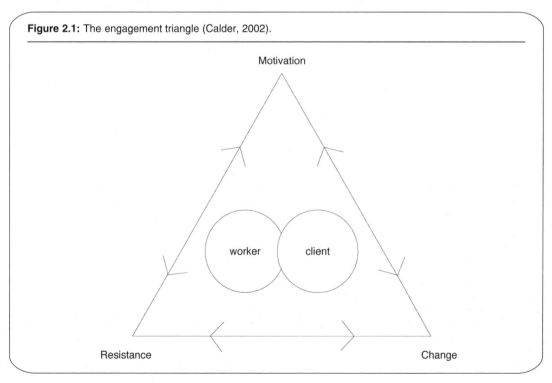

Figure 2.1: The engagement triangle (Calder, 2002).

Motivation

worker   client

Resistance   Change

the essential considerations for workers when seeking to engage clients in work deemed essential by professionals. His engagement triangle (see Figure 2.1) identifies a need to understand the concepts of resistance, motivation and change when approaching work with most clients within the child protection umbrella. The role of the worker in facilitating the ideal: reduced resistance, high commitment to change and motivation is recognised. Whilst some offenders will be static and resistant regardless of who does the work or which approaches are adopted, many offenders can be helped to change their attitude towards the suggested assessment and/or intervention.

The following represents a summary of the original work.

The origins of resistant behaviour
Research (such as Cleaver and Freeman, 1995) stresses the need for workers to begin by considering why the client appears resistant. It may simply be that the worker and the client are in the early stages of their relationship and insufficient trust has developed, or that they perceive the process as challenging and anxiety-provoking. Egan (1994) reminded us that 'involuntary clients' are much more likely to be reluctant or resistant. He provided some practical tips for managing the problem:

1. How might resistance show itself?

- By only being prepared to consider 'safe' or low priority areas for discussion.
- By not turning up for appointments or by being overly co-operative with professionals.
- By being verbally or physically aggressive.
- By minimising the issues.

2. When might resistance show itself?

- When there is fear of intensity and high levels of empathy being expressed by the offender.
- In situations in which lack of trust or fear of betrayal are present.
- When the offender feels they have no choice but to take part.
- When there is resentment of third-party referrers (such as other family members).
- When the goals of both parties are different.
- With people who have negative experiences or images of the professionals.
- When people feel that to ask for help is an admission of failure.

- When people feel that the rights are not respected.
- When people feel they are not participants in the process.
- If the worker is disliked.

3. What might we be doing or have done already to make matters worse?

- Becoming impatient and hostile.
- Doing nothing, hoping the resistance will go away.
- Lowering expectations or blaming the family member.
- Absorbing the offender and/or family member's anger.
- Allowing the offender to inappropriately control the assessment.
- Becoming unrealistic.
- Believing that the offender must like and trust us before assessment can proceed.
- By ignoring the enforcing role of some aspects of child protection work and hence refusing to place any demands on the offender.

4. Are there productive approaches to working with 'reluctant and resistant' people during assessment?

- Give practical, emotional support – especially by being available, predictable and consistent, thus modelling a secure attachment style.
- By seeing some resistance and reluctance as normal.
- By exploring our own resistance to change and by examining the quality of our own interventions and communication style.
- Establishing a strong and well-articulated relationship by clarifying all the rules of sharing records, by inviting people to meetings, by sharing with them how and why you have to make decisions and explaining the complaints procedure.
- Helping offenders to identify incentives for moving beyond resistance.
- Tapping the potential of other people who are respected as partners by the family member.
- By understanding that reluctance and resistance may be avoidance or a signal that we are not doing our job very well (147-53).

Strategies for reducing resistance
Resistance is a natural response to the fear of change. A worker who understands that resistance is part of the dynamics of a helping relationship will be able to help the client in the

process of making the desire to change their own behaviour. Even initially hostile and uncooperative clients prefer openness and honesty and a worker who shows concern and listens to their point of view. There will always be some clients that do not wish to work in partnership with the statutory agencies because they believe they have no problem or because of their hostility towards such bodies. Even with the most resistant of clients it should be possible to engage some in the child protection process and at the very least keep them informed about what is happening and how they could participate more fully. Low levels of client resistance are not only easier for the worker but it is also associated with longer-term change. By re-framing resistance as a feature of motivated behaviour, the workers can unlock an opportunity to help the client's change. It is important to identify the individual features of resistance to select a commensurate strategy of intervention, which may include:

Interviewing strategies

- Simple reflection – and acknowledgement of the disagreement, emotion, or perception can permit further exploration rather than defensiveness.
- Amplified reflection – or exaggeration can encourage them to back off a bit and reflect.
- Double-sided reflection – acknowledges what they have said and we then add it to the other side of their ambivalence.
- Shifting focus – away from the stumbling block by bypassing them.
- Agreement with a twist – offer initial agreement, but with a slight change of emphasis that can influence the direction and momentum of change.
- Emphasising personal choice and control – in the end, even where the current freedom of choice is threatened.
- Re-framing – information they offer so you acknowledge it but offer a new meaning of it or interpretation for them.
- Therapeutic paradox – where the resistance is designed with the hope of movement by the client in a beneficial direction.
- Handling missed appointments – seek them out and offer them a new appointment, regardless of the reasons (adapted from Miller and Rollnick,1991,104–11).
- Change the style of the worker to either increase or decrease the level of resistance.

- Where the offender and their family dispute the findings of the investigation, suggest that a fuller assessment would give them the opportunity to demonstrate evidence for their claims. It is important that any evidence the offender and their partner produce to support claims or demonstrate strengths and positive qualities is taken seriously and looked at together with evidence that demonstrates problems or confirms concerns, and use any high levels of anxiety to reduce any resistance to any ongoing work, e.g. where clients see their situation as beyond their control. Here, we can often get them to consider alternatives to their resistant behaviour or situation as a prelude to change.

Structural strategies

- Co-work to provide strength in numbers.
- The use of a consultant or 'expert' to emphasise the authority held by the workers. This needs to be done with care as otherwise it can become just an exercise in power.
- Promote effective inter-agency perspective to resist any transference of family anxieties onto the workers.
- Good intercommunication between the different professionals involved.

These need to be applied after careful consideration, particularly where the potential dis-empowerment may have a long-term impact on the client. It is important for the workers to try and bring the client's anxieties within working limits, and this can be achieved by getting them to list their anxieties. We can then agree goals that are likely to reward the client and act as a source of motivation to them. We need to be aware that motivation may fluctuate between real optimism and scepticism that change may create more problems than it resolves. It is the responsibility of the worker to persuade the client that it is worthwhile, and this can be encouraged by clarifying the goals, spelling them out clearly, and collectively working towards the same outcomes.

Small changes can be used to demonstrate that change is possible and rewarding, thus offering some pay off that will exceed the costs of change. Where the client does not accept that the benefits outweigh the costs, the worker can ask them not to change but to consider what changes would be desirable if and when they decided to change. This may activate their self-determination and the initiation of change

internally. For any assessment to have any
chance of success there must be at least some
motivation within the client.

A model of change (Prochaska and DiClemente).

This (1982, 1986) model offers an overview,
which allows for a range of change methods and
skills to be delivered by different professionals
according to the needs of individual offenders
and their families. It is a very useful model for
setting out realistic plans of work at the outset,
for setting attainable targets, and for reviewing
what progress, if any, has been made. Tony
Morrison (1991) originally applied the model to
the broader child protection arena, and it is very
appropriate to the child sexual abuse field as it
originated from work with addicts. The model is
set out visually below:

Pre-contemplation: This is where the client is
considering change far less than the
professionals, who are often reacting to the
presenting situation. Morrison (1995) pointed
out that this phase is characterised by blaming
others, denying responsibility, or simply being
unaware of the need to change, e.g. depression.
Whilst in this stage no change is possible.
Individuals thus require information and
feedback in order that they can raise their
awareness of the problem and the possibility of
change (Miller and Rollnick, 1991, 16).
Pre-contemplation is the point at which the
initial assessment takes place in order to
ascertain, and hopefully enhance motivation to
at least consider and contemplate, the need for
change. Whilst the professionals enter the work
at the action stage, the offender is probably only
in the pre-contemplation stage. Such a
combination cannot succeed as the two groups
are at incongruent stages of change. There may
also be a very different definition of the problem
between the two groups. For the client, they are
unlikely to be in a position to meaningfully
engage in the proposed assessment work and a
legal mandate often has to be sought. Offenders
are the prime candidates to be resistant to any
change efforts.

DiClemente (1991) identified four categories
of pre-contemplation. Reluctant
pre-contemplators are those who through lack
of knowledge or inertia do not want to consider
change. Rebellious pre-contemplators have a
heavy investment in the problem behaviour and
in making their own decisions. The resigned

pre-contemplator has given up on the possibility
of change and seems overwhelmed by the
problem. The rationalising pre-contemplator has
all the answers but have discounted change as
they have figured out the odds of personal risk,
or they have plenty of reasons why the problem
is not a problem or is a problem for others but
not for them (192–3).

Contemplation: Offenders in this stage are
most open to consciousness-raising
interventions, such as observations,
confrontations, and interpretations (Prochaska
and DiClemente, 1986, 9). Through this process,
their awareness of the problem increases, and
they are then free to reject or adapt to change.
The worker's aim is to tip the balance in favour
of change (Miller and Rollnick, 1991, 16–7).
Contemplation is often a very paradoxical stage
of change. The fact that the client is willing to
consider the problem and the possibility of
change offers hope for change. However, the
fact that ambivalence can make it a chronic
condition can be very frustrating. It is the stage
where many of the offenders will be waiting for
the one final piece of information that will
compel them to change. The hope is that the
information makes the decision for them.
Failing this, we need to offer them incentives to
change by looking at past changes and by
accentuating the positives (DiClemente, 1991,
194–6). It is only after such contemplation that a
viable contract for work can be made. There are
six steps to the contemplation stage before we
can move into the action stage and attempt
change. They are:

- *I accept that there is a problem.*
- *I have some responsibility for the problem.*
- *I have some discomfort about the problem and my part in it.*
- *I believe that things must change.*
- *I can see that I can be part of the solution.*
- *I can see the first steps towards change* (Morrison, 1998).

In this stage, the offender may now accept
that something has to change although they may
be unsure how it can be achieved. The task for
workers is to remove any barriers to change,
and create an environment where change is a
realistic possibility.

Change remains a very painful process.

Action: Is the stage where the offender
engages in structured work to bring about a
change, in a way that they believe they have
determined. Such a tact avoids dependency on

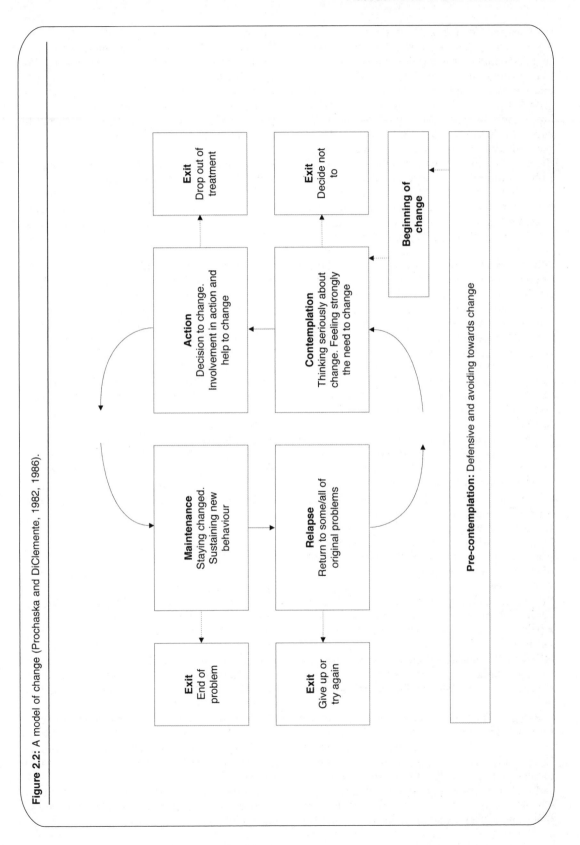

Figure 2.2: A model of change (Prochaska and DiClemente, 1982, 1986).

the workers. Yet action is a potentially stressful stage of change as they can fail and feel that they have failed or been rejected. We need to plan for relapse and involve the wider family and the community networks, for it is they who are most likely both to spot the early signs of lapse, and who will provide the most day to day support (Morrison, 1995). This stage is where the individual is seen 'in action', implementing the plan. It is where they feel able to make a public commitment to action; to get some external confirmation of the plan; to seek support; to gain greater self-efficacy; and finally to create artificial, external monitors of their activity (DiClemente, 1991, 198–9). For the worker, they should focus on successful activity and reaffirm the client's decisions. They should point out that change can be predicted where a person adheres to advice and the plan. The focus should be on learning, exploring and rehearsing ways of relating, thinking, behaving and feeling. All change is essentially a combination of these four basic human processes. This stage may take several months as new behaviour takes time to become established. At the end of the initial planning stage, the aim is to produce a longer-term plan of work.

Maintenance: Is about sustaining and consolidating change and preventing relapse. This is the real test. It occurs when the new ways of relating and behaving become internalised and generalised across different situations. They do not now depend on the presence of the workers, but become consolidated and owned by the individual/family as part of themselves. It is through this process that the client's sense of self-efficacy has been increased (Morrison, 1995). Successful maintenance builds on each of the processes that has come before, as well as an open assessment of the conditions under which a person is likely to relapse (Prochaska and DiClemente, 1986, 10). Stability and support will be essential to sustaining change, especially with the many families who have such poor experience of problem solving (Morrison, 1991, 96).

Relapse: The cyclical model of change allows for the reality that few people succeed first time round. Change comes from repeated efforts, re-evaluation, renewing of commitment, and incremental success. Relapse is thus part of, rather than necessarily hostile to, change. Change is a battle between the powerful forces that want us to stay the same, and our wish to be

different (Morrison, 1991, 96). It usually occurs gradually after an initial slip (often due to unexpected stress), rather than occurring spontaneously (DiClemente, 1991, 200). It can lead to a loss of all or most of the gains, resulting in a giving-up and a return to pre-contemplation. This can be counteracted by the worker, giving feedback, on how long it takes to accomplish sustained change. They should aim to keep the change effort going rather than becoming disengaged and stuck. Morrison (1995) noted that where it is noted quickly enough, and help is urgently sought and available from friends, family or professionals, all is by no means lost. This may lead to further work through the contemplation stage.

The assessment of change is a very uncertain process, and is often very fragile where it is achieved. Attitudinal changes are often the most noticeable to the workers, although we should also look for evidence of a willingness to engage and struggle with painful issues; a clearer understanding of their own continued potential for abusiveness; a willingness to share new information; and a clearer grasp of the victims experiences of the abuse (Willis, 1993). Workers do need to help the offender understand that the more they disclose, the likely reduction, rather, than an increase in, the risks they pose.

It is important that we acknowledge that change is very slow and it is often clearer to trust the lack of change as being an indicator of treatment failure than trusting change in a target area as evidence that the treatment is working.

Motivation

Motivation is defined as 'the probability that a person will enter into, continue, and adhere to a specific change strategy' (Miller and Rollnick, 1991, 19). It is about a state of readiness or eagerness to change, which may fluctuate from one time or situation to another. Motivation is not an attribute of the client but a product of the interaction of client, worker and environment. It is not a characteristic of the client's personality structure or psychological functioning. By viewing motivation as a transactional concept and a process rather than a trait, we are free to mobilise motivation in such a way as to build on and enhance the competencies of clients in their life experiences.

A transactional model of motivation enables us to assess several factors in relation to the change effort:

Figure 2.3: A continuum of motivation (adapted from Morrison, 1991, 34).

Internal motivators

I want to change.
I don't like things as they are.
I am asking for your help.
I have resources to help solve this.
I think you can help me.
I think things can get better.
I have other support, which I will use to encourage me.
I accept that I am doing something wrong.
I accept what you say needs to change.
I accept that others are right (family, friends, community, agencies).
You defining the problem clearly helps.
I understand what change will involve.
I accept that if I do not change, you will take my children away.
I can change if you do this for me.
I'll do whatever you say.
I agree to do this so the family can be reconstituted.
It's your job to solve my problem.
You are my problem.
I am right and you are wrong.
I don't have any problems.

External motivators

- Affective arousal – the level of emotional arousal related to the change.
- Directionality – the goals or direction of change/movement.
- The environment – as each person in the change effort perceives it.

None of these factors individually can explain or predict the level of motivation available for accomplishing a given task or for initiating change. Each of the components are interacting, interdependent forces affected and being affected by the others. As such, all components must be considered in assessing the motivation of a system, and each is necessary but not sufficient to explain motivation or to predict if change will occur. If we can identify the reluctant or disabling component, this can become the target for the initial intervention. Morrison (1991) has argued that motivation comes from the interplay of internal and external factors and it is rarely the case that real change is accomplished only on the basis of personal motivation without the assistance of external reinforcement (p93). Figure 2.3

provides a continuum which offers a useful way of locating the offender's motivation to change.

It is now clear that an assessment must include a family's motivation to change. Workers need to be careful not to label all involuntary clients as unmotivated. It is wrong to believe that work can only be accomplished with motivated clients, as there are strategies available to workers to help tap motivational elements in the family's social and extended family network. Workers need to believe that they can motivate the client and accept that this is more important than the client's pre-existing level of motivation.

Change has been defined as 'the elimination or substantial modification of the presenting problem'. One of the principal tasks for the worker is to reach some agreement about what will count as change in a particular case – when it starts, how it progresses and where it ends. In order to fulfil this task, the worker has to have some understanding of what conditions facilitate change, what barriers restrict change, and how we can measure change. If we are unable to set realistic targets we end up with shifting goalposts that often inflame clients who are unable to project forward with any certainty.

Strategies for enhancing engagement with involuntary clients (Ivanoff et al., 1994)

Prior to client contact

- **Problem orientation and worldview check** – workers need to identify, acknowledge and examine their negative biases and assumptions about clients as these can be dangerous and compromise effective practice.
- **Developing realistic expectations for practice** – many workers coming from academia are prepared for ideal, not real clients, and thus can become easily disappointed. The following self-statements can be helpful when beginning work with involuntary clients:
  - It is reasonable that involuntary clients resent being forced to participate.
  - Because they are forced to participate, hostility, silence and non-compliance are common responses that do not reflect my skills as a worker.
  - Due to the barriers created by the practice situation, clients may have little opportunity to discover if they like me.

– Lack of client co-operation is due to the practice situation, not to my specific actions and activities.

During initial contacts with the client

- **General guidelines** – start by adopting a general, non-defensive stance. Be clear, honest and direct, and acknowledge the involuntary nature of the arrangement. Clarify the role of the workers and the expected role of the client; the activity necessary to achieve mandated compliance; the structure and format of contacts; how the worker can be expected to respond to non-compliance; and the possibilities or options for rewards, incentives, early discharge etc.
- **Motivational congruence between worker and client** – is important to successful outcomes. This often involves preparing the client for their role, and can include some choices about selecting an intervention to promote their adherence to the plans.
- **Conversational responses** – for the worker to avoid. Common examples include:
  – Avoid expressions of over-concern.
  – Avoid moralistic judgements.
  – Avoid criticising the client.
  – Avoid making false promises.
  – Avoid displays of impatience.
  – Avoid ridiculing the client.
  – Avoid blaming the client for their failures.
  – Avoid dogmatic utterances.
  – Respect the right of the client to express different values and preferences from yours.

As Horwath and Morrison (2000) have pointed out, ' . . . engaging with the change process involves positively weighting, increasing or establishing motivators for change, whether these are material, psychological, individual or environmental. This can be understood only by recognising that motivation is an interactive phenomenon in which professionals are highly significant figures . . .'(83).

Interview dynamics

The interview dynamics of the assessment process are very important. This indicates the level of cooperation, attitude, current psychopathic characteristics, level of denial, etc. The interview process is a dynamic professional relationship, defined by a social context or exchange of communication. Likewise, interview behaviours indicate feedback on the worker's skill level to develop rapport, elicit information, gain cooperation, and work with denial issues (see Calder, 2002 for a detailed discussion of the engagement triangle).

Some specific guidelines and principles for assessment are listed below. This includes a set of attitudes and specific stages of assessment process. The responsibility for good assessment lays both with the offender and the worker.

Guidelines

1. Do your homework. Obtain thorough background information before seeing the client. Do not give away what you know until the client has given their account in the interview; this allows you to check for discrepancies.
2. Take control of the interview.
3. Stay relaxed and comfortable.
4. Tell the client the nature of the interview and inform them of the limitations of confidentiality before proceeding.
5. Structure the interview.
6. Establish yourself as professional and knowledgeable about the problem.
7. Utilise silence to create anxiety and gain power.
8. Use the client's anxiety to motivate them.
9. Change topics frequently to elicit spontaneous responses.
10. Focus clients on the themes of the interview.
11. Monitor client nonverbal responses at each point.
12. Ask who, what, where, when and how questions. Avoid asking why questions.
13. Respect the client as an individual capable of change.
14. Do not agree to keeping secrets or collude with justifications and excuses.
15. Do not trust the client or accept statements at face value, as symptoms of the problem of sexual offending is distorting information. Lying, minimising, denying, etc.
16. Avoid power struggles without giving in to intimidation and threat. Maintain control of the interview.
17. When working with the client do not express shock or disgust at their history. Separate the behaviour from the person. Do not model abusive behaviour.
18. Avoid giving up; maintain a high energy level.
19. Track the thinking errors, cognitive distortions and defensive structures used in each section of the interview.

20. Ask open-ended question rather than yes or no questions (adapted from Carich and Adkerson, 1995).

Interviewing styles

The confrontational approach

The confrontational approach to interviewing is characterised by the making of assumptions, by persistence and by structured confrontation. The emphasis is on the breakdown of denial, which is believed to be a manipulative strategy employed by the offender to deceive the worker. Here, the work needs to be structured and is usually characterised by painstaking dialogue with the offender – where every step, attitude and explanation is challenged unless it is a straightforward acceptance of responsibility. Structured confrontational interviews put the offender under pressure of questioning to describe the offending in detail and then have their account systematically questioned and the cognitive distortions pointed out. Mark (1992) argues that this is the approach to get to the heart of sex offending.

The worker is able to make 'safe' assumptions based on research evidence and clinical findings. The view usually adopted is that offenders will follow and will continue to follow, if uninterrupted, an identifiable pattern of behaviour that will lead them inevitably into other offences. Despite this position, workers do need to guard against an approach, which is over-controlling, un-empathic and defensive. At times it will become difficult to continue to maintain a legitimate use of authority without being persecutory (Sheath, 1990). Presumption is legitimate, but persecution is not.

The disadvantage of this approach is that workers frequently see the offender withdraw further and the relationship and future work become irretrievable. It has become clear that the way offenders are interviewed will determine the extent to which they co-operate with the assessment process which, in turn, will affect both the amount and quality of information obtained (Epps, 1993).

Motivational interviewing

Motivational interviewing is a style of intervention that is designed to strengthen the offender's commitment to change. It does not negate the use of confrontation, but this needs to come after a non-collusive working relationship has developed. NOTA (The National Association for the Development of Work with Sex Offenders) have recently issued a very useful guide applying motivational interviewing to work with sex offenders (Mann, 1996), whilst Kear-Colwell and Pollock (1997); Mann and Rollnick (1996); Miller and Rollnick (1991) and Taylor (1972) have described the approach well also.

Morrison and Print (1995) reproduced the principles of motivational interviewing stressed by Miller and Rollnick (1991):

- Motivation is the probability that a person will enter into, continue and adhere to a specific change strategy.
- Motivation does not reside within the client but involves an interpersonal context.
- Denial is a common functional behaviour not a personality trait.
- The worker is an important determinant of the client's motivation.
- Motivation is a key task for the interviewer.
- Therapist style is a major outcome of treatment success, and is often set in the very early stages of the client/worker relationship.
- Clients can be seen as unsuccessful self-changers needing help to change.
- Accurate empathy is a critical condition for an effective therapeutic relationship.
- Labelling people does not assist change, and is different to labelling behaviours.
- Confrontation is presenting a person with himself. It is a goal of intervention not a forceful/aggressive style.
- Working with the client's ambivalence about change is essential.
- The model is not personal combat with the client, and the object in motion is not a body but a perception, and
- Effective interviewing controls the process not the client (24).

Gray and Wallace (1992) offered us lists of 'dos' and 'don'ts' within this:

Examples of things to include:
- Do control the interview.
- Do remain objective at all times, monitoring all interactions and behaviours.
- Do be self-caring: keep your own body relaxed and comfortable.
- Do state immediately and clearly the nature of the interview.
- Do structure your interviews, or your client will.

- Do use silence for power in the interview, it can help build client anxiety.
- Do respectfully acknowledge client discomfort and anxiety and use it positively to motivate the client.
- Do change topics frequently to control the interview in an effort to elicit spontaneous responses from the client.
- Do keep the focus on the client and swiftly and repeatedly bring the client back to task.
- Do track the client's physiological changes closely (eye contact, posture, fidgeting, breathing, twitching).
- Do ask 'what and how' questions, not 'why' questions.
- Do confirm the client understands the question being asked.
- Do track your feelings during the interview.
- Do respect the client as a whole individual, capable of change, and
- Do respect the seriousness and harmfulness of the abusive behaviour (p7).

To this we can add:

- Do take a break if stuck.
- Do ensure a safe formal setting.
- Do work in detail, using hypothetical questions with positive assumptions.
- Do build on 'yes' sets of questions and use successive approximation/rapid fire questions.
- Do use paradox: 'I don't expect you will tell me but . . .'
- Do use ratings:'on a scale of 1 to 10, how aroused were you . . . ?'
- Do give positive feedback: 'you answered that very well' (Morrison and Print, 1995, 25).

Examples of things not to include:

- Don't become aggressive.
- Don't get into power struggles.
- Don't interview the offender without seeing the statements.
- Don't work harder than the offender.
- Don't continue an interview where the offender is completely un-co-operative.
- Don't collude: indicate you have a different understanding.
- Don't think that admission is the same thing as taking responsibility.
- Don't think your experience will protect your feelings, and
- Don't ever work alone or unsupervised (Morrison and Print, 1995, 25).

To this we can add:

- Do not agree to keep secrets.
- Do not ask yes/no questions: keep them open-ended.
- Do not ignore subtle changes in expression.
- Do not overlook 'thinking errors'.
- Do not make a rule you cannot enforce (but do set clear limits and act on them).
- Do not relinquish interview control.
- Do not be diverted.
- Do not abuse the client, avoid using confrontation in a manner that induces shame.
- Do not continue a weak strategy, change course, or 'up' your energy.
- Do not give up.
- Do not isolate yourself.
- Do not 'need or want' something from the client.
- Do not be exploited for what you do not know (Gray and Wallace, 1992, 8).

Ross (1989) pointed out the three most common mistakes made by assessors:

- The assessor loses control of the interview and allows the offender to take control. This can occur for a variety of reasons: fear of the offender, absence of accurate corroborative information about the offender's assaults prior to interview, discomfort in discussing sexual or abuse-specific issues, hostility towards the offender, pity for the offender, lack of confidence, or a lack of training to carry out the interview.
- The assessor assumes that they have the answer to the question instead of exploring in more detail. Here, excuses such as 'I can't remember',' I have a poor memory',' It was so long ago that I can't remember' need to be tackled strongly, with us spelling out that their style of response is unacceptable, and can only lead to a conclusion that they will be an unquantified, but serious danger in the future. We can leave them to think about this for five minutes or adjourn the session, and
- Assessors take sides by becoming either punitive or allied with the offender – usually when they have been severely abused themselves. Neutrality is the key and can be maintained through keeping up with theory, practice and assessment procedures.

Jones and Lewis (1990/1) argued that the middle-ground approach is optimistic when working with this client group, although the intention of shifting them from a passive to an active perspective of the offence is laudable (46). The worker needs to choose their approach bearing in mind the circumstances of the individual case. The worker may want to consider the offender's motivation in choosing a particular approach, and review this throughout the risk assessment.

Strategies within approaches

Pithers et al. (1989) developed methods for assisting sex offenders to admit to their offending by developing the following:

- Attempt to create 'yes' response questions.
- Demythologise stereotypes about sex offenders.
- Mix confrontations with supportive comments.
- Emphasise relief of acknowledging their secrets.
- Discuss the strength demonstrated by disclosure.
- Stress the importance of not making a second mistake.
- Make use of strong religious beliefs.
- Ask 'successive approximation' questions, e.g. offenders may deny that a specific act occurred yet acknowledge that they approximated the act; by leading them by successive, closer approximations to the act, they may reach the point of admitting it took place.
- Confront contradictions.
- Repeat questions periodically (83-5).

Beckett (1994) made several suggestions, which can be added to this list:

- Present as confident and familiar with the dilemmas they face in admitting the extent of their offending and the consequences of doing so.
- Convey that in your experience, many offenders feel anxious about fully disclosing and co-operating, but will often feel relief having done so, and are subsequently able to change and rebuild their lives, albeit in a way different to before, and
- Explain the benefits of collaborating in the assessment and how it will create the opportunity for treatment.

Burnham et al. (1990) told us to make sure that we:

- Use questions that are open and allow for exploration rather than questions that solicit what you want to hear.
- Be behaviour specific in comment and questions. Start with the 'what', 'when' and 'with whom' before the 'why' and do not just take the description on trust.
- Avoid the rule of optimism in responding to expressions of remorse. Be realistic about what you can achieve, e.g. letting them believe you can 'cure' them.
- Avoid work which only addresses the 'what' and 'when' and not the 'why'. This risks merely displacing the behaviour, or enabling the offender to be more successful in not getting caught.
- Avoid work or techniques that collude with social constructs of gender (109).

Prendergast (1991) used the 'four C's approach' to work with sex offenders:

- **Confrontation by the therapist** – whatever the offender says, it must be doubted and they must always be made to back up or prove their statements. When using confrontation, it is important not to interrupt the thought processes of the offender with long-winded statements or questions. In order to achieve this, he advocates the use of the following phrases: picture you're being vague, and I don't get a clear understanding off the situation; because I don't understand the motive or reasons for your actions/conclusions; pzzzzt: I don't believe you or don't buy your explanation, reason etc . . . ; show me: don't just tell me the changes you've made, give me proof that I can verify. Whatever you're telling me is incomplete; and tilt: You're off the subject or track! Get back to what we were discussing. The principle here is the less said by the therapist, the better!!
- **Cautions** – sex offenders are manipulative, seductive and con-artists. Never become too complacent or comfortable with sex offenders.
- **Confirmation** – believe nothing that they say. He coined the term 'partialisation' to reflect the persistent and compulsive practice of telling only part of the story. We should only confirm change when there is behavioural evidence to back it up.
- **Continuation/consistency** – of assessment is essential; as is the reinforcement that self-control is essential. Sex offenders are never cured and may experience recurrences

both easily and frequently, at least at the thought and fantasy level (105–21).

The ABC approach

If there is a need for a more structured approach to getting further information on the offences, the work of Bliss (1990, p31) is very useful. He formulated the 'ABC' method of interviewing sex offenders. It is a structured approach, which examines all facets of the client's sexual offending. This type of interview works on breaking down the different levels of denial and thereby enables the offender to become aware of his full and active responsibility in the offending.

It aims to establish and unpack the progression of the offenders' behaviour via looking at eliciting specific information as follows:

A – for antecedents

Here the client is encouraged to give a full account of the days, hours and minutes before the offence. The purpose of this is to set the scene and enable the offender to relive the experience; challenge any subsequent excuse of lack of recall; and to establish to progression of behaviour.

Include as much information as possible, however seemingly irrelevant:

Setting (at home? layout of furniture? other people around?) Time of day (dark or light? weather?) Events during the day (travelled on which bus? visited which pub?) Physical state (any illness?) Emotional state (what mood?) Stress points (a row with partner?) Fantasies about victim (sexually available?) Relationship to victim (why **this** person?) Description of victim (age, hair, clothes). Assumptions about victim (married?).

B – for behaviour

The actual offence is the focus of concern. It is important to establish the following at this point:

Degree and nature of planning., What actually happened, Internal state at the time (did he feel any relief? Or guilt?), Efforts made to conceal the offence, Degree of violence used, Attitudes towards the victim at the time.

Be careful to clarify any inconsistencies and watch the tendency to slide over issues. At this stage Bliss argues it may be counter productive to start challenging or confronting the offender.

C – for consequences

Imprisonment and Rule 43, Public humiliation, Losing job, Family break-up, Rejection by people of significance, Schedule 1 offender for life, Feelings of personal shame, disgust and regret.

Consider also at this stage what the benefits were for the offender. The reality for the offender is that there will have been some pay-off for him.

The complete paper describing the exercise can be found as an appendix to Garrison (1992, 32–6).

Other basic interview tactics in sex offender assessment

1. **Mind reading** – utilises information that is already known about the offender (and offenders), in effect, tells the client what he is thinking and feeling. Some examples of mind-reading statements in assessment interviews include:

'I'm sure you don't want to be here right now. You probably would rather be doing just about anything else. I imagine you are worried about whether you will be able to say and do the right things to make a good impression in their evaluation'.

'So often you've felt like you were all alone with this problem, maybe like the only person in the world who would ever have done these things or had these feelings.'

'These are still secrets; still things that others don't know about'.

2. **Prediction** – is used to establish credibility and lay groundwork for positive movement through the evaluation and treatment process by predicting behaviours and cognitive patterns of the offender. Most effectively used with mind-reading. Predication works through the use of suggestions to implant ideas and concepts in the offender's mind which will facilitate his progress. Some examples of prediction in the assessment interview include:

*'You will find yourself feeling some increasing discomfort and anxiety today when we first begin talking about the sexual offence, and other sexual issues which lead to your referral here. What you will find is, as you begin to talk more openly and honestly, you will become more comfortable as you talk more openly. When you start to tell what **really** happened, you will have a sense of relief.'*

'In treatment, you will find that each time you talk about the offence you become more and more comfortable . . .'

'I know you don't want to remember, and that is why it is hard for you right now. But as we talk more,

bits and pieces of the memories will return, triggered by my questions. Your memory of those bits and pieces will come back, they will come faster as we go on, building on each other. You will very likely remember all of what happened before we are through.'

3. **Leading** – is asking questions by leading or structuring a specific response. Leading presupposes a given direction for the answer of the question. It often involves double binds. Leading is most effective when used prior to asking direct details of the sexual assault. Some examples of leading are:

'What room were you in when it all began?'
'Who else was in the house when it happened?'
'How long before the incident had you been spending time at the park?'

4. **Use of current research as a direction** – Review current research (i.e., early history of sexual deviancy and multiple paraphilias) in order to logically direct the interview questions.

5. **Control the interview** – Do not allow offenders to sidetrack, detour, divert, stall, disrupt, interrupt, etc. When discussing victimology, specific offences, abuse history, etc., be firm and respectful. It is the worker's responsibility to keep on track. Diversion tactics may include: wearing dark sunglasses, tears (self-pity usually at this stage), stalling, going on irrelevant tangents, questioning the worker's credibility, non-verbal disruption, avoidance of eye contact, vague responses, confusion, memory lapse, focus on the client's molestation, etc.

6. **Don't tip your hand** – Prior to the interview, know the facts about the case. Tell the offender that you have much information, however, don't provide specifics. This alerts the offender to your database, without enabling them to figure out what you know and provide responses accordingly. This creates more influence or leverage in terms of drawing out accurate responses.

7. **Interview collaterals separately** – Do not initially interview the offender conjointly with family, victims, or others as they may control the responses of others (unless for specific purposes). Since offenders are manipulative, they could control the response of others, at verbal and non-verbal levels.

8. **Use multiple data sources** – Records, collateral interviews, psychological tests; and psycho-hysiological tests (phallometric evaluation or plethysmography and polygrams).

9. **Focus on 'What happened' instead of 'Why'** – 'What happened' questions pinpoints the specifics of the offences. It provides more indication of the risk, range of deviancy, victimology and offender profile.

10. **Use behavioural descriptions** – Define terms concretely, specifically, and in behavioural terms. Have offenders define terms. This eliminates confusion, misleading misinterpretation, etc. Use graphic language. Ask who, what when, where and how types of questions to get the specifics.

11. **Ask direct questions** – Ask questions in a straightforward fashion and in a matter-of-fact manner. Offenders will usually respond likewise. Avoid questions or statements implying hesitancy, apology, uncertainty, embarrassment, lack of clarity, etc. This implies incompetency, lack of confidence, weakness, etc., to the offender and enables them to be more dishonest.

12. **'Yes set' technique** – Erickson and Rossi developed a 'yes set' response technique as a means to gain cooperation. Yes set refers to selecting basic questions, safe questions, unimportant points, etc., that will elicit a series of yes responses. This sets up a response frame of agreement, compliance, and cooperation at both conscious and unconscious levels of awareness (see Rossi).

13. **Ignore untruthful responses** – The evaluator will eventually confront offenders on any type of dishonest answers, deceptions, confused responses, disagreements, inconsistencies, incongruencies, etc. Initially, these elements can be ignored and dealt with by repeat or re-phrased questions.

14. **Place burden of denial on the offender** – Assume the offender engaged in various offences. Phrase questions in terms of 'When did you first . . .?' or 'How often have you . . .?'

15. **Embed assumptions in questions** – Embedding assumptions increases the burden of denial. This is done through double binds to get the offender to admit to lesser deeds. For example, ask 'What percent of time did you, when masturbating, have deviant fantasies about the victim?'

16. **Employ 'successive-approximation' strategies** – This strategy consists of establishing facts related to the behaviour. Then facts or parts about the offence can be established leading up to the offence. This may involve a series of questions or questions interspersed throughout the interview.

17. **Repeat questions** – This refers to the re-asking of questions throughout the interview. Look for inconsistencies in the offender answers.

18. **Ask one question at a time** – Unless deliberate, avoid asking multiple questions at the same time. Multiple questions can induce confusion, interrupts the flow, and enables offender to dodge questions. Yet, at times multiple questions can be used to elicit spontaneous responses.

19. **Rapid-fire questions** – Asking questions quickly and one after another elicits spontaneous responses, without prefabricated answers, manufactured emotions and premeditated response.

20. **Fatigue factors/fatigue techniques** – Assessments and interviews can be structured in a way to wear down the offender. This enables one to see the offender's full range of coping strategies across situations. Resistance can also be eroded.

21. **Alternate support and confrontation** – Support and confrontation can be intermingled to enhance the stability/change dynamics. McGrath (1990, 517) states: 'Offenders generally disclose the most when they feel understood and supported but at the same time are held accountable for presenting a truthful personal history.' The offender can feel supported while being pressed.

22. **Frame disclosure as a positive action** – For offenders, admission is risky business (internally/externally) and thus admission can be reframed into initial stems in getting help, defining problems, etc.

23. **Test the limits** – Push and provoke offenders to have emotionally stimulated reactions. Compare accounts of offence histories.

24. **Saving face technique** – Give them a way out. If you back them against the wall, they may shut off forever or attempt suicide, hurt others, etc. This may include empathy.

25. **Planning for the future** – Install hope by breaking down complex problems into little problems.

26. **Dispelling myths** – Myths about offenders can be dispelled (i.e., single category offending).

27. **Offender mirroring** – Enabling the offender to see the mirror image of himself. This includes breaking denial, secrecy, minimisation, justification, and accessing other feelings (shame, confusion, inadequacy, etc.). For highly antisocial offenders, this will take much time and may not be feasible. This can be done by providing lists of problems, motivations, and

enabling the offender to see self through your eyes (developed from Adkerson, 1994; Carich, 1994c and McGrath, 1990).

Advanced paradoxical tactics

Utilising paradoxical techniques

A paradox is a message (or series of messages) that is logical at one level and illogical at another. It may also be a self-contradictory statement or message (O'Hanley, 1987).

1. **Reframe** – Providing a new conceptual frame to an event, that results in changing one's perceptual view (O'Hanley, 1987). This occurs when challenging thinking errors. For example, offender's denial statements can be reframed into protecting their children. In the course of treatment, reframing and relabeling will occur. Assessment and treatment will be new to the offender. Thus, the offender will be posed to a different framework.

2. **Relabel** – Changing the labels of descriptions of behaviours without changing one's frame of reference (O'Hanley, 1987).

3. **Deframe** – Defusing, taking away or demolishing one's frame without providing another (O'Hanley, 1987). The offender is left without meaning. A frame searches for meaning within the confusion. By using this intervention, the offender may become too confused, frustrated and then shut down.

4. **Double bind** – (Provide a force choice) Statements can be phrased in a manner in which the offender is provided a force choice with no escape (O'Hanley, 1987). For example, 'When you did this, this happened' or 'How did you feel when you did . . .' or telling clients 'We expect you to deny and lie so go ahead and talk about . . ., but don't lie.'

5. **Confusion tactics** – (O'Hanley, 1987) Offenders can be confused, thus allowing them to search for meaning. They may provide honest spontaneous responses. The confusion creates cognitive dissonance or conflicting beliefs. The risk is scaring the offender to the point of not responding.

6. **Parallel communication or metaphor** – Providing messages that at one level refers to another element, usually, in story form. It is a symbolic (communication) representation. This includes: jokes, puns, stories, analogies metaphor, etc. The risk is getting side-tracked.

7. **Taking the one down position** – Playing the one down role in order to control the interview and creating a facade that the offender

is in control. The risk is playing into a power game, and losing your position within the interview. Most offenders seem to thrive on the illusion, fantasy, and actuality of being in power and control of others. This tactic could reinforce or enhance the offender's perception and power-oriented behaviours. Therefore, this would be used on rare occasions, only when other tools are not working.

8. **Declaring hopelessness** – Giving up and taking the role of a hopelessness interviewer or that the client's problems are hopeless after the client begins to emote, change tactic. The risk is that the client gives up.

9. **Shock techniques** – Shock techniques involve inducing elements of surprise and psychological jolts to the individual's system (O'Hanley, 1987). Shocks are induced by out of context remarks. The risk is further withdrawal.

Detecting phoniness in sex offenders

Carich (1991) set out some helpful methods for evaluating phoniness in sex offenders. These include:

- Jumping from topic to topic and not focusing on, or staying with, one topic.
- Provides much verbal garbage or verbiage as if he was trying to impress others, avoid issues or present phoney self.
- They keep shifting stories, demonstrating contradictions.
- Distorted, twisted information compared to other reports.
- Taking long verbal trips to nowhere or not being relevant.
- They elaborate on leads with tangential verbiage.
- When information is left out and not volunteered.
- Inconsistency in behaviour in the past and present.
- Scanning others to look for cues on how to respond.
- Keeps shifting non-verbal behaviours, cues and responses, i.e. eye movements, body posture, limbs, etc.
- They scan the room looking for any type of confirmation and reinforcement.
- They avoid eye contact.
- They answer questions by asking questions as indicated by their non-verbal (voice-tone, pitch, rate, volume, etc.) in order to get confirmation.

- Hesitation in answering very intense questions.
- Pauses in responses to intense questions, as they construct an answer.
- Strong reactions and over-exaggerated reactions.
- The split second change or appearance of non-verbal cues, usually indicated in the offender's facial expressions.
- Incongruence in verbal or non-verbal behaviour in the here and now.
- Incongruence between cognitive/affective/ behavioural/physcho-physiological/social –domains of experience.
- Cutting off feelings – bland or blunted effect.
- Intellectualising.
- The 'chameleon effect' – changing feelings, behaviours or joining you or the group by mimicking what he thinks you want to hear. The changes have no meaning, and are superficial at best.
- Playing in the middle or being non-committed in responses.
- Agreeing on every topic or response.
- Presenting a superficial façade – no real depth in responses or just shallowness.

Four types of assessment

There are four basic types of sex offender assessment: general or basic assessments; progress assessments; risk assessments and recovery assessments (Carich, 1999). These are described below.

1. Basic Assessments
The initial, general, or basic assessment consists of collecting basic information or data. Emphasis is placed on the following: basic historical data collection, needs assessment, strengths/resources and problem areas, treatment planning, level of deviancy, patterns, etc. Methods used to elicit this information include: interviews, file reviews, paper and pencil inventories/tests/scales/instruments, psycho-physiological instruments. For a specific workbook style protocol see Carich and Adkerson (1995).

2. Progress Assessments
This is the evaluation of the offender's progress in treatment. This involves assessing the treatment goals and objectives, as compared to outcome criteria based on current behaviours. Emphasis is placed on meeting objectives and

thus making changes. For details see the comprehensive 11-point treatment plan (Metzger and Carich, 1999).

3. Risk Assessments

Risk assessment is the evaluation of the probability or chance that the offender could re-offend and it involves trying to predict the likelihood of them committing another offence. The probability or chance of re-offending is determined by both historical (static) and non-historical (dynamic) risk factors. The probability of re-offending is usually anticipated across a number of different levels (low, moderate, high, extremely high). Methods include interviews and inventories/scales/checklists. Further details are provided in Calder (2000; 2002) and Chapter 11 on risk assessment.

4. Recovery Assessments

Recovery assessments are evaluations of the offender's capability to maintain abstinence from sexual offending. Carich has been a pioneer in this area of assessment (see Carich, 1999 for details). Methods include interviews, inventories, psycho-physiological instruments, etc. For details of the 15 factors of recovery, see Carich (1997; 1999) and Chapter 11 in this book. Recovery assessments are not widely accepted by the leading authorities and most professionals use progress and risk assessments to evaluate recovery.

This chapter will provide further details in relation to the general or basic assessment whilst further discussion on the other three types of assessment will take place in Chapter 11, primarily to locate them at the appropriate point in the process and the book.

General or basic assessments

Historical and process elements

Assessment variables or elements can be categorised in terms of historical or non-changeable elements. Historical elements are past events that can not be changed. They are static in nature. Historical elements are data that has already occurred in time.

Historical data: biographical, personal, social developmental information

1. **Personal biographical data** – The key factors include: current age, date of birth, race, current location of residence, phone number, marital status, educational level, etc.

2. **Immediate family history** – The key factors include: marital history and other significant romantic relationships (i.e., spouses, partners, live-ins, etc.) along with names, dates, ages, dates of birth, descriptions of relationships, geographic locations, number of children by each partner, etc.; and children (i.e., names, current age, dates of birth, natural mothers and location of natural mothers, legal status of relationship, etc.). Key factors to consider include: quality and pathology of relationships, abandonment, losses, abusiveness (physical, sexual, neglect, emotional), type of termination, social service involvement, substance abuse, criminal histories of family members, history of mental illness, domestic violence, attitudes, enables offending, parental employment and impact, types of discipline, etc.

3. **Extended family history** – The key elements include: significant relationships during the developmental years, such as parental/parent figures, siblings, aunts/uncles, grandparents, cousins and any other significant relatives, characterisation of relationships, developmental impact and influences, names, ages, status of relationships, description of significant experiences, educational, occupational levels and status. Several key factors to consider include: type of experiences, supportive figures, enabling types of relationships and those factors listed for immediate family history.

4. **Social history** – The key elements include: current age, gender, occupation, leisure time, other types of activities, nature/type of relationships, interests, level of pathology (i.e., drugs/alcohol, etc.), along with support and also enabling dynamics in reference to significant peer group relationships in non familial relationships. Other factors to consider would be: lengthy relationships, conflict resolution, conflicts, values, how they were selected, aggression, sexual behaviours, group memberships, such as gangs and activities, shared values and beliefs, etc.

5. **Educational history** – The key elements include: age beginning school and ending school, school/names, dates, significant teachers and events, grades, interests, majors, vocational interests, learning problems and learning disabilities (i.e., special education, disabilities, mental retardation, I.Q. level of I.Q. functioning, literacy level, etc.) and significant relationships.

Key factors to consider include: attendance, truancy, dropout, re-entry, failure, disciplinary problems, aggression, sexual behaviours in school, sexual aggression in school, family involvement, attitudes, peers, extra-curricular activities and other significant events, etc.

6. **Work history** – The key elements include: name of employers, geographic locations, ages, positions held, duties, relationships with supervisors, unstable employment, terminations, absenteeism, attitudes, use of drugs and alcohol, along with these other factors to consider such as offending in work, sexual harassment, disciplinary measures, access to victims, sexual behaviours, etc.

7. **Military history** – The key elements include: branch of military, dates, ages, position, rank, combat history and experiences, status, level of authorised and non authorised violence, offences committed while in the military, disciplinary problems, type of termination, attitude, reasons for entering and exiting, activities while on leave, arousal to combat, stimuli on combat aggression, etc.

8. **Gang history** – The key elements include: name of gang, type of gang, rules, positions/rank, responsibilities and duties, attitudes, ages when involved, reasons for entering and terminating, how the termination was done current status, level of participation, level of allegiance and loyalty, types of sexual offences and relationships along with activities.

9. **Criminal history** – The key elements include: dates, ages, types of crimes, incarceration dates, security level and locations of prisons, sentences, sexual aggression and behaviours in prison, sexual experiences, current legal status, motivations of crimes, cognitive distortions involved, victim types, gang related crimes, weapons and other methods of criminal behaviours, attitude, number of crimes committed, crimes per year, range of crimes, sexual behaviours, aggression in prison, level of violence or sadistic behaviours, motivation of crimes (i.e., power and control, anger, revenge, attention, financial reason, etc.).

10. **Substance abuse and/or addictions history** – The key elements include: age, dates, types of substances, level of involvement, substances involved in offending, frequency, consequences, motivations/rationalisations, level of cognitive distortions, degree of use, period of use, current problems in that area, etc.

11. **Other addictions and indulgences** – The key elements include: types of addictions and indulgences, dates, ages, involvement of offending, sexual addictions, involves dangerous behaviour, etc.

12. **Psycho sexual history** – The key elements include: dates of events, ages, gender, names of significant sexual partners, specific perceptions, number of non adult/adult partners, type of exposure to sexual stimuli, length and depth of relationships, how/why partners were chosen, current sexual relationships, current partners enable and/or partake in sexual offences, victimised partners/sexual abuse survivors, etc.

13. **Developmental and sexual abusive history** – The key elements include: ages, dates, type of experiences, specific perceptions, traumas, relationship problems, disruptions, significant abusive relationships. Key factors include: dates, number of others involved, name of person involved, type of experiences, perceptions, behaviours, type of relationship with the perpetrator, the degree of anger and/or depression associated with those events, current perceptions, etc.

14. **Sexual problems history** – The key elements include: types of sexual dysfunction, dates problems began and ended, beliefs about the problems, specific distortions, attempted interventions, problems occurring involving offending, related physical conditions, specific patterns of why problems occurred, etc.

15. **Psychiatric history** – The key elements include: dates, locations of hospitalisations, locations of occurrences, types of occurrence, types of problems, type of pathology, outcome of hospitalisation, outcome of different types of treatment, other related psychotherapeutic problems, offence committed while in a treatment centre, etc.

16. **Medical history** – The key elements include: dates, types of problems, length of hospitalisations, operations, diseases, head trauma, outcome of head traumas, current medications, accidents, birth defects, chronic pain and conditions, serious burns, etc.

17. **Suicidal history of attempts** – The key elements include: dates, ages, methods, consequences, motivations, type of interventions, current suicidal ideation, number of times, actual attempts and ideations, etc.

18. **Self destructive history** – The key elements include: frequency, fantasies, dates, ages, methods, consequences, motivations, type

of interventions, if any, key perceptions, number of times, sexual arousal and masturbation in conjunction with self destructive behaviour, frequency, level of enjoyment, thrill seeking behaviours, etc.

19. **Spiritual history** – The key elements include: type of religion, dates, level of participation, current interests and degree of participation, stability of beliefs, and consistency/consistency of beliefs, religious views of sex/gender issues, access to victims, to religious activities, offending involved in direct religious activities, (and/or unusual practices), level of violence, sadistic behaviour, sexual aggression behaviour, secrecy, enabling patterns, etc.; religious community support and enabling (denial of offences) and overall religious views concerning sex offender treatment.

Historical data: a 9-factor assault profile (Carich, 1994b)

The purpose of developing the assault profile is to gather as much inner relating data as possible in order to indicate the individual's methods, selection process and other characteristics of the offending behaviour. A brief review of the nine factors include:

1. **Victimology** – non-documented/ documented history of victims (dates, gender, age, method, type of assaultive behaviour, age of offender during sexual assaults, relationships with the victim). Descriptions of the index crime are important. The key factors include: number of offences, index offence (current offences in question) dates of assaults, age of offender of each offence, age of the victim and gender of each offence, duration of each assault, number and type of assaults per victim, type of assaultive behaviours, perpetrator/victim relationships (i.e., stranger vs. family member, acquaintance, etc.), total number of victims, total number of assaults on victims, length of longest victimisation, total number of years offending, total number of assaults per year, gender, location, initial and last age of victim/offender, first and last assaults, etc.

2. **Victim profile** – Victim profiles include: type of victim (descriptions, characteristics, ideal/availability, age range, gender, relationship with the victim, etc.). This includes ideal victim profile. The key factors include: gender preferences and choices, average range of victims, ideal age range of victims, ideal victim characteristics, average victim

characteristics, characteristics of the relationship between perpetrators and victims, preferred and actual victim responses of both the victim and the perpetrator, vulnerabilities sought in victims, physical and emotional characteristics of victims, etc.

3. **Deviant fantasy profile** – The deviant fantasy profile includes: type and degree of deviancy in fantasies (fantasy theme, motives, detailed descriptions, frequency, masturbatory behaviour in conjunction with fantasies, arousal level, gratifications, insensory construction of a fantasy, etc.). The key factors include: frequency of fantasies, ideal deviant fantasy and the type of responses sought from the victim, fantasy structure in terms of sensory modes (such as visual, auditory, kinesthetic, tactile and olfactory), deviant fantasy themes, average deviant fantasies with the type of responses sought from the victim, masturbatory patterns, frequency of normal fantasies, processing aspects of fantasies, duration of fantasies, the fantasised assaultive behaviour and victim characteristics, etc.

4. **Violence profile** – The violence profile includes: type and degree of violence (level of violence, methods, history, age and gender of victims, level of sexual arousal and violence, etc.). The key factors include: type of violence, frequency of violence, age began using violence, arousal to violence, age/gender of target victims, history of violence, level of violence in sexual offences, etc.

5. **Sexual Interest** – Sexual interest is one's arousal patterns (range of sexual arousal/behaviour levels, paraphilias, types and levels of normal sexual behaviour). The key factors include: type of paraphilias, frequency of orgasm and methods, sexual dysfunctions, sexual identity issues, level of normal deviant arousal patterns, masturbatory patterns and stimulus sets, frequency of sexual contacts, gender preferences, age preferences, etc. Methods of data collection include: inventories, self-report, polygraph and plethysmography.

6. **Offending cycle data** – The assault cycle data includes: assault patterns (pre-cursers, aftermath of assault, enablers, risk factors, motive/early contributing factors, cues, triggers, patterns, etc.). The key factors include: enabling behaviours, cognitive distortions (i.e., justifications, rationalisations, denial), defences, mood states, any activity that helps feed and enhance pattern rituals, grooming behaviours,

ways of avoiding responsibility, disinhibitors, any other precursor to the offence, aftermath of offences, key perceptions of victim responses, etc.

7. **Victim selection** – The victim selection process is the ideal victim profile/type, symbolic representations and meetings, motives, perceptions of victims, vulnerability sought, set-up, grooming, the relationship with the victim, victim responses sought, etc. The key factors include: preference, ideal victim, ideal victim and fantasy, average victim, average fantasy, possible symbolic representations of victims, victims' vulnerabilities that are sought or perceived by the perpetrator, location of victims, availability of victims, stalking and patterns of searching, grooming behaviours, set-up behaviours, victim characteristics that are attractive, type of relationship dynamics between the victim and perpetrator, temporary satisfactions gained by the offender, perceived and/or requested type of victim responses, etc.

8. **Offending paraphernalia** – Offending paraphernalia is the extra elements and items enabling the offence. This includes: tools, pattern feeders or anything used to feed the pattern, including external (overt) behaviour, i.e., beer, porno, equipment, drug/alcohol, and internal (covert) behaviour, i.e., dysfunctional or distorted beliefs and defences). The key factors include: type of beliefs and/or distortions, peer group, pornography, drugs and alcohol, the vehicles, bondage materials, disguises, disposal material, weapons or any type of enabler, aid and/or pattern feeder, etc.

9. **Offending disinhibitors** – Any event lowering inhibitions (internal covert behaviour, i.e., dysfunctional thinking, defences and external overt behaviour such as drug/alcohol, etc.). The key factors include: thinking errors, cognitive distortions (justifications, irrationalisations, denial, etc.), mood states, drug and alcohol, pornography, withdrawal, excessive masturbation, etc.

Non-static or process elements

Process (or dynamic) elements are equally important in an assessment as this allows for variables to change over time. It has been suggested that we apply these factors two years after the offending incident and the collection of the historical information. The process elements are those behaviours observed during the interview. These include:

Social interest

Social interest is the general care and concern for others. In terms of sex offender treatment, it is the level of victim empathy and remorse towards one's own victims and also the empathy towards other victims. Victim empathy involves the compassion at both intellectual and emotional levels. This encompasses the understanding of the victim impact issues or the consequences of victimising other individuals. Key factors to look at would include: inconsistencies, self-pity, spontaneous responses of empathy and remorse, manufacturing feelings, emoting on cue, intellectualising, cognitive distortions (justifications, denial, rationalisation, or any sort of justification), etc. This includes the level of compassion, care and concern, victim empathy (compassion for victims, level of conscience/guilt, etc.).

Sexual interests and arousal patterns

These are sexual preferences or stimuli that one is attracted to. Arousal is historical and also current behaviours. The historical aspects are found in the 9-factor assault profile. Some key factors include: sexual preferences, age range, characteristics of sexual objects, stimulus sets, etc. A list of behaviours to look for, exhibitionism, voyeurism, obscene phone calling, frotteurism (unwarranted sexual touch or rubbing), kissing, breast fondling, genital fondling, own genitals fondled during the offence, dry intercourse, perform oral sex, receive oral sex, perform vaginal intercourse, receive vaginal intercourse, perform and receive anal intercourse, penetration with object, penetration by object, urination, defecation, being violent, binding partner, inflict physical pain, receive physical pain, mutilation of partner, mutilation of self, sexual homicide, necrophilia, stalking, acquaintance, rape, stranger rape, bestiality, private masturbation, cross dressing, photographing others, being photographed, use of pornography, shoe fetish, foot fetish, public masturbation, unwarranted masturbation to self and/others, sexual harassment, sex involving self-mutilation, attempted rape, adult rape/physical force, adult rape/verbal coercion, sexual attempted murder, sexual murder and necrophilia.

Mental health status

Key factors include: current mental health functioning in terms of orientation to time, person and place, speech patterns (logical, coherent, tangential, circumstantial, etc.); current reality testing/contact; history of psychosis; current hallucinations; history of hallucinations; delusions; history of delusions; memory problems; information processing problems; emotional states such as depression and bipolar disorders, manicky, irritability, depression, anxiety, flat affect, bland, agitation, hostility, anger, normal, pleasant; organicity (developmental problems and/or brain trauma/level of IQ functioning, behavioural problems). It is also helpful to consider psychopathy here. Hare (1983) defines psychopathy as an extreme antisocial personality disorder and outlined 20 factors that indicate the presence of psychopathy. Examples include:

1. **Glibness/superficial charm** – Tends to be amusing and entertaining conversationalist; tends to take interviewer off the subject; pseudo-intellectual flavour; at ease throughout the interview; superficial charm and insincere, may use technical jargon with superficial knowledge, appears to be slick, smooth talking 'gift of gab'.

2. **Grandiosity sense of self worth** – Grossly inflated view of abilities and worth; brags, self assured, opinionated, exaggerated self, victim stancing, superior attitude, overpower, interview behaviours may include: 'No comment', I'm not prepared to answer . . .'

3. **Need for stimulation/proneness to boredom** – Has excessive need for novel and exciting stimulation; likes to live life in the fast lane or on the edge, risking challenges; constantly starts new activities.

4. **Pathological lying** – Readiness to lie, deceptive, not embarrassed or perplexed when caught in a lie, changes stories; deception appears to have intrinsic value; look at discrepancies; false identities/aliases, fictitious like history.

5. **Conning/manipulative** – Use of deception and deceit to cheat, bilk, defraud, manipulate, schemes, scans, etc., for personal gain, tends to use people; he views others like they are prey and he is the predator.

Disowning behaviours and personal responsibility
Responsibility is holding oneself accountable for one's behaviour and owning up to one's behaviour. Key factors include: level of responsibility and accountability, specific cognitive distortions (i.e., justifications, denial, blame, rationalisation, entitlements,

personalises/depersonalises, etc.). Look at the offender describing offences and minimising behaviours, the level of admission and denial, look for lifestyle (chronic) behaviours versus offence-specific, look at specific defences.

Relationship dynamics
Interpersonal dynamics include both social skills and relational dynamics. Key factors include: interpersonal exploitation, possessiveness, withdrawal, alienation, jealousy, enmeshed boundaries, isolation, level of social skills ('I' messages, eye contact, active listening, paraphrasing, empathy, appropriate confrontation, respect, appropriate expression of affect, physical boundaries, etc.).

Developmental motivational dynamics
The offending dynamics are the motivations or reasons why the offender assaults, along with sexual gratification. Key motivational factors include: expression anger, power/control, inferiorities, self-worth issues, self-esteem/self-image issues, revenge, attention, acceptance, approval, ventilation, loneliness and other symbolic representations or deeper meanings of these specific items in relation to the offence. Developmental factors are specific events that occur during critical periods of time (i.e., physical abuse, sexual abuse, emotional abuse, deprivation, etc.).

Lifestyle behaviours
Lifestyle behaviours are specific behavioural patterns or tendencies including habits that involve belief systems or thinking patterns, overt activities, failing processes, emotional processes, etc. These behaviours presented below, may just involve the offences or may actually be chronic patterns present in the offender's lifestyle throughout his life. Primary categories include:

- Antisocial behaviours (themes of deviant patterns of victimising or hurting others).
- Narcissistic behaviours (themes of grandiosity, self-centredness and superiority).
- Borderline behaviours (i.e., unstable lifestyle, seeks immediate gratification, unstable in relationships, marked intense moodiness.
- Schizoidal behaviours (displays flat affect, engages in superficial relationships, isolates, lacks social skills).

These have been described in Chapter 1.

Level of denial and cooperation
Denial can be seen as one facet of an offender's disowning behaviours, distortions and defences highlighted by the following:

1. **Denial** – omitting information or not admitting to the truth, including the details of the offence; Secrets, holding out information, not telling . . .
2. **Lying** – any type of deliberate distorting of information; not telling the truth, twisting information . . .
3. **Justifying** – making bad deviant things 'okay'; making it alright.
4. **Excusing** – faulty reasons to avoid/evade responsibility and to justify one's behaviour; bad reasons, faulty reasons to get away with bad behaviour.
5. **Blaming** – blaming others or something else and thus avoiding responsibility, guilt feelings . . . pointing fingers at others.
6. **Minimising** – to make smaller less important; reduce the significance.
7. **Entitlement** – unwarranted requests, expectations, and an attitude of 'I want what I want when I want it and I want it right **now**! and I'm going to get it any way I can'.
8. **Power games** – being superior, dominant, controlling, bossy, defying authority, . . . (my way, no way).
9. **Depersonalising** – Not seeing people as people, but as objects to be manipulated, such as 'meat'.
10. **Narcissism/pride power** – overly inflated sense of worth usually at others expense; stuck up attitude; me first/me only attitude; self-centredness.
11. **Vagueness** – being unclear 'fuzzy' in order to avoid responsibility; being abstract.
12. **Poor me** – pity pot or sympathy for self; feeling sorry for self.
13. **Avoidance and distancing** – withdrawal, running away, distancing (staying away), not dealing with ducking issues.
14. **Dumping** – projecting or inappropriately taking your garbage out on others.
15. **Trashing** – rages in which, you tear up stuff and trash things.
16. **Musts/shoulds** – inappropriate unrealistic unwarranted expectations and 'set ups' of yourself and others . . .
17. **Walling** – putting up walls or defences to keep others out and/or information out; blocking out (others) stuff, stuffing feelings, twisted thoughts, defences . . .
18. **Ownership** – treating people as your own personal property. Pawns in a chess game.
19. **Negative thinking** – dysfunctional, irrational, inappropriate thinking that leads to a bad attitude.
20. **Extremes** – implies: rigidly held views, absolutes, perfectionism, all or none/either or type of thinking.
21. **Magnification** –blowing things out of proportion, making a big deal over nothing.
22. **Procrastination** – putting things off.
23. **Apathy** – who cares, lack of concern, giving up.
24. **'Phoney baloney'** – insecure, superficial.

Most sex offenders referred for assessment will have committed acts that they deny and it is not unusual for them to be more open as the process unfolds. We should anticipate their denial and incompleteness of information before it emerges and explain that this is usually a reflection of their current lack of acceptance of the need for change, their need to feel reassured by the process and the workers involved, or as a temporary memory lapse (Morrison and Print, 1995). It is important to spend some time explaining the content and process of their particular assessment and how we will expect and accept the release of more information as the process unfolds. It is important to generate self-belief that they can understand and change their presenting offending behaviours, whilst also making clear to them we have access to multiple sources of information which will allow us to compare, and challenge them, about their account as compared to others.

If we are to effectively respond to denial, it is important that we furnish workers with a detailed, yet practical framework, which sets out the offender's distorted representations of reality. Calder (1999) (see Figure 2.4) sets out 15 different dimensions of offender denial, reflecting the reality that it is a spectrum and not a single state. Workers should find that offenders move between these dimensions as the assessment (and treatment work) unfolds (Salter, 1988). These dimensions are not neat compartments as they **frequently overlap.** Denial is not therefore a 'yes' or 'no' phenomenon, but is rather a continuum. Between the two extremes, offenders vary considerably on the level of responsibility they take for their behaviour. Offenders who can project blame on others and find excuses for

Figure 2.4: A multi-dimensional typology of denial (Calder, 1999).

Hopeless   *Denial*

Complete denial of responsibility
attack
denial of facts
denial of awareness
denial of intent
denial of responsibility
  psychological
  behaviour
  denial of impact
  intrusiveness
  harm
  seriousness
denial of frequency
denial of fantasy or planning/grooming
oneself and the environment
denial of deviant sexual arousal
admission with . . .
  justification
  minimisation
  fabrication
  mental illness
guilty, but not guilty
after conviction
denial of denial
No denial/acceptance of responsibility

Hopeful   *Responsibility*

their behaviour basically are blocked from truly recognising the impact their behaviour has on victims. The typology we present is not a continuum given the real difficulty in grading the dimensions suggested.

A multi-dimensional typology of denial

Complete denial of responsibility
Here, the offender completely denies the behaviour described in the allegation, protests their innocence, and accuses others of fabricating lies about them. This is primary denial, and may include statements such as: 'I didn't do it, (even if I got blamed for it)'; 'I was out of the area at the time'; She's lying; she made it up'; and 'I was drunk, I must have blacked out'. This is the first reaction of most offenders: they act shocked, surprised, or even indignant about such an allegation. We should never be thrown by strong initial denial from the offender.

Attack
Some sex offenders can use this approach many times during an investigation or prosecution. This reaction consists of attacking or going on the offensive. The offender may harass, threaten, or bribe victims and witnesses; attack the reputation and personal life of the workers; attack the motives of the police or prosecutors; claim the case is selective prosecution; raise issues such as gay rights (if the child victim is the same gender as the offender); and enlist the support of groups and organisations. Physical violence also has to be considered a very real possibility (Lanning, 1992). These reactions are a severe example of denying the real truth of their abuse emerging and a denial of the process of justice.

Denial of facts
Denial of facts can take different forms. They may rationalise the fact that they have been convicted in a court by saying that they were framed. Alternatively, they may not deny that the sexual abuse occurred, they simply state that they were not the offender. It might occur when there is a denial of events on specific days and will often involve the use of alibis, which are clung to despite overwhelming evidence to the contrary. This denial may be aided by relatives, friends, neighbours, and others. They may claim that they did have sexual relations with the victims, but it was not an offence as they consented or did not resist, or because the victims received some emotional benefit from the sexual experience, or because they were tricked into thinking the victims were older. Another scenario is where they admit to the act but then go on to deny that the interaction was sexual in nature (e.g. they were administering cream). Typically, the offender will view themselves as the victim and will protest their innocence with righteous indignation. The denial of facts position is often assumed by the family when they act as if the abuse has not happened or they ignore salient facts about the abuse. The offender may own the offence of which they are accused, but may represent this offence as the only deviant act committed.

Denial of awareness
This is a process in which the possibility of offending behaviour is considered, although conscious knowledge of the abuse is denied. This type of denial is demonstrated by an offender claiming lapses in memory or through

alleged drug and alcohol induced blackouts. They may claim that they know nothing about it or that they do not remember. They may claim their judgement, as well as their memory, was suspended for periods of time, when they were intoxicated.

Denial of intent

Here, the offender may admit some parts of the offence, but they deny that there was any intent on their part to commit the offence. Examples would include: 'It just happened' or 'I didn't want it to happen, things just got out of control', or 'Is it a crime to hug a child?'. Workers challenging this view will need to refer to the concept of pre-offence planning as set out very clearly by Finkelhor (1984).

Denial of responsibility

This describes a process of inappropriate displacement of responsibility onto non-offending objects. A range of behaviours, emotions, and cognition in which the offender and significant others blame people, substances, or circumstances other than the perpetrator of the abuse. Offenders displaying this position will often attribute their participation in the offence to seductive behaviour by the victim, problems with the spouse, or benevolent intentions such as educating the child for future sexual encounters (Winn, 1996). This might include:

Psychological: This is a more general form of denial of responsibility. It is where the offender does not focus on the concrete details of the alleged offence, as they maintain they are not the kind of person to commit such acts. This 'nice guy' defence is built on the premise that they are the pillar of the community, a devoted family man, with no prior arrests, and a victim of many personal problems. This tactic can be effective where people retain the belief that most sex offenders are 'strangers' or societal misfits (Lanning, 1992). They may try to discredit the victims by calling the victims liars or vindictive.

Behaviour: This is where external factors and mitigating circumstances are put forward to explain their offending. They may make the child responsible for the abuse saying that the child triggered the abuse by their behaviour, or they may say 'Yes, I did it, but you can't blame me. If my wife hadn't left me, this wouldn't have happened'.

Denial of impact

This is a form of self-preservation in which the offender and significant members of his family or social network minimise or ignore the emotional, social, or physical ramifications of the offender's abusive behaviour. This process can relate to the offender's victims or to the impact of the crisis on the family as a consequence of disclosure (Winn, 1996). The offender may argue that the victim will fully recover and thus will not suffer any long-term effects, or that they have other sexual experience, thus rendering the abuse of no consequence. It might include:

Intrusiveness: Some offenders will admit some sexual acts and deny others. They may admit masturbating their victims and performing oral sex on them, but will deny actually penetrating them. Examples would include 'I only fondled her' or 'I didn't sodomise him, no matter what he says'. This is often noted when the offender minimises the extent of their previous offensive behaviour, the number of past victims, the frequency of their past offences and the degree of force they may have used.

Harm: This occurs when offenders may admit aspects of the offence, but deny that the victims were harmed. For example, they may say 'I did it, but it didn't hurt him, certainly not as bad as they say'; 'It didn't hurt me when I was abused'; 'When I had sex with my daughter I knew at the time it was my responsibility but I didn't hurt her'; 'She never asked me not to do it'; or 'It was a loving thing'. In this sense, they may portray the child as an active or willing participant in the abuse. They may deny any right of the child to say 'no'. The denial of harm allows the offender to pretend that their victims didn't suffer as well as preventing them from seeing their victims as people with thoughts and feelings about what happened to them. This will result in the offender seeing children simply as objects.

Seriousness: This follows on from where the offender has no concept of the severity of their acts, any long-term harm to their victims, or the difficulties involved in changing their pattern of offending behaviour. They may simply say 'It won't happen again', without accepting the likelihood of further abuse occurring; they may deny any abuse of power; they may deny any previous history of sexually deviant behaviour and/or any ongoing sexual problems. They may even present themselves as non-sexual beings. Offenders in this category are unlikely to want to change.

Denial of frequency

The offender's statement of how many times the abuse occurred may be much less than what the victim says occurred, for example, 'I did it, but only a few times, not the 20 times he says'. It is not unreasonable for the worker to double the frequency of admitted abuse, similar to a GP taking a history of alcohol or tobacco use.

Denial of fantasy or planning/grooming oneself and the environment

Some offenders admit the abuse, but deny any (internal) fantasy or (contextual) planning involved in organising the abuse. Offenders demonstrating this position will deny grooming themselves by fantasising deviant material or justifying the abuse to themselves. Similarly, they will deny any manipulation used in securing a victim. Rather, the abuse will be described as if it came 'out of the blue', with no warning to the offenders; or they may say 'I abused children, but the thought of it disgusts me' or 'I never get turned on when I think about it'. They may cite statements that the offence happened on the spur of the moment, for example: 'Her mother was out, she came downstairs in her night dress with no pants on, to watch her favourite TV programme and . . .' They may state that the offence was an isolated, inexplicable incident, or completely out of character, e.g. 'It's never happened before . . . it won't ever happen again . . . I don't behave like this, I'm happily married . . .'

Denial of deviant sexual arousal and inappropriate sexualisation of non-sexual problems

This describes a form of denial in which the offender and his family ascribe intentions for offending to non-sexual reasons. Instead of acknowledging the offence as sexual in nature, this position describes a range of thoughts, feelings, and behaviours which minimise or ignore the fact that the offender has a problem with paraphilic or inappropriate sexual behaviour (such as arousal, interest, or preferences), (Winn, 1996). Many offenders may deny only the sexual offence and intent and be candid about all the other requested information from the workers.

Admission, with . . .

Justification: A sex offender typically attempts to justify his behaviour to the police. This may be where the commission of the act is admitted, but where the extent and seriousness of the behaviour is often minimised and blame deflected onto life events or the victim. Consequently little guilt or blame is felt. This may involve pretending that the abuse was a normal/educational activity: 'I was teaching him about sex', or 'I was checking her out because she said she hurt down there'. They may outline the offence and argue that it included nothing unlawful (e.g. the child 'consented', or they did not know how old a certain victim was), or say that children often make up stories about being sexually abused. They may justify what they have done, saying 'She was sleeping with her boyfriend as well . . .' They may argue that the victim encouraged them, initiating the process and taking the lead, as well as enjoying the sexual encounter. Many argue that the victim hasn't disclosed until now because of these factors. Even where the offender has been seduced by a victim, and they are promiscuous, a crime has still been committed, and such a justification has no meaning. Others will simply believe they have done nothing at all wrong. The offender might claim that they care for these children more than their parents do and that what they do is beneficial to the child.

Minimisation: If the evidence against the offender rules out total denial, the offender may attempt to minimise what they have done, both in quantity and quality. Offenders minimise their own responsibility for their offences in three ways: attributing blame to the victim, making external (situational) attributions (such as stressful circumstances, social pressure or provocation) and making irresponsible internal attributions (such as their deprived childhood, their hormones or sex drive). It is also important to recognise that even seemingly co-operative victims may also minimise the quantity and quality of acts. If a certain act was performed 20 times, the victim might claim it only happened ten, and the offender might claim it only happened once. Victims may also deny particular sexual acts, such as anal intercourse by adolescent males. Limited and highly selective admission is commonplace, with the all-important planning and fantasising frequently being denied. Here, whilst the offender admits the offence, they use the device of making it sound much less serious than other evidence shows it to be: e.g., 'I only brushed up against her just the once', 'I only touched her', 'It wasn't a big deal', or 'I only put the tip in'.

When minimising the full extent of their behaviour, they frequently say that the child precipitated or collaborated with their own abuse. They may also minimise the full extent of their sexual problems. They may also be knowledgeable about the law and might, therefore, be motivated to admit to those acts that carry lesser consequences.

Fabrication: Some of the cleverest sex offenders come up with ingenious stories to explain their behaviour. For example, doctors saying they are researching male youth prostitution. A teacher claimed that his students had such a desperate need for attention and affection that they practically threw themselves at him and misunderstood his resulting affection for sexual advances. Another offender said that his sadomasochistic photographs of children were part of a child discipline programme. One offender claimed that some children made the sexually explicit videotape without his knowledge and he kept it only to show their parents. Workers clearly need to challenge such explanations and attempt to disprove them (Lanning, 1992).

Mental illness: When all other tactics fail, the offender may feign mental illness. Few do so until they are either arrested or charged. Such a diagnosis simply re-frames the need for treatment and never excuses their behaviour.

Guilty, but not guilty

This is where the offender will try to make a deal in order to avoid a public trial. Whilst this has the advantage of sparing the victim the trauma of giving evidence, it allows the offender to plead, in essence, to 'guilty, but not guilty'. In the UK, this can be plea-bargaining to a lesser offence. The offender might also say they are pleading guilty to spare the child, or that they cannot afford to contest the charges, but don't accept their guilt despite their pleas. This can confuse the victims further (Lanning, 1992).

After conviction

Post-conviction, and often incarceration, some offenders ask to speak to law enforcement officials in order to share information about organised abuse, including child sex rings, child pornography, abduction of children, etc., as this allows them to contextualise and minimise their abuses in the broader framework. It also allows them to plea for a reduced sentence (Lanning, 1992).

Denial of denial

Is a description of the offender's and the family's behaviour which minimises or disqualifies the fact that denial is a necessary means of psychological protection to cope with the shame generated in the maintenance of abusive behaviour. Accepting this fact often enables the offender to monitor themselves better, as they realise that denial has a purpose and cannot be cured but, rather, observed and managed (Winn, 1996).

No denial

This is where the offender's account of the events is essentially the same as the allegation. Examples include: 'I did it. It's my responsibility'; 'I did everything she said I did, and there are things I did that she didn't mention'; 'I'm sure I hurt him, though I don't know how badly', and 'Even though I hurt him, sometimes I still get turned on when I think about it.' It is very important that we don't allow offenders who start at this point to avoid some detailed assessment work, as it can be a clever tactic to avoid detailed internal enquiry.

Stages of denial

It is clear from the above framework that denial is a spectrum and never a single state. The worker would expect the offender to move between various positions as the work unfolds. As an excellent accompliment to this typology, Laflen and Sturm (1994) have looked at denial as a series of stages which the sexual offender will go through cyclically as the work unfolds. This will usually extend beyond the assessment phase into treatment.

The first stage is denial of the behaviour, in which offenders deny categorically that they committed any type of offence. The underlying function of the denial for the offenders is to protect themselves from rejection and to preserve the idealised self image. The goals in this stage are for the offenders to talk honestly about their behaviours, understand the concept of cycles of behaviour, begin improving their self image by beginning to take responsibility for themselves, and to begin trusting themselves and the relationship with the workers, by beginning to take small risks of honesty. For the worker, the goals are to provide clear, consistent structure in an honest, nurturing manner regarding the boundaries and expectations of the work.

The second stage is minimisation of the seriousness of the behaviours and is driven by their need to save themselves from the pain of facing the fact that they have a problem and that their behaviour hurts others, as well as from facing further shame. The goal of the second stage of denial is for offenders to realise that they have a serious problem and need help, and for them to realise their behaviours caused serious harm to their victims. An additional goal is for the offenders to begin to challenge the cognitive distortions, which is necessary for them to begin to move forward.

The third stage is denial of responsibility for their behaviours. The function of the denial for the offenders in this stage is to preserve their cognitive distortion that if they didn't plan the offence then they are 'not that bad'. This thinking error is intended to protect them from facing the shame and integrating a more reality-based self image. The goals of this stage are to work with the offender to continue to identify the cycle of their offence and to accept that through their thoughts, feelings, and behaviours they planned and executed their offence, as opposed to their offence having been impulsive and the result of some trauma they may have experienced as a child.

The fourth and final stage of denial is full admission of the behaviours accompanied by an acceptance of responsibility for the behaviours and genuine guilt about them. Upon resolution of this stage, the offender is are able to clearly identify the thoughts, feelings, and behaviours in their offence cycle and have begun to develop specific relapse prevention strategies. Offenders who are able to complete and begin to implement a comprehensive relapse prevention plan must necessarily be able to identify the cognitive distortions which allowed them to offend, and must accept responsibility for those distortions in order to be able to plan a healthy response to their reoccurrence. This would suggest that the offender is now able to accept as part of themselves the qualities which previously had to be denied. They now realise that they can be whole people, faults and all, without losing themselves, their connections to others in the world, and the opportunities to have their needs met. Their denial at this point tends to be centred upon their risk of relapse, and is addressed during the process of relapse prevention planning.

Taylor (1996) produced a model (see Figure 2.5) to assist workers locating the level of denial

Figure 2.5: A continuum of denial (Taylor, 1996).

Hopeless   *Denial*

- Nothing happened.
- Something happened but it wasn't me.
- Something happened but they wanted it to.
- Something happened but not as bad as they said.
- It happened, but at the time I didn't know it was wrong.
- It happened but it was an accident.
- It happened, I don't know what came over me.
- It happened, but it wasn't planned.
- It happened, but it never happened before and I haven't thought about it since.
- It happened, I planned it and I know how it hurt people so it won't happen again.
- It happened, I planned it, it hurt people. I understand now about my thinking so it won't happen again.
- It happened. I planned it. It hurt people. I understand my thinking. I think about it still, but this is my relapse prevention if I feel tempted again.

Hopeful   *Responsibility*

being displayed by the offender and then using it as the basis of determining interviewing approaches as well as attainable outcomes. Treatment of denial takes time and is often measured in terms of years, rather than months or weeks.

Social and life skills
Social skills is a broad term used to describe a wide variety of behaviours and cognitive phenomena presumed necessary for effective functioning in social situations (Conger and Conger, 1986, 526). It has been defined as 'the ability to maximise positive reinforcement and minimise punishment from others (Graves et al., 1992). Squirrel (1999) noted that social skills are largely about:

- Developing good communication skills: listening well, thinking about what is said, being aware of non-verbal cues, knowing how best to respond and anticipating the possible consequences of words and actions.
- Being aware of others' feelings, vulnerabilities, concerns, preoccupations and wants and knowing how best to respond to these.

- Being aware of one's own feelings, wants, preoccupations, ways of interpreting and shaping the worlds and the ways in which these impact on others and interactions with others.
- Knowing how groups work, knowing why people are different on their own, with friends or in social situations where they are dealing with authority.
- Developing the skills to understand, to channel and to manage personal feelings and emotions.
- Knowing how to manage interactions with others: to not be bullied or give in; to stop conflicts from developing; to make people less anxious or tense, to feel less threatened or concerned, to show power, status, rage or dominance.
- Being able to leave a social encounter knowing that you have done your best to express your feelings, ideas, needs, to have had them acknowledged and understood and not to have undermined anyone else in the process (1).

Social skills enable people to be more aware of others' feelings, the cues offered by others and to be more responsive to the range of social, work, living and other situations to which they are daily exposed. Developing social skills, being more adept at managing interactions, becoming more aware of ourselves and others are skills and which can never be considered as tasks completed or skills fully learnt.

Poor social skills can be a starting point for a host of difficulties, such as experiencing social isolation, desperation, a sense of not belonging or fitting into society; poor or dysfunctional intimate or sexual relationships; pursuing harmful or damaging lifestyles; not understanding emotions or managing them; not being able to communicate effectively with others and not reading social contexts or others' cues. Failures to communicate may lead to involvement in conflict situations and to escalating conflict (3).

The development of social skills is a keystone in successfully making life changes. They can be learnt, developed and do need to be practiced. Developing social skills is of immediate term benefit. It is a route to better self-image, improved self-esteem, improved social acceptability, less friction and fewer confrontations (3). Deficiencies in the offender's social skills are frequently cited as playing a key role in both the origin and then the maintenance of sexual offending – by excluding them from access to appropriate sexual partners or preventing them from changing their mode of sexual expression to a more normative one (Marshall, Barbaree and Fernandez, 1995). Marshall (1971) argued that if we wanted to help sex offenders change their behaviour, then we needed to equip them with the necessary skills to be successful.

Life skills are defined by Squirrel (1998) as covering the host of skills which all people need to develop in order to negotiate their lives successfully and to help themselves have a more fulfilled time. They are the essential building blocks for quality of life. Life skills form a whole mesh of inter-related skills, beliefs and ways of managing the world and oneself. They cannot be treated as separate skills divorced from one another. Thus, work on one area will be key to improving many other areas of life skills.

Sex offenders may present as being quite normal in their social functioning and beliefs. The interview itself can provide clues as to the offender's social skills behaviours (verbal and non-verbal). Deficits may be indicated where they look away excessively, fail to listen, interrupt readily, lack social pleasantry, appear socially awkward, jump topics suddenly, become over-familiar with the worker or ask personal questions of the workers which are unrelated to the background relevant to the inquiry (Carich and Adkerson, 1995, 8). However, we need to be mindful of Segal and Marshalls (1985) findings as they reported that the offenders' response and presentation within the interview situation may not accord with their behaviour elsewhere. Whilst role-play is advocated to counter this (Dougher, 1995), it is often difficult within individual sessions and may be more practical in a group setting.

Conclusions

There are a number of key differences in the remit of sex offender assessments from other types of assessment, reinforcing that specific frameworks are needed with this target group. This extends also to the interviewing of sex offenders, where a confrontational approach is unlikely to lead to positive outcomes. Whilst this chapter has focused primarily on general assessments, the other three types of assessment are addressed in more detail in Chapter 11. For a detailed framework that integrates theory, research and practical suggestions for information collection and then outcome measurement and evaluation, the reader is referred to Calder (1999).

References

Adkerson D (1994) *Training Handout on Mind-reading Prediction.* Unpublished Manuscript.

Beckett R C (1994) Assessment of Sex Offenders. In Morrison T, Erooga M and Beckett R C (Eds.) *Sexual Offending Against Children: Assessment and Treatment of Male Abusers.* London: Routledge, 55–79.

Blanchard G T (1996) *The Difficult Connection: The Therapeutic Relationship in Sex Offender Treatment.* Brandon, VT: Safer Society Press.

Bliss P (1990) *The ABC Exercise.* Derbyshire Probation Service.

Burnham D et al. (1990) Offending and Masculinity: Working With Males. *Probation Journal,* September 1990, 106–11.

Calder M C (1999) *Assessing Risk in Adult Males Who Sexually Abuse Children: A Practitioner's Guide.* Lyme Regis, Dorset: Russell House Publishing.

Calder M C (2000) *Complete Guide to Sexual Abuse Assessments.* Lyme Regis, Dorset: Russell House Publishing.

Calder M C (2002) The Assessment Framework: A Critique and Reformulation. In Calder M C and Hackett S (Eds.) *Assessment in Child Care: Using and Developing Frameworks for Practice.* Lyme Regis, Dorset: Russell House Publishing.

Calder M C (Ed.) (2002) *Young People Who Sexually Abuse: Building the Evidence Base for Your Practice.* Lyme Regis, Dorset: Russell House Publishing.

Carich M S (1991) Evaluating and Detecting the Phoniness of Clients. *INMAS Newsletter.* 4: 2, 13–4.

Carich M S (1994) Dissociative and Hypnotic Elements of the Offending Mode. *INMAS Newsletter.* 7: 3, 8–9.

Carich M S (1994b) 9-Factor Assault Profile or Typology. *INMAS Newlsetter.* 7: 2, 10.

Carich M S (1994c) Basic Types of Distorted Thinking and Behaviour. *INMAS Newlsetter.* 7: 3, 10–1.

Carich M S (1997) *Sex Offender Treatment and Overview: Training for The Mental Health Professional.* Springfield, Illinois: Illinois Department of Corrections.

Carich M S (1999) Evaluation of Recovery: 15 Common Factors or Elements. In Calder M C *Assessing Risk in Adult Males Who Sexually Abuse Children.* Lyme Regis, Dorset: Russell House Publishing, 279–81.

Carich M S and Adkerson D L (1995) *Adult Sexual Offender Assessment Packet.* Brandon, VT: Safer Society Press.

Cleaver H and Freeman P (1995) *Parental Perspectives in Cases of Suspected Child Abuse.* London: HMSO.

Conger J C and Conger A J (1986) Assessment of Social Skills. In Ciminero A R et al. (Eds.) *Handbook of Behavioural Assessment.* NY: John Wiley and Sons, 526–60.

Diclemente C (1991) Motivational Interviewing and The Stages of Change. In Miller W N and Rollnick S (Eds.) *Motivational Interviewing.* London: Guilford Press.

Dougher M J (1988) Clinical Assessment of Sex Offenders. In Schwartz B (Ed.) *A Practitioner's Guide to Treating the Incarcerated Male Sex Offender.* Washington, DC: NIC, 77–84.

Dougher M J (1995) Clinical Assessment of Sex Offenders. In Schwartz B K and Cellini H R (Eds.) *The Sex Offender: Corrections, Treatment and Legal Practice.* Kingston, NJ: Civic Research Institute, Inc.

Egan G (1994) *The Skilled Helper.* (5th edn.) Monterey: Brooks/Cole.

Finkelhor D (1984) *Child Sexual Abuse: Theory and Research.* NY: The Free Press.

Garrison K (1992) *Working With Sex Offenders: A Practice Guide. Social Work Monograph 112.* Norwich: UEA.

Graves R, Openshaw D K and Adams G R (1992) Adolescent Sex Offenders and Social Skills Training. *International Journal of Offender Therapy and Comparative Criminology.* 36: 2, 139–53.

Gray A S and Wallace R (1992) *Adolescent Sexual Offender Assessment Packet.* Orwell, VT: Safer Society Press.

Hare R (1983) *The Psychopathy Checklist.* Vancouver, CA: Department of Psychology: University of British Columbia.

Horwath J and Morrison T (2000) Assessment of Parental Motivation to Change. In Horwath J (Ed.) *The Child's World: Assessing Children in Need.* Reader. London: Jessica Kindley, 77–89.

Ivanoff A, Blythe B and Tripodi T (1994) *Involuntary Clients in Social Work Practice.* NY: Aldine De Gruyter.

Jones C and Lewis J (1990/1) A Pilot Prison Treatment Group for Sex Offenders At HMP Norwich. *Prison Service Journal.* 81: 44–6.

Kear-Colwell J and Pollock P (1997) Motivation or Confrontation: Which Approach to The Child Sex Offender? *Criminal Justice and Behaviour.* 24: 1, 20–33.

Laflen B and Sturm W R (1994) Understanding and Working With Denial in Sex Offenders. *Journal of Sexual Abuse.* 3: 4, 19–36.

Lanning, K V (1992) *Child Molesters: A Behavioral Analysis for Law Enforcement Officers Investigating Cases of Child Sexual Exploitation.* Arlington, VA: National Center for Missing Children.

Mann R (Ed.) (1996) *Motivational Interviewing With Sex Offenders: A Practice Manual.* Hull: Bluemoon Corporate Services.

Mann R and Rollnick S (1996) Motivational Interviewing With A Sex Offender Who Believed He Was Innocent. *Behavioural and Cognitive Psychotherapy.* 24: 2, 127–34.

Mark P (1992) Training Staff to Work With Sex Offenders. *Probation Journal.* 39: 1, 1–13.

Marshall W L (1971) A Combined Treatment Method for Certain Sexual Deviations. *Behaviour Research and Therapy.* 9: 292–4.

Marshall W L, Barbaree H E and Fernandez Y M (1995) Some Aspects of Social Incompetence in Sex Offenders. *Sexual Abuse: A Journal of Research and Treatment.* 7: 113–27.

McGrath R J (1990) Assessment of Sexual Aggressors: Practical Clinical Interviewing Strategies. *Journal of Interpersonal Violence.* 5(4): 507–19.

Metzger C and Carich M S (1999) Eleven Point Comprehensive Sex Offender Treatment Plan. In Calder M C (Ed.) *Assessing Risk in Adult Males Who Sexually Abuse Children.* Lyme Regis, Dorset: Russell House Publishing, 293–311.

Miller W and Rollnick S (1991) *Motivational Interviewing: Preparing People to Change Addictive Behaviour.* NY: Guilford Press.

Morrison T (1991) Change, Control and The Legal Framework. In Adcock M, White R and Hollows A (Eds.) *Significant Harm: Its Management and Outcome.* (2nd edn.) Croydon: Significant Publications, 85–100.

Morrison T (1995) *Core Groups: A Catalyst for Change?* Presentation to the National Conference on Core Groups. Manchester Town Hall, 14.7.95.

Morrison T (1998) Partnership, Collaboration and Change Under The Children Act. In Adcock M and White R (Eds.) *Significant Harm: Its Management and Outcome.* Croydon: Significant Publications, 121–47.

Morrison T and Print B (1995) *Adolescent Sexual Abusers: An Overview.* Hull: Bluemoon Corporate Services.

Mussack S E and Carich M S (2001) Sex Offender Assessment. In Carich M S and Mussack S E (Eds.) *A Handbook for Sexual Abuser Assessment and Treatment.* Brandon, VT: The Safer Society Press.

O'Hanley W (1987) *Taps Roots.* NY: WW Norton.

Pithers W D, Beal L S, Armstrong J and Petty J (1989) The Identification of Risk Factors Through Clinical Interviews and Analysis of Records. In Laws D R (Ed.) *Relapse Prevention With Sex Offenders.* New York: Guilford Press, 1–31.

Prendergast W E (1991) *Treating Sex Offenders in Correctional Institutions and Outpatient Clinics: A Guide to Clinical Practice.* NY: Haworth Press.

Prochaska J O and Diclemente C C (1982) Transtheoretical Therapy: Toward a More Integrative Model of Change. *Psychotherapy, Theory, Research and Practice.* 19: 276–88.

Prochaska J O and Diclemente C C (1986) Towards a Comprehensive Model of Change. In Miller W N and Heather N (Eds.) *Treating Addictive Behaviours: Processes of Change.* NY: Plenum Press, 3–27.

Ross J (1989) *Group Treatment Approaches.* Paper Presented at the Advanced Training for Treatment of Adolescent Sex Offenders. Toronto: Canadian Welfare Association.

Rossi E L (1993) *The Psychobiology of Mind-Body Healing. New Concepts in Therapeutic Hypnosis.* New York: W.W. Norton

Rossi E L and Cheek, D (1986) *Psychobiology of Mind-Body Healing: New Concepts of Therapeutic Hypnosis.* New York: W.W. Norton.

Rossi E L and Cheek, D (1988) *Mind-Body Therapy: Methods of Ideodynamic Healing in Hypnosis.* New York: W.W. Norton.

Salter A C (1988) *Treating Child Sex Offenders and Victims? Assessment and Treatment of Child Sex Offenders: A Practice Guide.* Beverly Hills, Ca: Sage.

Segal V and Marshall W L (1985) Heterosexual Social Skills in a Population of Rapists and Child Molesters. *Journal of Consulting and Clinical Psychology.* 53: 55–63.

Sheath M (1990) Confrontive Work With Sex Offenders: Legitimised Nonce Bashing? *Probation Journal.* 37: 4.

Squirrel G (1998) *Developing Life Skills.* Dorset: Russell House Publishing.

Squirrel G (1999) *Developing Social Skills.* Dorset: Russell House Publishing.

Taylor G (1996) *Working With Denial*. Workshop at the Barnardo's Conference, 'Learning to Change', Liverpool Town Hall, 14 March 1996.

Taylor R (1972) The Significance and Interpretation of Motivational Questions: The Case of Sex Offenders. *Sociology*. 6: 23–39.

Willis G C (1993) *Unspeakable Crimes: Prevention Work With Perpetrators of Child Sexual Abuse*. London: Children's Society.

Winn M E (1996) The Strategic and Systemic Management of Denial in The Cognitive/Behavioural Treatment of Sex Offenders. *Sexual Abuse: A Journal of Research and Treatment*. 8: 1, 25–36.

Chapter Three

Sex Offender Group Work

Group therapy is the primary modality of sex offender treatment although the rationale for this remains unclear. Behroozi (1992) suggests that groupwork is the preferred method of intervention with involuntary clients, as the group experience can reduce levels of denial, facilitate an acceptance of the fact their problems exist, increase their need for change, and help clients to develop more appropriate ways of dealing with their problems. He also states that due to issues of trust and authority being problematic with involuntary clients, confrontation which addresses the sources of their denial is far more effective when undertaken by their peers – all relevant with work with sex offenders. Calder (forthcoming) addresses the engagement of involuntary clients in some detail.

A cognitive-behavioural approach is the most evident of the groupwork approaches. However, whilst many programmes are generally successful in covering the specifically cognitive areas of therapy (such as enabling offenders to recognise patterns of their distorted thinking that allow them to enact illegal sexual acts, heightening empathy and understanding toward the victims of sexually abusive behaviour, and increasing the awareness of the harmful short-and long-term consequences of sexually abusive behaviour), there is often a narrow focus of behavioural features (such as reducing deviant arousal through masturbatory reconditioning or aversive therapies).

Despite the lack of empirical evidence on the effectiveness of groups, groups for sex offenders are believed to be effective because:

- By joining a group, a sex offender publicly acknowledges his need to change.
- Group therapy provides a context within which socially acceptable values are conveyed and normal social interactions are reinforced.
- Groups allow other offenders to challenge the offender's distorted pattern of thinking and behaviour.
- Group treatment provides a supportive environment in which new attitudes and behaviours can be rehearsed.
- There are less chances for the offender to maintain their lies.

- Offenders receive more feedback, often from fellow offenders.
- It intensifies the change context.
- Effective change occurs as a result of the integration of emotions, cognitions and behaviour. The group experience can offer a context within which to achieve this integration if the group process functions effectively (Cohen, 1997).
- Offenders help each other access/resolve issues, as well as learning how to develop skills from each other and maintain coping skills.
- The chances of worker collusion are reduced.

The responsibility of the worker is to provide or help develop a context for change, whilst the responsibility of the offender is to commit to change and do the things necessary to change. In this sense, individual change is encouraged within and outside the group context. Group work should never be seen as the sole form of intervention.

The pros and cons of individual and group therapy

1. *Pros of group therapy*
   - Learn the necessary skills more easily
   - Receive much more feedback
   - Much more intense therapeutic context
   - Easier context to access key issues/dynamics
   - Less likely to lie/distort/disown, etc. in group
   - Less likely to maintain 'dirty' secrets
   - More emotional/social support
   - Can learn from others
   - Easier to change lifestyle behaviours through group processes
   - More cost effective
2. *Cons of group therapy*
   - Less time for clients
   - Less confidentiality
   - Offenders learning new techniques from group members
3. *Pros of individual therapy*
   - More confidentiality
   - More client time

– More comfortable for the offender
– Reduces fear for those who have anxiety about groups
4. *Cons of individual therapy*
– Maintain secrets
– Easier to get away with crooked behaviours and entitlements
– More costly
– Less feedback reduced learning experience
– Less support

Not all offenders will benefit from inclusion in a groupwork programme and thus there needs to be some process for carefully considering those who should and should not join. Craissati and McClurg (1997) found poor treatment outcomes associated with more severe offence patterns and childhood experiences of abuse. In such cases, individual work has proved more effective in achieving progress and change, thus allowing the progression into a groupwork programme at a later stage.

Any assessment of the values and benefits of groupwork needs to consider both the individual treatment objectives and the group needs given that an offender may impact on the functioning of the group and its other members. This may embrace disruptive offenders who may well require the benefits of a supportive group to model more positive behaviour. Every offender must have received a substantial assessment to identify their needs (see Calder, 1999 for an outline) and the risks they pose to others should already be managed.

All offenders need preparing for admission to the group and this may best be achieved through a two-day pre-admission block to:

• Provide the offender with information about the problem of sexual offending behaviour and acceptable terminology.
• Further assess an individual's competence in a group setting.
• Provide a supportive, safe environment for the offender to start to talk openly about their offending behaviour.
• Provide the offender with information regarding the aims, rules and format for the group (Print and O'Callaghan, 1999).

All offenders require a contract pre-admission that addresses aims of the group, rules regarding attendance, confidentiality, behaviour inside and outside the group, personal goals, review of progress arrangements etc.

Groups

Since offender groups are different from non-offender groups, the structural differences need to be identified. In this section, we discuss the different types of group, group parameters, group structure and group rules.

Type of groups

There are two ways to categorise groups: by duration and by content. Duration usually differentiates between groups established for a specific timeframe and which are highly structured (time-limited groups) from open-ended groups, which allow some new members to be admitted whilst others may leave. This is appropriate for ongoing established programmes of work punctuated by different modules that can facilitate new admission points. It is often considered sensible to place offenders of the same sex with other offenders demonstrating diversity in victim type, patterns of offending and varying communication skills as such a group induces a dynamic atmosphere in which a higher level of intensity can be facilitated.

Group parameters

Group parameter considerations include size, co-facilitators, and group composition. The ideal group size ranges from 6-10 members, with eight being the preferred number. This provides an ideal context for group dynamics to emerge whilst facilitating participation by all group members. Any more than eight offenders seems to create ambiguity and confusion and leaves less time to work on the necessary issues. Some psycho-educational modules are extended to 15–20 members and are typically modelled on classroom contexts.

Group composition may be heterogeneous or homogenous, with some programmes integrating rapists with sex offenders against children. This mixture can give the group a unique set of dynamics. Groups can also be organised around IQ and developmental level. Slower functioning offenders need to be placed in their own group, separated from higher functioning aggressive offenders.

Co-therapy is recommended. Therapists can then support each other whilst offenders can learn to resolve conflicts by watching co-facilitators resolve theirs (concerning group terial). Carich (1998) outlined several useful regarding co-therapy:

It requires teamwork and team effort.
2. Both therapists are equal partners.
3. Power and control is equally distributed to both therapists.
4. The ideal is to have male and female teams largely because:
   a. This gives offenders exposure to both males and females in authority positions.
   b. Offenders could see how both males and females get along in harmony.
   c. Workers could more easily shatter myths surrounding females and relationships.
   d. Workers could model problem resolution and conflict resolution skills.
   e. It can model cross gender re-parenting.
   f. It shows that men and women are equals.
5. Both workers have to be on the same wavelength or have similar theoretical and therapeutic approaches. It follows therefore that workers should know each other and be able to anticipate what could get triggered in group. This includes any major hang-ups.
6. Workers can have conflicts in the group, as long as they are handled appropriately:
   a. Conflicts or disagreements can be used in therapy if resolved or left as each worker has an opinion and that is okay. However, try and avoid major conflicts in the group and address them elsewhere.
   b. Workers need to respect each other.
   c. Workers need to avoid power conflicts.
   d. Workers should never victimise each other.
7. Do not allow offenders to victimise each other.
8. Male workers should never overprotect females and vice-versa.
9. Workers need to develop agreed plans to handle problematic offenders.
10. Maintain flexibility, not rigidity.
11. Balance styles, roles of supportive versus confrontational.

Group structure

The structure of the group depends on the level of direction and guidance a facilitator(s) provide the group. For example, psycho-educational groups and newly formed groups are much more structured than advanced veteran, highly cultured groups with motivated offenders. It takes a while for the culture to develop and mature.

Groups can be structured any number of ways. For example, Loss (2001) and Ross (1998) emphasise using the group secretary concept. Offenders switch off the role of recording the main issues and responses within group. A portion of the next session is used to review the last session. Group rounds are used to quickly assess who has relevant issues. The time frame is divided.

All overly aggressive (i.e., disruptive, continuously challenging for poser, victimising, etc.) are controlled. Those individuals (usually highly antisocial and narcissistic in nature) dislike authority and control group.

The group culture is derived from a combination of the therapeutic attitude and group rules.

Many group oriented programs have rules in order to maintain a non-victimising orderly group process and culture.

Group purpose

Malekoff (1997) proposed four aspects of group functioning to measure the clarity of purpose:

- When the purpose of the group can be stated clearly and concisely by the workers and the group members.
- When the purpose has the same meaning for both the group members and workers.
- When the purpose is specific enough that both the client and worker will know when it has been achieved.
- When the purpose is specific enough to provide direct implications for group content.

Group rules

Carich (1998) identified the following group rules:

- No violence
- No overt/covert victimisation
- No confidentiality within the group
- No secrecy
- No sex with others
- No intimidation or threats
- Any and all significant security violations will be reported
- No lying
- Obey all program rules
- Offenders take responsibility for opening up and presenting material in the group
- So many major rule violations may result in members being terminated, suspended or

ejected from the group or given additional homework assignments

Issues that group leaders may face

- Silent members
- Conflicts between members
- Conflicts between leaders and members
- Power and control issues
- Complaints about stagnation or the lack of therapeutic movement
- Resistant or unco-operative clients impeding the groupwork programme
- Highly verbal members that monopolise group time
- Members who continually focus on others and not themselves
- Members who do not want to share or express their feelings
- Members who fear contamination

Stage of group development

It is important for workers to have some understanding about groupwork theory as well as knowledge about sexual offending when running a sex offender groupwork programme. Brown (1992) and Tuckman (1965) suggest that groups generally progress through a number of stages: forming; storming; norming; performing and mourning. Garland et al. (1965) also suggest a pre-group stage. The model of group decision making outlined by Douglas (1976) can be used in conjunction with stages of group development to highlight some of the tasks that each stage includes. We will now explore each of these stages in detail. Whilst we will address these sequentially, this is not to suggest that all groups will adhere to this flow, particularly where external influences impact on the group.

The pre-group stage

This is the time when the broad aims and membership of the proposed group are outlined. The manner in which group members are invited to participate and the information provided for them during this stage will affect significantly the group processes thereafter. What and how people are told about the purpose, procedures and tasks of the proposed group will influence, at least initially, the climate and style of the group and an individual's behaviour within it. The formation of a group and decisions regarding membership are therefore important tasks and should be given due consideration.

The forming stage

This period covers initial meetings. The forming phase is usually characterised by polite tense and restless behaviour whilst individual group members get to know each other, share information and attempt to understand how the group will behave and what their role will be. Group members will often engage in 'small talk' and social rituals, such as introductions, whilst they are establishing their status, seeking alliances, testing out whether their expectations will be met and how they compare to others'.

Some of the problems that can arise at the forming stage include:

- The forming of cliques, based on prior relationships, similar expressed opinions, etc.
- Mistrust, based on present or previous individual or agency relationships.
- Lack of confidence, individually or as a group. Groups or members without experience are less likely to risk decision making and may spend a disproportionate time contemplating alternative courses of action, their disadvantages and merits.
- Confusion regarding tasks, roles, resources and responsibilities.

Feelings of mistrust and a lack of confidence in the group can be minimised if group members spend time sharing information, clarifying aims and objectives, recognising skills and deficits and agreeing the most effective methods of achieving aims.

The storming stage

This can be a turbulent period during which individuals may have become disenchanted with each other, resentful of the demands made of them and less optimistic about outcomes. Whilst some groups will enjoy a strong feeling of integration and appear to move swiftly through to the 'norming' stage others will undoubtedly recognise that the honeymoon is over and will face conflict, anger, withdrawal and apparent disintegration. Even if the group does not demonstrate extreme negative behaviours it may not enjoy a strong 'team spirit'. Some members, for example, may feel very uncomfortable when disagreements and negative views are expressed. Others may be confused or uncomfortable with their role whilst some may consider the objectives to be unrealistic. Groups can easily become stuck at this stage and whilst some or all of the group's tasks may be subsequently completed, group members may be left feeling dissatisfied, angry or dispirited. Berne (1963) suggests that when problems occur at this stage it is essential that time is given to addressing the processes involved, even when this means delaying the completion of tasks.

Some of the problems that can occur during this stage include:

- Scapegoating of group members (group members or group convenors).
- Competitive behaviour or attempts to dominate.
- Rejection of original agreements, aims and tasks.
- Hidden agendas surfacing.
- Attempts by cliques to wield power.
- Previously active members may withdraw, remain silent or become inactive.

This stage of a group's existence requires positive, sensitive and careful management by the group leader. There is a strong need for structure and clear agendas for meetings in order that the group remains focused and to avoid becoming side-tracked or enmeshed in irrelevant issues. If, however, the group becomes so dysfunctional that it cannot operate effectively then Hartford (1971) suggests the worker may need to consider one or more of the following strategies:

- Help the group members refocus their attention by reflecting on the group, themselves and their expectations.
- Bring conflict to the surface to attempt to find a resolution by confronting the issues.
- Engage the group in reviewing its membership.
- Assist the group in renegotiating objectives, tasks, roles and timescales.

Kakabadse et al. (1988) recommended the following approaches to improve collaboration and understanding among groups of people:

- The use of reflective listening to improve the understanding of problems and build trust between individuals.
- Employing assertion skills which can have a powerful impact on people and help maintain their commitment to the work.
- Avoiding dominating, threatening or aggressive behaviours and making judgements only on the basis of fact can reduce communication blocks.

- Issues rather than inter-personal tensions should be emphasised which involves gathering facts, breaking larger issues into smaller workable units and confronting each problem separately.
- Careful appraisal of the agreed actions and an assessment of the consequences of those actions may deter individuals or groups from needless disputes in the future.

Groups which experience significant problems during the storming stage and manage to reach resolution can go on to achieve higher levels of integration, co-operation and satisfaction than some groups who sail through this stage without disturbance.

The norming stage

This is depicted by the development of a group culture and routine. Group members tend to refer to 'we' and often seek and offer each other support and approval. Relationships stabilise and defences are lowered so that group members become more cohesive, trusting, open and task focused. As described in the forming stage a 'cosy' atmosphere or complete lack of disagreement in the group can be a dangerous symptom and disagreement or suggestions should be consistently and actively explored. If conflict does arise its value in allowing alternative suggestions should therefore be recognised. By the 'norming' stage, however, it is usually dealt with as a shared problem rather than a head-to-head battle. The task of the worker is generally to enable the group leadership to be shared and to encourage all members to participate in decision making. Whilst this stage is often problem free it is important that the group remains focused on its objectives and tasks and that members are not tempted to rest in this comfortable stage.

The performing stage

This is the period of task focused activity conducted by a self-sufficient group. Problems that arise are often resolved within the group with members offering high levels of energy and positive attitudes. Creative solutions can often emerge since group members are now willing to collectively explore new suggestions. Ideas developed by the group may often result in more positive outcomes than the original suggestions individuals may have made.

It is important to regularly review the functioning and membership of the group throughout this stage so as to ensure that all members have clear, identified tasks. Changes in group membership, however, may involve the group in revisiting previous stages in the group's development.

The mourning stage

The prospects of the group ending, whether planned or not, can induce anxiety in its members. The need to pay attention to separation is no less significant if it involves a group rather than individuals. This can be most acute for offenders who have experienced a sense of belonging in the group, and the ending can resurrect other painful experiences for them, thus escalating their sense of anxiety and loss. This requires careful management. It is important to clarify from the outset that the group is a time limited exercise which will continue for a specified duration and no longer. Within the group's life, this needs to be periodically restated, so as to remind members and try to ensure that they do not become overly dependent on the support that the group can offer.

Garland (1992) identified five stages of 'collective competency' to groups in developing a genuine emotional content:

1. In the pre-affiliation stage offenders explore their perceptions of other group members. The workers need to set boundaries, agendas and establish opportunities for developing trust.
2. As the distance between group members closes power and control issues dominate with a need to re-state purpose and boundaries.
3. Once the group has progressed through these challenges to meaning and authority it can enter a more intimate stage 1 which is characterised by greater emotional depth and increased self-disclosure.
4. Successful and longer-term groups can develop a sense of identity, culture and values which survive membership and worker turnover. New members progress through these personal stages of group integration more rapidly.
5. The final stage is separation/termination, which can relate either to the group as an entity or to an individual in the group.

Loss (2001) outlines several phases of the group process. The first phase of the group process and business portion of the group is defined by analysis of offending patterns and dynamics, ongoing discussion. Specific details (i.e., intent, fantasies, specifics of the offence, reactions of the victim, victim selection process, cycle behaviours, etc.) of the offence are discussed. Offenders can be instructed to maintain journals and to complete a life history. The time in the group is provided to discuss day to day personal and interpersonal issues, since offenders tend to mismanage daily events (Loss, 2001). This phase may last from between six months and a year. The second phase lasts between nine months and two years and consists of focusing on their own lives, (core) problems, conflicts and other related issues. Their offending cycles emerge within the process and are detailed. The offenders complete and discuss their life history. Skill development occurs in this phase. The last phase lasts from 18 months and beyond and the focus is on the effect of their sexual assaults, victim impact, personal remorse and victim empathy.

Change and the group process

Most sex offenders enter treatment at a time of crisis: following their arrest or conviction, or whilst being denied contact with their children. Their admission into treatment is frequently mandated. Behroozi (1992) has noted that the offender is often reluctant to participate in treatment because they feel coerced into change; have different perceptions from others about the nature of their problems and of their need to change; and their pessimism about the achievability of the targets for change.

It is important for workers to:

- Develop self-motivation within offenders: many offenders entering the programme will be pessimistic and have low self-esteem. In order to enhance motivation for change, they have, first of all, to develop a sense of their potential for change. This involves the provision of regular and constructive feedback to enable the offender to recognise his attainments and his potential to achieve further realistic targets will become more motivated to succeed than someone who feels they are being punished, disempowered and failing.
- State that whilst the primary purpose of intervention is to prevent further victims, there is also an emphasis on the improvement of the quality of their lives and help them to ensure their needs are met in non-abusive ways.

- Offering positive regard to each group member and ensuring that their strengths and positive attributes are recognised and acknowledged. This may be achieved by separating out the individual from their behaviour giving rise to the concerns.
- Model desired behaviours which extend not only to the attitude that they express, the methods of control they exert and the behaviour they demonstrate but also includes the style of leadership they employ. It may also include the challenging of offender denial or inappropriate behaviours or beliefs.

Clark and Erooga (1994) articulated very well the phases of change within the group context:

Phase one – denial and resistance
Many men who are assessed as being suitable for groupwork continue to deny or minimise aspects of their behaviour, often as a self-defence mechanism to protect their self-image and preserve a view of the world designed to present their behaviour in the most acceptable light and to avoid, or reduce, guilt and responsibility. This distorted thinking prevents insight and defends against the feared consequences of facing the reality of their behaviour.

Phase two – guilt and false motivation
This phase is usually characterised by an initial presentation of remorse, guilt, embarrassment, self-pity, and possibly preoccupation with the further consequences of discovery – break up of the family, public shame etc. (see Calder, 1999 for a full discussion on this issue). This often creates a high level of compliance in the group and essentially represents 'false motivation' represented through unrealistic expectations about the nature of the problem and the extent of the changes needed; about the timescale for treatment; and about the chronic and entrenched nature of their offending behaviour. This can be a very lengthy phase.

Phase three – awareness and compliant resistance
The onset of this phase is characterised by an intellectual awareness of the issues and the beginning of an understanding of the work which needs to be undertaken. This may often start with the work on victim awareness issues. It can move forward thinking from a self-focus and breach the barriers and distortions they have created to block out the effects of their

offences on their victim. This may lead to a change from their emphasis on returning home to a desire to complete treatment to prevent relapse. At this stage, their understanding of many of the issues remains partial although their desire to continue treatment will form the basis of future work.

Phase four – awareness and internalisation
This is when distorted beliefs are owned and core constructs change, rather than responses being repeated parrot-fashion as the offender has learned that they are correct. This phase represents genuine and sustainable changes of attitude and beliefs and is difficult to evaluate in the short-term. It will be evidenced by a greater willingness to tackle painful emotional issues associated with facing up to the full extent of their responsibilities and the damage done to their victim and other significant relationships. Evidence of real change in behaviours as well as attitudes will need to be sustained over a period of time, and is likely to be a cumulative process, marked by indications of progress and slipping back.

Phase five – awareness and responsibility
This is when a possible return to the family can be considered as the offender actively takes responsibility for their behaviour, is aware of their cycle and triggers and has developed a relapse prevention plan. They will have accepted that the risk of relapse is life long.

Therapeutic issues

Offenders can often bring up relevant issues in the group setting and they need to be relevant to the theme of that particular group to enhance the therapeutic intent. The open-ended groups involve themes of offence disclosure, victimising behaviour, cognitive restructuring, deviant fantasies, daily management issues, lifestyle patterns and interpersonal issues. There are a number of common issues which arise in the group life including:

- Developing close relationships without: power trips, victimisation, sexual connotations, dependency, enmeshment, aggressive communication, etc.
- Developing victim empathy, social interest, remorse/guilt, and work through dysfunctional guilt.
- Develop effective domain or appropriate expression of feelings.

- Change antisocial/narcissistic/borderline, schizoidal lifestyles that promote victimisation.
- Identify and work through any victimising developmental factors and motivating issues.
- Develop appropriate self esteem/worth/ confidence, etc., without victimising.
- Victimising tendencies/aggressive behaviour.
- Unwarranted entitlements 'I want what I want when I want it'.
- Victims (reviewing cases).
- Empathy.
- Identify, challenge and change cognitive distortions (stinking thinking).
- Defensive behaviours.
- Review or look at most any daily event.
- Discuss and identify cycles of deviant behaviours or offending process.
- Discuss deviant fantasies.
- Discuss examples of crooked behaviours.
- Discuss examples of entitlement and self-centredness.
- Discuss relationships (specific problems, issues, dynamics or any significant issues, etc.).
- Discuss past relationships (i.e., marriages, family, etc.).
- Discuss past developmental life experiences.
- Work on specific motivations of sexual assault(s).
- Discuss any type of cycle behaviour.
- Methods of controlling deviant behaviour.
- Disowning behaviours (any way of avoiding responsibility and/or enabling offending).
- Discuss any relevant experiences.
- Discuss making and maintaining commitments.
- Discuss sexual preferences.
- Identify abusive relationships.
- Experiencing and expressing appropriate feelings.

*These issues are not all inclusive.

The therapeutic stance

The therapeutic stance often defines the group nature, culture, productivity level and cohesion. This includes both therapeutic attitude and the characteristics of the group leaders.

The attitude of the worker consists of firmness, fairness, responsibility, and supportiveness tempered with scepticism. The therapeutic attitude has to be one of taking control when needed and backing off allowing group members to process the group and take responsibility for the group process. Both workers and clients are responsible for facilitating change. The workers are responsible for creating a context for change. The offenders are responsible for their behaviour, making changes, taking an active role in the process and avoiding enabling others.

Characteristics of effective group leaders

Effective group leaders are not intimidated by the group process or by aggressive group members. They hold their own. A brief list of characteristics of group leaders might include:

- Courage and willingness to be vulnerable at times; admitting mistakes and imperfections; take risks; able to confront others on hunches; to act on hunches and personal beliefs; to be emotionally touched by others (but not drawn into emotional games); to draw upon one's own experiences in order to identify with others' situations; to continually examine one's inner self; to be direct and honest (to a degree) with others; able to express and deal with group fears, expectations, dynamic defiance, anxieties, disowning techniques, etc., concerning group process.
- Modelling – Leaders serve as models for members (at some level). Corey and Corey (1987, p15) state: 'Group leaders would do well to recognise the extent to which their behaviour influences the group. Through their behaviour and their attitude conveyed, leaders can create such group norms as openness, acceptance of others and the desirability of taking risks.'
- Emotional attendance/presence – Workers need to be emotionally present with their group and members (however, not emotionally drawn into problems in which one becomes stuck in problem area).
- Caring – Warmth, concern, support, respect, trusting and valuing people and viewing them as worthwhile (although you may disagree or strongly dislike).
- Belief in group process – The worker has confidence in therapy and the therapeutic outcome.
- Leader's openness – Open to new experiences, different lifestyles, opinions and values.
- Non-defensiveness in coping with attacks. Critics could be dealt with in a constructive manner.

- Personal power – Dynamic quality of leadership. This includes confidence, charisma and vitality; stamina – capability to withstand pressure, fatigue, burn-out, etc.
- Willingness to seek new experience – 'A narrow range of life experience restricts the capacity of a leader to understand the psychological worlds of clients who may have different values . . .' (Corey and Corey, 1987, p18).
- Self awareness – The worker should be clear on one's goals and motivations. They should be aware and pay special attention to their own needs, strengths, weaknesses, biases, values, feelings, problems, limitations.
- Sense of humour – Leaders can use a sense of humour as a therapeutic response.
- Inventiveness – Leaders need to be creative and spontaneous in order to maintain freshness.

In essence, it is important to have stamina, avoid personalising the work and maintain control.

Characteristics of effective groups

There are some similarities between sex offender and non-sex offender groups. Cohesion is a universal factor in most (if not all) group therapies as is interpersonal learning, some type of self understanding and perhaps problem solving. There are however several different characteristics of effective offenders groups versus non-offender groups. The following are some characteristics of working in sex offender groups:

- Offenders **disclose** offences.
- Offenders take risks to **share** reactions/reveal threatening materials.
- Offenders **trust** members/leaders.
- Offenders have a sense of **inclusion.**
- Leader **determines goals** based on offenders' needs/pathology/deviancy/issues . . .
- Leader maintains **control**, however, uses the group to facilitate change (i.e., senior group members can provide peer leadership roles as long as they follow the leader's direction).
- Offenders feel **hopeful**.
- High level of **cohesion** (togetherness/dynamic glue).
- Offenders accept **responsibility**.
- **Feedback** given/accepted without defensiveness.
- Groups are **confrontative** but confrontation is seen as a challenge and is often well received.

- **Communication** is **clear and direct** (unless otherwise set-up by the group leader).
- **There is respect** for individual and group differences.
- Group cultural **norms** are well established.
- **Conflict** is recognised, discussed and resolved.
- Offenders **work outside** of group.
- Leaders utilise all experiential domains to create a context for change (adapted from Carich, 1997 and Corey, 1987).

Primary factors for group therapy

- Hope – A belief that there is a chance to change.
- Universality – Others can understand others' problems.
- Guidance – Providing information.
- Altruism – Social interest (interest in others) support, encouragement.
- Corrective Recapitulation of primary family unit – Family re-enactment, reliving past relationship patterns/experiences.
- Development of socialising techniques/interpersonal learning – empathy, social skills, cooperation, interpersonal issues.
- Imitation behaviour/identification – modelling.
- Interpersonal learning – honest sharing, perception,
- Corrective emotional experience – Offender trauma resolves through a correctional experience.
- Group cohesiveness-solidarity or 'we-ness' of group, security, open to influence, more willing to listen, self-disclose, protective, less disruptive when members leave, higher level of participation.
- Catharsis – Ventilation of feelings.
- Self-understanding – Insight at all levels of self.

Non-effective working groups

Non-effective groups can easily occur with narcissistic and aggressive sex offenders. Common indicators of non-working groups are a sense of being 'out of control', much confusion and chaos, when group members continuously victimise each other, and when group members victimise staff and control the group. In these groups, quite often offenders get off on verbal tangents unrelated to the topic or theme of that group. Corey and Corey (1987) provided a list of characteristics of non-working groups:

- Mistrust is evidenced by the undercurrent of expressed hostility. Members withhold themselves, refusing to express feelings and thoughts.
- Goals are fuzzy, abstract and general. Members have unclear personal goals or no goals at all.
- Many members feel excluded and cannot identify with other members. Cliques are formed that tend to lead to fragmentation. There is a resistance to dealing with reactions to one another.
- There is a 'there and then' focus. People tend to focus on others and not on themselves and story telling is typical. There is a resistance to deal with reactions to one another.
- Members lean on leaders for all direction. There are power conflicts among members as well as between members and the leader.
- Participants hold back and disclosure is at minimum.
- Fragmentation exists; people feel distant from one another. There is a lack of caring. Members don't encourage one another to engage in new and risky behaviour, so familiar ways of being are rigidly maintained.
- Conflicts or negative feelings are ignored, denied, or avoided.
- Members blame others for their personal difficulties and aren't willing to take action to change.
- What little feedback is given is rejected defensively. Feedback is given without care or compassion.
- Members feel desperate, despairing, helpless, trapped and victimised.
- Confrontation is done in a hostile, attacking way; the confronted one feels judged and rejected. At times the members gang up on a member, using this person as a scapegoat.
- Communication is unclear and indirect.
- Members are interested only in themselves.
- Members or leaders use power and control over others.
- There is an indifference or lack of awareness of what is going on within the group and group dynamics are rarely discussed.
- Conformity is prized and individual and social differences are devalued.
- Norms are merely imposed by leaders. They may not be clear.
- The group relies heavily on cathartic experiences but make little or no effort to understand them.
- Group members think about group activity very little when they are outside the group.

Transference and counter-transference

Transference and counter-transference are issues that emerge in group work and in particular with sex offenders. Transference is the projection of various dynamics and issues onto another person unrelated or not directly related to the original experience. Transference issues could be the re-enactment of previous social-psychodynamic developmental situations. For example, an offender has mother/father issues and projects his unresolved anger/hostility onto the workers. The worker is the object of the ventilation process. Transference doesn't have to be based on hostile oppositional feelings, (negative transference), but positive transference (i.e., feelings of love, infatuation, etc.).

Counter transference is the projection of unresolved issues or past experiences with emotional changes by the worker onto the offender. For example, a worker who was sexually abused may project or dump feelings from unresolved issues back onto the offender.

Both transference and counter transference processes can be utilised in the treatment process. If unmanaged by staff, then the group dynamics can be explosive and lead to victimising. Yet, the dynamics can lead to the emergence of issues and the establishment of an emotional context for issue resolution. The key for the group worker is self-awareness and the development of both internal and external boundaries. External boundaries are the awareness of role differentiation between offender and worker. Each knows the 'rules' and 'roles' within the therapeutic relationship. Offenders know there will be consequences for crossing such boundaries. Co-therapy helps uphold externally the boundaries by supporting each other and ongoing processing of the dynamics. Internal boundaries rely on the worker to not only know when they are projecting past issues, but to have a set of internal responses (i.e., cognitive restructuring) to defuse feelings.

Therapeutic issues, group cohesion and group dynamics

It takes time to develop the group norms and culture. This is a maturation process established and guided by the group leader. The central premise is group cohesion. Cohesion refers to the solidarity of the group and occurs as the group gels and evolves over time. It is a necessary part of the change process. Although it is often difficult to isolate the factors which contribute to a sense of group cohesion, some likely factors may include offender honesty, non-victimising behaviour, offender self-disclosure and the development of empathy, identification, sharing and taking risks and confrontation. Influencing factors toward group cohesion include a sense of common purpose; open communication; skilled leadership; and a positive view of group efficacy.

Therapeutic issues and group dynamics often centre on the themes of power and control. Most offenders attend as a result of some kind of external mandate and this is the outcome of their abuse of power, manipulation or coercion of others. Trust is thus not the basis of the therapeutic relationship. Offenders tend to deliberately manipulate and control staff and the group process. Likewise, group leaders manipulate the situation, offender and group towards therapeutic goals. As such, both worker and clients manipulate each other. The very act of gaining cooperation is manipulation. Manipulation is inherent in every interaction. Offenders need to learn who is ultimately in control. They need to learn that they cannot control the group or others. In that respect, offenders need to learn how to deal with authority issues. There are a number of additional relevant factors around the power and control dynamics worthy of note:

- Power is influence through specific methods called control.
- Deviant manipulation is the crooked means of obtaining goals within hidden agendas.
- Offenders with aggressive tendencies will seek to victimise others.
- Offenders usually try and strive for power and controls in relationships (paradoxically out of inferiority feelings).
- Many offenders tend to consciously and unconsciously seek weaknesses in others and seize opportunities to control.
- Common examples of power tactics may include: the lowering of one's tone of voice so that everyone has to strain to hear; lying and deception; acts of violence; angry outbursts; legal threats; demands; heavy confrontation; self-pity and emotional tears (that occur on cue).
- Remember that power and control are sensitive issues for offenders.

Group therapy techniques: guidelines for workers

- Avoid being vulnerable and showing weaknesses that access vulnerability, especially with offenders.
- Limited self-disclosure – Self-disclose only information which cannot be used to victimise you. Rule of thumb: only disclose information which you want advertised to the world. Maintain boundaries.
- Flexibility – Be flexible in tolerance, strategy and technique.
- Neutral stance – Be aware of your own processes (feelings) and projection.
- Do not get overly emotionally involved or attached (i.e., enmeshed boundaries, dependency, or being sucked into the offender's emotions).
- Firmness/respect – Use firmness with respect. Do not victimise or let the offender off the hook. Find a comfortable balance.
- Respect – Respect the offender as a human being who behaved in unaccepted hurtful ways, unless for specified purposes. Find a balance between human value/worth as a being versus value in terms of one's behaviour equals self.
- Do not victimise.
- Keep the group focused. Stay on track of the designated issues (unless for strategic purposes).
- Utilisation of principle – Utilise the offender's behaviour, even resistance, to create a context of change or to facilitate an experience or response. Any response to an intervention can be used to facilitate change. Responses to unsuccessful techniques can also be used.
- Cybernetic dynamics – Use the cybernetic system dynamics of stability/change (support while inducing change differentness). Acknowledge their insecurities of change and use them.
- Avoid rescuing group members (unless person is totally inadequate and will collapse under pressure). Do not let offenders off the hook by giving them an opt-out.
- Confusion can be used when necessary. Plant seed of therapeutic message within the confusion. This enables the offender to sort out the confusion looking for answers.
- Do not support deviant thinking and/or dysfunctional behaviours. Don't enable deviancy.
- Don't play power games or engage in power struggles unless you can win.

- Don't take comments or 'stuff' personally.
- Metaphor construction – Choose appropriate metaphors, therapeutic goals and philosophy and get some agreement on it with your co-worker so that you do not cancel out each other.
- Get the group involved in therapeutic themes, topics discussion, processes, etc.
- One can do one-on-one in group, however, get the group involved.
- Do not enable dysfunctional behaviours through justifications and other enablers.
- Repetitive messages – Repeat messages as often as needed or necessary to drive the point home.
- Recycling – Recycle therapeutic messages, themes, topics, processes until effective learning takes place.
- Avoid secrets between group members. Play above board.
- Allow group members to take group responsibility for the group process. Group responsibility has to be directed.
- Directiveness – Since any therapeutic session can be demarcated into a series of behaviours and techniques (behaviours), and behaviour is goal-oriented, thus behaviour is directed. Any behaviour emitted from the worker can make a therapeutic impact and/or be used to make an impact. Directiveness is on a continuum ranging from deliberately direct to indirect. Indirect techniques can still be direct behaviour.
- Break big problems down into manageable ones. Smaller problems are easier to deal with.
- Do not let offenders drive wedges between co-workers. Conflicts can be worked out in group through appropriate methods, or else work them out outside the group.
- Whilst striving to be non-judgemental, offenders need to hear clear statements as to the unacceptable and harmful nature of their offending behaviours.

Worker tactics

1. Empathy – Responding in a warm understanding style or way. Put yourself in their situation and then respond. Sensing the subjective world of the client; such as 'grasping another's experience and at the same time maintaining one's separateness (Corey and Corey, 1987, p23).
2. Active listening – Responding, conveying to the speaker a full understanding of the

client. It involves absorbing content, noting gestures, subtle changes in nonverbal behaviour, paying full attention.
3. Paraphrasing – Summarising in your own words what the speaker said. Response statements include: 'I hear you saying . . .'; 'It sounds like . . .'
4. 'I' Messages – Using 'I' denotes one taking responsibility for one's own behaviour.
5. Carkhuff Dimensions
   a. Respect
   b. Immediacy (responding in the here and now present, instead of storing past garbage)
   c. Confrontation
   d. Concreteness/specificity (talk in concrete behaviour terms, by pinpointing behaviour)
   e. Empathy
   f. Genuineness
   Self-disclosure is done in levels. Typically, it is not recommended unless used superficially because offenders will tend to victimise the worker.
6. Mirroring – Reflecting the speaker's message by both verbal/nonverbal messages. This includes repeating or reflecting exactly what the client says or does. Mirroring facilitates a quick rapport. The mirroring process usually occurs in effective interactions. With awareness, one can use this toward therapeutic advantages, such as trance induction.
7. Clarifying – Sorting out confusing and conflicting behaviour or data. Pinpointing issues and goals.
8. Identifying and labelling of behaviour – Behaviour may be defined as (a) cognitive (non-operable covert, internal behaviour such as thoughts, perception, self talk); (b) emotional/feelings/affective behaviour (moods, emotional state); (c) overt observable behaviour (external) (Dyer and Vriend, 1980).
9. Proper questioning to invoke problem related responses – Avoid why questions when it tends to inhibit client responses. Ask who, what, where, when, how, how come, and what would be different type questions. Question formula: who + what + where + when + how + how come + why (when appropriate).
10. Use of humour – Humour does a number of things, including changing the client's worldview, relieving stress and tension.

11. Summarising – Summary statements facilitate a continuous flow, clarifies confusion, and helps proceed through.

12. Providing support and encouragement – Support is essential, just as encouragement is. This is done with confrontation. Narcissism is not supported or encouraged. With severe antisocial and narcissistic offenders, it is used sparingly at the beginning.

13. Linking technique – Connecting issues, goals, behaviour, problems, solutions, motivations, interactions, etc., by relating behaviours, events, themes or lines of communications to other members and their situations. This consists of generalising processes and transfer of learning.

14. Focusing techniques – Focusing on behaviour and problems until issues are resolved.

15. Interpreting – Behaviour ultimately has meaning, but there may be multiple meanings. Interpretation provides the client with a therapeutic frame to view problems and issues for resolution.

16. Blocking – The interruption of interactional process in order to re-channel, redirect, stop, etc., functional patterns of behaviour. Behaviours that are blocked include: gossiping, empathy, non functional story-telling, breaking of confidences, invasion of privacy, bombardment of others with questions, blaming, withdrawal, inaction, procrastination, continuous approval seeking a group spokesperson, rambling.

17. Reality testing – Reviewing of problem resolutions, alternatives, solutions, etc., in a realistic manner.

18. Diagnosing – Reviewing and defining problems and their appropriate goals.

19. Confrontation – It is the constructive provision of feedback to people, in which a disagreement is involved. There are many levels and types. This does not include criticising, attacking, destroying . . . which is destructive. It's most effective when rapport has been established. It is used when the following occurs: discrepancies are focused on; inconsistencies in verbal or nonverbal behaviour; to change self defeating behaviour and beliefs; to shift the client's perception of a problem defences; ineffective coping strategies; conflicts; and problem resolution.

20. Restating – Relaying data or information to members, in a way that they understand (Dyer and Vriend, 1980).

21. Advice giving (lecturing) – Providing of important information to members. This helps to establish a therapeutic frame (Dyer and Vriend, 1980).

22. Initiating – The taking of action when necessary; one needs a continuous plan of action.

23. Intervening – Intervening technique is literally intervening when inappropriate behaviour is committed, (see Blocking).

24. Using silence – Silence can be very effective. It allows members to think/process data; create tension to evoke material; control method as members may try to intimidate leaders by being silent. Leaders used to become comfortable with silence.

25. Recognising and explaining nonverbal behaviour – And relating to dynamics of the problems, clients awareness, etc.

26. Facilitating closure – Finishing business and moving on. One could use R. E. T. approaches when the offender is receptive emotionally.

27. Restraining, Subduing, and Avoiding Potentially Explosive Episodes and Dysfunctional Behaviour (Dyer and Vriend, 1980, p130).

28. Goal setting – Defining specific behavioural goals.

29. Self disclosure – Disclosing personal data can have a powerful effect on members, especially if problems are similar and resolutions are contained in their message.

30. Techniques for Drawing Out Members (Jacobs, Harvill and Mason, 1988) Drawing out – Eliciting participation, accessing issues, problems and dynamics.
    a. *When to draw out:*
       (1) Unmotivated members
       (2) Silent members
       (3) Shy
       (4) To develop group cohesion, trust, commitment
       (5) To get members involved
    b. *Hints in using drawing out techniques:*
       (1) Drawing out when it is necessary
       (2) Not all members need equal time and the same verbosity in groups
    c. *Techniques:*
       (1) Scanning the group and then focusing on specific inactive members
       (2) Eye contact

(3) Nonverbal looks or gazes of empathy
(4) Gazes
(5) Shifting voice tones, pitches
(6) Directly and verbally focusing and inviting members to comment
(7) Metaphoric messages geared to draw out
(8) Self disclosure
(9) Basic communication techniques and Carkhuff dimensions
(10) Nonverbal gestures (head nod, body posture, hand gestures, etc.)
(11) Confrontation
(12) Focusing on specific problems, issues associated with silence, lack of trust, intimidation, boredom, confusion, fear, insecurity, cognitive/emotional overload, personality, not attending, not prepared.
(13) Using silence and group silence (creating pressure to open up)
(14) Using rounds
(15) Dyads
(16) Cognitive behaviour interventions (writing, listing, journals, etc.)
(17) Paradoxical techniques (re-labelling, reframing, benevolent sabotage, paradoxical prescriptions, restraining, etc.)
(18) Metaphors

31. Techniques for Cutting Off Members (Jacobs, Harvill and Masson, 1988)
   a. *When to cut off members:*
      (1) Rambling
      (2) Member comments or responses conflict with the group purpose or therapeutic direction.
      (3) Inaccurate information
      (4) Leader shifts the focus of the group
      (5) Leader ends the session
      (6) Needless/useless arguing
      (7) Useless rescuing
      (8) Member responses are anti-therapeutic
   b. *Factors/elements of cutting members off:*
      (1) Timing
      (2) Use of voice (tone, pitch)
      (3) Clarify why you cut member off
      (4) Monitor your nonverbal behaviours (eyes, cues, minimal micro behaviour)
      (5) Refocusing the group to appropriate issues, members, etc.
   c. *Techniques/Strategies:*
      (1) Avoid eye contact with the group members

(2) Scan the group, thus inviting other response
(3) Confrontation (use the appropriate level)
(4) Give gestures, signals, therapeutic touches, minimal cues (nods, facial expressions, eye movement, shift in body positions)
(5) Refocusing the groups attention
(6) Ignoring or not attending to that particular member
(7) Shifting voice tone
(8) Pacing and leading
(9) Focusing on that member's needs for continuing in the non-productive direction (this can be very intense and the leader needs much confidence to follow through)

32. Utilising (leader directed) rounds – Rounds are structured activity in which the leader goes around the group soliciting responses or a member may go around the room gathering responses (see stationary rounds) (Jacobs, Harvill and Masson, 1988):
   a. *Subcategories include:*
      (1) Designated word or designated number round – Each member comments by single designated word (yes/no) response or by a number which is usually some sort of scale or rating system.
      (2) Word or phrase rounds – The leader provides an opportunity for each member to give feedback to the leader or other member only in brief phrases and words.
      (3) Comment rounds – The leader provides an opportunity for each member to make comments
   b. *Uses include:*
      (1) Gathering information
      (2) Assessing what individuals are experiencing
      (3) Locating energy
      (4) Summarising
      (5) Accessing needs
      (6) Deepening the intensity
      (7) Generating energy
      (8) Generating interest
      (9) Building comfort, trust, cohesion
      (10) Processing information
      (11) Drawing out quiet members

33. Shifting the focus of topics by utilising group opinions, comments or group dynamics.

34. Shifting the focus of group members – Shifting group attention from one person to another.

35. Shifting the focus of topics – Shifting group attention from one topic to another.

36. Using dyads – Dyads are the pairing of members together for specific reasons and tasks. This can be done by leader choice, member choice, seating arrangement, interest, etc. (Jacobs, Harvill and Masson, 1988). Purposes include: developing comfort and security, warming up members, changing topics and/or formats, provide leader/member interaction, provide time for leaders to think, processing information, finishing topics and placing members together. Procedures include: establishing specific amount of time, establishing goals, giving clear simple instructions, ensuring that members stay on the task, outlining your role as well as others, establishing an appropriate physical arrangement and follow-up.

37. Using triads – Triads consist of groups of three people and is similar to dyads (Jacobs, Harvill and Masson, 1988).

38. Written sentence completion tasks in group – The member is given an incomplete sentence (sentence stems) and asked to comment on it (Jacobs, et.al., 1988). These tasks are cognitive-behavioural. Examples are: 'I need to improve _____;' 'Five years from now, I want _____;' 'My biggest fear is _____;' 'I need _____' 'My greatest asset is _____.'

39. Listing – Listing techniques are cognitive behavioural interventions, in which members are instructed to write a list of designated items such as indicated within the below subcategories:
    (1) List likes/dislikes or positives/negatives of: self, others, significant others, group members, relationships, interests, ideal partners.
    (2) List (more or less) five members to be stranded with and why.
    (3) List (more or less) five members not to be stranded with and why.
    (4) List expectations of: self, others, other group members, significant others.
    (5) Listing statements (repetitive listing) – Instructing members to repeatedly list specific statements designed to create new patterns of behaviours. Usually statements consist of 'I choose . . .' and

are usually positive in nature (Carich, 1991).

40. Maintaining diaries, journals or reaction logs in which members can record significant experiences and their reactions.

41. Writing reports – Autobiographies, future autobiographies, reports of specific topics or issues, tracking symptoms or problems, fantasies, etc. (Carich, 1990a).

42. 'As if' techniques (Carich, 1989) – Instructing the client to enact (either cognitive/behaviourally) in 'as if' scenario. There are variations (Carich, 1989).

43. Imagery strategies (Carich, 1990a, 1990b, 1990c) – Imagery techniques can be delivered in group, for all members or for specific members. It is the mental reflection, visual rehearsal, etc., of some phenomena, event, behaviour, object, material, subcategories, etc., within any particular time frame.
    (a) Associating in or anchoring images with specific feelings/thoughts/behaviours, etc.
    (b) Guided imagery using all sensory modes (auditory, visual, kinesthetic, olfactory, taste) – projecting self mentally.
    (c) Futuristic projection – Projecting self into the future.
    (d) Taking journeys – Guided imagery in the form of visualising self/other taking some sort of journey.
    (e) Fantasies – Images of 'pretend' material.
    (f) Visual images – The internal visual representation of something, person or extent.
    (g) Fantasy door – Guided imagery using a door approach.
    (h) Collecting early recollections.

44. Magnifying issues – In this technique the leader tries to 'milk' what he can from the issue. The issue is magnified or blown up way out of proportion. A big deal is made out of something that is minor. This can create enough intensity to induce change.

45. Stationary rounds – 'This is a round in which the working members say something to each member of the group while remaining seated.' (Jacobs et al., 1988, p232). The working member goes around the room. Subcategories:
    (a) Using the same statement – The working member uses the same

statement (or question) with each member in the round. He thus gets a chance to hear self or gather more feedback.

(b) Using no specific sentences – The working member uses no specific sentences, but still goes around the group.

(c) The working member receives repeated questions – The working member responds to similar questions from each member.

46. The in depth round – In this round, the working member literally moves his/her chair in front of the other members. This intensifies the experience.

(a) Group asks the same questions – The working member moves the chair in front of group members asking the same question.

(b) Predetermined moves – The member is instructed to move in front of specific members.

47. Warming up – Techniques focusing on preparing the group to focus and discuss issues. This may be done by playing ideas, disclosing thoughts on topics, social conversation, developing trust, comfort, etc., social talk (Jacobs et. al., 1988).

48. Seeding ideas – An Ericksonian technique in which ideas are planted via suggestions, etc., and followed up later (Zeig, 1987).

49. Spinning off – When the focus is on one member for extended period of time, the leader gets others involved by seeking comments, tying into other members issues, inviting members to share, etc. This allows the leader to assess the interests of members, gain information, help the individual, and get members involved (Jacobs et. al., 1988).

50. Contracts – Used when the focus is on one person for extended periods of time. It is an agreement that the individual wants to work on a specific issue (Jacobs et al., 1988).

51. Clarifying problems through group interaction (Jacobs et al., 1988) – This includes specifically defining problems, in behavioural terms:

(1) Members ask questions – Group members take turns asking questions in order to probe.

(2) Members guess at problems – To probe further and enable the person to work through problems/issues, group members guess what the problem is.

(3) Clarifying round at assess problem – the working member addresses each group member stating what he thinks his problems are and perhaps addressing questions.

(4) Members 'role-playing' the member – Another group member plays the working member and then states what the problems are. This enables the working member to see self.

(5) Leader clarifies – The leader probes and clarifies issues and problems.

52. Information giving and mini lecturing – Providing brief five to ten minute mini lecture to the group. These are very short, brief, focused, relevant, accurate, and energising (Jacobs et. al., 1988).

53. Encouraging and support – Providing cognitive and emotional support by communicating warmth, respect, and empathy. This is not sympathy and does not reinforce inappropriate or self defeating behaviours (Jacobs et al., 1988).

54. Tone Setting – ' . . . the leader sets the tone by his actions, words, and what he allows to happen.' (Jacobs et al., 1988, p84).

55. Utilising eyes – Non verbal behaviour usually overrides verbal behaviour:

(1) Scanning for Cues – Leaders scout group looking for minimal cues (Jacobs et. al., 1988).

(2) Redirecting Members Comments – Through the leader's use of eyes, he can redirect a member.

56. Hot seat or hot chair technique – The group focus is on one group member. Typically that member is heavily confronted concerning their issues.

57. Psychodrama – This is the enactment of a group members problems via selected members of the group (Ohlsen, 1977). Primary component and roles:

(1) Protagonist – The client of whose problems will be enacted

(2) Auxiliary Ego(s) – Extensions of the protagonist who play key roles of the problem situations or areas of the protagonist's life

(3) Director – The facilitator/leader who prepares the participants and prepares them for the drama

(4) The Group – Provides the auxiliary egos, feedback, support, etc.

(5) Stage – The setting (Ohlsen, 1977)

Psychodrama techniques (Ohlsen, 1977):

(1) Self presentation – The protagonist's description of the problematic situation, including the specific roles to be played.

(2) Self realisation – The protagonist's version, review or view of their past, present, and future life.

(3) Direct soliloquy – A monologue given by protagonist, in which, they step out of the scene and speak freely to self and/or to the group about what is going on inside (Ohlsen, 1977).

(4) Therapeutic soliloquy (aside) – The protagonist shares hidden feelings and thoughts.

(5) Doubling – The auxiliary ego helps the protagonist to get into touch with his/her inner feelings more deeply, evaluate problems, etc. The auxiliary portrays an area of the protagonist's problem/personality.

(6) Multiple doubling – Several auxiliary egos enact different aspects of the protagonist's problem or personality.

(7) Mirroring – The auxiliary ego reflects the protagonist's behaviour/problem, etc., to enable them to see the pathology.

(8) Role reversal – The protagonist play their own antagonist in relevant scenes.

(9) Future projection – The protagonist projects himself via enactment, to convey hopes and wishes.

(10) Life rehearsal – Practicing for an anticipated event in the future.

(11) Psychodramatic hallucination technique – The protagonist portrays their own hallucinations.

(12) Psychodramatic dream technique – The protagonist acts out dream.

58. Role Playing – The playing of roles. Roles pertain to the group members problems, issues, past (scenes), future, etc. (Ohlsen, 1977).

(1) Early recollections – The individual recalls early memories and enacts various scenes. This enables the client to present self, overcome problems and define new behaviours.

(2) Expression of positive feelings – The client rehearses the expression of positive feelings toward others.

(3) Magic shop – To help uncover therapeutic material and issues the client pretends that they are in a magic shop and negotiates for personal characteristics of general desires.

(4) Intimacy exercise – Role playing the learning of how to be intimate.

(5) Pairing – Clients pair up and discusses the development of scripts.

(6) Fiddler game – Examining the pros/cons of decisions via role playing decisions.

(7) Self appraisal exercises – Developing scripts clarifying 'who that person is.'

(8) Autobiographies – Each group member presents self reviewing significant events and connections. Various roles and scripts can be enacted stemming for the autobiography.

(9) Future autobiographies – The client projects self into the future by writing out future roles and scripts. This includes: Future achievements, goals, behaviours, etc.

59. Milking an issue – This refers to stretching an issue (minor/major) in order to achieve other therapeutic objectives or specific therapeutic experiences.

Conclusion

Sex offender treatment should use group work coupled with individual pieces of work. Groupwork is never a panacea and it is never a sufficient intervention in isolation. Groupwork can offer support, safety and opportunity to explore thoughts, feelings and behaviours together with the chance to develop and rehearse skills and coping strategies. Peer pressure and challenge are powerful influences that can be used positively to induce change, create a sense of group cohesion and achievement to enhance an individual's self-esteem. The role of the workers in facilitating the group is critical, requiring considerable leadership skills, planning, programming, reviewing and evaluation.

References

Behroozi C S (1992) Groupwork With Involuntary Clients: Re-Motivating Strategies. *Groupwork*. 5: 2, 31–41.

Berne E (1963) *The Structure and Dynamics of Organisations and Groups.* Philadelphia: J.B. Lippincott.

Brown A (1992) *Groupwork.* (3rd edn.) Aldershot: Arena.

Calder M C (1999) *Assessing Risk in Adult Males Who Sexually Abuse Children: A Practitioner's Guide.* Lyme Regis, Dorset: Russell House Publishing.

Calder M C (Forthcoming) *Encouraging More Effective Practice With Involuntary Clients.* Dorset: Russell House Publishing.

Carich M S (1989) Variations of The 'As If' Technique. *Individual Psychology.* 45: 4, 538–45.

Carich M S (1990a) *Cognitive-Behavioral Approach.* Unpublished Manuscript.

Carich M S (1990b) Utilizing Task Assignments Within Adlerian Therapy. *Individual Psychology.* 46: 2, 217–24.

Carich M S (1990c) Hypnotic Techniques and Adlerian Constructs. *Individual Psychology.* 46: 2, 166–7.

Carich M S (1992) Categories of Behavioral Characteristics of Sex Offenders Based Upon Lifestyles/Personality Disorders, From A Linear View. *INMAS Newsletter.* 5: 2, 22–5.

Carich M S (1997) *Sex Offender Treatment and Overview: Training for The Mental Health Professional.* Springfield, Illinois: Illinois Department of Corrections.

Carich M S (1998) *Developing A Contemporary Context for Treatment.* Paper Presented At IDOC Sex Offender Training, Joilet, Illinois, 26th June 1998.

Clark P and Erooga M (1994) Groupwork With Men Who Sexually Abuse Children. In Morrison T, Erooga M and Beckett R C (Eds.) *Sexual Offending Against Children:Assessment and Treatment of Male Abusers.* London: Routledge, 102–28.

Cohen S L (1997) Working With Resistance to Experiencing and Expressing Emotions in Group Therapy. *International Journal of Group Psychotherapy.* 47: 4, 443–58.

Corey G, Corey S M, Callanan P J, and Russell M J (1988) *Group Techniques.* Brooks/Cole Publishing Co.

Corey S M and Corey G (1987) *Groups: Process and Practice.* (3rd edn.) Monterey, CA: Brooks/Cole Publishing Co.

Craisatti J and Mcclurg G (1997) The Challenge Project: A Treatment Program Evaluation for Perpetrators of Child Sexual Abuse. *Child Abuse and Neglect.* 21: 7 637–48.

Douglas T (1976) *Groupwork Practice.* London: Tavistock Publications.

Dyer W W and Vriend J (1980) *Group Counseling for Personal Mastery.* New York: Sovereign Books.

Garland J A (1992) The Establishment of Individual and Collective Competency in Children's Groups As A Prelude to Entry Into Intimacy, Disclosure and Bonding. *International Journal of Group Psyhchotherapy.* 41: 3. 395–405.

Garland J, Jones H and Kolodny R (1965) A Model for Stages in The Development of Social Work Groups. In Bernstein S (Ed.) *Explorations of Group Work.* Boston: Boston University.

Hartford M E (1971) *Groups in Social Work.* New York: Columbia University Press.

Jacobs E E, Harvill R L and Masson R L (1988) *Group Counseling: Strategies and Skills.* Pacific Grove, CA: Brooks/Cole Publishing Co.

Kakabadsde A, Ludlow R and Vinnicombe S (1988) *Social Working in Organizations.* London: Penguin Business.

Loss P (2001) The Sex Offender Treatment Group Process. In Carich M S and Mussack S (Eds.) *Handbook of Sex Offender Assessment and Treatment.* Brandon, VT: The Safer Society Press, 117–39.

Malekoff A (1997) *Group Work With Adolescents: Principles and Practice.* NY: Guilford Press.

Ohlsen M (1977) *Group Counseling.* New York: Holt, Rinehart and Winston.

Print B and O'Callaghan D (1999) Working in Groups With Young Men Who Have Sexually Abused Others. In Erooga M and Masson H (Eds.) *Children and Young People Who Sexually Abuse Others: Challenges and Responses.* London: Routledge, 124–45.

Ross J (1998) *Group Treatment Approaches.* Paper Presented At The Advanced Training for Treatment of Adolescent Sex Offenders. Toronto: Canadian Welfare Association.

Tuckman B W (1965) Developmental Sequence in Small Groups. *Psychological Bulletin,* LXIII, 384–99.

Zeig J (1987) Therapeutic Patterns of Ericksonian Influence Communication. In Zeig J K (Ed.) *Evolution of Psychotherapy.* New York: Brunner/Mazel. 392–406.

Chapter Four

Sexual Assault Cycles

Introductory comments

The cycle of offending has been a highly influential model for workers on both sides of the Atlantic. The exact origins of the cycle remain unclear and many adaptations are to be found. Historically, Lane and Zamora (1978) are credited with creating the cycle to explain juvenile sexual offences and this was subsequently applied to adult sex offenders, especially as it relates to the relapse prevention process. Indeed, the cycle is the foundation of the cognitive behavioural approaches of relapse prevention (see Chapter 8 for further details). Combined with relapse prevention, the offender can learn to anticipate the circumstances when they are likely to relapse into their offending behaviour again. The assault cycle then becomes the offender's life line as they are asked to develop some insight into their abuse precursors that then acts as the basis of formulating some suggested coping strategies when they are detected. It also can be the backbone of a treatment programme. Now there are nearly 40 different models of the sexual assault cycle. Clearly we do not have the space here to explore them all, and indeed this would probably induce confusion or paralysis among workers. Thus far we have referred to the cycles developed by Hilary Eldridge and David Wolf (see Chapter 1).

The assault cycle is the recursive chain of a connecting pattern of behaviours that lead up to the assault, including the assault and the aftermath. The belief is that the process towards offending has a number of clearly identified areas that become self-reinforcing (or addictive) cycle of thoughts and behaviours. This belief leads to many treatment programmes being highly structured.

The primary purposes of using the assault cycle in treatment are:

- To provide both clinicians and offenders with a framework and structure for treatment.
- To provide an easy method of analysing the assault process.
- To set up a framework so that the offender can stop their cycle. The offender can actually learn to identify specific aspects of their offending mode or process.

There are a number of specific applications in all sex offender work as follows:

- A tool to analyse and identify the offending process.
- A tool to help stop the offending process.
- A tool for the offender to monitor themselves.
- A tool for the others to monitor the offender.
- A tool that law enforcement can use to track and catch sexual aggressors. This last application has not been yet fully utilised.

With these points in mind, the concept of the sexual abuse cycle is presented in detail in this chapter. Several models are presented and the pros and cons of each discussed.

The concept of the cycle

Behind all the assault cycles are several common assumptions:

- There is no time frame, as cycles may occur in seconds, minutes, – up to years.
- Offenders can skip stages.
- Offenders can have multiple cycles, depending on victim types.
- Offenders can have sub-cycles.
- Stages can occur at same time.
- The cycle is an offending mode/pattern (of thoughts, feelings, and behaviours). It is a choice.
- The cycle is progressive and regressive in nature.
- The cycle can be defused at any point.
- The cycle feeds itself, as it is a series of choices. It may seem like the cycle is on automatic pilot.
- Whilst the stages described are general, the content varies across individuals.
- Cycle behaviours includes: enablers, defences, distortions (i.e., denial, justify, secrets), other disowning behaviours, disinhibitors, cues, risk factors, etc.
- This cycle applies to offenders of the 'lowest' level (non-contact) offences to the 'highest' level of offences (serial sexual murder).
- Offenders are held 100% accountable and responsible for the choices they make leading up to, during and after their offending behaviour.

- There may be multiple triggers and cues occurring throughout the cycle.
- There is no cure and thus an offender may be in a cycle at anytime.
- The cycle involves specific states of mind.
- The cycles may change over time.

Cycle behaviours

Cycle behaviours are any covert/overt and contextual event that involves the offending process or mode. Some cycle behaviours are automatic decisions and events. Offenders often describe being on automatic pilot. Automatic responses (i.e., thoughts, behaviours, reactions, etc.) are still choices that are made by the offender at unconscious levels of awareness. Cycle behaviours are sometimes referred to as risk factors. The concept of risk factors refers to anything/event/behaviour/decision that bring the offender closer to offending (and re-offending). Cycle behaviours that occur before the offence are called precursors. However, the post-assault cycle behaviours can be precursors to the next offence.

The following are cycle behaviours considered in more detail:

Disowning behaviours: defences and distortions

Disowning behaviours is a 'catch all' concept created by Carich (1993); Carich and Stone (1996a, b, c) to explain the strategies used by an offender to distance themselves from their abusive behaviour or to cognitively distort the reasoning to themselves. This can be both on a day-to-day basis as well as abuse-specific. Defences are thus adaptive and maladaptive coping responses that protect the individual. Applied to sex offenders, defences enable the offence and are maladaptive in this context. Defences can be traced to specific cognitive distortions. Cognitive distortions are covert behaviours that reflect twisted, destructive, irrational, or dysfunctional thinking. Distorted thinking and behaving are inappropriate/dysfunctional patterns of behaviour that enable the offender to offend.

The following list provides some ideas as to defences deployed by sex offenders:

- Denial – Omitting information or not admitting to the truth, including leaving out the details of the offence; secrets; holding out information; not telling . . .

- Lying – Any type of deliberate distorting of information; not telling the truth; twisting information to fit your needs . . .
- Justifying – Making bad deviant things 'okay'; making it alright; making excuses.
- Minimise – To make smaller or less important; reduce the significance.
- Entitlement – Unwarranted requests, expectations, and an attitude of 'I want what I want when I want it and I want it right **now**! and I'm going to get it any way I can.' This includes the 'shoulds', 'musts', 'oughts', and 'How awful'.
- Plays power games – Being superior, dominant, controlling, bossy, defying authority . . . (my way or no way).
- Depersonalising – Not seeing people as people, but as objects to be manipulated, such as 'meat'.
- Poor me/victim stancing – Pity pot or sympathy for self; feeling sorry for self; victim stancing is self-pity by playing the victim role to set-up another offence.
- Extremes – Implies: rigidly held views, absolutes, perfectionism, either all or none type of thinking.
- Apathy – Who cares: lack of concern; giving up.
- Rationalising – Seemingly okay excuses that you use to go on and act out.
- Fairness fallacy – Life should be fair and how awful it isn't.

'Detrimental D's'

The D's are Detrimental to maintaining abstinence (Carich and Stone, 1996) and include:
Defences/defensive
Degrading
Denial (not admitting to)
Depersonalise (make a non-person)
Despair
Depreciation (deteriorate, lower value)
Destructive behaviour
Deviant fantasy
Deviant planning
Devolve
Digress (wander from)
Dilate (magnify)
Dilute (minimise)
Discard (dismiss)
Discount (make less significant)
Discouraged
Disinhibitors
Dismiss
Disorder

Disowning
Disregard (not use)
Disrespect
Distance (isolation)
Distortion (twisted thinking)
Dodge
Dogging
Dominate
Don't care (apathy)
Drink and drugs
Dwell

Risk factors

A risk factor in general is any event that brings the offender closer to offending and/or re-offending In actuality, risk factors occur throughout the cycle.

Triggers/risk factors

Triggering events are a type of risk factors. They occur throughout the cycle. Triggers are any internal (covert) or external (overt) event, decision, response (i.e., urge, fantasy), situational, context, interpersonal, that 'causes', facilitates, stimulates, initiates any type of offending response (i.e., cycle behaviour, lapse, relapse). In terms of the assault cycle, it is most important to differentiate high risk versus low risk. High risk triggers have the potential to trigger a lapse or relapse, whilst low risks are events/decisions that seem low risk and insignificant, but can lead to high risk, lapse and relapse.

It is most important for offenders to identify their high risk factors (triggers) and low risk or seemingly insignificant or unimportant decision/event/lapse and relapse '**cues**'. Relapse or cycle cues are signals or warnings that indicate a potential or actual threat of lapse and/or relapse. These are red flags to the offender and warnings of danger. Cues are clues to the monitors of offenders that indicate they are lapsing and possibly relapsing. Cues have been analysed and categorised in terms of content or substance, and temporarily (time of occurrence). Offenders need to know their early warnings, mid/late cues and the last minute destructive warning line. Again, these issues are explored in more detail in Chapter 8 on relapse prevention.

Disinhibitors

A disinhibitor is any overt or covert behaviour that lowers the offender's barriers to offend. The offender's walls used to keep from offending are lowered. These barriers may be actual behaviours or thinking patterns that help maintain abstinence. Classical disinhibitors include alcohol/drugs, pornography, cognitive distortions, negative peer group, etc.

Patterned feeders

Pattern feeders are any type of behaviour/event that enhances or feeds the cycle. These could be reactions from others.

AVE responses

AVE (abstinence violation effect) responses are critical processes for offenders who want to or have stopped offending. In essence, AVE means that the offender violated their 'state' of abstinence. Freeman-Longo and Pithers (1992) outline five elements:

- Self-depreciation (disowning yourself).
- Failure expectation (expect doom).
- PIG (problem of immediate gratification or desires to offend).
- Erroneous attribution (overwhelming sense of guilt, sense of no control, blame).
- Increased probability (chance) to relapse.

The AVE is best viewed as a state of mind that encompasses a variety of internal struggles, between offending (violating someone) versus abstinence.

Deviant fantasy

Deviant fantasies are types of cycle behaviours that involve covert planning via imagery. It is the covert (mental) rehearsal usually through the internal imagination visualisation processes. It involves the offender's imagination processes. Fantasies range in terms of magnitude of time, degree of intensity, type of deviancy, quality, themes, etc. Deviant fantasies usually involve a theme, objectifying or targeting victim (depersonalising), re-personalising (placing the object of the fantasy in another role), deviant thoughts and images and using all sensory modes and unconscious elements. Ideal fantasies and the most deviant fantasies give indicators as to the severity level of the offender. Some fantasies may be flash (instant quick) fantasies or ongoing in nature.

Motivational/developmental cycle dynamics

The developmental dynamics of offending refer to the offender's specific and general life experiences (Carich and Stone, 1996a, b). These are the traumas and encoded behaviour from childhood and adolescence. The offender experiences perceptions of those developmental events lead to key core problems and issues. These issues are the motivational dynamics of the offences or specifically what emotional gratifications the offender gets out of offending. Examples include: attention, worth, esteem, revenge, power and control, recognition, acceptance, approval, etc.

Unconscious/dissociative behaviours

It seems that most contemporary leading authorities in the field largely ignore the unconscious processes and dynamics. The unconscious is a hypothetical constrict denoting materials, memories, thoughts, feelings, fantasies, artistic patterns, dissociation, etc. that are not in immediate awareness (Carich, 1993). It is also a process stemming primarily from right hemispheric functioning. Offenders (vs people in general) tend to operate their unconscious, expressing many dissociative behaviours. Dissociative behaviours are any form of detachment or a sense of splitting off. They are those behaviours including altered states, a sense of detachment, spacing out, etc., stemming from the unconscious right hemisphere. They are part of the cycle, as implied by Carich (1996) A brief list is presented below:

- Fixation of attention
- Total concentration
- Inner (internal) focusing of attention/highly focused
- Fantasy-sensory visualisation or imagery (pretending)
- High intensity of focus
- Oblivious to external surroundings
- Possible regression (trance like)
- Trance state of awareness
- Out of body experiences or hidden observer phenomena
- Possible catalepsy or rigidity in behaviour
- Ecstatic emotional states similar to euphoria
- Depersonalisation (i.e., people are objects, detachment) (Vetter, 1990)
- Detachment at cognitive and emotional levels
- Behavioural indicators: change in physiological response (heart rate, blood pressure, respiration, swallowing, muscular activity, etc.), glassy eyes, possible ideodynamic signalling processes, staring off into space, etc.

- Dream state/daydreaming (Vetter, 1990)
- Altered state of awareness/and heightened sense of awareness and sensory perception
- Unconscious processes, along with conscious processes
- State dependent memory learning and behaviour systems (i.e., context specific)
- High level involvement with right hemispheric functioning.
- Offending states tend to be triggered by stimuli indicated by cues
- Disinhibitors are suspended at least temporarily
- Offending patterns or states can be internally/externally interrupted or terminated
- There seems to be an internal switch box that the offender uses to turn on the offending mode state
- Sensory modes seem to be in tune with specific types of sensory experiences
- Anesthesia-numbing effect
- Flashbacks

*Note: This part of the list is based on clinical observation, unless indicated by reference.

Numbers 27–44 are taken from Dolan's (1991) work with sexual abuse victims and applies to offenders and also Harold Vetter's sexual killer research as indicated by the reference (Vetter, 1990).

- Amnesia
- Numbing-unfeeling
- Spacing out
- De-realisation (feeling of one's surroundings not real) (Vetter, 1990)
- Out of body experiences
- General disengagement from one's environment into a state of detachment observation (hidden observer phenomena)
- Memory lapses
- Flat affect
- Lapse in verbal response time, as if one is off somewhere else
- Perceptual distortion
- Hypnotic states
- Splitting off (Vetter, 1990)
- De-compartmentalising (Vetter, 1990)
- Ego state behaviour (Vetter, 1990)
- Spontaneous utterances (Vetter, 1990)
- Psychopathic glibness (i.e., superficiality, phoniness, lacking meaning) (Vetter, 1990)
- Absence of guilt (Vetter, 1990)
- Somatic dementia (words have/do not have acceptable meanings) Vetter, 1990)

Hypnotic behaviours are naturalistic behaviours stemming from right hemispheric functioning They often involve: disassociation, intense focusing/concentration/inner-absorption/fixed attention and often immobilised behaviour.

Abstinence, lapse vs relapse

A lapse is any slide towards relapse. It is when the offender cannot sustain changes previously made to their problem behaviour. However, many are inclined towards pursuing further change. The problem is that many hard core, chronic offenders use some types of offences (i.e., flashing, peeping, phone calling) as build-up behaviours to rape, attempt murder and serial killing. Thus, some offences are lapses to more severe crimes. Abstinence is the remission from sex offending. It is the time period in which an offender restrains from offending. Sex offenders are not always in their cycles. The period of abstinence and non-cycle behaviour is referred to as the adaptive life cycle. That is, the offender lives free from cycle behaviours, lapses and relapse.

Models of the assault cycle

This chapter will explore four models of sexual assault cycles: the original three-stage model developed by Lane and Zamora (1978), the classic four-stage model (Bays and Freeman-Longo, 1989) a six-stage model (Carich, Gray, Rombouts, Stone and Pithers, 2001) and the composite cycle (Carich, 1996).

The three-phase cycle

The first sexual abuse cycle was referred to as a 'rape cycle' where Lane and Zamora identified a predictable sequence that included:

An event or perceived event→an emotional response→stimulation of an emotional response which is an intolerable set of feelings or reactions for the offender→attempts to compensate with substitute feelings (thoughts, power behaviours, soliciting certain types of reactions from others that give the offender the feeling of being in control→feelings of anger, even rage→decision to rape→refinement of rape plan→selection of victim→selection of when and where to rape→rape or sexual assault→ internal feelings or reactions compensating for the original event.

Sandy Lane (1991) then went on to make several modifications to this rape cycle and the sexual assault cycle emerged. This included three stages:

1. The precipitating phase involves the exposure to an event, the subsequent interpretation of the event as having a negative feeling about oneself and the individual's initial efforts to cope with the situation by avoidance. Within this phase, certain sub-events may occur that propel the cycle forward. These include: events that evoke feelings of helplessness, accompanied by a diminution in self-image; negative anticipations that entail the expectation that others were going to reject them; and avoidance, which results in withdrawal and isolation.
2. The compensatory phase sees the offender attempting to increase his sense of self-esteem and reduction of anxiety through power-based or compensatory thoughts and behaviours which eventually culminate in the offence behaviour. The sub-events within this phase may include: power and control seeking via passive-aggressive behaviours, at which time the abuser begins to manifest a greater level of anger and uses this emotion to dominate others or retaliate against them; fantasy, which in addition to sexual or masturbatory thoughts, might include actual planning of offences or mental rehearsal of the plan; and the actual execution of the sexual abuse.
3. In the final integration phase the individual attempts to rationalise or support the offence behaviour in an effort to accept it without self-depreciation. The sub-events here might include transitory guilt, largely associated with fear of getting caught, and reframing.

The linkage within and across the phases for the offender are their cognitive distortions.

The four-phase cycle

The next model is the classic four-stage cycle. The four stages (set out in Table 4.1 overleaf) are build-up, acting out, justification and pretend-normal. This cycle is like a merry-go-round, where the offender can get on and off at any point. You can escalate the speed, decrease it or stop it.

Once the offender has engaged in a sexual offence, the offence cycle begins in the pretend normal stage. In this stage, the offender may

Table 4.1: The four-stage cycle.

Phase 1 – Build-up:
  (a)   Fantasy about pleasure/excitement →
  (b)   Building sexual interest (often with
         pornography) →
  (c)   Planning the sexual assault →
  (d)   Commitment to do the assault →

Phase 2 – Acting out:
  (a)   The sexual assault (In this phase some sexual
         offenders act out many deviant behaviours
         over a short time.)

Phase 3 – Justification:
  (a)   Fear and guilt →
  (b)   Rationalisation (or other defence mechanisms
         that are used to deny the problem) →
  (c)   Vowing never to do it again →

Phase 4 – Pretend-normal:
  (a)   Working hard to make up for the deviant
         behaviour →
  (b)   Return to daily routine →
  (c)   Boredom →
  (d)   Etc.

attempt to portray themselves as someone who has never had a problem with sexual abuse. They may attempt to 'build a new life' in which they distance themselves from everyone who is aware of their past acts, including those people who have lived pro-social lives and could be important sources of support. In the build-up stage, the offender begins to re-experience the internal and external stimuli that foster their interest in abusing (such as mismanaged emotions, disordered cognitions and accessible children). This process creates a momentum that culminates in another sexually abusive act. In the justification stage, the offender attempts to cognitively redefine the victimisation. An assumption appears to be made that the offender inevitably endeavours to excuse their abusive behaviour or even more powerfully create a 'rational' explanation for their conduct. If the offender's efforts are successful, they may continue to engage in abuse. If the attempt to rationalise the abuse does not succeed, or if outside influences (such as the court or family members) exert pressure for the offender to stop, they may enter the pretend-normal stage. This information can be visually presented as a cycle (see Figure 4.1 overleaf).

The six-stage cycle

Carich and Stone (Carich, 1991b; Carich and Stone, 1994a) mapped out a six-stage cycle along

with specific strategies to identify the cycle. Their cycle represents a refinement of earlier cycle models and was based on clinical observations of a wide range of offenders. They proposed a six-stage cycle in order to permit more precise specification of an offender's behaviours, processes and motivational dynamic to offend. However, one of the potential problems of this more precise model is that is potentially more difficult for offenders to understand and work through. The specific stages are set out in Table 4.2.

Although complicated for some offenders, this model provides much detail. The stages are:

1. Initial series of triggers and coping responses.
2. Pre-search (the emergence of issues of offending ideations and needs).
3. Search (hunt for victims).
4. Set up (grooming).
5. Sexual assault.
6. Aftermath.

Although the cycle begins with triggers, triggers and cues are dispersed throughout the cycle. Motivational factors are included under core issues as sexual gratification is fused with sexual aggression and psychosocial emotional needs (Salter, 1988). In the model, lapses and relapses are defined differently as there appears to be different levels of relapse. For some offenders, other offences are lapses to previous types and levels of offending. For example, rapists may make obscene phone calls, expose their genitals, peep, or engage in unwanted sexual touching prior to committing a rape.

The cycle has been described as a merry-go-round or a roller coaster, but at operating at different speeds. Each stage is connected to the next stage through behavioural chains in the form of lapses. The purpose of designating six stages serves to provide more sequential steps by which to show progression in the behaviours and the processes producing the offending behaviour.

The initial stage identifies the triggers or risk factors. Relapse cues are usually present. This stage encompasses the initial reaction or response to various triggers. Specific needs are expressed along with responses with which to fix these needs. These needs stem from core issues such as power and control, acceptance, approval, insecurity, inferiority, low self-worth, loneliness etc. Triggers or risk factors are events (overt/covert/contextual) or situations that evoke, stimulate, initiate, or facilitate a response,

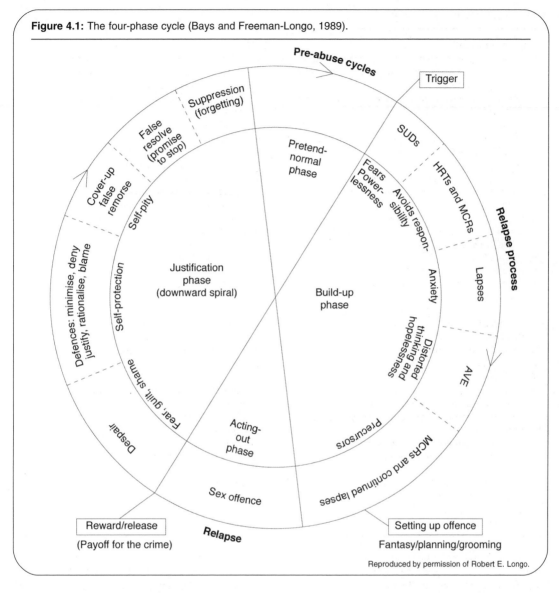

Figure 4.1: The four-phase cycle (Bays and Freeman-Longo, 1989).

Reproduced by permission of Robert E. Longo.

lapse or relapse. Triggers may include alcohol abuse, unresolved anger/resentment, angry outbursts, disagreements or any other stressors. The motivation includes jealousy/ possessiveness, power/control (need to over-control), feeling left out – all of which stem from deep-seated feelings of inadequacy, inferiority, low self-worth, insecurity, intense alones, dependency etc. Along with triggers, cues are present. Cues are warnings, signals or red flags from potential triggering situations. Cues can occur on individual, couple and family levels. Some types of individually-orientated cues include feelings of anger, recognition of faulty beliefs/perceptions (i.e. cognitive

distortions), feelings of jealousy, depression, specific behaviours, situational factors, etc. Couple, family or interpersonal cues include extended family communication, angry outbursts, disagreements, or interpersonal conflicts. Without appropriate intervention or coping strategies, the initial stage lapses into the pre-search stage. Maladaptive coping responses escalate the pattern.

Pre-search follows the initial stage. In this stage, the underlying issues emerge. Some of the underlining issues may be at both individual levels (e.g. inferiority, low self-worth/esteem, loneliness, inadequacy, insecurity etc.) and interaction levels (e.g. possessiveness, jealousy,

Table 4.2: Six-stage deviant cycle.

1. Triggering event
  a. Type of triggering events that set off the cycle
  b. Subjective processing of event (at conscious and unconscious levels)
  c. Needs evoked by triggering event (e.g., questions worth, needs reassurance)
  d. Initial attempts to cope – reactions to triggers may involve adaptive or maladaptive attempts to cope
  e. Trigger defused or lapse ensues

2. Presearch stage
  a. Abuse-predisposing ideation/feelings
  b. Problem/issues re-emerge (motivating purposes or needs, loneliness)
  c. Coping/disowning/enablers (e.g., rationalisation, denial, isolation, secrecy, blame, avoidance)
  d. Urges/cravings
  e. Deviant fantasy
  f. Buildup
  g. Depersonalisation/repersonalisation initiated
  h. Planning
  i. Pattern enablers/enhancers (e.g. pornography, masturbation, drugs or alcohol)
  j. Sexually 'turned on'
  k. Dissociation/detachment
  l. Lowering of inhibitions

3. Search stage
  a. Type of preferred/ideal victim
  b. Type of victim available/victim selection process
  c. Further depersonalisation and repersonalisation (distortion)
  d. Further planning the set up to fit or fix needs, problems, or issues at conscious/unconscious levels
  e. Implementation of plans: 'the hunt'
  f. Look for opportunity to offend
  g. Location of victim
  h. Defused/lapse

4. Set up stage
  a. Conscious/unconscious planning of the setup
  b. Manipulation of victim to the point of offending
  c. Engaging in the setup
  d. Grooming behaviour (e.g., developing false love, threats)
  e. Stalking
  f. Isolating victim(s)
  g. Commitment to offend
  h. Gaining access to victim(s)
  i. Defused/lapse

5. Relapse-offending behaviour stage
  a. Engaging in actual offending behaviour
  b. Some offences may be precursors to others (e.g., preparing to rape, rape to murder); one may have subcycles or multiple cycles
  c. Dissociated and detached
  d. Defused/relapse

6. Post offending experiential stage
  a. Aftermath
  b. Victim's response
  c. Distortion of victim's response (i.e., justification)
  d. Temporary solutions to needs
  e. Subjective processing (conscious/unconscious levels)
  f. Disowning/coping
  g. Pretend all is okay (and back to normal)
  h. False remorse (self-pity)
  i. False apology
  j. Daily routine
  k. Good-guy role
  l. Possible compensation (making up for offences)
  m. Possible celebration/trophies
  n. Defused/lapse

context etc.). Other behaviours may emerge such as fantasies, urges, cravings, anger, depressive responses, withdrawal etc. These include a variety of cognitive distortions (i.e. denial, justifications, etc.) and defences referred to as disowning behaviours. For example, sex offenders may express a variety of negative internal experiences and processes (i.e. loneliness, need to be accepted and loved, power and control, inadequacy, lack of self-worth, revenge, hopelessness, helplessness, etc.). They generate offending ideation and feelings, sometimes in the form of deviant fantasies. Urges and cravings emerge. Maladaptive coping responses lead to a lapse in the next stage.

As the goals and underlying issues emerge, the client system strives to fix it or to cope with

various core issues. The client system then seeks solutions to temporarily solve or fix problems. For example, the sex offender hunts for victims. Many of these processes remain unrecognised. A lapse leads to the set up stage.

The set up stage is initiated when the set up to engage is planned (at both recognised and unrecognised levels). Once the method of temporarily solving needs is established, the client moves to engage in targeting problematic behaviours. This may involve isolating a child; developing a rapport; giving special attention to the child by using candy, money, clothes, toys or by taking them places.

In the fifth stage, the offender engages in the sexual assault. The cycle does not end here and if uninterrupted continues as the cycle is recursive in nature. This stage lapses into the

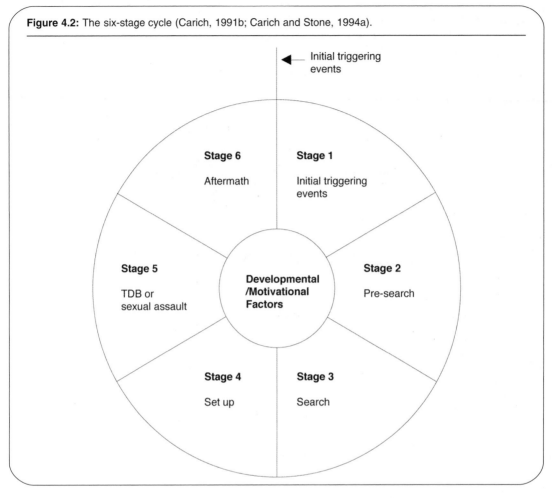

Figure 4.2: The six-stage cycle (Carich, 1991b; Carich and Stone, 1994a).

last stage, the aftermath. The aftermath consists of the consequences of engaging in the assaultive behaviour. The aftermath is the last stage of the cycle. If this stage is not interrupted or defused, the cycle continues. Within this stage, many things occur. Justifications and other cognitive distortions for the assault are further enhanced or used. When the assault violates another person's rights, either a rigid justification system or, sometimes, a sense of guilt and feeling bad may result. The assault is therefore a temporary solution to system problems that do not work. Many times the client system pretends that all is well, okay or normal. Other times, false apologies are proffered without behavioural change.

The composite cycle

In order to try and bring the information together from various cycles, Carich (1996)

developed an integrative model, which has three stages: the pre-assault phase, the assault phase and the post-assault phase (see Figure 4.3 overleaf). This cycle was developed for chronic offenders or those with numerous victims and types of offences.

The following characteristics can be identified within each of these three stages:

Stage 0: Non-offending phase
- Abstinence
- Commitment and motivation to maintain abstinence
- Adaptive coping responses
- Some adequate level of victim remorse
- Effective arousal control
- Utilising relapse interventions
- Appropriate interpersonal network or social peer group
- Appropriate companions
- Interpersonal issues neutralised

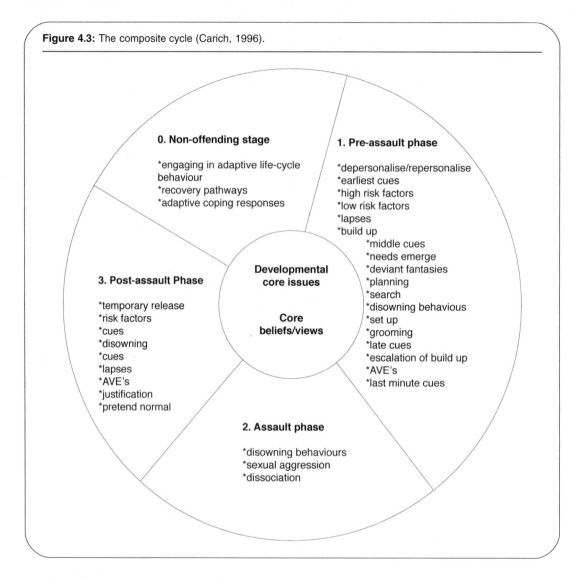

Figure 4.3: The composite cycle (Carich, 1996).

0. Non-offending stage

*engaging in adaptive life-cycle behaviour
*recovery pathways
*adaptive coping responses

1. Pre-assault phase

*depersonalise/repersonalise
*earliest cues
*high risk factors
*low risk factors
*lapses
*build up
    *middle cues
    *needs emerge
    *deviant fantasies
    *planning
    *search
    *disowning behavious
    *set up
    *grooming
    *late cues
    *escalation of build up
    *AVE's
    *last minute cues

3. Post-assault Phase

*temporary release
*risk factors
*cues
*disowning
*cues
*lapses
*AVE's
*justification
*pretend normal

Developmental core issues

Core beliefs/views

2. Assault phase

*disowning behaviours
*sexual aggression
*dissociation

- Sexual identity appears adequate
- Self-structure (self-concept; self-worth; self-esteem etc.) appears to be intact or adequate
- Rational thinking
- Maintain higher level inhibitors
- Lacks deviant behaviour
- Balanced lifestyle

Stage 1: Pre-assault phase

A. Trigger, risk factor and cues
- Triggers and/or risk factors
- Cues i.e. early, middle, late and content cues – cognitive, affective, behavioural; social; situational or contextual physical sensation
- Last minute warning and destructive line

B. Disowning behaviour
- Disowning behaviour (a way of enabling TDB and/or avoiding responsibility)
- Disowning behaviours, cognitive distortions and defences (i.e. denial, minimisation, justification, blame, rationalisation, entitlement, victim stancing, extremes etc.)
- Emergence of core issues, neediness and or motivating factors (i.e. acceptance, approval, attention, inferiorities etc.)
- Entitlement
- AVEs or abstinence violation effect (degrading, self-pity, failure expectation, toxic shame, problem with immediate gratification and sense of no control)
- Power and control needs emerge

- Dissociation or sense of detachment

C. Coping response
- Initial coping responses
- Maladaptive coping responses
- Urges and cravings

D. Depersonalisation/repersonalisation
- De-personalisation/re-personalisation (psychologically detaching victims real personal identity and replacing them with the object of their deviant fantasies)
- Deviant fantasies
- Overt disinhibitors (i.e. alcohol and drugs, use of pornography)
- Lowers inhibitors
- Dissociation and sense of detachment

E. Planning
- Deviant fantasies
- Urges and cravings
- Masturbation to deviant fantasies
- Planning
- Victim selection process (ideal victim type, preferred victim type, available victim type)

F. Search
- Victim selection process (ideal victim type, preferred victim type, available victim type)
- Location of victim (either ideal or available)
- Looking for an opportunity to offend
- Gaining access to victims

G. Setup
- Gaining access to victims
- Set up
- Isolating victim (manipulation, threats, buying materials for victims, providing false love, placing victim in abusive situation etc.)

Stage 2: Assault phase
A. Offence
- Any type of sexual aggression
- Level one offending (offences that are precursors to other offences such as flashing, peeping, frottage, stalking and rape)
- Level two offending (the ultimate and last offence)

B. Disowning behaviours and coping
- Disowning behaviours
- Maladaptive coping responses

C. Dissociative process and coping
- De-personalisation/re-personalisation
- Dissociated at some level

D. Risk factors
- Temporary fix of emerging needs and core issues
- More risk factors
- Relapse cues

Stage 3: Post-assault phase
A. Aftermath of offences
- Aftermath
- Further disinhibitors
- Further deviant fantasies
- More risk factors
- Relapse cues

B. Disowning behaviours
- Justifications of offence
- Other disowning behaviours
- False remorse (insincerely feeling bad with more self-pity)
- Further disinhibitors

C. Possible compensation
- Compensating for the offence or making up for offending (i.e. acting nice, doing good deeds, going to church, etc.
- False remorse
- False apologies, empty promises
- Playing 'good guy' roles

D. Pretend normal
- Pretend they are normal by acting as if everything is OK and nothing is wrong
- Returning to daily routine
- Playing 'good guy' roles

E. Celebration and collection of trophies
- Possible celebration
- Possible collection of trophies

Applying cycles into practice: some practical suggestions

The cycle can be interrupted and defused at any point. Interventions need to be structured in ways that enable the offender to terminate the cycle. The best time to intervene is at the earliest point in the cycle. This can be done by identifying specific risk factors, triggers or cues. There are a variety of ways to intervene, depending on the problem. Each individual has to accept responsibility for defusing the cycle. The following section provides some preliminary guidance on the identification of these points and there is then a link to Chapter 8 where the links between the cycle and the practice of relapse prevention are explored in further detail.

The three-stage cycle: questions to ask

Stage 1: Pre-assault behaviours
- How do you personalise (objectify victims, treat them like objects, etc.)?
- How does the victim fit into your fantasy?
- How do you plan your offence?
- What 'core needs' emerge when in your cycle?
- How do you select victims? What do you look for (i.e. characteristics, location, etc.)?
- Where and how do you search for victims?
- How do you groom victims?
- How do you set up the offence?
- What are some of your risk factors?
- What are some of your cues?
- What are your defence mechanisms and cognitive distortions?
- What are your deviant fantasies?
- What other build up behaviours do you have?
- What disinhibitors do you have?

Stage 2: Assaultive
- What were your assaultive behaviours?
- What were your thoughts?
- What were your feelings?
- What did you tell the victims?
- Did you detach and if so, what was it like?

Stage 3: Post-assault/aftermath
- What were your justifications and minimisations?
- What were your immediate gratifications?
- How did you pretend to be 'normal'?
- Did you have false remorse?
- What were your responses to then victims?

A sample profile for working directly with the offender to identify their basic three-stage cycle appears as appendix one to this chapter.

The four-stage cycle: questions to ask

Stage 1: Build-up
- What are some of your triggers or risk factors?
- What are some of your cues?
- What are some of your deviant fantasies?
- What are some of your seemingly unimportant or insignificant decisions?
- How does your sexual deviant interest or arousal build up?
- What types of plans do you create?
- What type of cognitive distortions do you use – denial, justification, entitlement, etc.?

Stage 2: Acting out
- What type of sexually deviant behaviour did you do?

Stage 3: Justification
- What type of fears did you have?
- Did you feel guilty or bad?
- What type of justifications did you use?
- Did you vow never to do it again and if so, how long did that last?
- Did you apologise to the victim after the offence?

Stage 4: Pretend normal
- How did you cover up your offending?
- What are your make-up behaviours?
- How did you pretend all was ok?
- What is your daily routine after an offence and how did you act?

The six-stage cycle: questions to ask

Initial stage
- What types of triggers (stressors/situations) do you have?
- How did you deal with them?
- What needs or issues emerged?
- What types of cognitive distortions did you use?

Pre-search stage
- What were your initial offending thoughts and feelings?
- What issues, problems, needs, etc. emerged?
- What type of offending urges and cravings did you have?
- How did you depersonalise (turn your victims into objects) and re-personalise (change the identity of the victims into someone else) and in what way?
- What type of deviant fantasies did you have?
- How did you plan your offence?
- What type of pornography did you use?
- How did you detach yourself?
- What disinhibitors (ways to lower your barriers to offend) did you use (drugs, alcohol, etc.)?

Search stage
- How did you select your victims?
- What is your preferred or ideal victim type?
- What type of victim will you settle for?
- How did you implement your plans?
- How did you hunt for your victim?
- How did you look for and locate victims?

Set up stage
- How did you gain access to victims?
- How did you set up the offence?
- How did you manipulate the victim?
- What type of grooming did you use?
- How did you stalk the victims?

Relapse offending stage
- What type of offence did you commit?
- What type of cognitive distortions did you use during the offence?

Aftermath stage
- What did you get out of the offence?
- What was the victim's actual response?
- How did you distort the victim's response?
- What type of justification and minimisation did you use?
- How did you cover up the offences?
- Did you have false remorse temporarily and if so, for how long?
- Did you apologise to the victim?
- How did you pretend that all was ok?
- How did you play the good-guy role?
- What is your daily routine after offending?
- Did you collect any trophies from the victim?

Steps in identifying cycles

Step 1 – Journals – Start and maintain an ongoing journal.* Journal is a diary or reactionary log. It is ongoing log of relevant, significant and insignificant events along with reactions that occur throughout the day. This includes one's events, thoughts, feelings and behaviours.* Topics include: any significant experiences (reflections of past and/or current events, seemingly insignificant or unimportant events/decisions, deviant fantasies, high risk factors/situations, stressors, relationship issues, lifestyle behaviours, deviant/non-deviant fantasies, crooked thinking, goals, jobs, anxieties, struggles, past victims, anger, potential victims, empathy, social interactions, positive events, etc.).

*Daily entry format: date, time, and entry (event/decision/experience – including: thoughts, feelings, behaviours, bodily sensations).

Likewise, in the journal, the offender can maintain an ongoing list of disowning behaviours, cues, triggers/risk factors, interventions and other cycle behaviours.

Step 2 – Life history – Instruct offenders to write a detailed autobiography or life history. This includes the details about victims, fantasies and offences, along with past significant events.* An autobiography is a life history or biographical statement about self. This includes all relevant or significant events, experiences, abuses, traumas, etc., including fantasies that occurred in one's life. These are the offender's perceptions of these events. These events may

not be accurate, but instruct offenders to try to reflect upon them as they occurred. These involve both positive and negative aspects.

The life history can follow the outline below:
(a) Consist of events from birth (first memories) to puberty.
(b) Consist of events from puberty to 18.
(c) Consist of events from 18 to the current time.

*Elements to include would be: dates or time frame – significant events in one's development, particularly your perceptions of the events. Significant events in one's development include family experiences (significant others, parents, relatives, siblings, etc.), experiences with significant others, sexual experiences, fantasies, offending experiences, past abusive experiences, both positive and negative experiences, etc.

Step 3 – Case reviews – Instruct offenders to write out a detailed description of all their offences and victim profiles. If they have hundreds or thousands, then write out the first ones, most significant (most meaningful to the offender) ones, the most serious offences, and the last ones. Include detailed fantasies. Highlight all cognitive distortions (justifications, minimisations, etc.), triggers, cues, etc. Make sure that the offender 'crashes' self, if they begin to get aroused on any of the assignments. Offenders who re-victimised any victim, need to write it out.

Step 4 – List events – Instruct offenders to make a list of all the precursors or events occurring prior to the offence, during the offence and aftermath, for each case or victimisation.

Step 5 – Identify reactions – Instruct the offender to write out their reactions (thoughts, feelings, and behaviours) (activities including physiological processes) to each event.

Step 6 – Cycle formats – Instruct the offender to take the above information for each case and plug into their specified cycle format of choice.

Step 7 – Summary cycles – Instruct the offender to develop a summary cycles for each victim type. This is a comprehensive cycle with sub-cycles.

Step 8 – Composite cycle – Offenders can develop ongoing cycles or a composite cycle of sexually aggressive behaviours Instruct them to note the differences when going into sub-cycles and perhaps multiple cycles. This can take the form of the three-stage cycle (pre-abuse, abuse and aftermath).

Step 9 – List cues and triggers – Instruct offenders to create an ongoing list of cues and categorise them early, late and/or as last minute warnings.

Step 10 – List disowning behaviours and ongoing cycle behaviours – Create an ongoing list of all types of disowning behaviours.

A summary strategy

These steps can be condensed into five critical steps:

1. Case reviews
   a. Selection of offences: if there are a few offences, write out all offences. If there are many offences, select first offences, average offences, last offences and most severe or significant offences. These are descriptions of victimisations.
   b. Write out a life history, including all significant developmental events and reactions (thoughts, feelings and behaviours).
   c. List all significant developmental events and reactions.
   d. Write out all deviant fantasies, average fantasies, and most deviant fantasies:
      – list what you are getting out of it
      – crash all arousal
      – notice the victim impact of offences
2. List of events per case
   a. Include all precursors to the offence; the assault, and post-assault or aftermath.
3. List all reactions
   a. List reactions to each event (i.e. thoughts, feelings and behaviours).
   b. List and identify all cognitive distortions.
   c. Identify and list all relapse cues (warnings).
   d. Identify and list key triggers (high and low risk factors or situations).
4. Cycle formats – Plug the information into any cycle format
   a. Identifying three-stage cycle by listing all (pre-assault) precursors, assault, and post-assaultive behaviours for each victim.
   b. Select designated cycle model of format.
   c. Identify cycle for each cycle component.
   d. Identify and define specific behaviours applied to the models.
5. Summary/composite cycle – Develop summary cycle. Develop a composite picture of all sexually aggressive related behaviours. Use the pre-assault/assault/post-assault format.
   a. List out all pre-assault events.

b. List out all assaultive behaviours and reactions.
c. List out all aftermath events.
d. Include key cycle behaviours:
   – disowning behaviours (maladaptive coping responses, cognitive distortions, defence mechanisms)
   – other disinhibitors
   – justification system
   – deviant fantasies
   – triggers
   – cues
   – developmental events/core issues and temporary needs met
   – AVEs
   – planning
   – searching for victim
   – de-personalise/re-personalise victims
   – victim selection
   – set up or grooming
   – celebration
   – collecting trophies
   – pretend normal

A basic intervention strategy

After identifying the cycle, the next step is intervention. By intervening, offenders interrupt their cycle and defuse triggers. It is important for them to learn to 'crash' deviant arousal or (offending) desires. This takes commitment, dedication and drive to avoid hurting others. A basic intervention strategy is discussed below and further details will be provided in Chapter 8 on relapse prevention.

Stop-strategy
The STOP Strategy is a basic format to help any offender change their behaviour and stands for:
   S – STOP! What you are doing or thinking.
   T – Think and rethink.
   O – Options, review all of your options and choices.
   P – Plan of action, select a plan and use it.
This easy simple strategy can be applied to changing your stinking thinking or cognitive distortions. For example:
   S – STOP, the steps what he is doing and thinking (self-talk).
   T – Think, and rethink the situation.
   O – Options, select better thoughts and behaviours.
   P – Plan of action – develop plans by using new thoughts and implementing them. Monitor the outcome.

Table 4.3: The pros and cons of the sexual assault cycle.

Pros	Cons
• Helpful framework to analyse the assault process.	• It can be used as an excuse: 'oh, well . . . I was in my cycle . . .'
• It provides an accessible conceptual framework to structure the treatment programme.	• It can help some offenders to gain greater insight into the offending process, especially when mixing with other offenders.
• It links very closely with relapse prevention approaches that aim to help offenders stop their offending.	
• It provides additional data to help monitor and track offenders.	
• It provides valuable assessment information.	

Conclusions

The assault cycle is a powerful concept and tool in sex offender treatment. Victim empathy, relapse prevention, cognitive restructuring, arousal control, skill development, etc., can all be based on the cycle. There are many reasons that promote the use of it in treatment and few that don't, as set out in Table 4.3 above.

The most effective treatment results occur when the cycle is introduced early on. Adequate treatment planning and timing is more critical when using the cycle as a basic building block. The cycle can be the backbone of any treatment programme. When used, professionals need to use the simplest conceptualisation that encompasses a variety of cycle behaviours.

When used properly, the concept of the cycle is the backbone of aftercare programming and external supervision. The offender, as well as, parole/probation monitors can quickly identify the level of cycling presented.

Mini-glossary

Abstinence: a lifestyle of non-offending.
Cycle: a chain of behaviours that are preclusively connected or linked together.
Risk factor: in general it is an event/behaviour that places the offender close to (at risk of) offending. Although it is often a trigger, it can be used to help determine the risk levels of an offender.
Detrimental 'D': any behaviour starting with a 'd' that threatens abstinence.
Pattern enabler: any event or behaviour that provides or helps (enables) the offender to commit an offence or increase the cycle.
Lapse: any slide toward relapse.
Relapse: any engagement of overtly sexually deviant behaviour.
Pattern enhancers: any event or behaviour that increases (makes greater, enhances) the speed of the cycle and/or offending.

Pattern feeders: any behaviour or event that is used by the offender to feed, nourish, or fuel the cycle.
Precursors: any event or behaviour that occurs prior to the assault.
Disinhibition: any event or behaviour that breaks the offender's barriers that prevents offending. They make the offending process easier.
Cycle behaviours: any behaviours or events that are part of your cycle.
Cognitive distortions: any deviant twisted thinking (thought, automatic thought, belief, idea, thinking error, etc.) that justifies and enables one to offend.
Defence: coping strategy or any way of coping with 'reality' including stress etc. These may include: denial, rationalising, religiosity etc. Defences are rooted into and traced to cognitive distortions.
AVE: Abstinence Violation Effect is a state of mind consisting of cognitive dissonance or conflicts between wanting and not wanting to offend.
Cues: signals, red flags, warnings of potential or actual triggers.
Triggers: events that evoke, stimulate, initiate, facilitate an offending response (lapse) and/or actual relapse.
Disowning behaviours (DBs): are any ways that enable one to offend and/or evade responsibility.
Recursive cybernetic: ongoing connecting patterns of behaviour.

References

Bays L and Freeman-Longo R (1989) *Why Did I Do It Again? Understanding My Cycle of Problem Behaviours.* Orwell, VT: Safer Society Press.

Bays L, Freeman-Longo R and Hildebran D (1990) *How Can I Stop? Breaking My Deviant Cycle.* Orwell, VT: Safer Society Press.

Carich M S (1991b) A Progressive Relapse Intervention Model: A Brief Review. *INMAS Newsletter*. 4: 2, 3–9.

Carich M S (1993) A List of Disowning Behaviours. *INMAS Newsletter*. 6: 1, 9–11.

Carich M S (1996a) *Identifying Risk Behaviours for Sex Offenders*. Springfield, IL: I.D.O.C.

Carich M S (1999) In Defence of the Assault Cycle: A Commentary. *Sexual Abuse: A Journal of Research and Treatment* 11(3): 249–52.

Carich M S, Gray A, Rombouts S, Stone M and Pithers W D (2001) Relapse Prevention and The Sexual Assault Cycle. In Carich M S and Mussack S E (Eds.) *Handbook for Sexual Abuser Assessment and Treatment*. Brandon, VT: Safer Society Press.

Carich M S and Stone M (1994) *Developing Sexual Assault Cycle Profile*. Unpublished Manuscript.

Carich M S and Stone M (1996) *Sex Offender Relapse Intervention Workbook*. Chicago, IL.: Adler School of Professional Psychology.

Carich M S and Stone M (1996b) *The Sexual Assault Cycles: A Booklet for Treatment Professionals*. Unpublished Manuscript.

Carich M S and Stone M (1996c) *The Sex Assault Cycles: A Booklet for Sex Offenders*. Unpublished Manuscript.

Carich M S and Stone M (1998) The Targeted Dysfunctional Behaviour Cycle Applied to Family Therapy. *The Family Journal*. 6: 4, 328–33.

Freeman-Longo R and Pithers W D (1992) *A Structured Approach to Preventing Relapse: A Guide for Sex Offenders*. Orwell, VT: The Safer Society Press.

Lane S (1991) The Sexual Abuse Cycle. In Ryan G D and Lane S L (Eds.) *Juvenile Sexual Offending: Causes, Consequences and Correction*. Lexington, MA: Lexington Books, 103–41.

Lane S and Zamora P (1978) *Syllabus Materials From In-Service Training on Adolescent Sexual Offenders*. Closed Adolescent Treatment Center, Denver, Colorado.

Salter A C (1988) *Treating Child Sex Offenders and Victims? Assessment and Treatment of Child Sex Offenders: A Practice Guide*. Beverly Hills, Ca: Sage.

Vetter H (1990) Dissociation, Psychopathy and The Serial Murderer. In Egger S A (Ed.) *Serial Murder: An Elusive Phenomena*. New York: Praeger.

Chapter Five

Cognitive Restructuring Approaches

Cognitive restructuring plays a central role in sex offender treatment. It is a critical aspect that helps modify the offender's behaviour. Cognitive restructuring is the therapeutic process of changing the offender's cognitions. Cognition in this context refers to a variety of phenomena related to thinking. This includes beliefs, belief systems, myths, attitudes, fantasies, automatic thoughts, perceptions, world views, frame of references, thinking errors, cognitive distortions, etc.

Ellis (1989) originated the concept of irrational beliefs. He claimed that one's behaviour is influenced by one's beliefs.

Irrational beliefs might include:

- The idea that it is a dire necessity for an adult to be loved by everyone for everything he does. Therefore, if I perceive I am unloved, I have a right to hurt others and seek approval.
  Rational – There is no research that shows that one needs the love or approval of anyone to survive. To be loved by everyone is the impossibility of perfectionism. To be unloved does not give anyone a right to hurt others.
- The idea that certain acts are awful or wicked, and that people who perform such acts should be severely punished is irrational. Therefore criminals may say, 'I have a right to do what I want to people' (distorted view).
  Rational – nothing is awful: things just are or are not and I added the labels awful, terrible, horrible, etc., which don't change reality. There is no evidence that punishment works – there are consequences of behaviour.
- The idea that it is horrible when things are not the way one thinks they should be (high expectations). Criminals say, 'therefore I have the right to do what I want. I'm entitled'.
  Rational – horrible is a label, people have little control over life and events and to control everything is an expectation.
- The idea that human misery is externally unrealistically caused and is forced on one by outside people and events. Offenders say, 'Therefore I can't change because . . .'
  Rational – The bottom line is that people create their own misery from their perceptions and belief systems or frame or reference of the activating event. This does

not give anyone the right to be irresponsible and infringe on other's rights.

- The idea that if something is or may be dangerous or fearsome one should be terribly upset about it. Therapy may be viewed as dangerous and thus too scary to be undertaken.
  Rational – People encounter dangerous events frequently and survive. The meaning that is attached to them depends upon their perception.
- The idea that it is easier to avoid than to face life's difficulties and self-responsibilities.
  Rational – Procrastination doesn't resolve the problem. Offenders may use this to avoid change.
- The idea that one needs something other or stronger than oneself to rely on something or someone outside of one's self. Offenders tend to engage in this belief.
  Rational – Everyone is responsible for their own behaviour.
- The idea that one should be thoroughly competent, intelligent, and achieving in all possible respects. Offenders say, 'If I can't be perfect, screw it'.
  Rational – Perfectionism is a myth that doesn't exist.
- The idea that because something once strongly affected one's life, it should indefinitely affect it. Offenders state, 'Therefore because this happened I have no other choice but to offend'.
  Rational – The past doesn't control one's life unless one consciously or unconsciously chooses to be controlled by the past. People are self-deterministic and make decisions. The past has influences and the individual chooses how to respond to them.
- The idea that one must have certain and perfect control over things and people including one's self. Offenders feel that they should control others.
  Rational – Perfectionism is a myth and no excuse to offend. One can't control others, just influence them, and it is up to that person to follow it.
- The idea that human happiness can be achieved by inertia and inaction. Offenders feel that there is magic in treatment.

Rational – There is no magic in life. Procrastination doesn't resolve problems.

- The idea that one has virtually no control over one's emotions and that one cannot help feeling certain feelings. Offenders feel helpless in that they can't control themselves.

Rational – My emotions are the results of my ideas, beliefs and philosophies (Criddle, 1975).

Disowning behaviours

Carich, Michael and Stone (1992) would argue that these irrational beliefs form a small part of a much broader concept of 'disowning behaviours'. These are any behaviour that enables the Target Dysfunctional Behaviours (TDBs) and enables the individual to evade and avoid responsibility. Disowning behaviours are a combination of coping/defensive structures, cognitive distortions and thinking errors. They play a significant role in the offending process. There appear to be two related components to disowning. These are irresponsibility and enabling factors. The first component refers to the offender not taking or accepting responsibility for his behaviour. The second component, enabling factors, are any overt/covert behaviours that enable or facilitate the offender's decision to offend. Both are related, as offending behaviours are irresponsible given the devastating consequences to others.

Carich (1993) set out several assumptions about disowning. Disowning behaviours are choices made by the offender. Disowning serves several purposes, including compensation dynamics, coping-strategies, maintaining psychological balance, and enabling target dysfunctional behaviours. Disowning occurs at both conscious and unconscious levels of awareness. It is learned at both levels. Disowning behaviours are integrated into the offender's lifestyle and usually operate automatically at unrecognised levels.

Carich et al. (1992) set out two basic categories: covert disowning behaviours and overt disowning behaviours. These are discussed in detail in their paper and address the following:

Covert disowning behaviours

These consist of any internal response that allows the offender to make choices to engage in offending behaviours and avoid responsibility. The sub-categories include:

- Cognitive DBs: are types of cognition or thought process that the offender has to avoid responsibility and engage in offending. The specific subcategories include: cognitive distortions and irrational beliefs, Samenow's (1995) criminal thinking defects, and other criminal thinking defects.
- Affective/emotional DBs: are any feelings, emotions or moods used to evade responsibility and enable or facilitate offending behaviours. For example, many offenders use anger, loneliness, apathy, boredom, depression, etc., to enable them to offend and behave irresponsibly. Offenders use these feelings, accompanied by cognitive distortions to engage in offending.
- Psychodynamic coping strategies: are specific 'protective' coping responses to stimuli that are usually threatening in nature. They involve elements of cognitive distortions.

Overt disowning behaviours

These are any observable activities or behaviours used to evade responsibility and engage in offending. They include:

- Overt Activities: referring to psychomotor behaviours, such as doing something, or engaging in doing some behaviour. They are typically accompanied by feelings and preceded by thoughts, perceptions, etc. They include avoiding things, alienating self, etc.
- Social DBs: socialising is a natural behaviour and a necessity for living. The type of peer group or social networking the offender has can either prevent or enable offending. Negative or dysfunctional peer groups tend to encourage distorted beliefs, and thus enable offending. For example, negative peer groups can enhance self-pity, unwarranted entitlements, a victim stance, blurring, rationalisations, etc.

Although cognitive restructuring techniques are often associated with identifying, challenging and changing distorted thinking to appropriate thinking; there are a number of techniques that directly or indirectly restructure cognitions. Most psychotherapeutic tactics involve some sort of cognitive restructuring process.

Theoretical overview

The cognitive restructuring approach has its cognitive roots in Pluto's philosophical perspective of idealism. In this perspective, Pluto emphasised that one can never know the real world objectively as it doesn't exist. It is merely a subjective observation.

The constructionist position is that people create their own realities. Adler (1941) strongly emphasised in constructivism, self-determinism and subjective uniqueness. Adler emphasised that people continuously make choices from their own unique perspective or world view. The person's world view (perspective) dictates their experience and behaviour. More specifically, their view of life guides them through life. Cognition influences perception, and together with elements of personality, greatly influences the components of physiological behaviour, social emotion, etc. The individual's perspective or frame of reference consists of beliefs and belief systems. Distorted, irrational or dysfunctional beliefs lead to irrational emotional/behavioural consequences.

Key assumptions

- Sex offending is rooted in and supported by distorted thinking, belief systems, attitudes, etc.
- Human behaviour and choices are largely influenced, affected, guided, etc. through cognitions.
- Cognition originates in the bio-physiological process of the brain, traditionally associated with left hemisphere functioning.
- A significant role and a large part of any type of sex offender treatment deals with restructuring distorted thinking processes.
- Cognitive restructuring affects every aspect of treatment and plays a big role in arousal control, relapse prevention, victim empathy, behaviour change, resolution of issues, etc.
- Sex offending is largely based on distorted thinking.
- The assault cycle is largely based on distorted thinking.
- Behaviour is a choice, as sex offending requires a series of choices. By definition, thoughts are behaviours and thus distorted thoughts are choices.
- Sex offending and distorted thinking are learned choices at all levels of awareness.
- Although the different experiential domains (affect/feelings, behaviour/activity, cognitions/thinking, physiological/bodily processes) are interrelated, cognition tends to dominate.

- Much of the offender's distorted thinking is unconscious or at some level out of awareness. The offender is still responsible for their behaviour. Thinking patterns exist at different levels of awareness and need to be changed accordingly.
- RET or any type of cognitive restructuring processes are vital key interventions.

Cognitive distortions

The work of Carich (1993) and Carich et al. (1992) have provided us with a much broader framework (set out above) for understanding 'disowning behaviours', of which cognitive distortions is just one component.

Most excuses are not simply excuses but are manifestations of underlying cognitive distortions or belief systems which may play a direct role in the initiation or maintenance patterns of sexual offending (Abel, Mittleman and Becker, 1985). Others, such as Quinsey (1986) believe that they are the consequence rather than the cause of offending. The term 'cognitive' refers to an individual's internal processes, including the justifications, perceptions and judgements used by the sex offender to rationalise their child molesting behaviour. Clinically, a child molester's cognitive distortions appear to allow the offender to justify his ongoing sexual abuse of children without the anxiety, guilt and loss of self-esteem that would usually result from an individual committing behaviour contrary to the norms of society (Abel et al., 1989, p137).

Cognitive distortions related to sexual offending are learned assumptions, sets of beliefs, and self-statements about deviant sexual behaviours such as child molestation and rape which serve to deny, justify, minimise, and rationalise an offender's actions (Bumby, 1996). These beliefs and cognitive distortions function to avoid negative self-evaluation and social disapproval and facilitate the disengagement of the offender's inhibitions regarding sexual offending (Ward, Hudson and Marshall, 1995). For example, offenders may attribute responsibility for offending to their marital problems or a child's supposed seductiveness, or exclaim that they are entitled to satisfy their sexual needs no matter what the cost is to others (Hanson, Gizzarelli and Scott, 1994).

Cognitive distortions can thus be defined as:

Thoughts which are based on erroneous perceptions; a misrepresentation of reality.

(National Task Force, 1993, p8)

or as..*a statement one makes to oneself, which contains distorted information about the reality of the situation (e.g. an offender who sexually abuses children says 'she seduced me', 'it's an education for the child', or 'it causes no harm).*

(Beck, 1976)

. . . particularly when they are used to deny, minimise, justify or rationalise their behaviour.

(Murphy, 1990)

When these distortions are processed by the offender, they are often represented as thinking errors, defined as 'patterns of thinking which are based on distorted perceptions, therefore seeming rational on the basis of some private logic, but irrational in the light of societal reality' (National Task Force, 1993, p12). It can be said that this mode of thinking is the means by which the offender is able to translate fantasy into action, and subsequently to maintain their behaviour. Thinking errors become a way of life for sex offenders. They are tempting to the offender as, when these thoughts are used they feel power and control, a sense of self-worth, and a general satisfaction. Cognitively distorting the offence allows the offender to overcome his own inhibitions and allows the offender to minimise and justify the offence, thus making the unacceptable behaviour 'acceptable'. Put simply, if the offender thought that there was nothing wrong with their behaviour they would see no reason for stopping it (Jones and Lewis, 1990/1, p44–5).

Cognitive distortions are arguably a partner for denial and minimisation for the offender. Most sex offenders deny the accusations against them, often despite overwhelming evidence to the contrary. Even in those who admit their guilt initially, there is often an effort to shift the blame from themselves. Related to this are the distorted perceptions related to the act itself. The sex offender typically sees the child as sexually provocative and as eagerly seeking sex with them. Innocent child-like behaviours (e.g. sitting in a manner, which exposes the child's underwear or excessively seeking physical contact) are often construed as indicating sexual intent. Similarly, when the offender is engaging the child in sexual acts, they will typically see passivity on the part of the child as active agreement to participate in the behaviours (Ward, Hudson and Marshall, 1995).

Sex offenders also engage in covert planning (Laws, 1989; Pithers, 1990) in which they make decisions, which they see as justified and unrelated to any explicit plan to offend. It is as though they are deliberately suppressing full awareness of their intentions to gain access to the victim, by rationalising to themselves that their decisions, at each of the steps, serves a nobler cause and then, when the ultimate opportunity to offend arises, it is an accident rather than a plan. Such rationalisations obviously allow circumstances to unfold in a way that facilitates offending, but no doubt, once offending has occurred, serve to avoid any sense of guilt (Ward, Hudson and Marshall, 1995). Sex offenders frequently suspend self-regulation during their offence chain, failing to consider long-term consequences for short-term needs. As a consequence, they do not experience any emotional incongruity between their behaviour and their self-image, nor do they feel any distress concerning the responses of the victim.

Hartley (1998) explored the cognition incest offenders in treatment use to overcome their initial inhibitions against offending and to maintain their offending once begun. The cognition identified is grouped into four separate categories (with some overlap):

Cognition relating to socio-cultural factors
Cognition related to socio-cultural factors typically involves beliefs based on messages offenders perceive, or misperceive, from society that they use to rationalise their offending behaviour. They include: the weak sanctions against sexual abuse in our society, particularly as few ever face severe consequences for their behaviour; the acceptance that the use of alcohol excuses their behaviour, as society is more tolerant and understanding of crimes committed while intoxicated; or that their behaviour wasn't serious as it doesn't extend to intercourse, based on societal tolerance of sexual interest in children as long as certain lines are not crossed. Knowing that the legal consequences for sexually offending are weak may make it easier for an offender to overcome initial inhibitions against offending.

Cognition used to reduce the fear of disclosure
Cognition used to reduce fear of disclosure typically involved some very real parent-child relationship problems that may have made it difficult for the child to disclose. For example, they may include: knowledge of conflict in the mother-child relationship, increasing the child's fear of maternal retaliation; fear by the child of

hurting their mother; or concern that the child's mother either wouldn't believe a disclosure or they could talk them out of taking action. The offender often uses these problems to his advantage in overcoming his inhibitions against offending. Offenders also used their perceptions that the child was somehow 'interested' in the contact to reduce their fear of disclosure. Interestingly, they found that the majority of offenders did not think about the possibility of disclosure, even though all knew what the possible consequences of their behaviour were, but they were able to set aside any concern and proceed with the offence.

Cognition used to diminish responsibility

Cognition used to diminish responsibility typically involved distortions related to the context in which the contact began. A perception that the contact started accidentally or innocently (i.e. a game), did not involve force or coercion, or that the child reacted 'positively' (or didn't react negatively) to the offender, served to reduce the offender's sense of responsibility for the abuse.

Cognition related to permission seeking

Respondents gave themselves permission to offend both by interpreting the child's reaction as neutral or favourable or by asking the child directly for permission. This does not imply that the child colluded with the contact; instead the offender typically observed and misinterpreted the child's response or reaction as permission to continue. Offenders described asking their daughters if the contact was 'OK' and only doing what she 'let him do'. If the child did not resist, displayed no reaction, or seemed interested, this was permission to ignore inhibitions and continue the abuse.

The study demonstrates that offenders do not just use these rationalisations to excuse their behaviour after disclosure. Rather, offenders reported using these rationalisations as a way of overcoming their internal inhibitions against offending.

Ward, Hudson and Marshall (1995) have proposed a theory on the role of cognitions in sexual offending that mirrors much of what was found in that study. Their theory suggests that offenders engage in a process of *cognitive deconstruction* related to offence events. According to Ward et al., cognitive deconstruction is a process in which 'people attempt to avoid the negative implications of

self-awareness in order to escape from the effects of traumatic or particularly stressful experience' (p71). In a cognitively deconstructed state, self-awareness is suspended or stunted and the person is typically focused on sensations in the here and now. While in this state, a person is not engaged in appropriate self-evaluative processes. This suspension of self-awareness may serve to help people reduce inhibitions and be more likely to violate their usual moral and personal standards. This theory of cognitive deconstruction may explain the offenders' lack of understanding of the child's or other's reactions to the abuse and their lack of fear about disclosure. Many offenders thus suspend their self-awareness of the impact or consequences of their behaviour so that this awareness would not inhibit them both beginning and continuing the abuse.

There is likely to be a relationship between cognitive factors and the offence chain. Models of the offence chain (e.g. Ward, Louden, Hudson and Marshall, 1995) typically specify the cognitive, behavioural, motivational, and contextual factors associated with a sexual offence. These models make explicit the temporal component of offending and suggest that the functional role of cognitive distortions may change over the offence cycle. Some of these cognitive processes change markedly throughout the offending sequence as a result of increased sexual arousal and fluctuating mood states. The ways in which offenders interpret, explain and evaluate both victims' and their own actions can function to precipitate and entrench offending behaviour (Johnston and Ward, 1996).

Ward, Fon, Hudson and McCormack (1998) provided us with a descriptive model to clarifying sex offenders' cognition concerning their offending behaviour. They argue that we need to extend our focus from post-offence cognition to **all** phases of the offending cycle, which consists of four sets of categories: offence chain, cognitive operations, cognitive content, and meta-variables. Given the detail of their arguments, the reader is advised to refer to the full paper for a detailed discussion of the points raised. The model aims to clarify statements made by the offender rather than to identify underlying distorting schemata. It offers the most advanced and dynamic conceptualisation of cognition.

Ward, Hudson, Johnston and Marshall (1997) provided us with an excellent review of the available literature on cognitive distortions using a social cognition framework. They argued that the study of cognitive factors in sexual offending has been hampered by the lack of a theoretical framework. They note that there are a number of cognitive variables in addition to distortions (which they define as offence supportive beliefs or attitudes): such as cognitive structures (e.g. schemata), operations (e.g. information processing) and products (e.g. self-statements, attributions) and sex offenders may differ from non-offenders on some, but not all, of these variables. They argued that we need to assess more of these components if we are to effectively intervene to treat these sex offenders. That being stated, it is clear that specialist assessment is clearly needed in these areas.

Common types of cognitive distortions

There are clearly many categories and types of distortions, ranging from basic irrational beliefs to thinking errors. A basic list is presented below:

- **Denial** – omitting information or not admitting to the truth, including the details to the offence; secrets, holding out information, not telling . . .
- **Lying** – any type of deliberate distorting of information; not telling the truth, twisting information . . .
- **Justifying** – making bad deviant things 'okay', making it alright.
- **Excuses** – faulty reasons to avoid-evade responsibility and to justify one's behaviour; bad reasons, faulty reasons to get away with bad behaviour.
- **Blame Game** – blaming others or something else and thus avoiding responsibility, guilt, feelings, . . . pointing fingers at others.
- **Minimise** – to make smaller, less important; reduce the significance.
- **Entitlement** – unwarranted requests, expectations, and an attitude of 'I want what I want when I want it and I want it right **now**! And I'm going to get it any way I can'.
- **Power Games** – being superior, dominant, controlling, bossy, defying authority . . . (my way, no way).
- **Depersonalising** – not seeing people as people, but as objects to be manipulated, such as 'meat'.
- **Narcissism/Pride Power** – overly inflated sense of worth, usually at others expense; stuck-up attitude, me first/me only attitude, self-centredness.

- **Vagueness** – being unclear 'fuzzy' in order to avoid responsibility, being abstract.
- **Poor Me** – pity pot or sympathy for self, feeling sorry for self.
- **Avoidance and Distancing** – withdrawal, running away, distancing (staying away), not dealing with and/or ducking issues.
- **Dumping** – projecting or inappropriately taking your garbage out on others.
- **Trashing** – rages in which, you tear up stuff and destroy things.
- **Musts/Shoulds** – awful inappropriate unrealistic unwarranted expectations and 'set ups' of yourself and others . . .
  Walling – putting up walls or defences to keep others out and/or information out; blocking out (others) stuff, stuffing feelings, twisted thoughts, defences . . .
- **Ownership** – treating people as your own personal property. Pawns in a chess game.
- **Negative thinking** – dysfunctional, irrational, inappropriate thinking that leads to bad attitude.
- **Extremes** – implies: rigidly held views, absolutes, perfectionism, all or none either or type of thinking.
- **Magnification** – blowing things out of proportion, making a big deal over nothing.
- **Procrastination** – putting things off.
- **Apathy** who cares, lack of concern, giving up.
- **Phoney Baloney** – insecure, superficial, facade, fake, unreal, etc.
- **Fallacy of Fairness** – the belief that life should be fair.
- **Victim Stance** – playing the role of a victim in order to justify and/or enable one's deviant behaviour. This leads to self pity or 'poor me'.

Traditional cognitive restructuring techniques

Basic strategies and tactics

Rational Emotive Therapy (RET)

This is a set of confrontational strategies in which one identifies, challenges, confronts and changes irrational beliefs to more rational beliefs (Criddle, 1974).

Basic Format: A B C D E

A. Activating Event – The activating event is the triggering stimulus or situation.
B. Beliefs – Beliefs are connected thoughts leading to perceptions about specific events and/or life in general. There are irrational or rational irrational (inappropriate,

dysfunctional) thinking leads to irrational, emotional and behavioural consequences. Rational beliefs lead to appropriate behaviour.

C. Consequences – Consequences stem from beliefs which are either irrational or rational behaviours and/or emotions.

D. Disputing – The basic theme of RET is identifying, challenging (disputing), confronting irrational beliefs and changing them to rational. Disputing refers to confronting and challenging old beliefs.

E. New Consequences – After changing irrational thinking to rational thinking, monitor the outcome of new consequences.

Basic cognitive restructuring approach

1. Identify the problem. The problem areas could range from arousal control, denial, responsibility, rage, self-destructive behaviour, assault cycle behaviour, etc. Once the problem behaviour is identified.
2. Identify the triggering event.
3. Identify beliefs about the event and/or problem behaviours (track self-talk, journal, etc.) Identify cognitive distortions.
4. Challenge dysfunctional beliefs or cognitive distortions.
5. Replace distorted thinking with functional thinking.
6. Monitor outcome.

The concept of RET is Rational Emotive Therapy. This theory is used to change distorted thoughts to rational clear thoughts. The process is (A) event, (B) belief or thought, (C) feelings, (D) dispute or challenge those thoughts, (E) behaviour, (F) goals, (H) action plan.

The process includes to examine the event or situation; then one's thoughts about the situation; check one's feelings about the situation; check out any cognitive distortions in one's thinking, and change those distortions to clear rational thinking. At this time, the offender can formulate a goal that one wants to achieve and make a detailed action plan of how to achieve this goal.

Basic RET procedure and format for offenders

1. Identify the activating event or triggering situation and problem.
2. Identify your current beliefs (self-talk or self-statements) about the activating event. Ask what you are telling yourself. Identify all

of your automatic thoughts or ideas and current self-talk.

3. Review the current consequences, both emotional and behavioural:
   (a) Are they functional or dysfunctional?
   (b) Are they rational or distorted/irrational?
   (c) Are they responsibility or irresponsibility?
   (d) Are they enabling sex offending or defuse the cycle?
   (e) Are they healthy and/or cycle or unhealthy?
   (f) Do they need disputing? Why?
   (g) If so, go to stem 4.
4. Action Plan – Dispute any/all distorted beliefs. These are counters that challenge and change your current distorted beliefs:
   (a) List how you are going to dispute or counter your distorted beliefs.
   (b) List some specific counters.
   (c) List your action plan.
5. Track and monitor new actions and feelings:
   (a) Note any and all new consequences.
   (b) Notice the difference.
   (c) You may have to repeat the process, to identify, challenge and change all distortions.

Disowning behavioural RET correctional process

Step 1 – A (Activating Event or Problem (Triggering) Situation): Describe (in detail) the problem situation or activating event that you become upset with. The details can include: who, what, when, where, how and perhaps how come or why.

Step 2 – B (Beliefs/Thoughts): Describe (in detail) your thoughts or beliefs, including automatic thoughts or ideas about A, the situation. This can be done by tracking your self-talk or self-statements about the situation.

Step 3 – C (Emotional/Behavioural Consequences): Part A – Describe, in detail, the consequences of your beliefs in response to A. This is your reaction. Reactions include: body sensations, emotions or feelings, more thoughts, specific behaviours or activities. Part B – Is your reaction appropriate, healthy, functional, helpful or deviant, inappropriate, dysfunctional, unhealthy, not helpful. Part C – Assess or analyse your thoughts (in Step 2) in terms of being helpful, healthy, appropriate, functional vs inappropriate, dysfunctional, unhealthy or not helpful. The latter leads to your deviant cycle.

Step 4 – D (Dispute) Dispute, challenge and change any distorted thoughts and/or behaviours: Identify all distorted beliefs and/or disowning behaviours in Step 2. Dispute them by developing counters. More specifically, dispute them by logically looking at the consequences. Replace the distortion with an appropriate belief.

Step 5 – E (New Action Plan): Develop an action plan to help cope with the problem situation. Include goals, plans/strategies with new beliefs, counters, etc. and monitor the outcome. See the format for specific process.

Specific applications

In sex offender treatment, the focus of cognitive-restructuring is used in three basic areas:

1. Offence-specific related issues (i.e., distortions supporting offence related behaviours and cycles).
2. Globally changing distortions (i.e., lifestyle behaviours).
3. Specific issues (i.e., changing any key beliefs or distortions supporting the issue).

The first area offence-specific issues includes:
- victim empathy
- denial and related
- defences
- arousal control
- defusing the assault cycle
- specific relapse interventions

These are directly linked to the offence.

The second area, global applications, includes lifestyle behaviours or personality characteristics (i.e., antisocial, narcissistic behaviours, borderline and schizoidal behaviours); coping skills with life stressors.

The last category, specific issues, applications include working through developmental traumas and issues; key core issues that directly and indirectly feed the offender's decision to offend (i.e., neediness, worth, esteem, loneliness, anger, revenge needs; recognition/attention, etc.) interpersonal issues and patterns.

At any rate, the offender's distorted part of their cognitive frame of reference or world view is restructured. The end result is that offenders think differently at all levels of awareness and thus behave differently. The above cognitive restructuring strategies apply to all three areas of issues that are normally seen in treatment.

There are many related techniques that can be used to restructure thinking. A few cognitive-behavioural tactics are discussed below.

Basic cognitive-behavioural techniques

Cognitive-behavioural techniques are techniques that primarily involve both thinking and behaviour (overt activity). Some of these techniques are used as methods of cognitive restructuring.

Journals

Journaling is a very powerful technique to initiate cognitive restructuring processes. This involves both behaviour (wanting activity) and thinking. A journal is a diary or reactionary log. It is an ongoing collection of relevant, significant and insignificant events along with the offender's reactions. This includes thoughts, feelings and behaviours. Topics include any significant experiences (reflections of past and/or current events, seemingly insignificant or unimportant events/decisions, deviant fantasies, high risk factors/situations, stressors, relationship issues, lifestyle behaviours, deviant/non-deviant fantasies, crooked thinking, goals, jobs, anxieties, struggles, past victims, anger, potential victims, empathy, social interactions, positive events, etc.). Offenders can then highlight and counter specific cognitive distortions.

Daily entry format: Date, time, entry (event/decision/experience) including: thoughts, feelings, behaviours, bodily sensations. Offenders can be instructed to maintain an ongoing list of disowning behaviours, cues, triggers/risk factors, interventions and other cycle behaviours.

Autobiographical/life history

Writing life histories or autobiographies is useful in restructuring the offender's thinking. A structure might be:

This is your life history. Write your story down on paper. More specifically, write out the most significant events in your life. Include dates and events. With each event, write out your reactions and perceptions (thoughts, feelings, behaviours, social implications). Use additional paper as needed. Also include a description of your offences and victims.

Begin with your first memories (pre-school years). The areas to cover include:

1. Pre-school years (age 1–5)
2. Early grade school years (kindergarten to 6th grade)
3. Junior grade school years (7th grade to high school)
4. High school years
5. Post high school (young adulthood) years
6. Middle adulthood years
7. Late adulthood years

Focus on different areas of your life, i.e., experiences and relationships with family members or significant others while growing up, job/work, traumas (past victimisations by others) your own victimisations, fantasies, etc. It may be best to outline the most significant events, place them in order, and then fill in the gaps.

By instructing offenders to write out their history, they can trace and identify distorted beliefs throughout their development. They can then employ traditional cognitive restructuring tactics to correct it. Change can be initiated by taking life histories into the future. The offender projects himself into the future, by writing out his future. Thus, specific issues and problems are tackled in this context.

Other writing and rewriting tactics

Rewriting tactics involve instructing the offender to rewrite specific elements; life scripts; and deviant fantasies to normal fantasies. The offender can rewrite their own life scripts, on how they want to be. Likewise, deviant fantasies can be rewritten with specific ways to 'crash' or alter the fantasy. Distortions can be countered in the fantasy. Negative images can be planted in the rewrite of the fantasy to lower the arousal level associated with deviant fantasy. Listing tactics involve writing out lists on selected themes and topics. For example, offenders can create lists of positives/negatives of self, distortions and counters.

Another related technique, repetitive listing, is the rewriting of one statement over and over. The offender may select an affirmation, new behaviour, counter to a distortion, a new belief, etc. and repeat writing that statement page after page. The limit of pages is usually 4 and 5 front and back. This is a good way to instil new beliefs and disconnect old ones.

Reports and metaphors

Written reports are task assignments, in which offenders are asked to write about a topic. It could be a specific topic of an animal. The offender would then write a detailed reflection report on that topic. The topic would directly and/or indirectly address an issue or behaviour inducing cognitive restructuring. Indirect methods reflect upon the use of metaphors. A metaphor is a parallel communication consisting of symbolic communication. The meaning of one element is transferred to another at different logical levels. It is a figure of speech that is normally used to mean another thing. With highly defensive offenders, metaphoric communication may be the best route to go. For example, using animal images and task assignments is using metaphors.

Conclusion

This chapter has attempted to locate cognitive distortions within a broader context of disowning behaviours and then explored the possible strategies and techniques used to try and restructure the cognitive and attitudinal factors that have allowed the behaviour to develop, be acted out and potentially justified and repeated. This is an area of sex offender treatment in its embryonic stages and further empirical work is needed to help refine and further develop practical options for workers.

References

Abel G G, Gore D K, Holland C L, Camp N, Becker J V and Rathner J (1989) The Measurement of Cognitive Distortions of Child Molesters. *Annals of Sex Research.* 2: 135–53.

Abel G G, Mittleman M S and Becker J V (1985) Sex Offenders: Results of Assessment and Recommendations for Treatment. In Ben-Aron M H, Hucker S I, and Webster C D (Eds.) *Clinical Criminology: The Assessment and Treatment of Criminal Behaviour.* Toronto: M & M Graphics, 191–205.

Adler A (1941) *Understanding Human Nature.* Cleveland, OH: The World Publishing Company.

Beck A T (1976) *Cognitive Theory and Emotional Disorders.* NY: Meridian.

Bumby K M (1996) Assessing The Cognitive Distortions of Child Molesters and Rapists: Development and Validation of The Molest and Rape Scales. *Sexual Abuse: A Journal of Research and Treatment.* 8: 1, 37–54.

Carich M S (1993) A List of Disowning Behaviours. *Inmas Newsletter.* 6: 1, 9–11.

Carich M S (2001) In Defence of Utilising the Construct of Cognitive Distortions: A Commentary. *Sexual Abuse: A Journal of Research and Treatment* 13(3): 221–23.

Carich M S, Michael D M and Stone M (1992) Categories of Disowning Behaviours. *Inmas Newsletter*. 5: 4, 2–13.

Ellis A (1989) Rational Emotional Therapy. In Corsini A and Wedding D (Eds.) *Current Psychotherapies*: Itasca, Il: Fe Peacock, 197–238.

Hanson R K, Gizzarrelli R and Scott H (1994) The Attitudes of Incest Offenders: Sexual Enticement and Acceptance of Sex With Children. *Criminal Justice and Behaviour*. 21: 2, 187–220.

Hartley C C (1998) How Incest Offenders Overcome Internal Inhibitions Through The Use of Cognitions and Cognitive Distortions. *Journal of Interpersonal Violence*. 13: 1, 25–39.

Johnston L and Ward T (1996) Social Cognition and Sexual Offending: A Theoretical Framework. *Sexual Abuse: A Journal of Research and Treatment*. 8: 1, 55–80.

Jones C and Lewis J (1990/1) A Pilot Prison Treatment Group for Sex Offenders at HMP Norwich. *Prison Service Journal*. 81: 44–6.

Laws P R (Ed.) (1989) *Relapse Prevention With Sex Offenders*. NY: Guilford Press.

Murphy W D (1990) Assessment and Modification of Cognitive Distortions. In Marshall W L, Laws D R and Barbaree H E (Eds.) *Handbook of Sexual Assault*. NY: Plenum Press.

National Task Force (1993) The Revised Report From The National Task Force on Juvenile Sexual Offending. *Juvenile and Family Court Journal*. 44: 4, 1–121.

Pithers W D (1990) Relapse Prevention With Sexual Aggressors: A Method For Maintaining Therapeutic Gain and Enhancing External Supervision. In Marshall W L, Laws D R and Barbaree H E (Eds.) *Handbook of Sexual Assault: Issues, Theories and Treatment of The Offender*. New York: Plenum.

Quinsey V L (1986) Men Who Have Sex With Children. In Weisstub D N (Ed.) *Law and Mental Health: International Perspectives (Vol2)*. NY: Pergamon Press, 140–72.

Samenow D (1995) *Errors in Thinking*. Unpublished Handout.

Ward T, Fon C, Hudson S M and McCormack J (1998) A Descriptive Model of Dysfunctional Cognitions in Child Molesters. *Journal of Interpersonal Violence*. 13: 1, 129–55.

Ward T, Hudson S M and Marshall W L (1995) Cognitive Distortions and Affective Deficits in Sex Offenders: A Cognitive Deconstructionist Interpretation. *Sexual Abuse: A Journal of Research and Treatment*. 7: 67–83.

Ward T, Hudson S M, Johnston L and Marshall W L (1997) Cognitive Distortions in Sex Offenders: an Integrative Review. *Clinical Psychology Review*. 17: 5, 479–507.

Ward T, Louden K, Hudson S M and Marshall W L (1995) A Descriptive Model of the Offence Chain for Child Molesters. *Journal of Interpersonal Violence*. 10: 452–72.

Chapter Six

Developing Victim Empathy and Remorse

Introduction

The purposes of this chapter are:

- To define victim empathy or remorse in the context of social interest.
- To distinguish victim empathy and remorse from toxic shame and self-pity.
- To identify specific elements of victim empathy.
- To provide specific techniques to enhance the development of victim empathy or social interest.

The aim is to furnish workers with sufficient information for the development of victim empathy in work with sex offenders. During the sexual offence, the offender lacks empathy for their victim and their level of social interest is low.

Victim empathy is an important element in treating sex offenders (Pithers, 1994; Hildebran and Pithers, 1989; Marshall and Fernandez, 2001, Hanson, 1997). This is highlighted by 94% of the treatment programmes in the U.S. using victim empathy components, designed to encourage the offender to accept some greater understanding of the impact of their behaviour on others (Knopp, Freeman-Longo and Stevenson, 1992, and Freeman-Longo, Bird, Stevenson and Fisher, 1995). The reasons for incorporating victim empathy in treating sex offenders centre around the issue of taking responsibility for the offence, the development of personal relationships and skills, and arousal control techniques. These factors act as inhibitors to acting out in a sexually aggressive manner in the future. These elements are fostered by the offender to develop by developing awareness for the impact that his actions have upon his victims at multiple levels:

- Primary victims, or the identified individuals directly involved in the offence.
- Secondary victims, individuals indirectly affected by the offence (e.g. family, spouse, friends).

Victim impact awareness additionally involves the experiencing of appropriate remorse or guilt for violating another individual. High levels of empathy and remorse are obstacles to the offender's re-offending.

There have been a number of different definitions of the concept, reflecting no consensus as to how victim empathy can be developed by the offender or about the theoretical basis for the treatment work.

Empathy comprises multiple components and processes, which need to be understood as a preface to any work in this area. Empathy has been defined as a cognitive ability to understand and identify with another's perspective (Cronbach, 1955; Taguiri, 1969), an emotional capacity to experience the same feelings as another (Clore and Jeffrey, 1972) or an interplay of cognitive and affective factors (Aronfreed, 1968). Briggs (1994) noted that cognitive empathy is where the offender has an intellectual understanding of the feelings of others without necessarily experiencing any emotional change themselves, whilst emotional empathy is where they experience the emotions of others in response to their situations and feelings. Other writers have argued that it should embrace communicative and relational elements. Freeman-Longo, Bays and Bear (1996) have argued that it is **not** about being self-centred, harsh, indifferent, resistant, discouraging, unsupportive, impatient, angry, inconsiderate, hostile, irritated, selfish, mean, abusive, cynical (p7).

George and Cristiani (1990) define empathy as the ability to tune in to the client's feelings and to be able to see the client's world as it truly seems to be to the client. The ability to be empathetic in a relationship requires that the counsellor responds sensitively and accurately to the client's feelings and experiences as if they were his own (p130). Egan (1986) defined empathy as 'the ability to enter into and understand the world of another person and communicate this understanding to them.' Egan goes on to differentiate several types: 'Emotional empathy is the ability to be affected emotionally by another person's state.' Role taking is the ability to understand a person's condition, frame of reference, or point of view. As a communication skill, it is the ability to communicate one's community of feeling (emotional empathy) and/or the understandings that flow from role taking (role-taking empathy). 'Specific elements include listening, understanding and the communication of that understanding. This requires attending, observing and listening (p95).

Carkhuff (1969) added a multilevel dimension to empathy as follows:

Level 1 'The verbal and behavioural expressions of the helper either do not attend to or detract significantly from the verbal and behavioural expressions of the helpee(s) in that they communicate significantly less of the helper's feelings and experiences than the helpee has communicated himself . . . In summary, the helper does everything but express that he is listening, understanding or being sensitive to even the most obvious feelings of the helpee in such a way as to detract significantly from the communications of the helpee.' (p174)

Level 2 'While the helper responds to the expressed feelings of the helpee(s), he does so in such a way that he subtracts noticeable affect from the communications of the helpee . . . In summary, the helper tends to respond to other than what the helpee is expressing or indicating.' (p174)

Level 3 'The expressions of the helper in response to the expressions of the helpee(s) are essentially interchangeable with those of the helpee in that they express essentially the same affect and meaning . . . In summary, the helper is responding so as to neither subtract from nor add to the expressions of the helpee. He does not respond accurately to how that person really feels beneath the surface feelings; but he indicates a willingness and openness to do so. Level 3 constitutes the minimal level of facilitative interpersonal functioning.' (p175)

Level 4 'The responses of the helper add noticeably to the expressions of the helpee(s) in such a way as to express feelings a level deeper than the helpee was able to express himself . . . In summary, the helper's response adds deeper feeling and meaning to the expressions of the helpee.' (p175)

Level 5 'The helper's responses add significantly to the feeling and meaning of the expression of the helpee(s) in such a way as to actively express feelings levels below what the helpee himself was able to express or, in the event of ongoing deep self-exploration on the helpee's part, to be fully with him in his deepest moments . . . In summary, the helper is responding with full awareness of who the other person is and with a comprehensive and accurate empathic understanding of the individual's deepest feelings.' (p175)

This can be represented clearly as a tabular continuum (see Table 6.1 overleaf).

Sex offenders are thought to suffer from deficits in their capacity to experience empathy – yet the extent is in dispute – and this is considered to be important in the development, and particularly the maintenance, of their deviant behaviour. The lack of any empathy clearly has a significant impact on the likelihood of repeat and escalatory offending. For example, it is clear that those sex offenders who deny any responsibility for their offences will feel little remorse or shame for what they have done. Indeed, the use of mechanisms such as denial preclude empathic interactions or awareness of the victims rights, and they also fail to appreciate (or lack) the basic information regarding the consequences of their behaviour – other than for themselves. Far worse than this, many offenders argue that they have helped the child they have abused, e.g. sex is educational and in the 'best interests' of the child. If the offender feels bad after abusing, the child victim, by simply surviving without psychological damage apparent to their offender, gives a covert message of 'it's OK'. The offender thus feels better, and this can make it easier for them to offend again. Victims may subsequently perceive the bad feelings held by the offender and feel responsible, even reassuring him (Calder, 1999).

Victim empathy can be viewed as a multi-dimensional and multi-levelled concept, with a complex set of interacting behaviours and processes. The highest level could consist of the offender's compassionate understanding and emotional expression of that understanding at both intellectual and emotional levels, of the victim(s) situation (i.e., victim impact) created by the offender. The offender understands what he did to the victim, the victim's suffering and can emotionally express those feelings. In order to reach this level, the following are required of the offender: responsibility (accountability) emotional recognition (identifying feelings) victim harm recognition (identifying the devastating impact of the offence), perspective taking (identifying with another and understanding their situation) and emotional expression (displaying feelings and communicating at emotional levels through feelings). These are discussed in more detail a little later in this chapter.

Table 6.1: The five-point multi-level model of victim empathy.

(i) Levels

5. Spontaneous emotional victim empathy
4. Generates consistent emotional victim empathy responses
3. Generates occasional emotional victim empathy responses
2. Intellectual understanding only
1. Superficial understanding and false remorse
0. Non-existent psychopathic

(ii) Descriptions of levels

Level 5
- Higher and deepest levels
- Spontaneous emotional victim empathy expression
- Consistent victim perspective/generates victim empathy
- Consistent global empathy
- Deep sense of remorse
- Balanced self worth/esteem with adequate sense of remorse
- Does not fear vulnerability
- Assumes responsibility/accountability
- Other centred
- Has fully developed conscience
- When focused on victims/victim impact, stays focused
- Understands full impact of behaviour

Level 4
- Generates emotional victim empathy response consistently
- Victim perspective
- Can be vulnerable
- Obtained responsibility, on an emotional level
- Holds self accountable/responsible
- Does not use cognitive distortions/defences to block victim empathy
- Does not victim stance
- Not self-centred and tends to stay other centred
- Has developed some level of self worth/adequacy/esteem and remorse
- Deep sense of conscience
- Tends to stay focused on victim empathy
- Realises victim impact on both primary and secondary victims
- Emotional recognition

Level 3
- Emotional recognition
- Occasional emotional victim empathy responses
- Does tend to feel for victims, but has difficulty expressing feelings except occasionally

- Struggles with being vulnerable
- Has obtained a victim perspective
- Fluctuates from self centred versus other centred
- Remains somewhat self-centred
- Has developed perspective taking skills
- Takes responsibility for offences
- May have emotional global empathy for crisis situations, however not concerning specific victims
- Gets distracted when focuses on victim empathy
- Recognises victim harm
- Conscience fluctuates

Level 2
- Intellectually understands victim perspective at best
- Limited use of some cognitive distortions (minimises, justification.)
- Fluctuates on responsibility/accountability
- Lacks emotional recognition and expression
- Fluctuates on victim perspective (intellectual at best)
- Limited global empathy
- Victim stances and self-pity
- Recognises victim harm at intellectual level only
- Continues to victimise others (non-sexually or even perhaps sexually)

Level 1
- Superficial empathy at best, with false remorse
- Cognitive distortions in offence disclosure
- Self-centred, does not consider others
- May try to act like he has victim empathy
- Enjoys distressing others and/or offending
- May pretend to care for victims and others only for ulterior motives
- Very insincere responses
- Limited global empathy

Level 0
- Psychopathic tendencies
- Lacks conscience (no remorse displayed)
- Self-centred or out for self
- Victimises (verbally/physically)
- Very manipulative
- Appears apathetic, cold callous, non-caring . . .
- Lacks global empathy
- Shallow and superficial
- Personality disorders anti-social and narcissistic
- Enjoys victimising and distressing others
- Does not care for victims at all

A model for understanding empathy

Marshall (1993) argued that empathy involves four processes: recognition of the other person's feelings, the evocation in the observer of those same feelings, the recognition of those states by the observer, and the acceptance of the shared feelings. It is no surprise that our understanding of empathy is often confused given the complexity of the concept. In response to this, Marshall, Hudson, Jones and Fernandez (1995) offered us a multi-component model to help us better understand sex offenders. They argued that empathy is a staged process involving:

1. emotional recognition
2. perspective-taking
3. emotion replication
4. response decision

Stage 1: Emotional recognition – requires that the offender be able to accurately discriminate the emotional state of the victim. The recognition of personal distress seems to be a necessary first step in the unfolding of an empathic response. Any failure to identify such distress prevents the subsequent stages of the empathic response following whilst also allowing a continuation of their sexually abusive behaviour.

In order for someone to 'feel' or experience the emotional state of another, they must first recognise the other person's emotional state.

Stage 2: Perspective-taking – is the ability to put themselves in the victim's place and see the world as they do In doing so, they are forced to recognise the unpleasantness of their actions, preventing any repetition from occurring. Those offenders who consistently offend against a particular group (e.g. children) or sex (male or female) may see them as quite different from themselves and, therefore, are unable to adapt the victim's perceptions.

Stage 3: Emotion replication – involves the vicarious emotional response that replicates (or nearly replicates) the emotional experience of their victim. This requires some emotional repertoire by the offender to allow them to replicate the observed state. It requires that they recognise the emotion (Stage 1) and adopt the perspective of that person (Stage 2).

Stage 4: Response decision – concerns the offender's decision to act or not to act on the basis of their feelings. They may have worked through the first three stages, yet decide against acting on their feelings (p101–3).

Empathy and social interest

Carich, Kassell and Stone (2001) examined victim empathy in the context of social interest and noted that they are closely related concepts. Social interest is comprised of the key elements of social embeddedness, a feeling of belonging or connectedness to the community, the ability and desire to cooperate with others, and the willingness to subordinate individual desires or needs for the good of the community. In addition, a person cannot be separated from his

social context and therefore he seeks to belong or fit into that social structure in some manner. The key element in this definition is the ability of the individual to subordinate his egocentric desires for the good of the community.

Marshall et al. (1995) defined victim empathy as the offender's ability to recognise an emotional state, replicate that emotional state within himself and behave in accordance with the emotional expressions of his victims. Victim empathy thus reflects the offender's ability to place himself subjectively in the position of his victims and to behave in a manner that is reasonably similar to the victims. This process requires complex cognitive and emotional abilities that are common in most individuals or society.

Carich et al. (2001) argue that victim empathy and social interest are similar in that each requires similar processes and abilities to exist within an individual. Victim empathy and remorse can be viewed as components of social interest. Social interest is largely accomplished through the ability to understand through shared experiences. The same abilities that are required to empathise with another individual are the abilities that are responsible for forming a feeling of connectedness or belonging with others. The desire or ability to cooperate with others must grow out of the understanding for the needs of others. In addition, that understanding must be significantly accurate and strong for the individual to put his or her needs and desires aside in order to assist the individual.

Carich et al. (2001) went on to distinguish victim empathy from remorse, toxic shame and self-pity. In the context of offender treatment, victim empathy is the compassionate understanding of what the victim experienced. Victim empathy involves understanding both the cognitive or intellectual and emotional levels of the impact of victimisation (victim impact) and the ability to express that understanding (see Calder, Peake and Rose, 2001 for a detailed review of these points). Remorse is the painful regret of violating another. A remorseful offender feels sad or guilty for violating another. Victim empathy and remorse involve an appropriate level of shame or feeling bad for violating another person. When an individual damages another person for his own gratification, that individual needs to experience levels of shame and guilt. Toxic shame is an excessive feeling of shame and guilt associated with the violation of another person to the extent that it lowers the offender's self-worth. Likewise, victim empathy and remorse can be differentiated from victim stancing and false remorse. Victim empathy is thinking and feeling in a manner that is other centred, while victim stancing is self-centred. False remorse is a superficial level of regret followed by insincere apologies and promises not to offend in the future. Real remorse implies a conscience in which a person generates guilt feelings for violating others.

Key components

There are several views of the key components of victim empathy, and some common elements. Karl Hanson (1997) outlined three components of victim empathy (note in his chapter he refers to empathy as sympathy):

- Offender victim relationship – The degree the offender can develop a caring relationship with the victim.
- Perspective taking ability – The degree one can cognitively understand another's thoughts and feelings. It is the ability to describe facial expression, body language, voice tone and other nonverbal behaviour and recognise the victim's suffering from their sexual transgression.
- Sympathy training – Working through distortions.

Marshall and Fernandez (2001) outlined four components of empathy:

- Emotional recognition of another's emotional state.
- An ability to see the world as the other person (perspective-taking).
- An ability to experience the same emotional state as the observed person (without effort) (the process of identifying with another person).
- The offender feeling impelled to act accordingly (i.e., stop victimising and comfort others).

Key elements

The key elements agreed by many writers include:

- **Emotional recognition** – An ability to recognise one's own emotions and others. Many offenders have difficulty recognising their own feelings and the feelings that others experience. They are able to dissociate or detach from their own feelings, thereby limiting or eliminating the emotional component of their experiences.
- **Victim harm recognition** – Ability to recognise the harm inflicted upon the victim through the transgression. Most offenders employ a variety of distorted private logic to deny, justify, and minimise the degree of victim impact or damage committed through their offending. The offender needs to restructure his private logic and recognise the amount of harm or victim impact: he must recognise the consequences of their offending.
- **Assuming responsibility** – Taking full responsibility (ownership without distortions) for one's offences. Responsibility is a crucial element in victim empathy work. The offender needs to assume full ownership of their behaviour by acknowledging that they have inflicted harm through their offences and by holding themselves accountable for their behaviour.
- **Perspective taking** – Identifying with the victim and developing a compassionate understanding of the other person. Perspective taking is another critical element of victim empathy. It involves taking the other person's point of view so that the offender understands what the other person was feeling and victim impact (both short- and long-term).
- **Emotional expression** – Emotional expression of the offender's compassion for the victim. Emotional expression is the outward display of feelings. In terms of victim empathy, the offender expresses the pain of the victim. He shares and displays his feelings concerning the victim's pain.
- **A guilt response** – The offender feels bad and guilty for violating another person.

Key assumptions

- Victim empathy is a series of choices at both conscious and unconscious levels.
- Victim empathy and remorse is a necessary component of treatment and recovery.
- The offender needs to find a balance in experiencing ongoing remorse/shame/guilt and self-worth inappropriate guilt is unhealthy.
- At the time of the offence, the offender did **not** have empathy for their victims. they may or may not have had empathy prior to the offence. Empathy is inconsistent with hurting others.

- Offenders vary on the degree and/or level of empathy (or lack of empathy) in general. The more socio-psychopathic (anti-social/narcissistic) the offender is, the less empathy they feel for people.
- Offenders may have totally blocked or numbed their feelings and thus may not be able to identify what they are experiencing.
- The blocking of empathy, involves the use of various distorted thinking patterns (cognitive distortions/defences).
- Victim empathy is a process and a learned behaviour. It is a skill and appears like a 'state' that can be turned off and on by the offender.
- Victim empathy and remorse are learned choices at multiple levels of awareness.
- In the course of treatment, it is hoped that empathy is self-generated and remorse is spontaneous. VE needs to involve another-centred perspective and behaviour.
- The less conscience one has the more anti-social/narcissistic (psychopathic) one is. VE enhances conscience and social interest.
- 'Being empathetic doesn't just happen to you It is not something you simply do or learn in a few minutes or a few days. It must be learned by feeling deeply and paying very close attention to the real feelings of others. It must be developed and cultivated over time.' Freeman-Longo, Bays and Bear (1996, p7)
- 'If you were a truly empathetic person before you sexually abused others, you would not have raped, molested, or sexually abused your victims. You may have occasional flashes of feeling concern and caring for people that you know, but either it doesn't happen very often, or it's always combined with figuring out how you can use the situation or the feelings to get something you want' (p8). These feelings may be false remorse, self pity, strings attached, to feel better, etc.
- 'To cultivate empathy, requires caring for and respecting others' (Freeman-Longo, Bays and Bear, 1996, p8).
- 'There are three things we can be in control of – our own feelings, our own thoughts, and our own behaviour. We are all responsible for everything we do' (Freeman-Longo, Bays and Bear, 1996, p9)

Treatment goals

Victim empathy can be facilitated in a number of ways depending upon treatment goals, processes and the steps taken to achieve their goals. Treatment goals may include the following:

- To develop basic empathy skills.
- To develop victim empathy for one's specific victim and victims in general.
- To work through offence specific distortion and defences that inhibit empathy.
- To help enhance the offender's conscience or guilt response mechanisms.
- Cognitive restructuring (offence specific and global distortions).
- Enable the offender to feel vulnerable.
- To enhance perspective taking skills.
- To enhance emotional recognition skills.
- To enhance emotional expression skills.

Treatment processes

There are several frameworks in which to use victim empathy techniques. Several are provided below:

Marshall and Fernandez (2001) outlined three segments of developing victim empathy:
1. Emotional expression/recognition:
   - Theme or goal:
     - To help offenders identify and recognise their own/other's feelings.
   - Therapeutic tasks:
     - Offenders are instructed to describe a significant past event (other than their arrest) and vividly re-live it.
     - Offenders may describe their own abuse and the consequences or impact, avoiding victim stancing.
     - Group members identify and rate the depth of each others emotional responses.
2. Victim harm:
   - The theme or goal:
     - To sensitise the offender to the harm of their offending and humanising the victim.
   - Therapeutic tasks:
     - Describe the differences and similarities between themselves and the victim.
     - Address specific needs, rights and feelings of the victims.
     - Describe offences from the victim's perspective. This may entail role playing the victim and expressing appropriate thoughts and feelings that would be expressed by the victim.
     - Address cognitive distortions.
     - Address victim impact (during the offence, short- and long-term consequences).

– Offenders are instructed to write two hypothetical letters, identifying the pain/hurt and evaluate and process the offender's response to the victim (i.e., apology letters, etc.).

3. Victim empathy
   - Theme or goal:
     – The focus of therapy is directed or focused on the actual victim(s) response and accounts.
   - Therapeutic tasks:
     – Offenders address, their own specific victims and the process is limited to group.
   - The process of victim empathy is simply an analysis of the victim empathy experience and steps taken to achieve that experience.

The steps are guidelines to facilitate the process. The process is outlined and followed by 10 steps.

Victim empathy process (Carich)

Carich (1997) has outlined a 12-stage process with 10 specific steps to facilitate victim empathy:

1. Accountability/responsibility.
2. Commitment to recover (at a significant level):
   - The offender wants to change.
3. Cognitive restructuring – Rethinking stinking thinking or changing cognitive distortions (i.e., justifications).
4. Emotional recognition:
   - Internal (self) – recognising feelings within one's self.
   - External (others based) – recognising feelings in others.
5. Focus and remain focused on victims, victim impact and related topics/themes.
6. Moving from self to other centred:
   - Respect for others.
   - Care and concern for others.
7. Perspective taking – Taking the other's view.
8. Describe and review victim impact issues (in general and victim-specific).
9. Recognise and acknowledge victim harm.
10. Identification process with the victim:
    - Taking the victim's perspective.
11. Experience and express feelings about victims:
    - Target and lower any walls or feeling inhibitors.
    - Enhance emotional expression.

12. Emphasise self value vs bad self (i.e., doing a bad deed vs being a totally bad person).

Steps in learning victim empathy (Carich)

Step 1: Exploring the myths involving empathy and offenders
   - Education
   - Commitment to recover

Step 2: Identifying and challenging offence-specific distortions
   - Case reviews
   - Identify distortions
   - List counters

Step 3: Emotional recognition
   - Differentiating thoughts from feelings
   - Identify feelings in self and others

Step 4: Moving from self-centred to other-centred
   - Learning respect
   - Learning basic empathy

Step 5: Perspective Taking
   - Listening skills
   - Openness and receptivity (lowering the defences)

Step 6: Review specific victim impact issues
   - Discuss victim impact issues in general
   - Discuss the impact of one's offending onto the one's victims

Step 7: Recognise victim harm
   - Focus on the impact and specific harm done to the victim
   - Feeling the victim impact

Step 8: Emotional expression: Expressing feelings
   - Offender vulnerability
   - Lowering inhibitions that prevent crying

Step 9: Express feelings about victims
   - Lowering inhibitions to express feelings for victims
   - Experience and express feelings

Step 10: Self concept and feeling bad
   - Differentiating behaviour from self
   - New me vs old me identities
   - Appropriate guilt and shame

The development of victim empathy: process and elements (Carich, 1997b)

Stage 1: Exploring empathy and the myths involving offenders and victims

Step 1   On a scale of 1 to 10 rate how much victim empathy (compassionate understanding of your victim and the victim impact of your behaviour).

Step 2   Review the commitment to recovery.

Step 3   Emphasise the role of empathy in recovery.

Step 4   Review myths of offending and empathy, and identify the ones that apply.

Stage 2: Identifying and challenging offence-specific distortions

Step 5   Case or offence reviews (review and write out offences in detail).

Step 6   Review basic distortions.

Step 7   Identify and list offender's distortions.

Step 8   List how each distortion blocks empathy.

Step 9   Define how the offender did and currently views victims and identify distortions.

Step 10   List counters to each distortion.

Stage 3: Emotional recognition

Step 11   Differentiate thoughts vs feelings.

Step 12   Identify basic feelings (mad/sad/glad/bad/bland/anxious/confused).

Step 13   Maintain journals.

Step 14   Identify feelings in self.

Step 15   Identify feelings in others.

Stage 4: Moving from self-centredness to other-centred

Step 16   List the ways that you are self-centred.

Step 17   List how you can be other-centred.

Step 18   Learning respect by listing 6 people who have problems and how they are affected.

Step 19   List 10 examples other than offending of how you have hurt others.

Step 20   Give 10 examples when you helped others, without selfish reasons or motives.

Step 21   How did you feel in 17?

Step 22   List the characteristics of being self centred and give examples.

Step 23   List the characteristics of being other centred and give examples.

Stage 5: Perspective taking

Step 24   Learn to be open and receptive by lowering your defences. List your defences/distortions that keep your walls up.

Step 25   List how you defuse your defensive walls (lower your walls). Practice lowering your walls.

Step 26   Learn listening skills by practicing listening to others. Do this five times per day.

Step 27   Learn to give and receive communication. Practice being the speaker (giving) and the listener (receiving). Use other skills (i.e., 'I' messages, active listening, paraphrase, respect, eye contact, etc.).

Step 28   Learn basic empathy skills by putting yourself in another's shoes and responding.

Step 29   Take turns and paraphrase what the speaker said.

Stage 6: Review specific victim impact

Step 30   List and discuss victim impact issues in general (the effects of abuse).

Step 31   List the short term effects of offending to the victim.

Step 32   List the long term effects of offending to the victim.

Step 33   List any effects of your own sexual abuse or any abuse.

Stage 7: Recognising victim harm

Step 34   Focus on the impact and specific harm of your behaviour by making a combined list of short and long term effects.

Step 35   Write about how each of your victims felt (if you have numerous victims, pick out the most severe, significant and as many as you can).

Step 36   If you were victimised (sexually or any other way) how did you feel then/now?

Step 37   When you violated your victim, what did that person go through?

Step 38   What is self-pity and how does that apply to you?

Step 39   What is guilt and remorse?

Stage 8: Emotional expression: expressing feelings

Step 40   If you have any problems expressing your feelings, analyse why? Look at why and how you are blocking feelings? Why and how you avoid the pain of your behaviour?

Step 41   Figure out how you can express your feelings by developing vulnerability.

Stage 9: Express feelings about victims

Step 42   Rewrite your victimisations with devastating victim reactions.

Step 43   Rewrite deviant fantasies and crash them by writing in how the victim was devastated and actually felt.

Step 44   Allow yourself to express your feelings.

Step 45   What is victim empathy and remorse? List the characteristics of victim empathy.

Step 46   List different ways that you can maintain victim empathy.

Stage 10: Self concept and feeling bad

Step 47   List the characteristics of the 'old me' or the victimiser.

Step 48   List the characteristics of the 'new me' identity with empathy.

Step 49   List how you can maintain the 'new me' identity with empathy.

Step 50   What can you do for restitution or making up for what you did?

Therapeutic process issues

Therapeutic issues involve both psycho-educational approaches vs therapeutic; and offender trauma abreactions.

Some professionals emphasise the importance of a strict empathy skill training regime while others prefer a therapy process. Most educational approaches tend to be cognitive-behavioural in nature. A well rounded victim empathy component will have both approaches built into it. Both educational and therapeutic approaches need to be combined, as the most effective victim empathy process entails both educational approaches combined with therapeutic experientially oriented tactics. The educational component sets up the experiential therapeutic experience and use of techniques. Thus, both approaches are intermixed, for the best results.

The second issue is offender trauma abreactions. Offender trauma abreaction (resolution) processes can play a significant role in facilitating victim empathy. There are several points to keep in mind:

- Avoid offenders using the victim stancing or playing the 'victim role' in order to avoid responsibility and issues.
- It is important to hold the offender accountable for their deviant behaviour.
- Continuously link offender trauma abreaction to their victims or victims in general.

Treatment victim empathy techniques

Developing victim empathy or social interest is not an overnight process. An offender may have to experience a variety of processes to develop empathy. No two offenders will share the same level of empathy or social interest at any one point in time. Therefore, the worker must encourage the offender by appreciating the point in the victim empathy process they are at.

Such behaviour encourages other offenders to understand and to tolerate individuals who are not at the same point in the treatment process.

Carich (1997b and 1999) suggested several basic techniques for developing victim empathy:

Utilising readings and videos

This involves instructing offenders to read selected readings and/or viewing selected videos/movies, victim impact materials, etc. The themes illustrate victim impact issues. Videos can be taken from T.V. documentation, talk shows, movies, etc., that illustrate the devastating experiences of the victim. For example, the Safer Society's RP Modules have a '911' victim empathy segment, in which the actual rape of a woman was taped during her 911 call for help. This kind of example carries a huge potential impact on the offender. With this tactic, offenders are instructed to recognise their own feelings and the feelings of the victim. Victim harm and victim impact are emphasised. Empathetic responses are encouraged and developed. The group context needs to consist of vulnerability, support, cohesion and compassion. Since offenders are at different points in the treatment process, arousal to victim distress and deviant behaviour may occur. These issues need to be addressed and safeguards need to be in place. If not addressed, it can be a reinforcing experience. Any deviant arousal needs to be addressed, probed and crashed or interrupted. This can be done through probing questions, cognitive restructuring tactics, confrontation selecting aversive elements (for that particular offender) pairing them with the victim's distress and paraphilia.

Victim clarification letters

Victim clarification letters are letters written by the offender to their victim (but not mailed, unless under direct supervision and consideration with the victim's therapist) taking full responsibility for the offence. There are no excuses, minimisations, blaming, etc., or any cognitive distortion in the letter (Freeman-Longo and Pithers, 1992). Letters are processed in a group setting, as empathetic and remorseful responses are evoked. Letters may be sent to the victim based upon the survivor's needs, level of stability, therapeutic focus or victim's direction, and with permission from the victim and/or victim's therapist.

Victim letters

Victim letters are letters written by victims and directed toward a specific offender or offenders in general. These letters can have a huge impact as the victim shares their experiences and impact of the offence. The most significant impact occurs when the offender receives a letter from his own victim outlining their devastating experiences. Offenders are instructed to identify the victims' feelings and are then able to recognise the harm done to the victim. In group, offenders are expected to identify and share their feelings concerning the victim's experience.

Role play

There are a number of role play tactics and variations. One set of role playing techniques involve instructing the offender to enact the offence (without actually perpetrating). Usually, another offender plays the victim. Obviously, safeguards are taken to avoid placing anyone in physical danger. The primary goal is to create an abreaction, in which the offender feels disgusted perpetrating the victim and recognises the damage done. The feelings of disgust are then linked to feelings of empathy and remorse. As specific cognitive distortions can be identified, countered and defused empathetic feelings are explored. Offenders can play various roles, depending upon what direction therapists want to go. Specific scenarios can be designed to meet the offender's needs.

Reverse role plays

Reverse role playing techniques centre around instructing the identified offender to play the role of one of his selected victims. Another offender plays perpetrator. Scenarios are designed in advanced based upon the identified offender's case. The offender is then able to enhance his awareness of victim harm, perspective taking, emotional recognition and expression, by playing the victim's role. These tactics break down distortions and defences at emotional levels as, feelings of pain are linked to the actual victim's experience. Of course, safeguards need to be taken in to consideration to ensure or address that offenders playing the perpetrator role, do not become aroused and that no one is re-victimised. Some may not be able to identify their emotional reactions. As with any of these tactics, offenders may need assistance in emotional recognition skills.

Answering victim questions

Typically, victims have numerous questions. Victims tend to blame themselves and feel shameful (toxic shame). Offenders can address these questions in role play situations, by instructing one or more offenders to play the victim. Typical questions and comments include:

- Why me?
- What did I do to deserve this?
- Is this my fault?
- Why do I feel so guilty?
- How could I have prevented it?
- Did he/she love me?
- Why did he/she do it?
- Why do I feel so dirty and ugly?
- How could this happen?

Basic confrontational tactics

Confrontation involves pointing out specific issues, materials, behaviours, etc. to the offenders or bringing it to their attention. At one level, confrontation is explaining and challenging, yet at another level superficial. There are levels of confrontation ranging from addressing issues to 'attack' forms of confrontation. The latter are shame based approaches, which are no longer recommended Intense and rigorous confrontation tactics can be used in the appropriate context. Specific therapeutic factors include:

- non-victimising
- cohesive group
- peer pressure
- therapeutic rapport
- offender is hooked into treatment
- use of support, along with confrontation

Specific areas that can be targeted include: specific behaviours, congruencies, inconsistencies, lack of empathy/remorse, denial, lack of responsibilities, cognitive distortions (i.e., minimisation, blame, justifications, self pity, victim stancing, false remorse, etc.), supporting offences and inhibiting empathy. Empathy inhibitors need to be addressed. For example, an offender may distract himself from feelings, by placing his hand over his face, fumbling a pencil, etc.

Using victim impact statements

Victim impact statements are specific statements from the victim. This is the victim's version of the offence. It is a written statement discerning their experience. Quite often, the offender's version is different from the victims. When the offender is presented with the victim's version, he can become quite emotional. Inconsistent views are explored. The offender's emotions are linked back to the victim's experience and usually what they are still experiencing. Distortions and inconsistent accounts are explored and challenged.

Using statement of facts
Similar to victim impact, the 'statement of facts' provides another dose of reality for the offender. These are the facts of the offence, as presented in court. This is the court's version. The rapists can compare their facts to the offender's story. This view closely represents a presentation of the victim's view. A variety of issues can be addressed including accountability, distortions, responsibility, avoidance strategies, victim impact, etc.

Focusing on specific times when the offender was wronged or offender trauma
This is an intense method to enhance empathy. It is also dangerous for offenders to develop self pity and victim stancing. It involves selecting specific times or events in which the offender was violated or wronged. Similarly, the offender's own abuse (offender trauma) can be used. Once the offenders are at an emotional level, then the offender's reactions are explored and linked to their specific victim's experiences. Emphasis has to be placed on the victim's experience and victim impact issues. This is done by linking the offender's own abusive experiences (emotional reactions) to their own specific victim's experiences. This can be linked to victims in general. It is extremely important to avoid victim stancing (the offender taking the victim role), thus leading to self pity and justifications to offend. This actually creates a victim perpetrator cycle. It is recommended that offender trauma and related core issues need resolving or worked through to a less intense level, in another context. Victim empathy group or work is not usually the appropriate time and place to work on offender trauma issues. As a rule, the offender's traumatic experiences are continuously linked to victim empathy. This prevents victim stancing, which needs to be challenged.

Personalising the victim as a human being or person
In the assault, typically the offender depersonalises the victim into a non person and/or may re-personalise (mentally place) the victim into another identity. The new identity fits the deviant fantasy and motives for offending. In the offender's mind, the victim loses their true identity and takes on characteristics of another. Many offenders see the victim as an object to be manipulated and the offender feels entitled to manipulate. For most, it is the object of one's fantasy or possibly symbolic representations of specific figures from the past. Re-personalising the victim is placing them as a symbolic representation of someone/something else. As a tactic, emphasis is placed on viewing the victim as a real person with an identity, their own unique identity. When the offender's distortions are challenged, the victim takes on the characteristics of a real person. Then emotional recognition, victim harm and perspective taking can be targeted.

As if technique
The as if technique was originally developed by Alfred Adler and has many variations (Ansbacher and Ansbacher, 1956). It is a cognitive futuristic intervention in which the client projects themselves into one's future and responds accordingly. The client is instructed to pretend or enact a scenario using the linguistic framework of 'act as if you . . .' or 'what if you . . .' This applies to victim empathy and remorse. Offenders are instructed to project themselves into the future by psychologically enacting a what if/as if scenario, involving victim impact themes. Typically, the scenario is based on placing the offender in a victim role. The offender's experiences are processed.

The offender's immediate feelings and experiences are directly linked to the offender's specific victim's experiences.

Survivor or (victim)/offender interactional groups
The victim/offender interactional groups are comprised of therapeutic groups with both adult survivors (victims) and offenders. With adult offenders, groups are composed of both adult survivors and offenders. These groups can have very powerful impacts. These types of groups have to be constructed in a way that survivors do not get victimised. Likewise, it is just as important to minimise the offenders getting victimised by survivors. However, survivors may tend to ventilate their feelings towards offenders and offenders need to utilise those experiences. For optional results, both

offenders and survivors need to be at a certain level. Survivors need to be stable and not self destructive. Likewise, offenders need to be at a certain level (i.e., motivated and committed towards recovery, willing to take some responsibility, less distorted, etc.) or
they may react with anger, defensiveness, deviant arousal and try to re-victimise the survivors.

Specific group parameters are established. Group themes involve survivors discussing their experiences and victim impact issues. Survivors may ask offenders why they were assaulted and offenders are encouraged to answer. A basic group rule of no victimising needs to be in place and enforced: violators are confronted. If survivors ventilate their feelings towards the offenders, the offenders need to link their reactions to the survivors reactions. In other words, the ventilation is used therapeutically to reinforce empathy and remorse. Survivors can get a sense of relief, perhaps as a burden has been lifted. The healing effect may take the following forms: answers to their questions, confidence to deal with the life, self-esteem, validation, alleviation of guilt/toxic shame, fears, all generated from the perpetration. It is important for the survivor's therapist to attend and help provide a sense of security and stability for them. This also allows the survivor to process the experience within their own treatment context. Offender/survivor groups provide the offender with an opportunity to take responsibility, feel for their victims and provide emotional restitution. In essence, offenders witness the pain of their victims.

Victim's voice technique
The victim's voice tactic consists of the offender describing his offence from the victim's perspective. The offender writes out the offence from the victim's perspective using the victim's words. In group, the offender then verbalises the offence using the victim's words. Each event is described along with their reaction. Intense feelings of empathy and remorse can be elicited. The written description needs reviewing and any distortions addressed, prior to reading the offence to the group.

Creating victim impact collages
A collage is a collection of pictures, symbols, words, sayings, images, etc., glued together on a poster board. Victim impact collages are collected pictures, symbols, sayings, etc.,

involving victim impact themes. These types of interventions access right hemispheric and unconscious processes. This reminds the offender of the devastating impact of offending. The trauma, pain and issues felt by the victim, along with other short and long term impact behaviour are being displayed. Safeguards are taken into consideration, to prevent the offender enhancing his deviancy.

Victim empathy process curve
The VE curve is based on the following assumptions:

- Victim empathy is both a complex skill and process.
- The skills involve (and compliment) the process of learning victim empathy.
- The curve consists of various offender 'states' and behaviours.
- The curve begins with denial/lack of empathy (self-centred focus) and ends with self-actualisation (defined as responsibility and empowerment with empathy or other centred focus).
- Offenders can move back and forth.
- The victim empathy process is plotted on the curve.
- Similarly to cycles, there is not a specified time frame.

The victime empathy curve is conceptualised as an inverted statistical normal curve. Both the victim empathy learning process and behaviours involved are plotted on the curve. The left side of the curve consists of typical behaviours that new offenders display in treatment (see Figure 6.1). As they progress in treatment, offender proceeds further down the left side of the curve, he develops initial remorse and responsibility. He assumes a victim-focused perspective. The offender obtains the desire to avoid sexual aggression. The offender displays emotional recognition, emotional expression and some perspective taking skills. Arousal control is targeted throughout the process, as the offender now displays some arousal control skills. The bottom of the curve reflects the offender possibly 'hitting bottom' and crashing with suicidal ideation. A strong guilt response is displayed.

As treatment continues, the offender then moves up the right side of the curve with an 'other' centred perspective. The offender is humble, empathetic (both victim specific and globally), and self accepting of the victim impact

Figure 6.1: Victim empathy process curve.

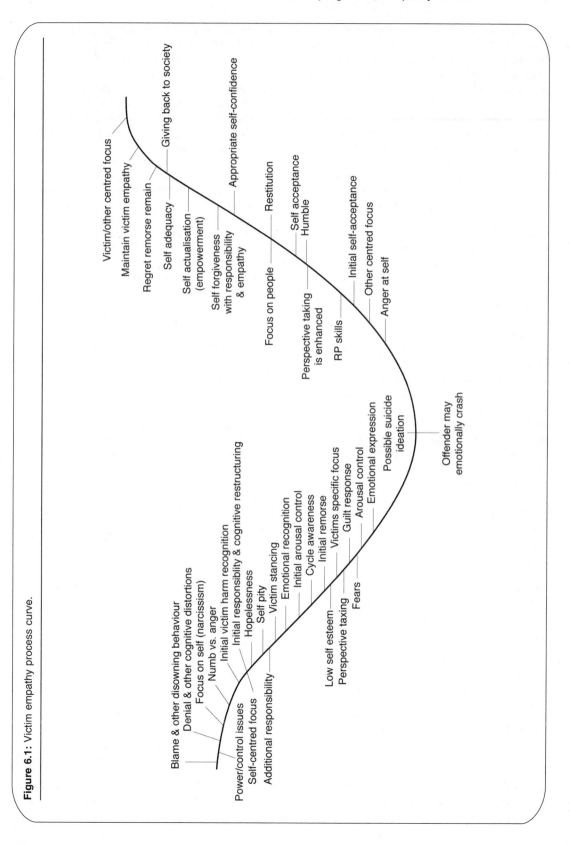

with a set of restructured cognitions at the emotional level. At the upper end of the curve, the offender is 'self actualised' in terms of empowerment and responsibility with victim empathy. He has appropriate levels of self-esteem/worth/confidence, as well as empathy and remorse.

The authors found the VE curve to be an interesting way to visualise and understand the victim empathy learning process. By using the VE curve, the clinician can alleviate potential offender 'resistence' by conjointly reviewing the model and instructing the offender to plot himself on the curve. Prior to plotting the offenders behaviour on the curve, the offender can list his current perceptions and behaviours. The group can provide valuable feedback as to where they see the offender on the curve. The VE curve can be used as an assessment tool to evaluate the offender's progress and establish both immediate and long term treatment targets.

The VE process curve can also provide a unique conceptual framework to understand the victim empathy learning process. Thus, the mystery is dispelled, as the curve can be linked to other components of treatment (i.e. assaule cycle/RP skills, cognitive restructuring, social skills and restructuring, responsibility, arousal control, and recovery). Clinical observation indicates successful utilisation with both adolescent and adult sex offenders.

Conclusions

Victim empathy is considered an important and perhaps a critical component of sex offender treatment.

However, the overall research has not absolutely supported the effectiveness or necessity of victim empathy interventions, nor discounted it. The use of victim empathy in treatment is best justified through clinical experience. Eight clinical justifications and observations include:

- Victim empathy appears to enhance the offenders' commitment and motivation to the treatment goals of 'no more victims' (Hildebran and Pithers, 1989; Pithers, 1994).
- Victim empathy enhances interpersonal relationships and social skills (Hanson, 1997; Marshall and Fernandez, 2001).
- Victim empathy creates a resource for the offender, to use as a disinhibitor towards offending.

- Victim empathy enhances relapse prevention skills (Hildebran and Pithers, 1989).
- Victim empathy facilitates and reciprocally involves cognitive restructuring of the offender's offence specific distortions/defences, including denial, justifications, minimisations, global distortions, etc.
- Victim empathy facilitates and reciprocally involves emotional recognition, expression and the experience of feelings (Hanson, 1997; Marshall and Fernandez, 2001).
- Victim empathy can be used in conjunction with covert arousal control techniques. Victim empathy is an excellent fantasy crasher. Recognising victim harm and feeling the pain of the victim does not correspond with deviant arousal.
- Victim empathy enhances the development of the offender's conscience or 'guilt' faculties and mechanisms.

References

Ansbacher H l and Ansbacher R R (Eds.) (1964) *Superiority and Social Interest*. Evanston, Il: Nortwestern University Press.

Aronfreed J (1968) *Conduct and Conscience: The Socialization of Internalised Control Over Behaviour*. NY: Academic Press.

Briggs D I (1994) Assessment of Sex Offenders. In McMurran and Hodge J E (Eds.) *The Assessment of Criminal Behaviours of Clients in Secure Settings*. London: Jessica Kingsley, 53–67.

Calder M C (1999) *Assessing Risk in Adult Males Who Sexually Abuse Children: A Practitioner's Guide*. Lyme Regis, Dorset: Russell House Publishing.

Calder M C, Peake A and Rose K (2001) *Mothers of Sexually Abused Children: A Framework for Assessment, Understanding and Support*. Dorset: Russell House Publishing.

Carich M S (1999) *Enhancing Victim Awareness and Empathy*. A Pre-Conference Workshop Presented at The Annual Meeting of The Association for The Treatment of Sexual Abusers, Chicago.

Carich M S, Kassell M E and Stone M H (2001) Enhancing Social Interest in Sexual Offenders. *The Journal of Individual Psychology*. 57: 1, 18–25.

Carich M S (1996) Facilitating and Developing Victim Empathy and Remorse: Basic Goals and Tactics. *INMAS Newsletter*. 9: 1, 4.

Carich M S (1997) Utilizing Victim Empathy Techniques in Sex Offender Treatment:

Training Module. In Carich M S (Ed.) *Sex Offender Treatment and Overview: Training for The Mental Health Professional*. Springfield, Il, Illinois Department of Corrections.

Carich M S (1997b) *Sex Offender Treatment. Psycho-Educational Module Developing Victim Empathy and Remorse*. Unpublished Manuscript.

Carkhuff R R (1969) *Helping and Human Relations: A Primer for Lay and Professional Helpers Volume I Selection and Training*. NY: Hold, Rinehart and Winston, Inc.

Clore G L and Jeffrey K M (1972) *A Descriptive Study of Incarcerated Rapists and Paedophiles Report of The Solicitor General of Canada*. Ottowa, Canada.

Cronbach L J (1955) Processes Affecting Scores on 'Understanding of Others' and 'Assumed Similarity'. *Psychological Bulletin*. 52: 3, 177–93.

Egan G (1986) *The Skilled Helper: A Systematic Approach to Effective Helping*. Monterey, CA: Brooks/Cole Publishing.

Freeman-Longo R, Bays L and Bear E (1996) *Empathy and Compassionate Action Issues and Exercises: A Guided Workbook for Clients in Treatment*. Brandon, VT: The Safer Society Press.

Freeman-Longo R E, Bird S, Stevenson W F and Wand Fiske J A (1995) *1994 Nationwide Survey of Treatment Programs and Models: Serving Abuse-Reaction, Children and Adolescent and Adult Sex Offenders*. Brandon, VT: The Safer Society Press.

George R L and Cristiani T S (1990) *Counselling Theory and Practice*. Englewood Cliffs: New Jersey

Hanson R K (1997) Invoking Sympathy: Assessment and Treatment of Empathy Deficits Among Sexual Offenders. In Schwartz B K and Cellini H R (Eds.) *The Sex Offender: New Insights, Treatment Innovations and Legal Developments*. Kingston, NJ: Civic Research Institute. Il: 1, 1–12.

Henderson N V and Carich M S (2001) Victim Empathy Process Curve. *The Forum* XIII(1), Spring 2001, p3.

Hildebran D and Pithers W D (1989) Enhancing Offender Empathy for Sexual Abuse Victims. In Laws D R (Ed.) *Relapse Prevention With Sex Offenders*. NY: Guilford. 236–43.

Knopp F H, Freeman-Longo R and Stevenson W (1992) Nationwide Survey of Juvenile and Adult Sex Offender Treatment. *Psychology*. 14: 119–24.

Langevin R, Wright P and Handy L (1988) Empathy, Assertiveness, and Defensiveness Among Sex Offenders. *Annals of Sex Research*. 1: 533–47.

Marshall W L (1993) A Revised Approach to The Treatment of Men Who Sexually Assault Females. In Nagayana-Hall G E, Hirschman R, Graham J R and Zaragoza M S (Eds.) *Sexual Aggression: Issues in Aetiology, Assessment and Treatment*. Washington, DC: Taylor and Francis, 143–65.

Marshall W L, Hudson S M, Jones R and Fernandez Y M (1995) Empathy in Sex Offenders. *Clinical Psychology Review*. 15: 2, 99–113.

Marshall W L, Jones R, Hudson S M and Mcdonald E (1993) Generalised Empathy on Child Molesters. *Journal of Child Sexual Abuse*. 2: 61–8.

Marshall W L and Fernandez Y M (2001) Empathy Training. In Carich M S and Mussack S (Eds.) *A Handbook on The Assessment and Treatment of Sex Offenders*. Brandon, VT: The Safer Society Press, 141–7.

Pithers W D (1994) Process Evaluation of A Group Therapy Component Designed to Enhance Sex Offenders' Empathy for Sexual Abuse Survivors. *Behaviour Research and Therapy*. 32: 5, 565–70.

Taguiri R (1969) Person Perception. In Lindzey G and Aronson E (Eds.) *The Handbook of Social Psychology (Volume 3)*. Reading, Mass: Addison-Wesley, 395–449.

Chapter Seven

Arousal Control Via Behavioural Interventions

One of the primary goals of sex offender treatment is to help the offender reduce deviant or inappropriate arousal. The purposes of this chapter are providing an overview of types of conditioning theory as well as discussing a number of interventions or techniques designed to reduce or control sexual arousal.

Conditioning theory

Conditioning theory involves incorporating and increasing or decreasing and eliminating targeted behaviours. Behavioural interventions were originally based on working with overt or observable behaviour and covert behaviour. Conditioning was (is) commonly referred to as learning through association and/or by consequences. The cognitive mediators are largely overlooked. There are several basic assumptions of this approach:

- Learning is viewed as observable behaviour.
- The individual is passive in the environment.
- The individual is made by the environment.
- Learning is a mechanistic process of learned sequences.
- Emphasis is on physical environment.
- Behaviour/learning is determined by the environment.
- Learning is a culmination of conditioned responses.
- Learning can be reduced down to stimulus response/response stimulus sequences.
                                    (Martin and Pear, 1983).

There are several basic principles involved in applying behavioural techniques:

- Specify the target behaviour.
- Decide rather to increase or decrease it.
- Decide rather to use associative or consequential learning or both.
- Use the immediacy principle.
- Close proximity of stimuli – response or response stimuli.
- Use perpetuation.

Behavioural Learning Theory can be divided up into three distinct categories:
1. Classical learning (conditioning by association)
2. Operant learning (learning by consequences)

3. Social learning

Since most behavioural-oriented tactics involve one or more of these theories, a brief typology is presented below:

1. Learning by association, called classical conditioning:
   - Vicarious learning – physical or physiological learning by association.
   - Traditional Pavlovian (S–S) classical conditioning (stimulus–stimulus association).
   - Respondent conditioning (Thorndike) or S–R associative conditioning (stimulus–response association).
   - Verbal associative learning.
   - Imitation (modelling).
   - NLP Anchoring and behaviours, sensory modality, content.
   - Rote memory (memorisation).
   - Generalisation (transfer of learning via association).
   - Social learning (imitation).
2. Learning by consequences. Operant conditioning:
   - Instrumental conditioning R–S (learning by response followed by a stimulus reinforcer).
   - Ratio (schedules based upon number of reinforced responses):
     - Fixed ratio (fixed number of reinforcers).
     - Variable ratio (varied number of reinforcers).
   - Internal (schedules based upon time):
     - Fixed interval (fixed amount of time for reinforcement).
     - Variable interval (varied amount of time for reinforcement).
3. Social Learning:
   - Modelling.
   - Rehearsal.

Each of these areas will now be explored in some further detail.

Learning by association

Learning by association refers to learning by connecting together stimuli and/or responses. The classical paradigm is 'classical conditioning', created by Pavlov. Classical conditioning or respondent conditioning is the learning by association. Typically, stimuli are paired to create new responses. For example a dog barks when you feed him/her. The dog then associates the rattling of papers with food. The dog then barks when you rattle the papers. Pavlov noted that reflexive reactions (unconditioned responses or UCR) may be activated by a previously neutral stimulus (conditioned stimulus or CS) after repeated pairings with a stimulus (unconditioned stimulus or UCS) which unavoidably produces the response (Kratochwill, 1985). Time, immediacy, contingency (the connection of association) etc. between the UCS and CS followed by a response elicited by the UCS. The conditioned stimulus (CS) and newly conditioned response (CR) become associated together. Martin and Pear (1983) state

> ... that any learned response was a response to a conditioned stimulus (CS). The CS had acquired the ability to elicit the conditioned response (CR) because that CS has been paired with an unconditioned stimulus (US) that elicited an unconditioned response (UR) that was similar to the CR.

The procedure consists of the following steps:

1. Identify a stimulus (S) that reliably elicits the response that you desire to condition.
2. Identify a stimulus (S) that does not presently elicit the response, but that would be convenient or desirable to have elicit the response.
3. Repeatedly pair the two stimuli by presenting S first and quickly (within 0.5 to 1.0 seconds) follow it with S2.
4. Gradually decrease the number of trials during which S2 is presented but continue to present S so that it alone will eventually elicit the response (Martin and Pear, 1983, p243).

Basic steps:

1. Set up stimulus (or stimuli) with the appropriate target response (behaviour).
2. Strengthen the connection by:
   - Using close temporal (spatial) proximity between the stimuli and response.
   - Immediacy in the connection or association.
   - Repetition of presentations between stimuli and response.

A related technique is covert conditioning. Cautela (1985) defines conditioning as a

behavioural change and covert conditioning 'refers to a set of imagery-based procedures which alter response frequency by manipulation of consequences ... Covert conditioning focuses on imagery, thoughts, and feelings are also included as covert processes that can be manipulated by covert conditioning procedures.' (p86). Covert refers to internal behaviours or non-observable behaviours. Covert psychological responses include thinking, verbal behaviour, imagery or imagining, feeling, bodily cues or reproducing sensations (learned sensations), etc. Overt is observable noticeable behaviour. Cautela (1985b) outlines three main assumptions:

- Homogeneity: that there is continuity between covert and overt processes. They share similar properties in maintaining, explaining, and modifying behaviour. This is called the continuity assumption or assumptions of functional equivalence.
- Interaction: these are interactions between overt/covert behaviours. These are different levels of activity.
- Learning: covert behaviours are governed by the laws of learning.

Behaviour can be decreased and extinguished through covert extinction. Cautela (1983c) defines covert extinction as 'a covert conditioning procedure employed to decrease the probability of target behaviours. In covert extinction the client imagines the behaviour to be reduced in frequency and then imagines that the reinforcement that usually overtly follows this behaviour does not occur.' This would include decreasing or eliminating the pairings of stimuli to the targeted behaviour.

Learning by consequences

This sub-category involves the presentation of a stimulus or consequence following the response to increase or decrease in the behaviour. The most significant and classical model is operant or instrumental conditioning. Operant conditioning is defined as 'the probability of the reoccurrence of a response is increased if the response is followed by a reinforcing stimulus.' (Kratochwill, 1985). The frequency of the response is influenced by the schedule of reinforcement (a) continuous; (b) intermittent (1) interval; (a) fixed interval; (b) variable interval; (2) ratio; (a) fixed ratio; (b) variable interval; (3) ratio: (a) fixed ratio; (b) fixed ratio; differential reinforcement, DRL, DRO. Behaviours or responses followed by contingent stimuli (events) will increase the behaviours (reinforcers) or decrease them (punishment). Miller (1975) defines a reinforcer as 'any event that quickly follows a response and increases the probability (or rate) of that response.' The essence of operant conditioning is that a response can be increased or decreased by the addition or removal of a stimulus event. The event may be a punisher, reinforcer, blocking a reinforcer or punisher, etc.

Rules for learning by reinforcement are:

1. Contingency: the response must be connected to the stimulus reinforcer.
2. Continuity: reinforcement needs to be in close approximation to the response.
3. Immediacy: reinforcement needs to follow the target response immediately.
4. Law of frequency: or repetition (the more repetitions, the stronger the response).
5. Law of reinforcer deprivation: the more a person is deprived of the reinforcer, the more effective it is.
6. Law of reinforcement size: 'The larger the amount of any single reinforcer, the more effective that reinforcer will be (Martin and Pear, 1983).

Operant conditioning: learning by reinforcement: responses or behaviours that are strengthened by (connected to) stimuli or events.

The rules of reinforcement include the following:

- Contingency: the response must be connected to a positive reinforcing stimulus.
- Immediacy: the reinforcer immediately follows the TARGET response.
- Frequency: repetition of the reinforcer.
- Close proximity with regards to the response and reinforcer.

Application of reinforcement (behaviour modification)

1. Selecting the behaviour to be increased/decreased
   - Target behaviours
   - Specific behavioural concrete goals
2. Selecting a reinforcer
   - Stimuli (or events, objects, social events) avoidable.
   - Able to be immediately followed by the target behaviour.
   - Repetition.

3. Application
   - Instruction.
   - Reinforcer in close proximity to behaviour.
   - Reinforcer contingent (connected to) on target behaviour.
   - Repetition of reinforcer and behaviour.
   - The subject could be in a state of deprivation in regard to the reinforcer.
4. Warning form reinforcer
   - Reinforcers gradually withdrawn.
   - Look for/apply natural reinforcers to maintain behaviour (Martin and Pear, 1983).

Summary of application of reinforcement (Martin and Pear, 1983)
Rules:

- Identify target behaviour.
- Identify reinforcer (example a star, money, award).
- Ratio schedule: give a reinforcer (star) for each of the behaviours emitted or vary it intermittently.
- Interval schedule: set up a specific period of time that you want the behaviour to occur or not to occur. Reinforce the behaviour by giving a star for each period of time that the behaviour occurred or did not occur (depending upon your goal).
- So many starts equal something.

Several classical operant conditioning tactics are briefly described below.

Positive reinforcement. 'Positive reinforcement is an operant conditioning procedure in which a response is strengthened by the onset of an event (positive reinforcer) which follows the responses in time' (Poling, 1985). A positive reinforcer strengthens the response. 'A reinforcer is any event that quickly follows a response and increased the probability (or rate) of that response' (Miller, 1975). Schedules include: (a) continuous reinforcement; (b) intermittent: (1) interval; (a) fixed interval; (b) variable interval: (2) ratio; (a) fixed ratio; (b) variable ratio, differential reinforcement, DRL, DRO.

'Continuous reinforcement is a schedule of reinforcement in which every response is reinforced' (Miller, 1975). The procedure of reinforcing every response is used initially then moved to intermittent schedules.

Intermittent reinforcement. 'Intermittent reinforcement applies to schedules of reinforcement in which only some responses are reinforced' (Miller, 1975). This type of reinforcer strengthens the response more than continuous reinforcement.

Fixed interval. Interval refers to time and thus the client is reinforced in intervals of time. 'Fixed interval is a schedule in which a person is reinforced for making a response only after a fixed period of time has passed since the previous reinforcement' (Miller, 1975). The client usually pauses after reinforcement and then gradually engages in the targeted behaviour and speeds up until reinforcement. The intervals of reinforcement are fixed.

Variable interval. 'Variable interval is a schedule in which a person is reinforced for making a response only after a varying period of time has passed since the previous reinforcement' (Miller, 1975). Clients typically respond at a uniform rate. The intervals of reinforcement vary.

Fixed ratio. Ratio refers to the amount of behaviour emitted. Reinforcement is based on the amount of behaviours. Miller (1975) states: 'Fixed ratio is a schedule in which a person is reinforced for making responses without reinforcement.' Clients typically pause after reinforcement and then work at a high rate until reinforced again. Reinforcement schedules are based on a fixed number of targeted behaviours emitted.

Variable ratio. 'Variable ratio is a schedule in which a person is reinforced for making a response only after he has conditioned reinforcement and generalised reinforcement to ensure that immediate consequences support those behaviours that lead to long-delayed reinforcers that we might not otherwise obtain' (Miller, 1975).

Differential reinforcement. 'Differential reinforcement involves two or more, physically different responses; one response is reinforced, and all others are extinguished' (Miller, 1975).

Differential reinforcement of low rate behaviour (DRL). 'Differential reinforcement of low rate behaviour (DRL) is a schedule of reinforcement which results in the reduction but rarely the elimination of behaviour' (Deitz, 1985).

Punishment

An argument can be made that they are the same, except derived from different conditioning modules. Punishment is similar to aversive conditioning and perhaps punishment can be effective when used correctly. There is some possible negative fall out if used alone.

Punishment is an operant procedure contingent upon the deviant response, whereas aversive therapy is based upon respondent procedures of pairing stimuli together to decrease targeted response.

Punishment is defined as 'an operant conditioning procedure in which the future rate or probability of occurrence of a response is reduced as a result of response-dependent delivery (positive punishment) or removal (negative punishment) of a stimulus (punisher). Punishment may weaken, strengthen, or have no effect on other response classes, but the procedure by definition weakens the response class for which it is arranged' (Poling, 1985). A punisher is any event that follows a response and decreases the rate of that response. Punishment typically employs an aversive stimulus or consequence contingent upon the target behaviour, but doesn't have to be. Punishment is the decrease of the targeted behaviour.

Miller (1975) describes four basic laws of using punishment:

- The Law of Contingent Punishment states that a punishing event will be more effective if it is delivered when, but **only when** the particular response to be punished occurs.
- The Law of Immediate Punishment states that a punishing event will be more effective if it is delivered quickly (within a minute) after the response to be punished occurs.
- The Law of Punisher Deprivation states that a punishing event will be more effective if it has **not** been delivered frequently in the near past.
- The Law of Punisher Size states that a punishing event will be more effective if it is **strong** (of large magnitude).

Miller (1975) uses the term punisher as any event that involves presenting or withdrawing a stimulus that decreases the response.

Guidelines for Using Punishment (Martin and Pear, 1983):

1. Selecting a response: Punishment is more effective with a specific behaviour, rather than a general category of behaviour.
2. Maximise the conditions for a desirable (non-punished) alternative response:
   a. Select a desirable alternative behaviour that competes with the behaviour to be punished such that alternative behaviour can be reinforced. If possible, select a behaviour

that will be maintained by the natural environment after the termination of your reinforcement programme.

b. Provide strong prompts to increase the likelihood that the desirable alternative behaviour will occur.

c. Reinforce the desirable behaviour with a powerful reinforcer on an appropriate schedule.

3. Minimise the causes of the response to be punished:

a. Try to identify and eliminate many or all of the stimuli controlling the undesirable behaviour, early in the training programme.

b. Try to eliminate any possible reinforcement for the undesirable behaviour.

4. Select an effective punisher:

a. Choose an effective punisher that can be presented immediately following the undesirable behaviour.

b. The punisher should be one that will in no way be paired with positive reinforcement following every instance of the undesirable behaviour.

5. Delivering the punisher:

a. The punisher should be presented immediately following every instance of the response to be decreased.

b. The individual administering the punisher should do so in a calm and matter-of-fact manner.

c. The person doing the punishing should also be associated with a lot of positive reinforcement for alternative behaviours, so that the person does not become a conditioned punisher.

6. Carefully monitor by checking for side effects and collecting data.

Punishment contingence can be established for sex offender behaviours. This can be effective within individual settings and also in residential settings. For example, specific negative consequences can be contingently set up for target behaviours.

Social learning

The last major classical behavioural learning theory is social learning. Social learning is based on learning through observation. People observe behaviour and imitate them. There are several tactics listed below.

Modelling. Modelling encompasses observational learning and imitation:

Imitation is the observation and then displaying of this series of responses. Observational learning . . . refers to the learning that occurs from the observation of others, and often the behaviours learned are not precisely imitated . . . there are several steps that seem to be of considerable importance. These include: (1) The attentional process itself (e.g., sensory capacity, arousal level, perceptual set and post reinforcement); (2) Retention processors (symbolic coding, motor rehearsal, and cognitive organisation; (3) Motor reproduction processes (e.g., physical capabilities, accuracy, feedback, and availability of component responses); (4) Motivational processes (external reinforcement, self-reinforcement).

(Matson, 1985).

The effectiveness of modelling depends upon clarity and proficiency.

Imitation Training.

Imitation training is a specific form of discrimination training consisting of three parts: (1) The teacher demonstrates what behaviour the learner is to engage in (called the imitative stimulus); (2) The learner is called on to produce a similar behaviour (called the imitative behaviour); and (3) The teacher arranges for some type of reinforcement for the imitative behaviour. The imitative stimulus is an S d for the imitative behaviour.

(Miller, 1975).

Observational Learning.

Observational learning . . . refers to the learning that occurs from the observation of others, and often the behaviours learned are not precisely imitated . . .

(Matson, 1985).

Behavioural Rehearsal.

Behavioural rehearsal is the term used to describe a specific procedure which aims to replace deficient or inadequate social or interpersonal responses by efficient and effective behaviour patterns. The patient achieves this by practicing the desired forms of behaviour under the direction of the therapist.

(Lazarus 1985)

Behavioural Role Rehearsal. Role rehearsal is instructing the client to enact or act out a behaviourally-oriented script.

Behavioural Reverse Role Rehearsal. Clients are instructed to reverse roles or scripts (Lazarus, 1985).

Participant Modelling.

This approach requires the client to be exposed to and actually practice gradually approaching phobic situations. However, social reinforcement is not emphasised. Instead, the critical variable is thought to be a therapist model who shows graded approaches to the phobic stimulus in the presence of the client.

(Martin and Pear, 1983).

The above discussion outlines the basics concerning behavioural theory. Originally, most arousal control techniques were strictly behavioural in nature. Of course, many of the techniques and strategies listed in this book can be used for arousal control.

Aversive conditioning

Aversive conditioning was defined by Marshall (1983) as 'a variety of techniques involving systematic presentation of noxious stimuli in cases marked by an inability of the patient to either control or resist enacting certain behaviours . . . This common process is usually thought to be conditioning of one kind or another . . .' Various applications of aversive conditioning share certain features in common. The stimulus conditions which elicit the unacceptable behaviour, and perhaps the unacceptable behaviour itself, are recreated or allowed to occur, and they are associated with an unpleasant experience. Typically, the unpleasant experience follows the onset of the aberrant stimulus or behaviour. It is used to counteract the power of undesirable reinforcer (Martin and Pear, 1983). It 'involves the repeated pairing (that is, over a number of trials) of an undesirable reinforcer with an aversive event' (Martin and Pear, 1983). It de-potentiates the unwanted reinforcer.

Aversive conditioning is a derivative of classical conditioning and learning by association via the pairing of a deterrent stimuli with deviant response/stimulus. It is also a derivative of operant conditioning (learning by consequences) as an event follows the deviant response.

Applications for aversive therapy (Martin and Pear, 1983):

1. During conditioning trials, the onset of the stimulus to be made aversive (that is, the undesirable reinforcer) is generally followed 0.5 to 1.0 seconds later by the aversive stimulus. The pairing continues for a few seconds, and then the two stimuli terminate at approximately the same time.
2. The client is encouraged to experience the undesirable reinforcer (or its symbolic representations) as fully as possible while also experiencing the aversive stimulus. The aversive stimulus must be strong enough to transmit its effects to the undesirable reinforcer, rather than the other way around.

3. The termination of the aversive stimulus is usually paired with a stimulus that the client wishes to have as a positive reinforcer that will replace the undesirable reinforcer.
4. Reinforcement is normally arranged in the natural environment so as to follow instances when the client chooses the desirable alternative reinforcer over the undesirable reinforcer.
5. Occasional booster aversion therapy sessions may be required to maintain the low reinforcing value of the undesirable reinforcer . . . (p237).

Electric shocks are used because: (a) easy to use; (b) instant delivery; (c) intensity and duration can be controlled; (d) used repeatedly; and (e) is aversive to most people.

There are several different applications for sex offenders as set out below:

Aversive stimuli vary across six dimensions:
1. Intensity
2. Duration
3. Individualised adverseness and uniqueness
4. Economised or economical
5. Ease of use
6. Acceptability (Maletzky, 1991)

Goals of aversive conditioning include:
- Reducing sexual arousal levels.
- Reducing the ability to generate deviant (pleasurable) sexual fantasies.
- Reducing excitement associated with devious behaviour.
- Producing anxiety for offenders in the proximity of deviant stimuli (Jensen, 1994).

Effective elements of aversive conditioning:
- Diminish arousal to zero during each treatment.
- Be self-administered.
- Requires a brief period of time.
- Be administered daily.
- Be administered in the morning.
- Should generalise to similar stimulus.
- Should not be offensive to the client's values.
- Should not be extremely uncomfortable.
- Should include specific description of the client's behaviour and fantasies.
- Should not reinforce cognitive distortions.
- Should include methods to control spontaneous fantasy arousal.
- Should work without conscious violation to control arousal (Jensen, 1994).

He goes on to emphasise five effective elements of any aversion:

1. Self-administered any time or place.
2. Doesn't require special apparatus.
3. Simple to learn.
4. Cost effective and ethically applied.
5. Reduction of arousal that can be measured.

Jensen, (1994) outlines several legal/ethical issues concerning enforced consent:

- Explanation of procedures/purposes.
- Descriptions of expected discomforts.
- Descriptions of benefits.
- Disclosure of appropriate alternative procedure.
- Answer enquires about the procedure.
- Instruction about the subject and withdrawal from the process.

We would recommend the following procedure, which has been adopted from Jensen (1994):

1. Identify inappropriate deviant response pattern or deviant arousal as indicated by a thorough assessment.
2. Select the most effective (ethical) aversive stimulus to the offender.
3. Elicit the deviant response.
4. Follow it immediately by an aversive event.
5. Repeat the procedure.

Olfactory aversion

Olfactory aversion is the use of odour as the aversive stimulus is presented with the targeted undesirable behaviour and stimulus. The pairing of the intense odour disrupts inappropriate arousal. Maletzky (1991) outlines several advantages of olfactory aversion:

1. Precise timing of presentation.
2. Little technical equipment needed.
3. Odour is long lasting, stable and made more effective.
4. High client acceptance.

Minimal Arousal Conditioning (MAC) (Jensen, 1994)

MAC was developed and perfected by Steve Jensen and is presented below in its entirety.

1. Treatment is preceded by the inmate writing a detailed description of his arousing deviant fantasy. The description is two to three pages in length including:

- Use of all physical senses.
- A description of the setting.
- How the victim was groomed for the assault.
- The victim's response during the assault.

- An exact accounting of the progression of sexual behaviour.
- The offenders thoughts and feelings throughout the assault.
- How the assault was terminated.

An inmate having multiple paraphilias is instructed to develop a description representing all forms of his inappropriate behaviour and fantasies.

2. Upon completion of the written description, the offender's arousal level to the material is assessed with the plethysmograph.
Non arousal or low arousal, less than 20%, is evaluated to determine casual factors. Remedial steps are taken including rewriting the description so that it is more arousing.

3. Treatment consists of the offender reading the deviant scenario in the privacy of his own room.

The primary premise of MAC is that inappropriate behaviour will be more effectively reduced and controlled if the punishment is powerful enough to inhibit the undesirable behaviour (arousal) after a few trials. To accomplish this goal, the reinforcing value of the behaviour cannot exceed the potency of the punishment.

Noxious odors (spirit of ammonia) were identified as the simplest and most portable method of punishment for deviant arousal. Due to the difficulty in securing a more potent and efficient means of aversion, and the health hazards associated with intensifying the level of noxious odour used, it was decided that the level of stimulus would be reduced. This resulted in the punishment consistently impacting the stimulus with such force that deviant arousal was repeatedly and significantly reduced. This caused a reduction in arousal to near baseline levels within one to ten aversion trials in a single setting.

The second limitation observed in traditional approaches to arousal control was the use of stimulus that was not directly related to the individual's deviant act or fantasies. The use of descriptions of the individual's actual behaviour or fantasies more effectively impacts his ability to regenerate these fantasies and pair them with arousal.

Jensen describes Minimal Arousal Conditioning (MAC) below and provides a description of the actual procedure as it is currently being used:

1. The offender is asked to write a detailed description of one of his most arousing deviant

experiences. This description is usually a 2–3 page long detailed narration of the events surrounding and including the offence. The narration should include the setting, how the victim was approached and their responses during the entire incident, an exact accounting of the progression of sexual behaviour, the offender's thoughts throughout the offence and a description of how the offence was terminated.

2. If the offender has been involved in multiple paraphilias, he is instructed to develop descriptions, which will represent all forms of his inappropriate behaviour and fantasies.

3. The worker reviews the description to determine whether or not it contains sufficient detail and to eliminate cognitive distortions, which would continue to support his deviant thinking. The client is then assessed on a penile plethysmograph, while he is reading his description out loud to determine where in his description significant arousal begins. Significant arousal is considered to be 5% to 10% of full erection. After the assessment the offender and worker identify the point in his description at which significant arousal was first detected. This is the point in his description at which significant arousal was first detected. This is the point at which aversion will be applied. The offender places this segment on audiotape or reads the written description, whichever produces the most arousal.

4. The offender is then instructed in the daily practice of **Minimal Arousal Conditioning**. It is suggested that he find a private, comfortable setting where he reads or listens to an audio tape version of his description. It is stressed that he read **only up to the point of significant arousal** and then immediately punish this arousal by inhaling 'spirit of ammonia' 20 times in succession. After each repetition, the offender logs his estimate of arousal and estimation of effectiveness of punishment on his 'aversion chart'. This process is performed at home on a daily basis, at his own convenience. It appears as though this process is most effective if performed shortly after the client wakes up. The clients' progress is reviewed every two weeks and he is assessed on his entire description. It may be necessary to move the client further on in his description to achieve control over his entire description. Regardless of whether it is necessary to read further through their description, most offenders have reduced arousal to their entire description in 12 to 18

weeks. This same procedure continues to be used with each description until arousal to all the descriptions are below the 5% level.

5. When the offender demonstrates at least four weeks of deviant arousal below 5% and, has equally low responses to similar stimulus material he moves to the second stage of arousal control which is described as 'maintenance'.

6. The maintenance phase involves application of the same basic technique but utilises covert aversive scenes in place of inhaling ammonia spirits. As the offender demonstrates continued control over his undesirable arousal he is instructed to diminish the frequency of his daily aversion programme.

Most offenders can effectively maintain control over arousal by continuing covert sensitisation or olfactory aversion (20 repetitions) one to two times per week. All offenders are cautioned that deviant arousal will return and they should be prepared to use olfactory aversion on a daily schedule to again reduce this arousal to maintenance levels. This will usually require less than two weeks.

Descriptions of olfactory aversion techniques in the literature usually end at this point. However, application of any arousal control technique alone will not maintain arousal control over time without the employment of other treatment techniques (Jensen, 1994 p1–3).

Jensen (1994) warns that aversion techniques alone lead to a response suppression, however do not necessarily eliminate the response. In the absence of a rewarding alternative sexual response (healthy sexual relationships), the suppressed response will return.

Covert sensitisation

Covert sensitisation is a popular covert technique based upon classical conditioning theory. Offenders are carefully instructed to imagine an aversive scene or events that are 'negative' to the offender. The aversive stimulus is imagined and not a real physical entity as defined below.

Cautela (1985b) defines covert sensitisation as 'procedure that is analogous to the operant procedure of punishment . . . The term covert is used because both the behaviour to be reduced in frequency and the consequence are imagined . . .' Martin and Pear (1983) state that 'covert sensitisation . . . involves having the client imagine both the undesirable reinforcer and the aversive stimulus. This procedure is so named because the pairing of the stimulus occurs only in the client's imagination (in other words, it is covert) and the anticipated result of this covert pairing process is the undesirable reinforcer becomes aversive (that is, the client becomes sensitised to it.)'. For example the client who wants to quit smoking is instructed to imagine smoking and while inhaling becoming violently sick, gagging while everyone is staring in disgust. He then imagines turning away from the cigarette. Technically, this is not punishment. Punishment is the decrease of a response followed by a stimulus. Sensitisation refers to being sensitised or taught to avoid maladaptive behaviour (Cautela, 1985b).

The general procedure consists of:

- Selecting a target response to be decreased.
- Instructing the offender to imagine performing the target behaviour.
- Instructing the offender to imagine an aversive stimulus.
- Pairing the target behaviour with a covert aversive stimulus several times to numerous times until the targeted response is decreased.

Jensen (1994) has outlined a procedure for covert sensitisation as follows:

Covert Sensitisation
1. Selection criteria:
   - Offenders are unable to use ammonia treatment due to medical conditions.
   - Offenders who have reached the maintenance phase of minimal arousal conditioning.
   - Offenders who are to be released into the community within six months.
2. Treatment procedure:
   - Offender verbalises into tape recorder one of his arousing deviant fantasy scenes up to the thought of sexual offending.
   - The scene is then shifted to an extremely aversive scene.
     - Aversive scenes focus on situations, which may be painful, frightening, sickening or humiliating to the offender.
     - Scenes should focus on as many sensory images as possible.
   - Aversive scenes are then shifted to an escape scene.
     - The escape scene pairs appropriate behaviour with cognitive and material rewards.
     - Positive rewards might include:
       (a) Not responding to deviant stimulus situations.

       (b) Assertive behaviour.
       (c) Appropriate sexual behaviour.
       (d) Using skills learned in treatment.
   - The offender does one session daily, three to five days per week.
     Sessions consists of two complete cycles. A cycle is defined as:
     – Deviant lead up.
     – Aversive scene.
     – Escape scene.
   - During each session, inmate records on the covert sensitisation chart his levels of arousal to deviant scene, level of discomfort to the aversive scene and level of sensitisation to escape scene.
   - Tapes are reviewed by staff after the offender has filled one tape (one hour of tape of four 15 minute sessions) to ensure compliance and effectiveness of procedure.
3. Completion criteria:
   - The procedure continues until offender has successfully completed 10 tapes, with minimal arousal to deviant scene and maximum discomfort to aversive scene.
   - Assessment on plethysmography reveals below 10% arousal to deviant scene.
   - Upon completion of procedure offender writes a three to five page paper describing the effectiveness of the treatment and how to use the technique in the community e.g., high risk factors, cues, etc., which suggest the need to implement it.

The essence of covert sensitisation is sensitising the client to a noxious stimulus event via imagery in the presence of deviant response and for stimulus. Marshall (1993) emphasises the importance of cataloging the sequence early. A summarised procedure includes:

- Constructing deviant scripts with response sequences (cycle).
- Writing them out on index cards.
- Constructing several possible catastrophic/negative consequences.
- Writing them out on cards.
- Offenders carry cards around.
- Reading each card and consequence at least three times per day.
- Reporting progress and problems.

Another simple procedure includes:

- Identifying and defining a targeted deviant response (i.e., some aspect of offending and the excitement of the offending).

- Identifying a covert behaviour (image of something) that effectively interrupts, defuses, spoils and decreases the deviant behaviour. Remember many offenders get 'off' or turned on by 'negative, painful, gross' events.
- Instructing the offender to pair off associate (through imagery) deviant response (i.e., fantasy or some aspect of offending) with the selected image (of an event) that decreases or spoils the behaviour.
- Monitoring the outcome to ensure the offender is decreasing the deviant response.
- Repeating the pairing numerous times. The goal is to spoil the pleasurable deviant behaviour. This is an excellent fantasy crasher for motivated offenders.

Maletzky (1991) outlines three components to any covert conditioning scene:

1. Build up on sexual arousal associated with deviant stimulus.
2. Negative affect connected with deviant response such as disgust, (i.e. sores, vomit, fear, etc.) pain of some sort, causing emotional/physical pain to others (remorseful responses), embarrassment and natural adverse consequences.

Maletzky (1991) outlines several factors to be considered:

- De-condition important sexual fantasies.
- Construct scene from the offender's own language.
- Don't need overly detailed scenes, just enough to facilitate imagery.
- Include offender participation in arranging negative images (the most unpleasant).
- Use flexibility as offenders vary on timing and detail of scene.
- Realistic presentation.
- Sessions could include three scene presentations with hypnotic relaxation induction to facilitate the imagery process.
- Stop or interrupt the chain early.

Assisted Covert Sensitisation (ACS)

ACS involves the covert processes along with a physical event. A classical definition is 'ACS is a form of aversive therapy in which noxious stimuli are combined with descriptions and fantasies of unwanted behaviour . . . and extension of covert sensitisation . . . However, only the presenting or unconditioned stimuli are covert; the aversive or conditioned stimuli are real and can consist of electric shock' (Maletzky, 1985).

There are three basic steps:

1. Relaxation training.
2. The generation of scene depicting the target behaviour.
3. Pairing of scenes with aversive stimuli.

Applied to sex offenders, it is used with offenders that cannot develop a list of covert scenes (Krauth and Smith, 1989). Typically, a noxious odour is used to enhance the covert imagery.

A specific procedure includes:

- Offenders list noxious unpleasant covert scene.
- Offenders engage in deviant fantasies/imagery.
- Arousal may be monitored.
- Offenders engage in noxious images and exposed to noxious stimulus.
- Responses are monitored.

Aversive behavioural rehearsal

Aversive behavioural rehearsal has also been referred to as shame aversion. Aversive behavioural rehearsal or shame aversion is defined as the individual who engages in the targeted behaviour for attention or reinforcement by others and is instructed to perform the behaviour in front of selected staff, and staff respond neutral, non-emotional, etc. (Bellack, 1985b). This is used with exhibitionists. This technique involves offenders re-creating offences in a different context, thus inducing a different meaning or meanings (or a meaning of demeaning). For example, Maletzky (1991) describes some authors instructing exhibitionists to expose themselves to staff (who have been previously instructed to respond neutrally) and thus neutralising the offenders expected victim response.

Dougher (1988) outlines a seven-step strategy:

1. Offenders describe offences in detail.
2. Appropriate props (mannequins, clothing, etc.) are obtained.
3. The offender relives the offence in the presence of staff and group.
4. The session may be video taped.
5. The offender verbalises the following specific plans, methods of control, grooming, type of dress, feelings and thoughts, etc.
6. If the sessions are emotionally charged, then debriefing or processing may be needed.
7. The tapes are played and narrated by the offender, explaining thoughts, feelings and actions.

The responses are to be processed in group therapy. Maletzky (1991) provides several advantages of this approach:

- It requires no equipment.
- It is inexpensive.
- It works quickly and effectively.

The drawbacks include:

- Difficulty in getting consent in some cases.
- Difficult in getting staff to observe.

Masturbatory satiation

Masturbatory satiation has been referred to us as masturbatory reconditioning, orgasmic reconditioning, directive masturbation (Marshall, 1993). The purpose is to reduce subjective and psycho-physiological distress associated with obsessional thoughts or images. 'The treatment procedure essentially consists of prompting or instructing clients to form or image the obsession for prolonged periods of time. Often, clients are asked to verbalise the disturbing thought continuously while focusing on the image representing the thought' (Last, 1985).

'Masturbation therapy involves the offender's masturbating to ejaculation in response to appropriate fantasies' (Krauth and Smith). If arousal occurs, then offenders switch to appropriate images.

A procedure was developed from Dougher (1988), Krauth and Smith (1989) and Marshall (1993):

1. Identify targeted deviant behaviour.
2. Instruct offenders to masturbate to appropriate stimuli.
3. Verbalise fantasy into tape recorder during entire masturbation session.
4. Masturbate to ejaculation (to appropriate stimulus).
5. Allow for a two minute relaxation period and continue to masturbate with a flaccid penis to deviant fantasy for 50 minutes to two hours.
6. Closely monitor responses.

The overall goal enhances appropriate responses and decreases deviant response. Maletzky (1991) discusses the essence of the technique: 'This type of reconditioning relies on the belief (not yet objectively verified) that sexual drive is lowest just after ejaculation. Masturbating at that time, the sexual offender begins to associate deviant fantasies with a low

sex drive. Indeed to have to masturbate then is quite likely to be an aversive event . . . The post-ejaculation masturbation period should be prolonged to enhance the boredom, extinction of, or aversion toward deviant arousal.

Maletzky (1991) outlines two elements of satiation:

1. Masturbation to non-deviant fantasies at the time of maximal arousal.
2. Masturbation to deviant fantasies at the time of minimal arousal.

Verbal satiation

Verbal satiation is similar to masturbatory conditioning except the procedure is verbal. Verbal satiation involves the offender repeatedly verbalising deviant fantasies for at least three minutes on at least three occasions per week (Krauth and Smith, 1993).

A procedure was developed from Dougher (1988) and Krauth and Smith (1989):

1. The deviant behaviour is targeted.
2. Offenders masturbate and ejaculate to appropriate fantasies.
3. Offenders then engage in deviant fantasies in the post-refectory period.
4. Fantasies are recorded as the offender verbalises them, the entire period of time (30 minutes).
5. The responses are unconditioned.

Fantasy alteration

Fantasy alteration provides a bridge for offenders who do not get aroused to appropriate stimuli or fantasies, in order to learn new responses. Offenders are instructed to initiate arousal through masturbation to deviant fantasy and then switch to appropriate fantasy (Maletzky, 1991). It is important to switch before and maintain the switch during ejaculation. All fantasy work can be taped to ensure compliance.

A procedure consists of:

1. Identifying a deviant fantasy.
2. Briefly writing the deviant fantasy out.
3. Identifying a 'normal' non-deviant fantasy.
4. Writing the fantasy out in detail.
5. Instructing the offender to begin masturbating to the deviant fantasy.
6. Upon obtaining arousal, instruct the offender to quickly switch.
7. Ensuring the offender switches, by perhaps using tape recorders, etc.

Each time the offender switches early, monitor the offender early (Maletzky, 1991).

Vicarious sensitisation/conditioning
Dowd (1985) defines vicarious conditioning as 'a social learning procedure in which behaviour or emotional reactions are altered by observation of modelling displays, rather than by direct performance . . . In vicarious operant conditioning, the model is observed being reinforced (or punished) for performance of the target. Thus, learning occurs indirectly from observation only.

Boredom techniques in general
Boredom techniques have been associated with satiation techniques (Jensen, 1994). Both techniques play on boredom as an aversive element paired to deviant fantasy/arousal. A detailed procedure was outlined by Jensen (1994):

Boredom Treatment/Verbal Satiation
Selection Criteria:
- Offender is unable to use ammonia treatment due to medical condition.
- Offender who demonstrates 10% arousal to various deviant stimuli.
- May be used in conjunction with MAC.

Treatment Procedure:
1. Treatment is preceded by the offender writing a detailed description of his most arousing deviant fantasy.
   - The description is two to three pages in length.
   - Uses all senses, written in first person, present tense.
   - Is a description of the setting stating:
     - How the victim was groomed for the assault.
     - Victim's responses during the assault.
     - An exact accounting of the progression of sexual behaviour.
     - The offender's thoughts and feelings throughout the assault.
     - How assault was terminated.
2. Upon completion of the written scenario, the offender arousal level is assessed with penile plethysmography.
   - Non or low arousal (below 20%) is evaluated to determine causal factors.
   - Remedial steps are taken including rewriting the description to increase arousal.

3. The offender numbers each statement in the scene and then rates the statement from the lowest to the highest arousal.
4. The offender writes detailed description of an appropriate adult consenting sexual fantasy.
   - The description is two to three pages in length.
   - It is written in present tense, first person, using all senses.
   - It focuses on mutually caring aspects of the relationship, including phrases of affection.
   - It includes a description of the sexual responses of the partner and the offender.
5. Upon completion of the written description, the offender's arousal level is assessed by the plethysmograph.
   - Non or low arousal (below 50%) is evaluated to determine causal factors.
   - Remedial steps are taken including rewriting the description to increase arousal.
6. The offender begins the procedure by masturbating to his appropriate fantasy in the privacy of his cell.
   - Once the offender ejaculates or reaches orgasm, he records his level of arousal on his Boredom Tape chart.
   - The offender is instructed to stop masturbating to the fantasy if he does not believe he is going to achieve an orgasm (after 10 to 15 minutes) and is beginning to feel frustrated and is losing sexual interest/arousal to the appropriate fantasy.
   - This is to be recorded on the chart.
7. After the offender records his arousal level and whether he ejaculated, he turns on tape recorder.
8. The offender begins reading the statement in his deviant scene, which was assessed to be the least arousing.
9. At the end of the session, the offender records his beginning and end arousal level, overall highest arousal and boredom level at end of the session.
10. When the offender's arousal to the deviant statement is rated at zero arousal and boredom level at ten, he begins reading the next highest arousing statement at the next session.
11. Treatment is done five to seven days per week. (Tape recorders are not issued on weekends but inmates can do the procedure without a recorder).

12. The offender will be assessed monthly on the plethysmograph to determine if arousal levels to appropriate scenes are sufficiently high and if arousal to the deviant scene are decreasing.
13. Once the offender has completed all of his statements in the scenario, he completes the same process for another deviant scenario which is part of his deviant arousal pattern.

Boredom techniques involves pairing the boredom with the deviant behaviour so that the offender loses interest in the deviant sexual behaviour.

Conclusions

This chapter has set out a handful of selected behavioural techniques used specifically for arousal control and management. Arousal control is supported by Marshall (1996, 1999); Laws (1995, 1999) and McGrath (2001) supports both arousal control and covert sensitisation, assisted covert sensitisation and verbal satiation. The primary focus is on decreasing (if not extinguishing) deviant responses and increasing appropriate responses. The selected techniques include: aversion therapy, covert sensitisation, minimal arousal conditioning, olfactory aversive, assisted covert sensitisation, aversive behavioural rehearsal, masturbatory satiation, verbal satiation, fantasy alteration, and boredom techniques in general.

The general purposes of using these techniques are to alter the client's arousal. Timing is of the essence. Offenders have to be ready to use behavioural tactics. They have to have the desire, commitment and motivation, to get rid of their deviant behaviour. For the best results, in essence, the offenders have to have a desire to give up offending and maintain the goal, **no more victims**.

There are several warnings and contraindications. Behavioural tactics are not the entire treatment. It is only one component of treatment. These tactics are not magical. It is important to help offenders develop appropriate arousal patterns while decreasing and eliminating deviant behaviours. Behavioural approaches work best with motivated non-psychopathic offenders. It is recommended that a full evaluation (i.e., instruments, interview, penile plethysmography, phallometric assessments, self-report, polygraph, etc.) be given. It is very important to know the offender's deviant arousal patterns to establish an individualised treatment plan.

There are several contradictions. First, it is important that the behavioural treatment does not reinforce deviant behaviour. Thus, what is average to one offender may not be average to another. When using aversive approaches, the aversive stimuli need to be aversive or non-sexually/emotionally stimulating.

A second contradiction applies to the psychopathic offender. Psychopathic and chronic offenders would be more aroused to some behavioural techniques. Thus, boredom satiation techniques could increase deviant arousal as the offender would use them for deviant purposes. The third contradiction is medical condition. For aversion therapy, MAC or any related technique, offenders need to be periodically evaluated. Offenders who are sensitive to noxious odours or have breathing problems could increase health problems.

Behavioural treatments have been demonstrated to be effective, in conjunction with other components. Jensen (1994) suggests five steps for arousal control. They include:

1. Adversive Conditioning – in particular olfactory conditioning using ammonia.
2. Minimisation of Stimulus – the offender needs to minimise contact with persons and situations that produce deviant arousal.
3. Control of desire, fantasies and arousal – offenders are urged when faced with deviant response to: (a) remove self from the situation, (b) punish the behaviour with ammonia and (c) discuss with treatment personnel.
4. Cognitive restructuring – offenders are urged to identify and replace distorted thoughts that support deviancy.
5. Adult relationships – offenders are urged to develop appropriate intimate relationships.

References

Cautela J R (1985) Covert conditioning. In Bellack M and Hersen M (Eds.) *Dictionary of Behavior Therapy Technique*. NY: Pergamon Press.
Cautela J R (1985b) Covert sensitization. In Bellack M and Hersen M (Eds.) *Dictionary of Behavior Therapy Technique*. NY: Pergamon Press.
Cautela J R (1985c) Covert extinction. In Bellack M and Hersen M (Eds.) *Dictionary of Behavior Therapy Technique*. NY: Pergamon Press.
Deitz S M (1985) Differential reinforcement of low rate behavior. In Bellack M and Hersen M

(Eds.) *Dictionary of Behavior Therapy Technique.* NY: Pergamon Press.

Douglas M (1988) Behavioral techniques to alter sexual arousal. In Schwartz B (Ed.) *A Practitioner's Guide to Treating the Incarcerated Male Sex Offender.* Washington, DC: NIC, 109–14.

Dowd E T (1985) Vicarious conditioning. In Bellack M and Hersen M (Eds.) *Dictionary of Behavior Therapy Technique.* NY: Pergamon Press.

Hersen M (Eds.) *Dictionary of Behavior Therapy Technique.* NY: Pergamon Press.

Jensen S H (1994) Minimal arousal conditioning. Unpublished manuscript.

Kratochwill T (1985) Classical conditioning. In Bellack M and Hersen M (Eds.) *Dictionary of Behavior Therapy Technique.* NY: Pergamon Press.

Krauth B and Smith R (1988) *Administrator's Overview: questions and answers on issues related to the incarcerated male sex offender.* Washington, DC: NIC.

Last C (1985) Satiation training. In Bellack M and Hersen M (Eds.) *Dictionary of Behavior Therapy Technique.* NY: Pergamon Press.

Laws D R (1995) Verbal satiation: Notes on procedure with speculations on its mechanism of effect. *Sexual Abuse: A Journal of Research and Treatment.* 7: 155–66.

Laws D R (2001) Olfactory aversion: Notes on procedure with speculations on its mechanism of effect. *Sexual Abuse: A Journal of Research and Treatment.* 13 (4): 275–87.

Lazarus A (1985) Rehearsal. In Bellack M and Hersen M (Eds.) *Dictionary of Behavior Therapy Technique.* NY: Pergamon Press.

McGrath R (2001) Utilizing behavioral techniques to control sexual arousal. Carich M S and Mussack S E (Eds.) *Handbook of Sexual Abuser Assessment and Treatment.* Brandon, VT: Safer Press.

Maletzky B M (1985) Assisted cover sensitization. Bellack M and Hersen M (Eds.) *Dictionary of Behavior Therapy Technique.* NY: Pergamon Press.

Maletzky B M (1991) Treating the sexual offender. Newbury Park, CA: Sage.

Marshall W L (1985) Aversive conditioning. In Hersen M (Ed.) *Dictionary of Behavior Therapy Technique.* NY: Pergamon Press.

Marshall W L (1993) Personnal communication to Mark S Carich.

Martin G and Pear J (1983) Behavioral modification: what it is and how to do it. Englewood Cliffs, NJ: Prentice Hall.

Matson J (1985) Modelling. In Bellack M and Hersen M (Eds.) *Dictionary of Behavior Therapy Technique.* NY: Pergamon Press.

Miller S (1975) Principles of everyday behavioral analysis. Monteray, CA: Brooks/Cole Publishing Company.

Poling A (1985) Positive reinforcement. In Bellack M and Hersen M (Eds.) *Dictionary of Behavior Therapy Technique.* NY: Pergamon Press.

Chapter Eight

Relapse Prevention and Intervention Strategies

Introduction and overview

Since 1985, relapse prevention (RP) models have been very popular in the treatment of addictions, including alcohol (Marlatt and Gordon, 1985) and more recently sex offenders (Carich et al., 2001; Laws, 1989; Pithers and Gray, 1996). The traditional RP model has undergone major revisions as professionals have realised that there are multiple pathways to facilitate and learn self-management strategies (Hudson and Ward, 1996a; 1996b; Ward and Hudson, 1996b). It emerged to help offenders avoid risky situations and rehearse coping strategies to mitigate the influence of high-risk situations that could not be avoided.

RP was originally seen as a linear process compared to the assault cycle, which was a circular concept. It was not until 1992 that the two concepts were used together (Freeman-Longo and Pithers, 1992). The cycle has become an important component of relapse prevention strategies. The offender needs to identify triggers for high- and low-risk factors by using relapse cues or warning signals. The offender identifies his cycle and learns various coping behaviours to defuse and intervene. By using the assault cycle concept (outlined in Chapter 4), RP can also be used to initiate change and maintain treatment gains. Indeed, the RP model can be seen as an extension of the cycle or relapse process, enhancing supervision at both internal and external levels, coping strategies, competence and self-efficacy (Laws, 1995).

It has now come to be used as a primary (but not exclusive) component in the treatment of sex offenders. For example, nearly 90% of all programmes in North America used RP as a component in treatment (Freeman-Longo, Bird, Stevenson and Fiske, 1995). There have, however, been a number of changes made to Marlatt's original model when applied to sex offenders.

The self-management model only applies if the offender's life remains free from notable distress. Many offenders deviate as a response to distress or maladaptive attempts to alleviate perceived distress; a belief that external support is necessary to help offenders, particularly as others are more reliable informants about risk factors than offenders themselves (highlighting also that relapses are due to both internal as well as external factors); and a belief that offenders need to begin to demonstrate recognition of the importance of employing their knowledge, even during those moments when they would rather not.

The focus of this chapter is to highlight and apply the primary elements of traditional RP as applied to sex offenders, along with some variations and modifications. The emphasis of this chapter is on applications of the assault cycle concept and RP.

Goals of treatment

The goals of RP are divided up into generalised and specific goals. The general goals of RP include:

- Teaching the offender appropriate skills to prevent a relapse, including an enhanced ability to detect the earliest signs of risk and reliable coping responses that may be used to lessen risk.
- Developing external sources of supervision, including people who are explicitly aware of the offender's crime, risk factors, and coping strategies and who have been trained in the relapse prevention model.
- Reducing the risk of re-offence, relapse and deviancy by utilising relapse interventions.

Some specific goals of relapse prevention or intervention programmes include the following:

- The offender understands the concepts of RP and the assault cycle.
- The offender understands how to apply the concepts of RP and in particular the assault cycle or patterns of the offence; as this includes all precursors and cursors to the offence and the aftermath.
- To learn effective methods of monitoring self.
- To learn specific indicators or cues of offending patterns, that signify when risk factors are present or imminent.
- To identify specific risk factors, triggering events and other precursors to the offence

Figure 8.1: A cognitive-behavioural model of the relapse process.

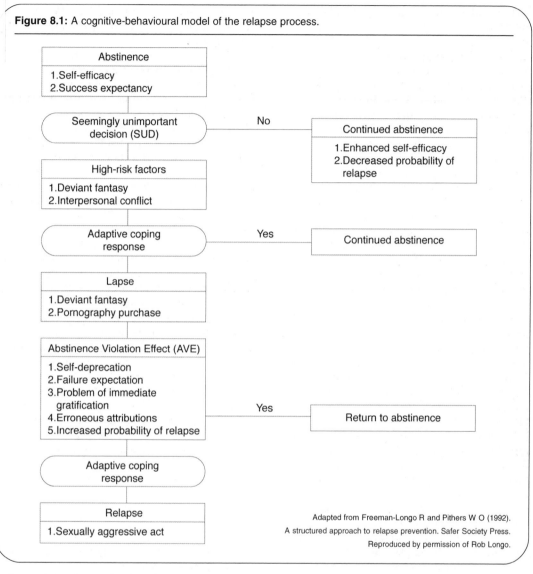

Adapted from Freeman-Longo R and Pithers W O (1992).
A structured approach to relapse prevention. Safer Society Press.
Reproduced by permission of Rob Longo.

(i.e., motivating and other developmental factors).

- To learn specific interventions to defuse the relapse process.
- To learn specific coping strategies.

In essence, RP and its modifications centre on creating and providing multiple sources of supervision (Pithers, 1990); enhancing the offender's skills in identifying various risk factors and/or situations when they may re-offend (Carich, Steckel and Stone, 1994; Freeman-Longo and Pithers, 1992; Laws, 1989; Gray and Pithers, 1993), and enhancing the offender's management or coping skills to prevent a relapse.

An overview of traditional RP

Figure 8.1 offers a sequential guide to the specific relapse determinants that sex offenders may experience as they progress closer to the point of re-offending, within a cognitive behavioural framework. It represents initial attempts to explain the chain of cognitive and behavioural events experienced as sex offenders move from being in adequate behavioural control to abusing again. Not all offenders proceed uniformly through the stages in sequence or indeed through all the stages before they offend. Although the figure presents a common pathway toward offences, the essence of RP is that it must be applied uniquely to each offender, thus maximising the likely outcomes.

Abstinence, lapse and relapse

Abstinence is the primary goal in sex offender treatment. It is the state of non-offending (Pithers, 1990) and is violated by a lapse, any slide toward re-offending. For example, generating deviant fantasies is considered a lapse. Given the seriousness of sexual offending and relapse behaviour, the concept of relapse has been defined as any sexual offence or violation. With other types of problems, relapse is referred to as the return to previous levels of the particular problematic behaviour. Yet there are multiple levels of relapse with sex offenders. The lowest level includes non-contact sexual offending behaviours, while the highest exceeds the previous level and seriousness of offending (Ward and Hudson, 1996 a and b). For example, obscene phone calling or exhibitionism is not considered as serious as rape or physical abuse. Most rapists and child molesters engage in several less serious offending behaviours prior to rape or physical sexual violation of another individual. In essence, lapses are precursors to relapse. In learning that relapse is a process occurring over time, offenders discover that they have many opportunities to control their behaviours to avoid abusing again. Offenders report experiencing greater hopefulness about their potential to change as they begin to unearth the patterns of behaviour that precedes their abuse, with each precursor to past offences now viewed as an opportunity to avoid re-offending (Carich et al., 2001).

RP is based on the approach that offenders learn strategies to maintain abstinence. Abstinence for sex offenders, is a lifestyle of not committing sexually aggressive behaviours (Freeman-Longo and Pithers, 1992). Abstinence hinges on at least two essential ingredients: (1) self-efficacy and (2) successful expectancy. Both are based on the assumption that the offender has the skills and the motivation to maintain abstinence. Self-efficacy is the offender's perception that can appropriately handle situations to prevent relapse. This involves a successful expectancy (self-fulfilling prophecy) that the offender will maintain abstinence. Abstinence is maintained by skills, commitment and the belief in oneself. The offender thus believes they have a sense of control while maintaining abstinence and this perception remains until they encounter a high-risk

situation. There are a number of different ways to look at offence precursors within the offending process:

Risk factors and triggering events

A high-risk factor (or trigger) is any event that brings the offender closer to offending (Hanson, 2000), threatening the offenders sense of control. If an offender in a high-risk situation enacts a coping response the probability of relapse decreases. However, if they fail to cope successfully with a high-risk situation, a decreased sense of hopelessness ensues. If these behaviours occur in a situation containing cues associated with past sexually abusive behaviours, relapse is likely.

Pithers et al. (1988) noted that the first determinant of relapse in many sex offenders was a change in predominant affect: frequently a response to disruption in their lifestyle, such as a critical interpersonal event or negative emotions such as anger and depression. Offenders who respond to a disruptive influence positively (exercising, asserting concerns) are utilising an adaptive coping response and are thus less likely to lapse or relapse. Those who respond negatively (e.g. masturbating as an escape from loneliness) utilise a maladaptive coping response and are more likely to lapse and beyond, to relapse. By definition, risk factors can be both offence cursors and precursors and the terms risk factors and triggering events are often used interchangeably.

A triggering event is any internal or external event or situation that initiates, stimulates or 'triggers' an offending-related response (i.e. cycle behaviour) or any part of the offence chain. Triggers may be categorised based on:

Content: Content refers to a substance type of trigger. Content categories include physiological, cognitive (thoughts and ideas), affective (feelings and moods), social or interpersonal), contextual or environmental, and behavioural or situational responses (Carich and Stone, 1996).

Magnitude: Magnitude refers to the intensity of the actual trigger in terms of stimulating an offending response. The magnitude ranges from low-risk (including seemingly unimportant, insignificant decisions or events that can lead to high-risk, lapse or actual relapse) to high-risk factors or situations (such as a high potential to trigger and lapse and/or relapse). Low-risk-factors appear to be low in magnitude of

Table 8.1: Examples of high-risk and low-risk triggers for child molesters and rapists.

Type of sexual offender	High-risk triggers	Low-risk triggers
Child molester	Jobs around children Babysitting Viewing programmes or movies about or for children Walking through parks or near schools alone Losing a job Losses in relationships Working with children Boredom Using drugs or alcohol Hanging around amusement parks	Adult pornography Living Walking through schools and parks with friends Being in close proximity to children for a short duration Negative peer group
Rapist	Sadistic pornography Sadistic fantasies Being out at night alone Picking up hitchhikers Using drugs or alcohol Getting insulted Working alone at night Conflict relationships Harbouring bitterness Using any pornography Negative peer group Losing a job Rejection Boredom	Going to a bar to socialise Running errands at night Engaging in power struggles Everyday stressors Pressures on a job Being out at night with peers Going to parties with peers

intensity; however they can escalate into high-risk or actual relapse behaviours. Traditionally it was thought that seemingly unimportant decisions occurred prior to high-risk.

Temporal factors: Freeman-Longo and Pithers (1992) and Gray and Pithers (1993) outlined three types of temporal factors subsumed under the risk factor umbrella: (a) predisposing risk factors (historical and developmental risk factors), (b) precipitating risk factors (occurring immediately prior to the offence) and (c) perpetuating risk factors (ongoing situations). Each type is sub-categorised with feelings, thoughts, behaviours and situations.

It is important for offenders to understand the concept of SUDs and low and high risk factors so that they can identify their own as a preface to developing strategies to effectively deal with them as and when they appear.

Relapse cues

Another major type of offence precursor is relapse cues. Relapse cues are any type of event that serves as a warning of a potential or actual risk factor or situation, lapse or relapse (Carich

et al., 2001). Cues are warnings, signals or red flags to the offender concerning potential problems and problematic situations. Like triggers, cues can be categorised by content, process and temporality of time of occurrence. Content cues include cognitive, affective, behavioural, social, physiological, contextual or situational. Temporal cues consist of (a) early warnings, (b) mid and late cues and (c) last-minute cues or warnings (Freeman-Longo and Pithers, 1992). Early warnings include putting blame on others, being argumentative and stubborn, being unable to concentrate, objectifying women or other targets, and experiencing loneliness. Mid and late cues include having deviant fantasies, drinking alcohol, walking around at night, seeing people as objects, looking at pornographic magazines, engaging in sex frequently, and feeling nervous. These may all reduce the offender's own prohibition against abusive acts. Last-minute cues include rapid heartbeat, shortness of breath, sweaty palms, excessive masturbation, having an erection and searching for victims. Cues are not triggers, although triggers may serve as cues. Cues do not initiate cycles. Several cues may occur with one trigger. This is referred to cue convergence (Gray and Pithers, 1993). Examples of various cues are outlined in Table 8.2.

Deviant fantasy is frequently identified as a principal determinant of relapse especially when accompanied by masturbation. This may

Table 8.2: Cue examples

Examples of early warning signals or cues

1. Putting blame on others
2. Being argumentative
3. Selective hearing
4. Being stubborn
5. Increased smoking
6. Being bored
7. Feeling restless
8. Spacing out
9. Loss of concentration
10. Eating a lot or not eating
11. Watching a lot of television
12. Self talk; 'I'm dumb, ugly' etc.
13. Worrying about things I have no control over
14. Horseplay
15. Feeling sleepy or tired a lot
16. Missing a shower
17. Not looking at someone talking
18. Gambling, cards, etc.
19. Objectifying women
20. Withdrawn
21. Isolation
22. Alienation
23. Feeling powerless
24. Feeling hopeless/helpless
25. Feeling weak and inadequate
26. Not using assertiveness
27. Paranoia
28. Needs to be on top
29. Jealousy
30. Loneliness
31. Confusion
32. Worthlessness
33. Missing work
34. Mind reading
35. Justifying
36. Blaming
37. Missing groups
38. Avoiding people
39. Searching for TV sex
40. Fallacy of fairness
41. Tunnel vision
42. Entitlement

Examples of mid/late warnings
Aid and late cues include the following:

1. Masturbating
2. Justifying
3. Deviant fantasies
4. Drinking alcohol, smoking pot
5. Being around kids
6. Being alone with women
7. Scanning
8. Walking around at night
9. Driving around at night
10. Flirting with needy women
11. Apathy
12. Feeling excited
13. Feeling pumped up
14. Heart beating fast
15. Seeing people as objects
16. Tunnel vision
17. Looking at porno magazines
18. Having a lot of sex
19. Believing I'm dumb
20. Looking for poofs
21. Quit going to group
22. Not going to work
23. Not taking care of yourself
24. Shortness of breath
25. Breathing really hard
26. Hand sweaty
27. Hands and legs shaking
28. Butterflies in stomach
29. Objectifying

Examples of DEW lines or last minute warnings
Last minute cues include the following:

1. Heart beating really fast
2. Mouth dry
3. Lump in my throat
4. Shortness of breath
5. Hands twitching
6. Hands and legs shaking
7. Butterflies in my stomach
8. Having an erection or hard on
9. Masturbation to deviant fantasies
10. Excessive masturbation
11. Searching for victims

be because the fantasy was congruent with the offenders state (angry or lonely) and this can allow the refinement of a proposed act of abuse.

Again it is important for offenders to identify their earliest cues and last-minute warnings to allow a plan for management to be effective. The earlier in the offending process the cycle can be broken, the better.

There are a variety of ways to help offenders identify triggers and cues. These include: journaling, life histories using any type of tracking formats, verbal/written case or offence reviews, creating general lists of triggers and cues, lists of precursors, etc. Triggers and cues can be highlighted from journals, offence reviews, and life histories (aspects pertaining to sexual deviancy). High and low risk factors can be distinguished by scaling or rating the magnitude of the trigger.

Abstinence violation effect

Whether a lapse becomes a relapse depends on a number of factors, one of which is called the AVE. A major source of the AVE is a conflict between the individual's self-image as an abstainer and their recent experience of a prohibited behaviour (e.g. a deviant sexual fantasy).

Pithers (1990) outlined a negative reaction that the offender experiences when he violates any type of internalised abstinence rules. It is predicated on the offender's desire to maintain abstinence. This concept encompasses five elements: self-depreciation, failure expectation, problem of immediate gratification erroneous attributions and increased probability of relapse (Freeman-Longo and Pithers, 1992, p56). When lapsing, the offender's thoughts, beliefs, feelings and behaviours change, to the point, that one may conclude a lack of willpower and a destiny of failure. Offenders learn that there is no 'cure' or absence of sexual deviant problems. This leads to the PIG. The PIG is the problem of immediate gratification. This occurs as part of the AVE. PIG experiences are urges or cravings to commit sexual offences (Pithers, 1990). It is the perceived need for immediate gratification. Offenders are taught to 'ride out' the PIG and these needs will disappear.

Ward and colleagues have re-analysed the AVE Concept (Ward and Hudson, 1996b; Ward, Hudson, and Marshall, 1994) and concluded that the AVE only applies to those offenders who fit the following criteria:

- Have a commitment to abstinence.

- Have some form of empathy and remorse.
- Offenders who are not further in treatment.
- Offenders with high levels of psychopathic characteristics (antisocial and narcissism).
- Offenders who enjoy and desire pleasure from the pain of others.
- Offenders who are deep in their cycle.

They also noted that the AVE in which the offender engages self-recrimination occurs only after the abuse has occurred. The AVE can best be viewed as a state of mind, struggle on multiple levels with the desire to offend and abstain. The AVE response consists of the following experiences:

- Violation of one's own rules about abstinence.
- State of mind consisting of internal struggles or conflicts between desires, urges, cravings, problems of immediate gratification.
- Creates cognitive dissonance or confusion.
- Involves self-pity and victim stancing.
- Increased possibility of lapse/relapse.
- Self-depreciation.
- Failure expectation.
- May justify offending.

Most sex offenders set the scene for relapse by placing themselves in high-risk situations, either by making a sense of seemingly important decisions (SUDs) or seemingly unimportant decisions (SIDs), each of which represents a step toward a high-risk situation. Although sex offenders can deter relapse once they are in high-risk situations, it is far more difficult.

Motivational/developmental dynamics of relapse prevention

Added to complete the RP model (Carich and Stone, 1996) these psychodynamic factors were broken down into aetiological factors (perceptions of developmental life historical experiences; also called contributing factors) and teleological factors (purposes of the offending behaviours). Developmental experiences are based on the male sex offender's perceptions of the developmental event. The reality of the situation does not matter as much as the perception of the offender. From these developmental perceptions, the offender formulates the teleology of the offending behaviour. Emotional needs appear to be fused with sexual aggression. An offender gains more than sexual gratification from offending. The sexual deviances are intertwined with other core and emotional issues. For example, one offender had witnessed his father's raping and beating of his mother; as a result, he felt the need to control women with whom he interacted, treating them as sub-entities. These dynamics are not excuses or avenues of blame; rather, they suggest reasons for the offender's mistaken beliefs. The offender must become aware that these early childhood lessons were inappropriate so that he will see his sexual offending behaviour stemming from these lessons is also inappropriate. Having identified a cause of the behaviour, the offender may engage in victim stancing, suggesting that he should be the object of pity instead of the person he sexually assaulted. However, at no time is the offender allowed to avoid full responsibility for his sexual offending behaviour.

Adaptive and maladaptive coping responses
Maladaptive coping responses are inappropriate, dysfunctional coping mechanisms to risk factors. MCRs are lapses and lead to relapse. Maladaptive coping responses (MCRs) involve the concept of disowning behaviours (DBs). DBs are any way the offender evades responsibility and/or enables the offender to offend. Typically, DBs involve cognitive distortions (i.e., denial, justifications, blame, rationalise, minimising, entitlement, and defences). For more detailed information see Chapter 5. Adaptive coping responses are appropriate behaviours or responses with regard to coping with triggers or risk factors, stressors, AVE and PIG phenomena.

A self-regulation model of the relapse process

Ward and Hudson (1998) proposed a revision of the cognitive-behavioural model of relapse. Their aim was to provide a model of relapse that would:

- Incorporate various pathways to relapse involving different types of goals and planning, and different affective states throughout the offence cycle.
- Provide an integration of cognitive, affective and behavioural factors.
- Account for the dynamic, temporal nature and the various phases of the offence process.
- Provide a description of the mechanisms inhibiting or encouraging relapse.

They identified nine distinct phases in their model incorporating differences in offenders'

goals, offence planning, and levels of affect (attached either to pre-offence, high-risk situations or to post-offence behaviour).

Phase 1: This is where a life event (ranging from minor to major stressors) activates knowledge structures related to the offender's goals and needs, which in turn trigger patterns of thoughts, emotions, and intentions.

Phase 2: A desire for deviant sex is then activated and this includes sexual and/or aggressive fantasies.

Phase 3: The offender establishes offence-related goals and goals and strategies are then selected either unconsciously or automatically.

Phase 4: Four offence pathways to relapse are proposed:

- Avoidant-passive: desire to avoid offending plus failure to actively prevent this from occurring (the traditional cognitive-behavioural model of relapse).
- Avoidant-active: desire to avoid offending plus direct attempt at mental control which itself is inappropriate and actually enhances the likelihood of re-offending (maladaptive coping responses).
- Approach-automatic: desire to re-offend plus under-regulation (planned impulsive).
- Approach explicit: conscious planning (intact self-regulation) toward inappropriate goals.

Phase 5: The offender then enters a high-risk situation (such as contact with a victim) which is either the result of earlier planning (either implicit and explicit) or it may be unexpectedly.

Phase 6: Is a lapse and includes the immediate precursors to a sexual offence. All offenders experience positive affectivity during this phase due to a combination of high levels of arousal and cognitive deconstruction.

Phase 7: Is the sexual offence.

Phase 8: Involves post-offence evaluation (guilt and shame as well as positive self-evaluation).

Phase 9: This represents the offenders attitude toward re-offending, and it incorporates the idea that offenders learn from each offence and may either continue on an avoidant path (resolving not to persist offending) or move to an approach or acquisitory path (resolving to offend again in the future).

Such a model clearly sets out some worker challenges in that we need to adapt our traditional interventions to help the offender identify which type of offender pathway they follow as a preface to a more individually tailored treatment plan. They make some suggestions as to what this may involve:

- Avoidant-passive: requires the acquisition of relationship skills, problem solving, mood management, self-efficacy and the development of greater meta-cognitive control to more effectively monitor and remediate various components of their offence cycles.
- Avoidant-active: also requires skill acquisition, especially with respect to meta-cognitive control, as well as interventions aimed at increasing the offender's awareness of the effects of current coping strategies and developing adaptive coping styles.
- Approach-automatic: demands a strengthening of meta-cognitive control and the need to be taught not to rely on over-learned behavioural scripts. Perspective taking and cognitive restructuring also play an important role in changing these offender's goals.
- Approach-explicit: requires the focus become the offender's goals and as such core schemata (e.g. self, intimacy, sexuality etc.) with the aim of reconditioning their urges and cravings.

Relapse interventions

Relapse interventions are methods or ways that one uses to defuse or interrupt any relapse (deviant responses, lapses or relapse) (Carich et al., 2001). Interventions are adaptive coping strategies, responses, and skills that we have categorised in terms of experiential modalities, cognitive, social, behavioural, cognitive-behavioural, and imagery and futuristic interventions. Each category can be combined with others to create more effective interventions. These are set out in Table 8.3 overleaf and then discussed in more detail in the next section.

Cognitive interventions

Cognitive interventions primarily involve thinking covert behaviours. These interventions range from simple thought stopping techniques to problem solving tactics. Several primary interventions include: thought stopping, cognitive restructuring, problem-solving, word storming, and catching self.

Thought stopping refers to teaching offenders to stop patterns of behaviour by thinking STOP. Typically, offenders practice yelling 'stop' out loud until targeted deviant responses are interrupted. The offender gradually learns to internally yell 'stop' and interrupt the deviant behaviour. This is a type of conditioned response in which yelling 'stop' is paired with deviant responses (i.e. distortions, deviant rumination, craving/urges, fantasies, or any other cycle behaviours, etc.). The STOP strategy can be used as follows:

S   Stop!   Immediately stop what one is doing.
T   Think   Think and assess or evaluate what is going on.
O   Option   Review options and select one or more. Options are choice points and interventions.
P   Practice   Implement selected options and do something different. Assess or evaluate the outcome.

If needed, repeat the process.

Cognitive restructuring techniques involve restructuring dysfunctional beliefs, cognitive distortions and constructing functional beliefs. Cognitive distortions or distorted beliefs need to be identified, challenged and replaced with rational functional beliefs. Hopefully, over time the corrected thinking turns into automatic thoughts or beliefs ingrained unconsciously. Thinking occurs at both conscious and unconscious levels of awareness. Typically, the sex offender's distorted thinking is ingrained at all levels of awareness. A list of common distortions include: denial, blame, rationalisation, victim stancing, minimisation, justification, entitlement, etc. Jenkins-Hall (1989) provides an excellent synopsis of using restructuring techniques in RP. Likewise, for more details on these techniques, refer to Chapter 5 on cognitive restructuring in this book.

Problem solving strategies provide simplistic plans to identify and solve problems. These strategies range from word storming to highly technical strategies.

Catching self is the Adlerian technique of self-monitoring. Offenders learn to carefully monitor or mentally 'catch' themselves engaging in any type of cycle behaviour, risk factors, etc. and terminate the behaviour immediately. There is a variety of tracking systems available, as noted in the cognitive-behavioural section.

Table 8.3: A list of relapse interventions*.

I. Cognitive (thought-oriented interventions)
1. R.E.T. strategies of challenging specific irrational beliefs
2. Challenging and changing basic cognitive distortions
3. Challenging and changing criminal cognitive distortions
4. Challenging and changing D.B.'s
5. Challenging and changing perceptual distortions
6. Thought stopping
7. As if/what if
8. Cognitive self-monitoring
   a. Catching self
   b. Reality checks
9. Cognitive preparation
10. Humour
11. Brainstorming
12. Problem solving

II. Cognitive–behavioural (thinking/activity)
1. Writing interventions
   a. Journals/logs (self-monitoring)
   b. Autobiographies
   c. Future autobiographies
   d. Dichotomy listing interventions (positive or likes/negatives or dislikes)
   e. Reminder cards, notes (with plans/goals)
   f. Lists (triggers, cues, interventions, D.B.'s, etc.)
   g. Tracking (self-monitoring)
   h. Reports
   i. Fantasies with interventions
   j. Letters
   k. I choose statements
   l. Script or role aspects
2. Cognitive–behavioural formats
   a. Reprogramming thoughts
   b. Reprogramming behaviour
   c. Futuristic scenarios
3. Art

III. Affective interventions
1. Catharsis
2. Expressing feelings

IV. Social interventions
1. Support groups
2. Positive peer networks

3. Communication skills (i.e., assertiveness, direct expressions, empathy, respect, appropriate confrontation, active listening, paraphrasing, etc.)

V. Imagery
1. Single images
2. Scenarios
3. Scenes
4. Metaphoric images as support
5. Creative imagination
6. Review of past scenarios for future handling and coping
7. Review past trigger scenarios
8. Journeys

VI. Hypnotic interventions
1. Relaxation (imagery)
2. Self-hypnosis
3. Deep breathing
4. Futuristic projection

VII. Behavioural
1. Operant conditioning (reinforcement)
2. Classical conditioning (covert association)
3. Assertive conditioning
4. Covert desensitisation
5. Covert sensitisation
6. Time out
7. Stimulus control
8. Avoidance
9. Escape

VIII. Psychodrama
1. Role play
2. Reverse role play

IX. Futuristic interventions
1. Futuristic scenarios
   a. Structured
   b. Unstructured
2. Future autobiographies
3. Futuristic cognitive
   a. Triggers and interventions
   b. Trigger, dynamics and interventions
4. Imagery
   a. Journeys
5. Age progression
6. Hypnotic 'as if'
7. Covert rehearsal
8. Futuristic role play

---

*Adapted from: Carich, M. S. & Stone, M. (1992). A List of Relapse Interventions. *INMAS Newsletter*, 5(3), 8.

A strategy summarised from D'Zurilla (1988) is presented below:

- Problem definition.
  - identify the problem
  - establish goals
- Generate alternative solutions or word storm ideas.
- Select a solution, by ranking and listing the most workable solutions first with the anticipated outcomes.
- Implementation of the solution.
- Monitor the results.

Social interventions

Social interventions consist of a variety of techniques involving interpersonal skills and types of interpersonal relationships. Interpersonal skills refer to specific communicational and social skills. These include: empathy, victim empathy, active listening, paraphrasing, eye contact, 'I' messages, respect, appropriate confrontation skills, assertiveness training, listening skills, appropriate expression of affect, etc. The other aspect is the development of positive peer network and support groups. It is very difficult for offenders to survive without support peer group networks. Peer group networks need to consist of peers that do not enable deviant behaviours, but can also be supportive.

Behavioural interventions

Behavioural interventions involve using the principles of conditioning and overt activities. Covert (internally-oriented) interventions are considered behaviourally based upon the conditioning procedures of instrumental or operant conditioning, classical conditioning and their variations (i.e. modelling). Operant conditioning procedures involve learning through reinforcement or the consequences of behaviour. Offenders can learn to set up behavioural modification schedules, thus reinforcing positive behaviours, while reducing negative behaviour. Classical conditioning is the learning through the pairing of two or more stimuli and/or stimuli with responses. Thus, deviant responses are reduced, while appropriate behaviours are enhanced. It is learning through association. Some of the variations include self-aversive conditioning techniques, covert sensitisation, stimulus control, escape, and avoidance.

Self-induced aversive conditioning techniques involve setting upon an overt event following any target deviant response (i.e., urges, cravings, deviant fantasies). Aversive events may include 'popping' rubber bands around the offender's wrist, using noxious odours, pinching, etc. Staff should monitor the process to ensure that the offenders are not selecting aversive events that stimulate deviant behaviour.

Covert sensitisation is the pairing of a negative internal covert stimulus with deviant responses. The offender imagines a noxious negative 'turn off' type of image (i.e., event, specific person). Covert images need to be strongly aversive and immediately following the deviant response. Over time, the deviant behaviour is reduced.

Stimulus control techniques cent controlling the risk factor and/or si involves the offender controlling th environment to reduce the risk of re-offence. There are two related tactics avoidance and escape. In RP, avoidance refers to the offender avoiding specific high-risk situations or factors. These may include: baby sitting, frequenting bars, viewing pornography, going out at night, etc. Escape refers to getting out of or leaving a high risk situations.

Cognitive-behavioural interventions

Cognitive-behavioural interventions encompass a variety of techniques that involve both primarily thinking and behavioural (activity) experiential domains. There are several tactics that offenders can use as relapse interventions. These include: writing techniques, such as, journals/logs, or tracking systems, lists, letters, repetitive listing, reminder cards and notes, crashing fantasies, and reprogramming formats.

Writing techniques include any form of writing. The most popular tactics are listed above. Journals, logs or any type of tracking systems are methods of self-monitoring. More specifically, offenders track significant events, throughout their day and record their reactions. Their reactions consist of thoughts, feelings, social behaviours/behaviours or any overt activities and physiological responses. Offenders can also monitor risk factors, coping skills, and distorted thinking. Specific RP journals can be designed to enable offenders to analyse triggers and reactions, along with keeping an ongoing list of risk factors, cues, distortions, interventions, etc.

Listing techniques are also helpful. Offenders can make single lists (i.e., triggers, risk factors, interventions, cues (early, late and DeWs), consequences of decisions, common distortions, etc. These are double lists and can be comparative and non comparative in nature. Some examples include positive/negatives or like/dislikes, of situations, decisions, people, events, things, self, etc. This helps the offender analyse decisions, events, relationships, etc.

Writing and utilising letters can be a very effective way to interrupt or defuse a cycle. Letters or notes consisting of victim impact statements or by the offender. Letters (can be written by one's own victims, other victims) can be powerful ways to remind the offender about the consequences.

Repetitive listing is the repetitive/or repeatedly written) rewriting of specific statements. Statements usually begin with 'I choose to . . .' and completed with something meaningful (i.e. to avoid certain situations, learn new coping behaviours, etc.). Typically, offenders are instructed to write 4 or 5 pages front and back. The basis of this intervention is the unconscious reprogramming of the offender.

Reminder notes and cards are written out statements, messages, goals, risk factors and interventions, placed on index cards or notes. Offenders can write out specific key messages on notes and hang them up in their living quarters. Likewise, key messages can be written on index cards and carried on the offender. Messages may consist of: risk factors with interventions, key risk factors, positive affirmations, key support group numbers, key interventions, etc.

Reprogramming formats are specific formats designed to reprogram the offenders thinking and behaviour. Typical, formats include identifying specific distortions, behavioural consequences, replacement statements and new consequences (see the cognitive restructuring chapters for specific formats).

Lapse contracts are specific agreements with built-in plans. Offenders agree to follow certain plans and sign the agreement. The plans usually consist of goals, options, plans or interventions and a commitment.

Imagery and futuristic interventions

Imagery and futuristic interventions refer to the specific internal visualisations and representations of behaviours, thoughts, feelings, behavioural sequences with themes, events, situations, objects, animals, scenarios, etc. Imagery involves using all five sensory modes (visual, auditory, kinesthetic, olfactory, taste) and can take the form of single images or actual scenarios. For example, specific images of animals that provide the offender with strength (confidence, competence, and esteem) are paired. Images of places can be associated with relaxation, i.e., pleasant places, mountains and beaches. Through imagery, specific interventions can be reviewed and rehearsed. Similarly, futuristic risk situations or scenarios with appropriate coping strategies and plans are rehearsed through imagery. Thus, the offender projects himself into the future by rehearsing specific scenarios.

Basic treatment stages of relapse intervention

RP can be utilised in a variety of ways. Gray and Pithers (1993) provided a brief overview of nine basic stages. RP can be done within a supervised peer group, context and/or formal treatment group. If the RP peer group is used, peer group facilitators need to be knowledgeable senior program members and under the supervision of treatment staff.

Stage 1: Identify offending patterns and processes
- Case reviews (detailed descriptions of assaults/victims).
- List of events (breakdown of each case into events).
- Identify reactions (thoughts, feelings, behaviours of each event of each case).
- Select cycle model or format for each victim.
- Develop a summary cycle for each victim type/profile and a composite cycle of offending (using pre-assault, assault and post assault patterns of all offences).

Stage 2: 'Identifying Developmental/Motivational Factors' is an added dimension to RP. It is not a necessary component. In stage five 'Identifying Triggers', professionals may use any risk factor or triggering event typology available. It is important for offenders to identify motivational factors and significant developmental experiences:
- List significant developmental experiences (use life history or autobiography, journal, early recollections).
- List motivations of the offences.
- List the emotional gratifications obtained for the offence.
- List the reactions wanted from the victim during the offence and in the deviant fantasies.
- List needs being met by offending.

*This stage is optional and is not found in traditional RP.

Stage 3: Identify and list all distortions, defences or any type of disowning behaviours (was to evade responsibility and/or enable offending):
- Keep a journal and highlight distortions/defences.
- Review offences and fantasies, highlight distortions.

- Track and identify offence-enabling behaviours.

Stage 4: Dispute and change distortions
- Develop specific counters.
- Use cognitive restructuring tactics.

Stage 5: Identifying triggers
- List high-risk factors/situations or triggers.
- List low-risk factors/situations or triggers (seemingly unimportant decisions or events).

Stage 6: Identifying relapse cues
- List early warning cues.
- List mid and late cues.
- List last minute warnings (DeW Line).
- List content cues (i.e., cognitive, affective, social, physiological, behavioural, situational).

Stage 7: Develop Relapse Interventions
- Learn a variety of interventions.
- Select and adapts interventions that are most effective.

Stage 8: Review specific triggers, cues and effective interventions
- List each trigger with related cues.
- Develop effective interventions.
- Group evaluation of the effectiveness of interventions.
- Review triggers/cues/interventions until interventions are near automatic response.

Stage 9: Develop and review possible high and low risk futuristic scenarios
- Review any existing scenarios with interventions (Carich and Stone, 1996, have 26 futuristic scenarios).
- Develop effective interventions.
- Group evaluation of the effectiveness of interventions.

Stage 10: Develop relapse intervention aftercare plan
- Outline key risk factors and relapse cues.
- Outline support system and resources.
- Outline supervision system.
- Outline aftercare treatment system.

Holistic approaches and wellness planning

Recently, some of the more traditional approaches to treating sexual abusers have come under criticism, including relapse prevention (RP) the most widely used treatment

model by programmes treating adult sexual offenders (Ward and Hudson, 1996; Laws et al., 2000). First, they have noted the limited ways to account for offence behaviour, second the presentation of the offence chain is overly rigid and leaves no room for individual differences in behaviour (there is no flexibility in the chain of behaviours and events leading to sexual assault). The model is very academic (it intellectualises sex offending) with abstract concepts and complex terms and language, and it relies on coping strategies that are not positive goal oriented i.e., avoidance and escape. Although the model has many limitations, it is a viable model that when modified can be used in conjunction with a holistic approach. Longo (2001) set out the essential ingredients of a holistic approach. Teaching clients about relapse prevention and the cycle of sexual abuse can be readily blended into a holistic model (Freeman-Longo, 2000). The relapse prevention model has already been adapted to teaching the sexual abuse cycle for many years (Freeman-Longo and Pithers, 1992). Recent modifications to this model enable the blending of the four universal needs, the four aspects of self, and the use of core values and beliefs (Figure 8.2) to teaching clients about cycles of abuse (Figure 8.3). By developing a four phase cycle, the four universal needs and the four aspects of self can be readily adapted.

The 'pretends-to-be-normal' phase of the cycle represents the universal need for belonging and the spiritual self. When a client is in this phase of the cycle, basic life areas are not being managed and problems are ongoing. They are likely to be withdrawn from others, and the spiritual self not developed.

In the 'build-up' phase of the cycle, the client is engaging in a variety of risk factors, lapses, and maladaptive coping responses. The emotion self is not healthy and the client mismanages emotions often leaving him or her with feelings of anger, rejection, low self-esteem etc. The universal need for mastery is malfunctioning as the client continues to lose control of their life, thoughts feelings and behaviours.

The 'acting out' phase of the cycle is the sexual abuse behaviour. The universal need for independence is not met as the client needs a victim in order to act out their feelings and problems. The physical self is acting irresponsibly.

The 'justification phase' of the cycle or the 'downward spiral' represents the universal need for generosity and the mental self. During this phase the client is engaging in denial and other defence mechanisms and the mental self is filled with unhealthy thoughts and cognitive distortions. The need for generosity is replaced with a selfish impulse to protect the self and the

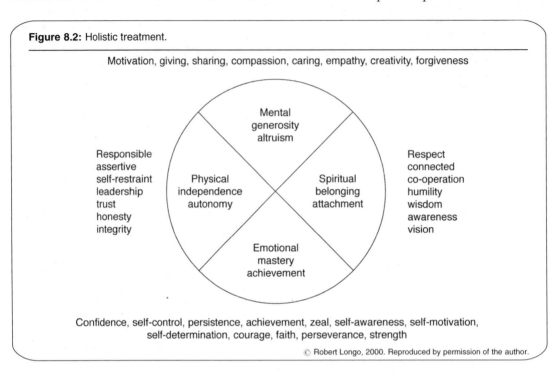

Figure 8.2: Holistic treatment.

Motivation, giving, sharing, compassion, caring, empathy, creativity, forgiveness

Mental generosity altruism

Responsible assertive self-restraint leadership trust honesty integrity

Physical independence autonomy

Spiritual belonging attachment

Respect connected co-operation humility wisdom awareness vision

Emotional mastery achievement

Confidence, self-control, persistence, achievement, zeal, self-awareness, self-motivation, self-determination, courage, faith, perseverance, strength

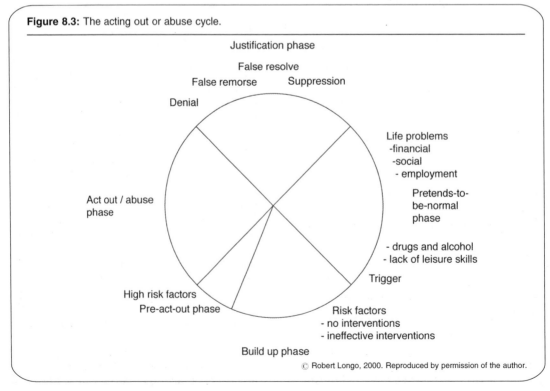

Figure 8.3: The acting out or abuse cycle.

Justification phase

False resolve

False remorse   Suppression

Denial

Life problems
-financial
-social
- employment

Pretends-to-be-normal phase

Act out / abuse phase

- drugs and alcohol
- lack of leisure skills

Trigger

High risk factors
Pre-act-out phase

Risk factors
- no interventions
- ineffective interventions

Build up phase

client takes from others if he engages others at all and he or she does not give or share.

Holistic treatment focuses on wellness. When we label others by the behaviour or with a particular diagnosis, we potentially brand them for life. We see this most clearly with psychiatric diagnosis. People become known as bi-polar, paedophiles, mentally ill, etc. We know from the literature that as many as 20-25% of child victims of sexual abuse who enter treatment emerge into adulthood with little or no residual trauma. We meet adults who have been sexually abused that are thriving today and have happy healthy and productive lives. If we work in this field long enough we are blessed with the opportunities to meet women and men who have been brutally raped as children or adults and have not only worked through the horrific trauma of these experiences but also celebrate life.

We know from our experience and the experience of other professionals that many sexual abusers go on to lead productive happy lives after going through treatment. There are literally hundreds of thousands of sexual offenders who have been through specialised treatment programs and live productively and happily in our communities. As most adult sex offenders have experienced childhood abuse and/or neglect, what messages are we giving them when we talk about life long damage, and no cure? These powerful statements are debilitating and do not give clients a sense of hope and potential for recovery any more than the statements we give people in medicine that they have a terminal illness. Holistic treatment has a focus on wellness with messages of hope. It gives clients a clear message that they can heal, that they can go forward, and that they are human beings worthy of respect and dignity.

A return to basics

Holistic treatment, in the simplest of terms is a return to basics; looking at the four domains or aspects of self; mind, body, spirit and the emotional self (see Figure 8.2). In addition, a holistic model addresses the four universal needs for generosity, belonging, mastery, and independence (Brendtro, Brokenleg, and Van Bockern, 1990). The need for generosity is then for people to give and share of themselves. This is not a giving of materialistic goods, but rather a giving and sharing of time, of one's feelings and one's self.

The need for belonging transcends all cultures and societies. Human beings are social animals with a need to belong to a family, a community, a society, and the need to feel connected to the universe. The lack of belonging leaves one feeling isolated, lonely and intimacy suffers. Our spiritual self begins to die.

The need for mastery is essential for personal growth and learning. Each of us has a need to feel we have the courage and strength to master tasks from the simple to the more complex. We need to feel in control of ourselves and assured that we can master the tasks that will take us through life.

Finally, the need for independence is that need to operate our lives in a fashion in which we are free from dependence upon others. This is not to say that we don't need or depend on others from time to time, we all do. However, to depend upon others consistently especially in co-dependent ways is unhealthy. A healthy independent self is being responsible for ourselves and assertive in getting our needs met.

The teaching focus of a holistic approach takes into account several core values and beliefs that address the four aspects of self and the four universal needs. These concepts also fit nicely with four leading theories in psychology; altruism, autonomy, attachment, and achievement (see Figure 8.2).

Holistic treatment uses a 'wellness' approach, and looks at the 'whole' person, not at damaged parts. It pushes personal growth while noting that one's problems are a 'part' of the whole, not the whole person. Holistic treatment is a strengths based model, and seeks to find what one can do (approach goals) versus looking at the person's weaknesses alone using a deficit-based model that addresses only what one should not do (avoidance and escape goals) which comes from the criminal justice/forensic model and is often focused on punishment.

While looking at the whole person, the holistic model works with all parts of humans. There is a focus on the physical part of self instead of viewing the client as a sex offender and focusing on just the genitals. It sees the connection between a healthy physical self and a balanced whole person including a healthy mental, emotional and spiritual self.

Unlike most sex offender treatment programmes in existence today, a holistic model incorporates spirituality into the treatment process. Incorporating spirituality into treatment does not mean engaging clients in organised religious activities, although that may be the path in which many clients chose to develop their spiritual self. In a more global sense, addressing the client's spiritually means as professionals we need to address the client's need for 'belonging,' his yearning, sadness, etc., which is a part of one's spirituality.

The holistic model recognises that to be healthy and keep a balanced life, the client must also work on developing his mental self and emotional self. These two parts of the whole can only be healthy when the physical self is healthy and the two combined make up a healthy spiritual self. The mental self feeds denial systems and when unhealthy supports the client's cognitive distortions and unhealthy thinking processes. While most programs for youth who sexually abuse address thinking errors, they must also be sure to develop and enhance the client's healthy thinking process.

The emotional self is probably one of the most difficult aspects of self to heal and make healthy. Most programmes have a treatment component that addresses teaching empathy, but there is more to healthy emotions than the ability to have empathy. In fact, to have empathy for others mean one must first have empathy for one's self, an aspect of treatment often overlooked by sex-offender specific treatment programs. A holistic model teaches clients about feelings, how to recognise feelings in one's self and others, how to express one's feelings, and utilises a variety of modalities to help clients explore their feeling self.

Holistic treatment is process oriented and looks at the Gestalt. It is interactive and experiential, not something we do to clients but rather a process of change, growth and healing we experience with clients. It facilitates change while including goals and the process/journey is equally as important. It recognises the client's need for a connection to others and the community. It incorporates a wellness plan focused on wellness activities in each of the four aspects of self, mental, spiritual, emotional and physical. Traditional sex offender treatment is very structured and directive, focuses on target goals and thus is very goal oriented. This type of treatment has the potential to isolate the client. Prevention plans are focused on avoidance and managing risk factors.

Wellness plans utilise approach goals with a focus on healing and self-improvement. While wellness plans may suggest avoidance of certain behaviours or activities, these restrictions are always followed by what the client should do in order to change the behaviour into a healthy one. For example, a wellness plan may incorporate the following: (Adapted from Ellerby, 1999).*

How to maintain **Emotional** health and balance to stay well and manage risk:

- Be more aware of how you experience feelings, both yours and what you observe in others.
- Explore your feelings so you can better understand them and where they are coming from.
- Avoid overreacting to situations. Learn to respond with appropriate assertiveness.

How to maintain **Mental** health and balance to stay well and manage risk:

- Challenge irrational thoughts.
- Try to keep in harmony with your head, heart, gut, and environment.
- Avoid 'all or nothing' thinking, be flexible.

How to maintain **Spiritual** health and balance to stay well and manage risk:

- Participate in spiritually related activity (meditation, church, meetings, etc.) regularly.
- Take time for yourself.
- Realise what you can control and what you cannot control. Give what you can't control to God or a higher power.

How to maintain **Physical** health and balance to stay well and manage risk:

- Continue on medications you are taking.
- Don't isolate or withdraw, seek others for companionship and activities.
- Keep active, spend leisure time wisely, exercise regularly and take care of your physical health.
- Eat on a regular and healthy basis.

It must be noted however that holistic treatment recognises that some individuals are damaged to the point that the holistic method may be difficult for them to use or they may not be willing to use it. Like any other model in mental health, some client's will offer resistance or an unwillingness to engage in any type of therapy, or in the case of persons assessed and

---

* Adapted from Lawrence Ellerby. *A Holistic Approach to Treating Sexual Abusers*/Workshop. ATSA 18th Annual Conference 9/24/99. Lake Buena Vista, Florida.

determined to be psychopathic personalities, the model will not work.

Conclusions

RP approaches have proven effective in helping offenders maintain abstinence (Marques, Day, Nelson and Minor (1989) and Pithers, Martin and Cumming (1989), Pithers and Gray (1996). There are several points worthy of repetition here:

The first point concerns the use of RP as the entire treatment programme. Although RP may be used as the backbone of a programme, it cannot represent the entire treatment programme. It is only a set of approaches within a programme used to help the offender maintain abstinence. RP provides resources to establish effective management and supervisory components.

A second point involves treatment planning. Effective treatment planning involves forming treatment around individual differences. RP can be adapted to the uniqueness of the offender population.

The last point concerns the best circumstances to use RP. Based on clinical experience, the best results occur with internally motivated offenders who are committed to abstinence. It is also strongly recommended that the offender consistently experience victim empathy at both cognitive and emotional levels, prior to using RP (Pithers and Gray, 1996). Although victim empathy is considered critical in using RP, teaching the assault cycle concept can begin early in treatment.

The future of RP in sex offender treatment hinges on the use of the assault cycle, modifying and adapting RP strategies to specific client populations, and refining and adding different RP concepts as needed. The bottom line is that offenders need to identify triggers/risk factors, cues, cycle behaviours and develop automatic relapse intervention or prevention responses.

Useful texts

Eldridge H (1995) *Maintaining Change: A Relapse Prevention Manual for Adult Male Perpetrators of Child Sexual Abuse.* Birmingham, England: Lucy Faithfull Foundation.

Freeman-Longo R E (2000) *Paths to Wellness.* Holyoak, MA: Neari Press.

Laws D R, Hudson S M and Ward T (Eds.) (2000) *Remaking Relapse Prevention Who Sex Offenders: A Sourcebook.* Thousand Oaks, Ca: Sage Publications

References

Brendtro L, Brokenleg M and Van Bockern S (1990) *Reclaiming Youth at Risk: Our Hope for the Future.* Bloomington, Indiana: National Education Service.

Carich M S and Stone M (1996) *Sex Offender Relapse Intervention Workbook.* Chicago, Il: Adler School of Professional Psychology.

Carich M S, Gray A, Rombouts S, Stone M and Pithers W D (2001) Relapse Prevention and The Sexual Assault Cycle. In Carich M S and Mussack S E (Eds.) *Handbook of Sexual Abuser Assessment and Treatment.* Brandon, VT: Safer Society Press, 77–104.

Carich M S, Steckel S and Stone M (1994). *Relapse Interventions & Prevention for Sex Offenders: A Monograph.* Unpublished Manuscript.

Carich M S and Stone M H (2001) Using Relapse Prevention Strategies to Treat Sexual Offenders. *The Journal of Individual Psychology.* 57: 1, 26–36.

D'Zurrilla T J (1988) Problem Solving Therapies. In Dobson E S (Ed.) *Handbook of Cognitive-Behavioral Therapies.* New York: The Guilford Press. 85–135.

Ellerby L (1999) *A Holistic Approach to Treating Sexual Abusers.* Workshop. ATSA 18th Annual Conference 9/24/99. Lake Buena Vista, Florida.

Freeman-Longo R E (2000) *Paths to Wellness.* Holyoak, MA: NEARI Press.

Freeman-Longo R and Pithers W D (1992). *A Structured Approach to Preventing Relapse: A Guide for Sex Offenders.* Orwell, VT: The Safer Society Press.

Freeman-Longo R E, Bird S L, Stevenson W F and Fiske J A (1995) *1994 Nationwide Survey of Treatment Programs and Models.* Brandon, VT: Safer Society Press.

Gray A and Pithers W D (1993). Relapse Prevention With Sexually Aggressive Adolescents and Children: Expanding Treatment and Supervision. In Barbaree H E, Marshall W L and Hudson S (Eds.) *The Juvenile Sex Offender.* NY: The Guilford Press. 289–319.

Hanson R K (2000) *Risk Assessment.* Beaverton, OR: The Association for The Treatment of Sexual Abusers.

Hudson S M and Ward T (1996a) Relapse Prevention: Future Directions. *Sexual Abuse: A Journal of Research and Treatment.* 8: 249–56.

Hudson S M and Ward T (Eds.) (1996b) Special Issue: Relapse Prevention. *Sexual Abuse: A Journal of Research and Treatment.* 8: 3, 171–256.

Jenkins-Hall K (1989) Cognitive Restructuring. In Laws D R (Ed.) *Relapse Prevention With Sex Offenders* NY: Guilford Press. 207–15.

Laws D R (1989) (Ed.) *Relapse Prevention With Sex Offenders.* NY: The Guilford Press.

Laws D R (1995) Central Elements in Relapse Prevention Procedures With Sex Offenders. *Psychology, Crime and Law.* 2: 41–53.

Laws D R (1999) Relapse Prevention: the State of the Art. *Journal of Interpersonal Violence* 14(3): 285–302.

Laws D R, Hudson S M and Ward T (Eds.) (2000) *Remaking Relapse Prevention With Sex Offenders: A Sourcebook.* Thousand Oaks, Ca: Sage Publications

Longo R E (2001) A Holistic Approach to Treating Young People Who Sexually Abuse. In Calder M C (Ed.) *Young People Who Sexually Abuse: Building The Evidence Base for Your Practice.* Dorset: Russell House Publishing, 218–30.

Marlatt A and Gordon J (Eds.) (1985) *Relapse Prevention.* NY: Guilford Press.

Marques J K, Day D M, Nelson C and Miner M H (1989) The Sex Offender Treatment and Evaluation Project: California's Relapse Prevention Program. In Laws D R (Ed.) *Relapse Prevention With Sexual Offenders.* NY: Guilford Press. 247–67.

Pithers W D (1990) Relapse Prevention With Sexual Aggressors: A Method for Maintaining Therapeutic Gain and Enhancing External Supervision. In Marshall W L, Laws D R and Barbaree H E (Eds.) *Handbook of Sexual Assault: Issues, Theories, and Treatment of the Offender.* NY: Plenum Press. 343–61.

Pithers W D and Cumming G F (1989) Can Relapses Be Prevented? Initial Outcome Data From The Vermont Treatment Program for Sexual Aggressors. In Laws D R (Ed.) *Relapse Prevention With Sexual Offenders.* NY: Guilford Press. 313–25.

Pithers W D and Gray A S (1996) Utility of Relapse Prevention in Treatment of Sexual Abusers. *Sexual Abuse: A Journal of Research and Treatment.* 8: 3, 223–30.

Pithers W D, Marques J K, Gibat C C and Marlatt G A (1983) Relapse Prevention With Sexual Aggressives: A Self-Control Model of Treatment and Maintenance of Change. In Greer J G and Stuart I R (Eds.) *The Sexual Aggressor: Current Perspectives on Treatment.* NY: Van Nostrand Reinhold. 214–34.

Pithers W D, Kashima K M, Cumming G F and Beal L S (1988) Relapse Prevention. A Method of Enhancing Maintenance of Change in Sex Offenders. In Salter A C (Ed.) *Treating Child Sex Offenders and Victims: A Practical Guide.* Newbury Park, CA: Sage. 131–70.

Pithers W D, Kashima K M Cumming, G F, Beal L S and Buell M M (1988b) Relapse Prevention of Sexual Aggression. In Prentky R S and Quinsey V L (Eds.) *Human Sexual Aggression: Current Perspectives. Annals of The New York Academy of Sciences 528.* NY: New York Academy of Sciences.

Ward T and Hudson S (1996a) Pithers' Relapse Prevention Model: A Response to Gail Ryan. *Sexual Abuse: A Journal of Research and Treatment.* 8: 162–6.

Ward T and Hudson S M (1996b) Relapse Prevention: A Critical Analysis. *Sexual Abuse: A Journal of Research and Treatment.* 8: 177–200.

Ward T, Hudson S M and Marshall W L (1994) The Abstinence Violation Effect in Child Molesters. *Behavior Research and Therapy.* 32: 431–7.

Ward T and Hudson S M (1998) A Self-Regulation Model of The Relapse Process in Sexual Offenders. *Journal of Interpersonal Violence.* 13: 700–25.

Chapter Nine

Social Skills, Life Skills and Interpersonal Relationships

Introduction

Social skills, life skills and interpersonal relationships are a common and necessary part of society. One cannot escape the social context. Social skills are a broad term used to describe a wide variety of behaviours and cognitive phenomena presumed necessary for effective functioning in social situations (Conger and Conger, 1986, p526). It has been defined as 'the ability to maximise positive reinforcement and minimise punishment from others' (Graves et al., 1992). Squirrel (1999) noted that social skills are largely about:

- Developing good communication skills: listening well, thinking about what is said, being aware of non-verbal cues, knowing how best to respond and anticipating the possible consequences of words and actions.
- Being aware of others' feelings, vulnerabilities, concerns, preoccupations and wants and knowing how best to respond to these.
- Being aware of one's own feelings, wants, preoccupations, ways of interpreting and shaping the world and the ways in which these impact on others and interactions with others.
- Knowing how groups work, knowing why people are different on their own, with friends or in social situations where they are dealing with authority.
- Developing the skills to understand, to channel and to manage personal feelings and emotions.
- Knowing how to manage interactions with others: to not be bullied or give in; to stop conflicts from developing; to make people less anxious or tense, to feel less threatened or concerned, to show power, status, rage or dominance.
- Being able to leave a social encounter knowing that you have done your best to express your feelings, ideas, needs, to have had them acknowledged and understood and not to have undermined anyone else in the process (p1).

Social skills enable people to be more aware of others' feelings, the cues offered by others and to be more responsive to the range of social, work, living and other situations to which they are daily exposed Developing social skills, being more adept at managing interactions, becoming more aware of ourselves and others are skills and which can never be considered as tasks completed or skills fully learnt.

Poor social skills can be a starting point for a host of difficulties, such as experiencing social isolation, desperation, a sense of not belonging or fitting into society; poor or dysfunctional intimate or sexual relationships; pursuing harmful or damaging lifestyles; not understanding emotions or managing them; not being able to communicate effectively with others and not reading social contexts or others' cues. Failures to communicate may lead to involvement in situations of conflict and to escalating conflict (p3).

The development of social skills is a keystone in successfully making life changes. They can be learnt, developed and do need to be practiced. Developing social skills is of immediate term benefit. It is a route to better self-image, improved self-esteem, improved social acceptability, less friction and fewer confrontations (p3).

Life skills are defined by Squirrel (1998) as covering the host of skills which all people need to develop in order to negotiate their lives successfully and to help themselves have a more fulfilled time. They are the essential building blocks for quality of life. Life skills form a whole mesh of inter-related skills, beliefs and ways of managing the world and oneself. They cannot be treated as separate skills divorced from one another. Thus work on one area will be a key to improving many other areas of life skills.

Social competency is defined as 'the capacity to integrate cognition, affect, and behaviours to achieve specified social tasks and positive developmental outcomes. It comprises a set of core skills, attitudes, abilities, and feelings giving functional meaning by the contexts of culture, neighbourhoods, and situation. Thus social competence can be viewed in terms of 'life skills for adaptation to diverse ecologies and settings' (Haggerty et al., 1996, p275). Social competency is difficult to define as it embraces both skills as well as outcomes. Graham et al. (1997) defined social competency as encompassing 'the ability of the individual to develop and maintain social relationships appropriate to his age and situation. In particular, it refers to skills the individual possesses for use in establishing and maintaining social relationships, which may form a prelude to 'normal' sexual relationships. Poor social competency is recognised as a contributory factor predisposing toward sexual abusiveness' (p61).

Social skills are necessary to develop appropriate relationships. Relationships are patterns of communication between one or more people bound within social context or social system. It is based on interactive patterns. Interpersonal communication is a dominant human function, and many of our problems stem from our concerns over the way we relate to other people, and the manner in which they respond to us (Lazarus, 1976, p42). It is not surprising, therefore, that interpersonal relations are a central part of dealing with a sexual perpetrator, particularly since the abusive behaviour is an interpersonal act (Groth, 1979). The nature of their problems will vary from case to case and thus need to be isolated if we are to tailor our intervention to the individual.

Weiss (1974) identified six key areas which isolated people miss out on. They are: attachment, provided by close affectionate relationships, which give a sense of security and place; social integration, provided by membership of a network of persons having shared interests and values; the opportunity for nurturing others, usually children, which gives some incentive for continuing in the face of adversity; reassurance of personal worth, which promotes self-esteem and comes both from those at home as well as from colleagues; a sense of reliable alliance, which is obtained mainly from kin; and obtaining help and guidance from informal advisors when difficulties have to be resolved. Examples of the items include: at present, do you have someone you can share your most private feelings with (confide in) or not? Who is this mainly? Do you wish you could share more with them, or is it just about right the way it is? Would you like to have someone like this or would you prefer to keep your feelings to yourself?

The role of socialisation in sex offender treatment

Just like social skills and interpersonal relationships are critical or key aspects of society, they are necessary skills for sex offenders. Clinical experience and research suggests that many sex offenders have deficits or problems in this area (Hudson and Marshall, 1997; Marshall, 1989; Marshall, 2001; Ward, McCormack and Hudson, 1997). The very crime or behaviour of sex offending involves a social component. Offending occurs in a social relationship, in which the perpetrator violates another individual.

Research and clinical experience demonstrates that offending is not solely motivated by sexual gratification (see chapter 1), but also by urgent needs and unresolved issues. Some of the unresolved issues and urgent needs involve dysfunctional relationships, interpersonal issues, lack of skills and ways of attracting to others. This can be summarised best by reference to attachment theory. Attachment theory is based on the way or ways people relate, bond or become attached to each other. It is based on relationship styles and the ways one seeks intimacy. Satisfaction of this need occurs with stable, frequently pleasant and affective interactions. Attachment theory is based on the human needs to belong, bond and develop intimacy (Ward, McCormack and Hudson, 1997).

Attachment theory and intimacy

Whilst we still have a long way to go before we are clear about the roles played by intimacy and relationship problems in the development and maintenance of sexual offending, it is clear from the work of Finkelhor (1984) that any blockage to the development of satisfying adult relationships is part of the offender's motivation to sexually offend. Such blocks might include there being little or no communication between the partners; and there being no sexual relationship between the partners or that it is not emotionally gratifying. Such problems in adult relationships may contribute to the gravitation toward children for emotional and sexual gratification (Faller, 1988).

People attach to one another in the form of relationships. Marshall (2001) and Ward, McCormack and Hudson (1997) all emphasise the need to belong and to be intimate (close) to another is a fundamental human motive. Most sex offenders have deficits in these areas. There are a number of potential causes of offending: deviant arousal or preference; developmental adversity; and interpersonal competency deficits (including social skills, self-esteem, empathy and intimacy).

Interpersonal dyadic relationships can be defined by three relatively independent dimensions: boundary, power and intimacy. Since the development of intimacy is a process, boundary and power cannot be isolated from any definition of intimacy (Waring and Reddon, 1983). A healthy intimate relationship is characterised by the capacity for constructive, respectful expression of positive and negative emotions. These expressions should be mutually acceptable and promote the psychological well-being of the individuals involved; their function is primarily to define boundaries, to communicate concern and commitment, to negotiate roles, and to resolve conflicts. Offenders with a history of being abused themselves have often lacked healthy role models, and boundaries between family members are too weak or too firm. The boundary difficulties resulting from these factors may lead to two distinct problems with intimacy: they may be needy, intrusive, enmeshed, or controlling resulting from a lack of clear boundaries between self and others, or the person may be avoiding and distancing, the outcome of boundaries too tightly drawn.

Intimacy is clearly important in establishing effective emotional and sexual relations with other adults (Brehm, 1992), and those who are able to develop it are seen to be warm and sincere; less aggressive, and better able to resist stress. Their relationships also provide them with a sense of security, emotional comfort, shared experiences, an opportunity to be nurturing plus a sense of self-worth (Marshall, 1993). Intimacy is a universal human characteristic. If thwarted in adult relationships, then sex offenders may seek intimacy in other less appropriate ways. This failure to achieve intimacy leads to the experience of emotional loneliness, which causes considerable frustration. If this frustration is experienced as emotional isolation from effective relations with women, adult females may be seen by these men as the cause of their loneliness (Marshall, 1989. Offenders who report a low sexual satisfaction with their adult partners are clearer more likely to overcome the resistance to sex

with children (and therefore inappropriate partners) in their quest for intimacy.

Intimacy can be understood as being an enduring motive that reflects an individual's preference or readiness to experience emotional closeness, warmth and mutual regulation in close relationships (Ward, McCormack, and Hudson, 1997). Intimacy is important to us all, bringing with it the following:

- Provision of a sense of security and emotional contentment.
- Companionship and shared experiences.
- A chance to be nurtured.
- Reassurance of self-worth.
- Support during adversity.
- A sense of kinship or belonging.

High levels of this motive result in more intimacy enhancing behaviours such as self disclosure, displays of affection, and support (McAdams, 1980). The concept of intimacy with its emphasis on mutuality, commitment, vulnerability and knowledge of the self and other (Morris, 1983) is not seen as being appropriate to describe the abilities of a child and it is from adolescence onwards that the desire for intimacy is thought to become an increasingly important aspect of human behaviour. Having said this, the capacity for intimacy and the skills necessary to attain it develop through attachment relationships during childhood (Marshall, 1989). Intimacy can also be conceptualised as an outcome of interpersonal skills and experiences, developing from attachment styles that arise from important attachment related experiences (Ward et al., 1997). This outcome can be seen as a continuum with high intimacy at one end, and emotional loneliness and intimacy failure at the other (see Table 9.1 overleaf).

Emotional loneliness leads to hostile attitudes towards women and children as well as acceptance of violence and inter-personally aggressive behaviour (Diamont and Windholz, 1981). Check et al. (1985) also found that loneliness was significantly related to an acceptance of violence directed at women and anger at rejection by women; whilst others have related it to externalising behaviour problems such as anger and aggression, and internalising problems such as self-doubt, shame, anxiety, depressive feelings and paranoia (Becker-Lausen and Mallon-Kraft, 1997).

In a series of publications Marshall and his colleagues have outlined a general theory of

Table 9.1: Comparison of high vs low intimacy individuals.

High intimacy individuals – 1 seen as:	High intimacy individuals – 2 characterised by:
• Warm and sincere • Egalitarian • Cooperative • Confident • Rarely need psychiatric help • More frequent positive contact with others (p2) **Low intimacy individuals** • Emotional loneliness • Aggression and hostility • Distrust of others • Low self-esteem • Poor interpersonal skills • Lack of depth in relationships • Low empathy (p3)	• Ability to withstand stress • A sense of meaning to their lives • Resistance to depression and anxiety • Interpersonally skilled • Non-aggressive (p2)

sexual offending in males. In this model insecure childhood attachment relationships and the capacity for intimacy are seen as essential links in the chain of development underlying the emergence of an inappropriate sexual disposition.

Marshall (1989, 1993) has developed a theoretical framework integrating research on attachment theory, intimacy deficits, and sexual offending. He argues that the failure of sex offenders to develop secure attachment bonds in childhood results in a failure to learn the interpersonal skills and self-confidence necessary to achieve intimacy with other adults. Attachment theory is concerned with the bond between children and their caregivers. A child often displays discomfort and anxiety when separated from an attachment figure. If attachment bonds are insecure in childhood, individuals do not acquire the necessary skills to establish close relationships, and may fear, rather than desire, intimacy with another adult.

Poor attachments also lead to low self-confidence, poor social skills, little understanding of relationship issues and a decided lack of empathy for others (Garlick, Marshall and Thornton, 1996), as well as deficiencies in adult intimacy and are far more prone to violence than are intimately effective persons (Seidman, Marshall, Hudson and Robertson, 1994). Deficiencies in social skills (i.e. problems in accurately perceiving social cues, problems in deciding on appropriate behaviour, and deficiencies in the skills to enact effective behaviour) seriously restrict the opportunity for attaining intimacy

Marshall's model (1989; 1993) can be divided into two dimensions, the development of 'vulnerability', and 'priming' that sexualises vulnerability

Vulnerability

Through an insecure attachment relationship with the primary caregiver, children are thought to experience difficulties in learning the interpersonal skills necessary to attain intimacy, such as developing appropriate empathic capacities. The initial attachment relationship allows an affective/cognitive representation or internal working model to develop that holds concepts for how loveable the child is and how available others are in times of emotional need (Bowlby, 1969). Failure to establish a secure attachment with parents is therefore thought to often lead to low levels of self-esteem. The failure to develop intimate relations during adolescence and early adulthood may lead to emotional loneliness and the experience of alienation. Individuals who are emotionally lonely may have many superficial relationships. However these relationships often remain emotionally unfulfilling. Emotional loneliness is known to be related to hostile attitudes and interpersonally aggressive behaviour (Diamant and Windholz, 1981) and the acceptance of violence and hostility toward women (Check, Perlman and Malamuth, 1985). This developmental pattern can lead to the state of 'vulnerability'

Vulnerability is not exclusive to sexual abuse Marshall (1989) originally argued that it was not specific to sexual abuse but to a risk state which could lead to other problems, such as non-sexual offences. Research has found that sexual offenders do have intimacy deficits (Garlick et al., 1996) but these deficits are found in men who have committed non-sexual offences (Ward et al., 1997). The concept accounts for the sexualised nature of vulnerability.

Priming

The 'priming' dimension is not made so clear in the model. It accounts for the sexualised nature of 'vulnerability' often found in men who commit sexual offences. If the individual is 'pre-primed' to view situations in sexual terms, then the fusion of intimacy and sex may result in him seeking to gain intimacy through inappropriate sexual behaviour. The fusion can lead to persistent promiscuity and increasing sexual deviancy as attempts to meet intimacy escalate (Ward et al., 1995). Social and cultural factors are also thought to be import in the development of priming. Media images may convey inappropriate messages to vulnerable young men (Ward et al., 1996; Marshall, 1989). Brownmiller (1975) has presented a case for the association between rape and power in patriarchal societies. Anthropological evidence has been provided by Sanday (1981) to suggest that some societies are 'rape prone', while others are 'rape free'. Gender roles and power relations are likely to influence the development of individuals within a society. It would be useful to explore these avenues further in an attempt to examine the association between intimacy and sex, as well as providing more of understanding of the attitudes and cognitive distortions often held by young people who sexually abuse.

Hudson and Ward (1997) developed an attachment-based model that relates four types of attachment to a set of offending styles and related interpersonal goals. This follows on from the comprehensive attachment model of intimacy deficits articulated by Ward, Hudson, Marshall and Siegert (1995). They found that it was more important to consider attachment styles rather than the types of offences committed in considering intimacy difficulties in sex offenders. They suggested that securely attached individuals (positive self/positive others) have high levels of self-esteem and view others as generally warm and accepting and, as a result, experience high levels of intimacy in their romantic relationships. Preoccupied people (negative self/positive others) see others

in positive terms, but their own sense of unworthiness leads them to seek the approval of valued others to an undue level. They typically are sexually preoccupied and prone to sexualising the need for security and affection through sexual interaction. Because this style is unlikely to lead to satisfactory relationships for either partner, high levels of loneliness are expected together with low levels of aggression (Bartholomew and Horowitz, 1991). If a preoccupied man crosses the boundaries with a child and begins to fantasise about a sexual relationship, he will begin the grooming process, and may well view the child as a lover, although any sexual involvement will follow the courtship ritual. Fearful individuals (negative self/negative others) desire social contact but avoid such interactions because of their distrust and fear of rejection, often keeping their partners at a distance. They are likely to express their aggression indirectly rather than directly (although they may use force to attain their goals), experience loneliness as their relationships will tend to be impersonal and be rather un-empathic towards their victims as a result of their negative views of others. They rarely experience any guilt in relation to their offending behaviour. Finally, dismissing individuals (positive self/negative others) are sceptical of the value of close relationships and place considerable value on independence and autonomy from others in order to remain invulnerable. Therefore, they are unlikely to report being lonely and are more likely to fear intimacy; whilst others will view them as aloof and cold. They are likely to seek relationships or social contacts that involve minimal levels of emotional or personal disclosure. They also blame others for their lack of intimacy and tend to be angry and overtly hostile towards potential partners. They often exhibit profound empathy deficits and, when they do offend, they do so aggressively, even sadistically as an additional measure of their hostility (p325).

Ward, McCormack and Hudson (1997) identified a very important issue in relation to intimacy – its complexity. They identified 12 categories from their research: relationship commitment, evaluation of the partner, self-disclosure, trust, and expression of affection, sexual satisfaction, giving and receiving of support, empathy, conflict resolution, autonomy, and sensitivity to rejection. They found all of these to be significant aspects of sexual offenders' perceptions of their intimate relationships. Interestingly, they did not find any evidence for an independent category of loneliness. They concluded that 'intimacy might usefully be viewed as a state or consequence of other factors, for example, self-disclosure, expression of affection, or commitment to a relationship' (p68). The offences of the sexual group reflected a greater degree of impairment in relationships and sense of social cohesion. They imply a serious violation of others' physical integrity and boundaries and would expect to be mirrored in more profound interpersonal dysfunction.

Basic social skills

The interview itself can provide clues as to the offender's social skills behaviours (verbal and non-verbal). Deficits may be indicated where they look away excessively, fail to listen, interrupt readily, lack social pleasantry, appear socially awkward, jump topics suddenly, become over-familiar with the worker or ask personal questions of the workers which are unrelated to the background relevant to the inquiry (Carich and Adkerson, 1995, p8). However, we need to be mindful of Segal and Marshall's (1985) findings as they reported that the offender's response and presentation within the interview situation may not accord with their behaviour elsewhere. Whilst role-play is advocated to counter this (Dougher, 1995), it is often difficult within individual sessions and maybe more practical in a group setting.

It is also important to explore the relationship of any social skill deficiencies to their pre-assault cycle. In assessing the offender's perceptions, a number of questions need to be asked: Do they tend to be involved in insular activities? Do they value spending time with others? Has the influence of others been experienced primarily in negative or positive terms? Are there any differences in the way they describe interactions with children, same-sex adults, and opposite-sex adults?

The skills discussed in this chapter include:

- 'I' messages
- eye contact
- respect
- immediacy
- reflecting
- active listening
- paraphrasing
- direct expression

- behavioural description
- requesting or behavioural prescription
- deferring attention
- requesting clarification
- empathy
- confrontation
- basic conversational skills
- summarising
- closed statement/questions
- open-ended questions
- confrontational assertion statements
- assertive communication
- empathetic assertive statements

These skills will help you be both a giver and receiver.

'I' Messages – the use of saying I when referring to self. This denotes taking responsibility.

Eye contact – establishing and maintaining eye contact is the behaviour in which both the speaker and listener look into each others eyes. It is noted that in some cultures, eye contact may be a form of disrespect and thus inappropriate. In American and UK society, maintaining eye contact is a form of connecting, communicating, listening and respect for eye contact demonstrates to the speaker and/or receiver that you are interested in the conversation. It is also a good indicator of self esteem, inner security, lack of inferiority, etc.

Respect – respect is recognising and demonstrating the value of another person. You see and treat the person as a human being with dignity and worth. This means you do not discount, objectivy (see someone as a sexual object or 'piece of meat', degrade, etc.).

Immediacy – immediacy is staying in the here and now. This requires staying focused and on topic. The speaker uses here and now language. When you are talking about past issues or history then do not use immediacy, unless you are tying the past with current time frame.

Reflecting – reflecting is also called mirroring. As a listener, it is repeating back to the speaker what was said, as if you were a mirror to the speaker. When done appropriately, this can enhance communication. The problem with mirroring is that some offenders have learned to communicate by simply reflecting back what was said, without any meaning. It has no meaning, it reinforces the 'chameleon' responses. This becomes a form of mimicking, allowing yourself to hide.

Active listening – the listener or receiver allows the speaker or other person to feel understood. You do not need to use the exact words of the speaker. This requires looking the speaker in the eyes and indicating to the other person that you understand what is being said by using both own words and the speaker's.

Paraphrasing – related to active listening, paraphrasing is summarising what the speaker said in your own words. There are several common phrases used. The speaker feels understood. Specific types of introductory phrases include:

I hear you saying . . .
It sounds like . . .
I understand you to say . . .
Are you saying . . . ?
What I think you mean is . . .

Direct expression – direct expression is simply making a statement using 'I' messages. Direct expressions indicate one's taking responsibility for their behaviour. Feelings are expressed directly, but not in a victimising manner. Some examples include: 'I am mad' and 'I am sad'.

Behavioural description (concreteness) – a behavioural description is the use of concrete specific words that describe a thing, person, place or event, Examples: 'Bill, I am irritated with you, (direct expression) you interrupted me before I finished talking' (behavioural description).

Requesting or behavioural prescription – a behavioural prescription is a request for future behaviour. More specifically, when using this technique, you are asking someone to do or not to do something in the future. It is a request using specific terms and behavioural descriptions. Examples:

In the future, Bill, please do not cut me off.
Please ask before you take something.

An example of using the last three skills includes: 'Mary, I am irritated with you (direct expression) you interrupted me when I was talking (behavioural description). In the future please do not interrupt me' (behavioural prescription).

Deferring attention – deferring attention is simply stating that you don't have time to talk now, but would like to talk some other time. It is important to set a specific time down, to get together. By using this skill, the other person doesn't feel left out, abandoned, discounted, or

disrespected. Use this skill, when you can not give the other person your full attention or if you are currently busy. For example, letting the other person know that we are interested in them, and what they want to talk about, yet we are unable to give them our full attention, thus a specific time in the future to talk was given. Example: 'I am currently busy. I would like to talk to you. Can we get together at another time? Perhaps tomorrow at 2 p.m.?'

Requesting clarification – requesting clarification is the skill of simply asking another person to clarify or make his/her statements and meaning clear. This helps clear up mis-communication, mis-perceptions and prevent misunderstanding.

Empathy – empathy may be the most difficult skill to learn. This depends on how self-centred or into your self that you are. Empathy is a basic component in relationships. Empathy is the expression of care and concern for the speaker, while indicating that you understand what was said. This requires being warm. Empathy involves caring for others, being concerned, careful listening and expressing your care and concern. The basic steps of empathy skills are:

1. Listen to what the speaker is saying.
2. Observe the nonverbal behaviours and feeling.
3. Put yourself into the speaker's position or shoes.
4. Respond appropriately, expressing both care and concern for the speaker, along with the understanding of what the speaker said.

Confrontation – confrontation is the skill in which, you firmly discuss issues, problems, inconsistencies, discrepancies, etc. with another. Confrontation involves assertiveness skills. Appropriate confrontation requires empathy, respect and taking responsibility. It is constructively pointing out inconsistencies and discrepancies in a non-attacking manner. Most people think that confrontation is being overly critical or aggressive. The following are kept in mind when using confrontation:

- be respectful and positive
- maintain eye contact
- do not degrade/discount
- listen to what is said
- be warm
- use specific concrete words
- use behavioural regression
- use 'I' messages

- state the purpose of confrontation
- use direct expression

Basic conversational skills – conversations can be subdivided into three components:

A. initiating conversations
B. maintaining conversations
C. terminating conversations

You can use the above skills to implement, continue and terminate conversations.

A.   Initiating conversations – is important to start the interactive process. Appropriate conversational openers may include: hello, hi, waves, excuse me/pardon me (if the person is already in a conversation). This is followed by bringing up a topic.

B.   Maintaining conversations – the above tactics and skills will help you maintain conversation. To maintain a conversation, you need to talk about some theme. You need to stay focused.

C.   Terminating conversation skills – terminating conversational skills are tactics that close out the current conversation. This does not mean the relationship is terminated. Your typical terminating the conversation or exiting the interaction methods include: saying bye, making arrangements to talk again, closing out the conversation. You want to leave the conversation, sending out messages of respect, thus avoiding discounting the other person.

Summarising – this refers to selecting the highlights of details and restating these back to the sender. This is a listening skill.

Closed statement/questions – are statements or questions that require one word or phrase responses, such as 'How many brothers do you have?' 'Have you been in treatment before?'

Open-ended questions – are statements or questions that encourage the responder to elaborate.

Examples:

What do you like about sex offending?
What do you not like about being a sex offender?

Confrontational assertion statements – these statements are especially useful when you feel someone has broken rules or tend to avoid responsibilities and/or commitment that he has committed. These are not attack statements. These statements involve three to four steps:

A. Describing the obligation or commitments objectively.

B. Describe what the other person actually did or didn't do.
C. Express what you would like to happen.
D. Identify the consequences of the other person's actions or persistence in behaviour.

You may choose to omit C depending upon the situation.

Assertive communication – communication style that allows one to state opinions, express beliefs and values without victimising others. Aggressive communication is a communication style that victimises others and demonstrates disregard for their individuality, opinions and values.

Empathetic assertive statements – these statements include two parts. The initial pattern involves communicating concern and compassion for your listener. Expressing genuine concern for your listener encourages more communication. The second pattern describes your situation, thoughts, feelings or needs. In communicating negative feelings, most frequently it is best to identify your feelings initially before you describe the behaviour of the one you are upset with. Be accountable. Own the responsibility for your own emotions. Avoid dumping on others.

I want/need statements – these statements are designed as a means of clarifying your specific desires involved in the communicating process. You will need to be specific regarding the information you convey. This will allow the individual receiving the necessary information needed to determine whether or not they will be willing or able to meet the desire or need requested. An example of such could include: 'I want you to help me with this assignment' or 'would you please type this memo', or 'I would appreciate it if you would refrain from talking loudly in the cell when I am sleeping'. Check voice tone, body language that you are giving, to avoid indications of demand. Ask about avoidance and willingness. Identify the intensity of your need.

Methods to initiate and respond assertively: suggestions for working with sex offenders

Use 'I' statements that convey your ownership of thoughts, feelings and behaviours. Steps involved in developing an appropriate 'I' statement include:

- Identifying your thoughts and feelings. Know your wants and needs.

- Recognising any behavioural responses involved you may have acted on prior to your decision to communicate assertively on this issue.
- Approaching the individual you have conflict with.
- Acknowledging your thoughts and feelings concerning the issue you have conflict with.
- Describing the behaviour of the person while avoiding any temptation to attack the character of this individual.
- Listening to the response of the one you are communicating with. Avoid defensiveness by focused listening to the needs and wants of the other.

Assertive statements do not attack the character of the listener. Attacking statements are victimising and evoke a defensive response from the listener.

You will encounter situations in which you have both positive and negative feelings about what you are communicating. For example:

I feel happy and excited that you are going to be released from prison soon, but I feel sad that I won't be seeing you.

Methods of assertive interaction
You have developed a style and pattern of communicating that you have become accustomed to over the years. Change is not easy, but essential. Sex offending is a lifestyle and your poor communication skills are a significant factor involved in the development in enabling and perpetuation of your offending cycle. Learning new patterns of communication will aid you in breaking old self-defeating patterns of behaviours. Assertive communication training provides opportunity for you to learn skills that enable you to express ones needs, desires, values and opinions while demonstrating respect for the people you interact with.

There are a number of ways to communicate that mutually benefit you and those you interact with. After you have identified your inappropriate communication patterns, you will need to replace your dysfunctional patterns with non-victimising and self-motivating communication. Listed below are several illustrations of patterns that you can utilise to initiate a response to others.

Basic feelings statements: happy, mad, sad, anxious statements
These statements convey your feelings to others. Identifying and labelling your emotional

response is mutually beneficial in how you feel and also verbalisation can also increase self-awareness and validation.
Examples:

I felt very uncomfortable when you talked about our financial difficulties during the company party.
   I like it when you shared your bad day experience with me.
   When you pick your nose, I feel very irritated.

Suggested guidelines
Be specific when using feeling words. You are more likely to be successful at gaining and maintaining interest of your listener if you choose feeling words that correlate the intensity and avoid redundancy.

Do not over-elaborate during the empathetic portion of statements. Focusing too much on the empathetic portion may take away from the latter part.

Avoid shaming or condescending messages.

Focus on the behaviour of the other person. Avoid using this occasion to bring up unrelated incidences or temptation to tell them everything that ever annoyed you about them.

Avoid assumptions and personalisation.

Basic components of social skills
Communication is the exchange of information in the form of verbal and nonverbal between one or more individuals to another. There are several basic components of social skills. These include: emotional recognition, behavioural recognition, reception and behavioural expression. We propose that these components are inherent in most if not all social skills.

Emotional recognition
Emotional recognition is the capability, ability and behaviour of identifying emotions, feelings, sensations, or any physiological sensation with energy. There are two dimensions: (1) self and (2) others. In sex offender treatment, emotional recognition is the key to victim empathy, remorse, insight, managing anger, coping skills, commitment, issue resolution, and relating to others.

Some basic feeling states or categories include:

- Mad – anger to rage types of feelings.
- Sad – depressing, sorrow or down feelings.
- Glad – happy, gay, excited.
- Bad – not feeling good or okay. This may include guilt, low self-worth.

- Apathy – don't care attitude.
- Confused – mixed-up feelings.
- Anxiety – nervousness, tension.
- Had – victimised, put down, hurt.
- Scared – fears, insecurity.

Typically, primary feelings are basic feelings (i.e. hurt, pain, sad, glad, bad, scared) from which others can be generated, such as secondary feelings (anger, bad, apathy, confused, anxiety). See list of different types of feelings that fall under those primary feeling states.

Behavioural recognition
Just like emotional recognition is imperative to social skills so is behavioural recognition. Behavioural recognition is the process of perceiving and decoding or interpreting the other's behaviour. Offenders often have problems deciding what others are saying and doing. Quite often, problems stem from misunderstanding the decoding process.

Reception
Communication is based on one person being receptive to another, not shutting each other out.

Behavioural expression
Behavioural expression is the communicational process of expressing self to another. Just as recognition (decoding processes) and reception are half of communication, expressing oneself is the other half. Communication involves the process of expressing information from one person to another.

Interpersonal issues

In exploring interpersonal relationships, we need to consider:

- The nature and quality of the offender's relations with peers.
- The nature, quality and duration of the offender's friendships.
- The relative age, gender and number of the offender's friends and the kinds of friends they select as associates. Are they susceptible to the influence of others?
- The nature and extent of social isolation – which may possibly indicate a more severe psychopathology.
- Whether the offender is active or passive in social relations, e.g. social interests, activities and memberships. Are they self-centred? Excessively controlling and competitive?

- The nature and stability in their relationships. Obtain a relationship history, including the ages and sexes of the ex-partner's children (adapted from Dougher, 1995; and Groth, 1979).

The worker – offender communication dynamic within the assessment should not be disregarded either. These interpersonal communications involve not only overt acts and statements, but also a range of unspoken, non-verbal, covert and connotative elements such as body posture (Lazarus, 1976). There may be reactions from workers, induced by the offender, which highlight a problem in the way in which they relate to others. Conversely, the offender may react aggressively either to male or female worker and this needs to be understood.

Interpersonal issues are issues that emerge in relationships or within social contexts. Sex offenders have a number of social problems attaching to others and interpersonal issues. Typical examples include: power struggles, jealousy, possessiveness, trust, enmeshed boundaries, etc. For details, see Table 9.2 overleaf.

Appropriate social-sexual relationships

Whilst we all vary in our motivation for intimacy, many sex offenders do present as isolated loners or as having superficial or unsatisfying relationships. The assessment of intimacy deficits and loneliness may facilitate a more thorough understanding of the factors associated with the initiation and maintenance of sexually deviant cognition and patterns of behaviour.

A good way to approach this part of the assessment is to employ questions similar to those asked about children.

What is your partner like or what kind of a person is she?

What about her pleases you?

What displeases you?

What kind of things do you do together? Do you enjoy these?

Do you ever do things together without the children?

Are there things about your partner you would like changed?

Do you tell her things you don't tell anyone else?

How do you show her when she pleases you or you are happy with her?

Table 9.2: Interpersonal issues.

1. Jealousy – is the striving for, desire to or want (drive) to obtain something or characteristics another has. They typically feel inferior.
2. Loneliness – is not being attached to others. Marshall (2001) outlines two types: 1) social loneliness (isolated socially from others) and 2) emotional loneliness (separated or detached from others over a period of time).
3. Boundary issues – a boundary is a set of patterns or interactions defined by overt and covert (implied) rules and roles. It is an established demonstration based on rules and roles in a relationship.
4. Enmeshed boundaries – two or more individuals' identities merge together. Each smothers the other. This leads to co-dependency.
5. Possessiveness – wanting to own and control another individual, as if they belonged to the one possessing them.
6. Power and control issues – the need to control or strongly influence another. The underlining core issues involve inferiority striving for superiority via controlling others and often authority issues.
7. Passive-aggressive – the ventilation of anger or hostility indirectly or 'sideways', instead of directly,
8. Alienation/isolation – the offender maintains social and emotional distance from others.
9. Dependency – one individual 'depends' or 'overly counts/needs' on another for physical things, emotional needs, worth, etc., to the point where the dependent one can not function by one's self without another. One's existence hinges on another.
10. Rejection – feeling one doesn't belong, or not wanted from a particular group.
11. Co-dependency – the dynamic in which both individuals mutually depend upon each other. Their personal identities are merged and lost. Neither can function without the other.
12. Intimacy – an emotional bonding between two or more individuals. Bonding refers to an intense attachment based on trust, respect, warmth, affection, care, closeness, and ability to share deeply (Ward, McCormack and Hudson, 1997).

How does she show you when you please her or that she is happy with you?

How does she know when you are displeased?

How do you know when she is displeased?

What do you have arguments about?

Have you ever used physical force with each other? If yes, please describe (Faller, 1988).

The marital relationship needs to be specifically targeted for information, eliciting how they met their partners; how they were attracted to them; how long it lasted (if it has ended, why and when); how many serious relationships they had before they married; why they decided to marry; how their relationship changed after marriage; what were the good and bad parts of the marriage; did they or their wives have other sexual relationships? Why? When?; the number of children and their relationship with them; their attitudes and expectations regarding marriage; any history of rape, domestic violence, etc.; the quality of their relationships, their ability to see their spouse as a separate individual with her own needs, and the extent to which their descriptions correspond with information elicited from other sources. Marriage failures may reflect an inability to form lasting relationships, or to meet someone else's needs.

How is their sexual relationship with their wife?

Can they describe the kinds of sexual activity they engage in and their approximate frequency?

How often do they engage in sexual activity?

Has this relationship been more or less the same over the years or changing?

Who initiates sex?

Nature and age of partners (girlfriend, wife, child prostitute).

Level of sexual satisfaction with different partners.

The importance of sex to them in their relationships.

The aspects of their sexual relationships they would change, and how.

Their ability to discuss their sexual likes and dislikes with their partner.

Their desired sexual competency (Calder, 1999).

It is very important to establish what each individual offender understands by intimacy and relationships whether they have any blocks or fears in these areas, and whether these are related to one or multiple relationship types (e.g. partner, friends, etc.). We should always point out any examples of inappropriate intimacy, e.g. with children or young people.

How the offender reacts to the workers (and vice versa) may provide us with vital clues as to their ability to form adult relationships – as should parallel areas such as observations of supervised contact, joint interviews with their partner, etc. Workers do need to be conscious of the likelihood of different responses to the degree of loneliness and/or intimacy experienced by the offender, at the time of their work as compared to the time of their offending.

Workers need to model, and stress the importance in understanding, the close relationship between emotions, behaviours and intimate relationships. It may identify 'chains' of emotions and behaviours associated with their intimate relationships and can lead to interventions tailored to them, e.g. addressing specific relationship deficits rather than the broader emphasis on social skills training (Ward et al., 1995).

It is well worth spending some time on this area as, once identified, there is the potential to help the offender make huge changes in the areas of relationships and intimacy deficits (Marshall, 1993).

Many hard core chronic offender's lifestyles are constructed from deviant behaviours. They struggle with decreasing deviant arousal and replacing it with appropriate arousal and behaviour. Much of their arousal is expressed through deviant fantasies. The social context or deviant fantasies involve violating or hurting someone else. We emphasise that while decreasing inappropriate deviant fantasies and behaviours, the offender needs to replace them with appropriate ones. We have provided some guidelines on appropriate sexual fantasy below:

Guidelines in the development of appropriate social sexual fantasies:

1. Elements of an appropriate sexual fantasy:
   - Mutual consenting partners
   - Age appropriate
   - Non-threatening or manipulative
   - Emphasis on relationship elements (care, concern, intimacy, etc.)
2. Relationship contextual elements:
   - Relationship elements
     - honesty (including acknowledging past history)
     - mutual attraction and affection
     - care and concern
     - respect
     - mutual consent
     - equal knowledge of sex issues
     - communication
     - give and take
     - self disclosure
     - the type and kind of relationship wanted

- trust
- romantic feelings
- acceptance
- Partner's characteristics:
  - facial features
  - build of body
  - hair color
  - body characteristics/features
  - dress
  - psychological behaviours
  - personality characteristics
  - ideal partner characteristics
- Relationship time line:
  - time line of the relationship
  - time frame of actual sexual behaviours ranging from talking, foreplay to after play
3. Sexual fantasy components (Ross, 1992)
   Step 1 – appropriate sexual build up:
   The actual sexual encounter:
   - Include who, what, where, when, how etc., in the scenario.
   - Mutual consent and age appropriate (with no manipulation, deviant behaviour, etc.)
   - Privacy – privacy is necessary, thus choose an appropriate place.
   - Foreplay – foreplay is the behaviour leading up to more intense sexual contact (i.e., oral sex, intercourse) include: talking, touching, holding, kissing, etc.
   Step 2 – Sexual Activities:
   - Sexual behaviour/birth control – Non aggressive sexual activities or behaviours need to be non aggressive, non hurting, non-'scary', no fetish behaviours (i.e., urine, faeces, cross dressing, sadism, etc.). Include birth control devices.
   Step 3 – After play
   - After sexual encounters, then engage in affectionate behaviours, such as, holding, touching, kissing, similar elements as in foreplay. This reinforces the care, concern, respect, love . . . intimacy element of the relationship.
   Step 4 – Specific guidelines:
   - When developing fantasies and imagery use all sensory modes (i.e., visual, looks, auditory/sounds, movements/touch/ feeling, smell, taste).
   - First person, present tense or the here and now.
   - Very detailed description.
   - Check for cognitive distortions, any type of victimising elements to ensure non-victimising elements are present.

- For conditioning appropriate arousal, the adult-adult sexual scenes need to be explicit – within the relationship context.

Conclusions

This chapter has attempted to address the areas of social and life skills and the allied concepts of attachment and intimacy. Each of these is potentially seen as part of the development and maintenance of sexual offending. The key is the link between good assessment and treatment work.

References

Bartholomew K and Horowitz L M (1991) Attachment Styles Among Adults: A Test of a Four Category Model. *Journal of Personality and Social Psychology.* 61: 226–44.

Becker-Lausen E and Mallon-Kraft S (1997) Pandemic Outcomes: The Intimacy Variable. In Kanber G K and Jasinski J L (Eds.) *Out of The Darkness: Contemporary Perspectives on Family Violence.* Thousand Oaks, Ca: Sage, 49–57.

Bowlby J (1969) *Attachment and Loss: Vol. 1 Attachment.* New York: Basic Books.

Brehm S S (1992) *Intimate Relationships.* (2nd edn.) NY: McGraw Hill.

Bretherton I (1985) Attachment Theory: Retrospect and Prospect. In Bretherton I and Waters E (Eds.) *Growing Points of Attachment Theory and Research Monographs of The Society for Research in Child Development, 50,* (Serial No 5–38).

Brownmiller S (1975) *Against Our Will: Men, Women and Rape.* London: Penguin.

Calder M C (1999) *Assessing Risk in Adult Males Who Sexually Abuse Children: A Practitioner's Guide.* Lyme Regis, Dorset: Russell House Publishing.

Calder M C (2001) *Juveniles and Children Who Sexually Abuse: Frameworks for Assessment.* (2nd edn.) Lyme Regis, Dorset: Russell House Publishing.

Carich M S and Adkerson D L (1995) *Adult Sexual Offender Assessment Packet.* Brandon, VT: Safer Society Press.

Check J V P, Perlman D and Malamuth M N (1985) Loneliness and Aggressive Behaviour. *J Soc Person Relations.* 2: 243–52.

Conger J C and Conger A J (1986) Assessment of Social Skills. In Ciminero A R et al. (Eds.) *Handbook of Behavioural Assessment.* NY: John Wiley and Sons, 526–60.

Diamont L and Windholz G (1981) Loneliness in College Students: Some Theoretical, Empirical and Therapeutic Considerations. *Journal of College Students Personality.* 22: 515–22.

Dougher M J (1995) Clinical Assessment of Sex Offenders. In Schwartz B K and Cellini H R (Eds.) *The Sex Offender: Corrections, Treatment and Legal Practice.* Kingston, NJ: Civic Research Institute, Inc.

Faller K (1988) *Child Sexual Abuse: An Inter-Disciplinary Manual for Diagnosis, Case Management, and Treatment.* London: Macmillan.

Finkelhor D (1984) *Child Sexual Abuse: Theory and Research.* NY: The Free Press.

Garlick Y, Marshall W and Thornton D (1996) Intimacy Deficits and Attribution of Blame Among Sexual Offenders. *Legal and Criminological Psychology.* 1: 251–8.

Graham F, Richardson G and Bhate S (1997) Assessment. In Hoghugi M S, Bhate S R and Graham F (Eds.) *Working With Sexually Abusive Adolescents.* Thousand Oaks, Ca: Sage Publications, 52–91.

Graves R, Openshaw D K and Adams G R (1992) Adolescent Sex Offenders and Social Skills Training. *International Journal of Offender Therapy and Comparative Criminology.* 36: 2, 139–53.

Groth A N (1979) *Men Who Rape: The Psychology of the Offender.* NY: Plenum.

Haggerty R J, Sherrod L R, Garmezy N and Rutter M (1996) *Stress, Risk, and Resilience in Children and Adolescents.* NY: Cambridge University Press.

Hudson S M and Ward T (1997b) Intimacy, Loneliness and Attachment Styles in Sex Offenders. *Journal of Interpersonal Violence.* 12: 3, 323–39.

Lazarus A A (1976) *Multi-Modal Behaviour Therapy.* NY: Springer Publishing.

Marshall W L (1989) Intimacy, Loneliness and Sexual Offenders. *Behavioural Research and Therapy.* 27: 491–503.

Marshall W L (1993) The Role of Attachment, Intimacy, and Loneliness in The Aetiology and Maintenance of Sexual Offending. *Sexual and Marital Therapy.* 8: 109–21.

Marshall W L (2001) Enhancing Social and Relationship Skills. In Carich M S and Mussack S (Eds.) *Handbook of Sexual Abuser Assessment and Treatment.* Brandon, VT: Safer Society Press, 149–62.

McAdams D P (1980) A Thematic Coding Scheme for The Intimacy Motive. *J Resperson.* 14: 413–32.

Morris D (1983) Attachment and Intimacy. In Stricker G and Fisher M N (Eds.) *Intimacy.* New York: Plenum Press.

Ross J E (1992) *Deviant Sexual Fantasy Group Handout.* The Waypoint Program at New Hope.

Sanday P R (1981) The Socio-Cultural Context of Rape: A Cross-Cultural Study. *Journal of Social Issues.* 37: 4, 5–27.

Segal V and Marshall W L (1985) Heterosexual Social Skills in a Population of Rapists and Child Molesters. *Journal of Consulting and Clinical Psychology.* 53: 55–63.

Seidman B T, Marshall W L, Hudson S M and Robertson P J (1994) An Examination of Intimacy and Loneliness in Sex Offenders. *Journal of Interpersonal Violence.* 9: 4, 518–34.

Squirrel G (1998) *Developing Life Skills.* Lyme Regis, Dorset: Russell House Publishing.

Squirrel G (1999) *Developing Social Skills.* Lyme Regis, Dorset: Russell House Publishing.

Ward T, Hudson S M, Marshall W L and Siegert R (1995) Attachment Style and Intimacy Deficits in Sexual Offenders: A Theoretical Framework. *Sexual Abuse: A Journal of Research and Treatment.* 7: 4, 317–35.

Ward T, McCormack J and Hudson S M (1997) Sexual Offender's Perceptions of Their Intimate Relationships. *Sexual Abuse: A Journal of Research and Treatment.* 9: 1, 57–74.

Ward T, Hudson S M and Marshall W L (1996) Attachment Style in Sex Offenders: A Preliminary Study. *The Journal of Sex Research.* 33: 17–26.

Waring E M and Reddon J R (1983) The Measurement of Intimacy in Marriage. *Journal of Clinical Psychology.* 39: 53–7.

Weiss R S (1974) The Provisions of Social Relationships. In Rubin Z (Ed.) *Doing Unto Others.* Englewood, Cliffs, NJ.: Prentice-Hall.

Chapter Ten

Aftercare Programmes

Introduction

Aftercare treatment is the (often time-limited) follow-up treatment, management and care of a sex offender from an intensive primary treatment programme. The intensive programme encompasses both residential and outpatient facilities, recognising there are some crucial differences. For example, offenders making the transition from inpatient to outpatient care are moving from a peer network of similar offenders and a regimented culture that disappear on their release. In either case, aftercare programmes are usually less intensive compared to the original primary intensive programme, although it is often higher for those moving out of prison. A rule of thumb is to reduce the frequency of contacts by no more than 50% and the aftercare should continue for a minimum of one-year after the transition.

Sex offender treatment is best viewed as a continuum of care, ranging from intensive treatment through aftercare and lifelong maintenance. The initial intensive treatment is aimed at reducing the deviant behaviour, enabling the offender to develop a state of abstinence, while the aftercare programme helps ensure an offender's continued success in maintaining himself within the community. Aftercare can thus be seen as a transitional therapeutic process (Mussach and Carich, 2001). It is not usually aimed at developing new life changes, although early releases may require a re-adjustment be made to embrace the work or monitoring needed. It is important to discuss the aftercare programme with the offender so that they see it as one part of a longer process and that they have graduated successfully from the intensive treatment programme. This is important since we know that any perceived stresses by the offender are related to lapses and relapses (see Chapter 8 for further details on these points). Aftercare is predicated on the assumption that there is no cure, thus an offender could relapse anytime. The offender needs continued care, as recovery is a life long process. As such, professional support and monitoring should remain immediately available to constructively intervene when lapses, relapses or difficulties arise, particularly since most lay people remain ignorant of the cycles used by sex offenders and the specific warning signs for this particular individual.

The purposes of this chapter are to discuss aftercare as a component of sex offender treatment; discuss some goals and potential mechanisms for aftercare programming.

Components of aftercare

There are several components of successful aftercare programmes. These are a residential placement or living arrangement; supervision and management via monitoring; and treatment. These components all work together, to help externally manage the offender and enabling the offender to manage himself. This is important when the release and choices facing the offender often seem overwhelming. Aftercare, especially for post incarcerated sex offenders, needs to be carefully structured within a network of support systems. It is hoped that the offender will have started to develop new support networks and life skills during their treatment programme. Teamwork among management providers is absolutely necessary. All people working with the offender need to be on the same wavelength and such teamwork and communication can help the offender make his transition from primary treatment to aftercare.

Residential placement and structure

The primary purpose of a structured living environment is to facilitate the offender's successful reintegration into society. Food and lodging, as well as emotional support, are provided while the offender obtains gainful employment, develops support networks and works out constructive means of coping with influences to return to a destructive lifestyle (Carich, 1991a and b; 1992).

Residential placement is used broadly to refer to the living arrangements of the offender. All post-incarcerated offenders need to reside in a structured setting. If they have done 'time' in a prison or other institutional setting, they may be institutionalised. Institutionalisation refers to the offender's dependency upon a set structure. In essence, the offender doesn't know how to live independently. In this case, a halfway house, work release, or structured group home is recommended. In order to be effective the establishment needs to inherit the details of the treatment work undertaken previously. From a highly structured environment, the offender is gradually weaned and moved to independent living. Part of the gradual process may be a halfway house with limited staff supervision. Another middle step could be group homes. Some specific considerations concerning the structure of residential places include:

- Maintain a set of rules and multi-level consequences for rule infractions. This may range from verbal reprimand through the restriction of whereabouts within the community to re-incarceration (Mussach and Carich, 2001). Provision of a definite structure is essential.
- Train staff in the management treatment of sex offenders.
- Maintain and monitor house restriction/privileges/movement.
- Maintain individual levels of restricted and monitored privileges.
- Monitor 'phone privileges.
- Monitor movement.
- Supervise travel.
- Carefully select and screen employment.
- Screen peer group.
- Assign house chores and work assignments.
- Supervised phases of progression, privileges and responsibilities.
- Monitor and/or supervise visits.
- In-house treatment (i.e., life skills, social skills, house meetings, drug/alcohol support groups/SA, special groups, etc.)
- Carefully developed policies and procedures including specific consequences for rule infractions and the obtainment of privileges.
- Polygraph and evaluation as required.
- Assess and screen, as needed.
- Maintain a firmly established hierarchical system.

For intensive offenders from intensive outpatient programmes, residential issues centre on re-unification problems and protecting victims. In reunification situations, things need to progress slowly, gradually and be carefully monitored. The family needs to be in treatment for successful re-integration (Thomas and Wilson, 2001).

Treatment-specific components

The components of aftercare treatment may not be as intense as the primary programmes and the offender's issues are often dealt with as they arise, although any unfinished business from the primary treatment programme should be addressed. In reality, offenders come into aftercare programmes with issues. Even offenders from the most intense and in-depth residential programmes, will have issues to work through. For post-incarcerated offenders, issues emerge as the offender makes the transition from prison into society. Treatment plays several roles. One role is work on issues. Another role is to help monitor and supervise the offender. A third role is to provide a support service that enhances the offender's capability of maintaining abstinence through problem solving and coping strategies.

A specific list of treatment components include:

- Support groups (AA/NA/SA, house meetings, other group types).
- Individual counselling.
- Group therapy.
- Relationship/family therapy.
- Types of therapy:
  - Relapse intervention approaches are dynamic cognitive/behavioural strategies that help the sex offender enhance skills to identify assault cycles, triggers and/or risk factors, relapse cues, cognitive distortions and defences or disowning behaviours, and using interventions to interrupt or defuse deviant responses, lapses and relapses. This is a critical area of aftercare since aftercare is a time of difficulties and mistakes for offenders.
  - Cognitive restructuring approaches identifying, challenging and changing distorted beliefs.
  - Behavioural interventions – overt/covert conditioning and stimulus control methods.
  - Medications – use of Depo-Provera and/or other anti depressant medications that would alter the psychological responses and thus reduce sexual arousal. This is effective for those offenders who struggle with extremely frequent, intrusive sexual fantasies coupled with compulsive or impulsive acting-out. It is likely to be used for those who started their prescription in the substantive treatment programme since a speedy withdrawal is contra-indicated.

– Cognitive behavioural strategies – using thought process and activities (such as writing, maintaining notes, etc.) to induce and maintain change.
– Psychiatric consultation as needed.
– Life skills training, to help re-integrate back into society.

Most offender treatment is done in small group settings, with supportive individual counselling as needed. Aftercare groups typically work with relapse prevention related issues. They are cognitive-behavioural in nature, with an integrated RP component. The offender can discuss triggers or risk factors, cues and interventions. Thus, the offenders evaluate existing coping strategies and develop more interventions. Occasionally, some offenders may need medication to stabilise various psychopathologies and reduce deviant arousal. In these cases, psychiatric intervention is necessary. In some cases, sex offender specific family therapy may be required to help the offender's transition back into the family or at least resolve family related issues.

Peer support groups such as AA, NA, GA, SA, etc. can be beneficial. Offenders have to be prepared to go to these types of meetings. They will meet all sorts of people. Some will be using drugs, prostitution, or will be very needy and clingy. Offenders need to prepare for these scenarios with some specific interventions.

Supervision and monitoring

The cohesive link between residential care and treatment is supervision and monitoring. Supervision is usually composed of some type of community service parole or probation agents. In these cases, guidelines are established by specific conditions. Residential care staff and treatment professionals can also participate in formally supervising offenders. They can keep tabs on the offender's behaviour and level of cooperation. Some specific elements of supervision are outlined below, but are detailed more in Cumming and Buell (1997).

Two types of supervision include:

1. External supervision – Monitoring from external or outside sources.
   - Residential placement site.
   - Employer cooperation and monitoring.
   - Treating agencies.
   - Support systems.
   - Community services/probation/parole – the level of supervision varies from area to

area. Typically agents monitor the offender on a monthly basis or as needed.
2. Internal supervision – Monitoring from within the offender.
   - Use of relapse intervention/prevention strategies.
   - Maintaining journals and logs (entries include date, time, entry of significant events and reactions).
   - Use of daily tracking sheets or systems (name, date, ID number, page number, list each significant event with reaction, thoughts/feelings/behaviours and overall responses with the rating of appropriate and inappropriate coping strategies) to be given to staff.

A detailed description of the legal process for offender release and monitoring in the UK is available in Calder (1999).

External supervision

External supervision involves people monitoring the offender. There are several methods, besides residential staff and treatment staff monitoring his behaviour. Community service agencies can use the following:

- drug drops
- home monitors (i.e., ankle bracelets)
- alcohol checks
- telephone checks
- check in/out system
- drop-in checks
- travel logs
- teaching methods

Those who monitor the offender must be prepared to confront the offender when they observe lapses or relapses. Sanctions are an important component of aftercare just as support is, and frequently acts as a motivator to the offender. The aim is to shift the offender from external sanctions to internal control, although this will not be appropriate for all offenders. For this latter group, there is a need to develop an ongoing external network with a remit to remind the offender of the risks for them as well as the sanctions available.

Internal supervision

Aftercare presents an opportunity for the offender to assess the effectiveness of self-monitoring skills developed in treatment. Internal supervision involves the offender monitoring themselves. This is contingent on several criteria: commitment towards recovery, level of RP skills, level of coping skills and other skills. There are several methods that can be used for self-monitoring. These include: journals, travel logs, relapse plans, and tracking deviant fantasies: all of which provide valuable ongoing information about the offender's current state and level of functioning. The offender tracks his own encounters with risk factors. This method is good unless the offender starts their cycle again.

Carich and Stone (1996) developed a 'future autobiography' in which the offender records their history, including coping strategies employed and the risk of re-offence. The offender then identifies any new coping strategies developed and how they will be used in the future.

Conditions of release for post-incarcerated offenders

The offender needs the structure. In fact, the changes in their life style 'should' correlate and fit with the conditions of supervision, imposed by the system. Several elements can be considered: substance abuse monitoring, agency monitoring, polygraph, supervised travel, travel logs, check-in/out systems, telephone monitoring, etc. Conditions of community supervision need to consider the offender's specific risk factors. Supervision plans can be tailor-made.

There are levels of restriction, depending upon the offender's victimology, assault cycle, risk factors, available resources, etc.

There are a number of issues for post-incarcerated offenders. These can be placed in several categories:

Self worth issues

Self worth can be viewed in a number of ways. For practical purposes, at one level worth/ esteem can fluctuate in any given situation. At another level, worth is constant or stable. Most offenders had/have major issues with worth. They may have based worth on their deviant behaviour, as a means of compensation. The offender needs to feel good and value himself, and they face enormous amounts of stress. They need to continue to feed their self worth with appropriate behaviour. Self worth can act as an internal guide to the offender in avoiding high-risk situations by reinforcing responsible, accountable behaviour. At the aftercare stage, it

is hoped that all contact will validate the offender's ongoing gains rather than the need for further intervention (Mussach and Carich, 2001).

Lifestyle issues

The successful treatment and management of the sex offender depends upon the level and amount of antisocial characteristics. Hard core psychopathic offenders have less of a conscience. They tend to be more narcissistic or self-centred. These (and other) tendencies may flare up from time to time

Adjustment issues

Adjustment issues emerge for post-incarcerated offenders. The issues with institutionalisation or dependency on a structure emerge as the offender has to cope with a new environment. The challenges and choices of a new environment are very stressful. A simple task of ordering food can be overwhelming. The offender needs to be moved from dependency or structure to independence with lower levels of monitoring.

Cycle issues

Cycle issues refer to the lapses that offenders will experience. These lapse issues will emerge from time to time and the offender needs to use these issues to develop self-awareness and competency skills. Cycle behaviour needs to be continuously addressed.

Interpersonal issues

Sex offenders may be socially starved of appropriate sexual partners. Their own needs may emerge and mate selection processes need to be monitored. Developing new relationships can be stressful. The offender's relationships need to be addressed in order to monitor enabling and risk situations.

Discontinuing the aftercare provision

Mussach and Carich (2001) provided us with some helpful criteria upon which to take the difficult decision as to when and how to end the aftercare provision. They are:

- Regular attendance at aftercare sessions.
- Regular attendance at meetings with their supervising officer.
- Maintenance of behaviours that were part of the decision criteria to move the offender into aftercare.

- Recognition of lapses or relapses with immediate efforts to use healthy coping strategies.
- Maintenance of the support network.
- Maintenance of stability within the community in areas of employment, education, relationship and family.
- Agreement between the professionals and the support network that termination is appropriate.

Behaviour changes to be observed in the offender when they return home include:

- Starts to abuse alcohol or drugs.
- Stresses the impossibility of re-offending.
- Interested in pornography.
- Stresses the innocence of his sexual contact with children.
- Begins to minimise the impact of his past offending.
- Keeps leaving the house for no apparent reason.
- Lies in other areas of his life.
- Gets involved in youth activities.
- Wants to be left alone with the children.
- Changes noticeably in his sexual functioning.
- Discusses sexual issues in front of the children.
- Starts to use innuendos.
- Becomes paranoid and stresses the fact that you don't trust him (Wyre, 1987).

Carich has developed the notion of recovery assessments in some detail (see Chapter 11) that should form an integral part of any aftercare treatment programme.

Conclusions

Aftercare treatment plays a vital role in the management and treatment of sex offenders. It is a time of polishing and solidifying the safety, support, non-destructive coping and self-monitoring strategies developed by the offender during treatment. It is also a time to clarify areas needing further therapeutic focus.

Identifying these areas of concern – situations that occur prior to re-offence and during aftercare – further clarifies environmental triggers in offender's assault cycles. Offenders can then get help in developing additional constructive coping strategies to increase the likelihood of long-term safety (Mussach and Carich, 2001)

References

Calder M C (1999) *Assessing Risk in Adult Males Who Sexually Abuse Children*. Dorset: Russell House Publishing.

Carich M S (1991a) Aftercare Programs: An Essential Element for Post-Incarcerated Sex Offenders. *INMAS Newsletter*. 4: 1, 15–8.

Carich M S (1991b) Some Notes On Individualized Aftercare Programming. *INMAS Newsletter*. 4: 2, 9–11.

Carich M S (1992) Developing A Sex Offender Aftercare Program. *INMAS Newsletter*. 6: 1, 12–3.

Carich M S and Stone M (1996) *Sex Offender Relapse Intervention Workbook*. Chicago: Adler School of Professional Psychology.

Carich M S and Stone M (2001) Aftercare for Medium and Hardcore Sexual Offenders. *Journal of Individual Psychology*. 57: 1, 60–6.

Cumming G F and Buell M (1997) *Supervision of the Sex Offender*. Brandon, VT: Safer Society Press.

Mussack S E and Carich M S (2001) Aftercare Programming. In Carich M S and Mussack S (Eds.) *Handbook for Sexual Abuser Assessment and Treatment*. Brandon, VT: Safer Society Press, 225–36.

Thomas J and Viar C W (2001) Family Treatment of Adult Sexual Abusers. In Carich M S and Mussack S E (Eds.) *Handbook for Sexual Abuser Assessment and Treatment*. Brandon, VT: Safer Society Press, 163–92.

Wyre R (1987) *Working With Sex Abuse*. Oxford: Perry Publications.

Chapter Eleven

Risk, Recovery and Progress Assessments

Risk assessments

Risk is about the uncertainty of outcomes. As life contains a multitude of uncertainties, and part of our personal growth comes out of our success or otherwise in learning from experiences of coping with these situations, then philosophically it could be argued that as uncertainty has an irremovable place in human life, then so does risk. When workers talk about risk, they are referring to the likelihood of serious or even irretrievably harmful consequences, which could arise from a dangerous situation. Uncertainty, by definition, cannot be fully knowable. Thus, no professional can be held to be negligible for not realising what is unknowable. Similarly with dilemmas: dilemmas are risks where there are no harm-free options, and a decision is needed, as delay would be harmful. However, where past knowledge provides a reasonable basis for the likely prediction of such an uncertainty or dilemma, then the question arises if it was knowable in this way, why was action not taken to avoid it? Ignorance is therefore not always an excuse (Stafford and Hardy, 1996).

Wald and Woolverton (1990) pointed out that there is a lack of clarity about the meaning of risk assessment. They argued that the proper meaning of risk assessment is 'a process for assessing the likelihood that a given person (usually a parent) will harm the child in the future' (p486). The goal of risk assessment is thus to: guide workers in better identifying situations wherein children are vulnerable to abuse or neglect; improve consistency or service delivery; aid managers in their decisions about priorities for services; and help staff design outcome orientated plans and target resources effectively (English and Pecora, 1984).

The term risk assessment is used to define a number of different assessment and decision-making processes in various agencies. We believe that it is the systematic collection of information to identify if risks are involved, and if so, what these are; identifying the likelihood of their future occurrence (prediction); whether there is a need for further work; and what form this should take. It can also be used to predict the escalation of the presenting behaviour as well as the client's motivation for change.

Features of risk

The previous chapters will have reinforced that sex offenders are a heterogeneous group. It follows, therefore, that a comprehensive assessment is needed to pinpoint the specific problems within the presenting individual. Each sex offender has a specific profile that needs to be accurately identified, and the worker needs to identify the interplay of numerous factors, which have predisposed the offender to abuse a child. In line with this, McEwan and Sullivan (1996) have set out 21 important features of risk that need assessing:

- Level and types of denial.
- Type of offences committed.
- Category of offender – extra-familial, intra-familial, sadistic, non-sadistic.
- Target (victim) group.
- Duration of offence pattern. Age at onset of offending.
- Variation of offence pattern.
- Motivation to change. Experience of previous treatment and acceptance of worker assumptions.
- Presence of external factors affecting motivation, e.g. a collusive or 'well-groomed' family will block an offender's progress.
- Level of acceptance of responsibility for the abuse.
- Level of victim empathy.
- Mental illness.
- Drug and alcohol misuse.
- Non-sexual offending. Previous convictions.
- Sexual aggressiveness.
- Abusive personality.
- Seriousness of sexually abusive behaviour (often different from conviction or offence charged).
- Cultural issues – target group. It is important to note that the power base of most institutions is white and this may impinge on the ability of black victims to disclose.
- Learning disability – psychological testing required as many programmes are cognitive/behavioural. Relapse prevention

techniques require direct consequences rather than victim empathy.

- Level of self-esteem/social isolation.
- Own victim experience.
- Links with other sexual offenders – co-defendants, paedophile rings? (p149).

The specific focus of risk assessment changes depending upon the particular step in the process, ranging from being concerned at whether and how fast to respond to the report at intake, to ensuring child safety during the investigation phase, to assessing whether the risk factors have been addressed before returning the child home or closing the case. In order for the protection process to be effective, the process must be related to the original situation. For example, the risk may be controlled after investigation, but the risk does not go away until the sources of the risk are altered.

It is a term which is often misused because it focuses exclusively on the risk of harm, whereas in any other enterprise a risk equation also includes a chance of benefit resulting (Carson, 1994). Any risk assessment, should, therefore, be concerned with weighing up the pros and cons of a client's circumstances in order to inform decision-making as to what should happen with regard to intervention and protection. It involves examining the client's situation to identify and weigh various **risk factors** (such as the influences that increase the likelihood that a child will be harmed in a certain way), strengths, resources, and available agency services. This assessment information can then be used to determine if a child is safe, what agency resources are needed to keep the child safe, and under what circumstances a child should be removed from the family. Risk assessment is a feature of all assessments, as risk needs to be continuously re-assessed as the circumstances change and/or more information becomes available to the workers.

There have been many attempts to develop risk assessment models and guidance in order to assist professionals in making decisions about individual children. Whilst research-derived models are better than those built on professional consensus, both struggle to embrace the diversity of practice situations, particularly in sexual abuse situations. Since many models tend to err on the side of over-prediction, professionals need to accept that they represent a tool, which is not an end in

itself, merely an aid to professional judgement. The term risk assessment can thus refer to both a structured form of decision-making as well as to specific instruments or frameworks that are used in the process (e.g. Calder, 1997; 1999a and b; Calder, Calder, 2000; Calder, 2001; 2002a).

Developments in risk measurement

What is clear is that there have been some important developments on how we should conduct risk assessments in the sexual abuse field (see Calder, 2000 for a detailed review). There has been a shift toward meta-analyses, providing an alternative to the narrative review in seeking to produce a standardised overview of a large number of empirical studies. Meta-analysis is 'a technique that enables a reviewer to objectively and statistically analyse the findings of each study as data points ... The procedure of meta-analysis involves collecting relevant studies, using the summary statistics from each study as a unit of analysis, and then analysing the aggregated data in a quantitative manner using statistical tests' (Izzo and Ross, 1990: p135). The meta-analyses as they apply to sex offender work have provided a framework upon which to construct the next generation of risk measurement tools. In doing so, they can inform the design of interventions for use with offenders that may have an impact on the rates of offending that is significantly greater than chance. Given the serious consequences of sexual abuse, special care is justified in the evaluation of sexual offenders. Future behaviour can never be predicted with certainty. Nevertheless, a growing body of research indicates that well-informed practitioners can predict sexual recidivism with at least moderate accuracy.

Meta-analyses highlight two issues with respect to assessment: the importance of the assessment of risk and the need to assess criminogenic factors (Andrews and Bonta, 1994). With respect to the former, these authors formulated the risk principle for effective programme delivery. The risk principle states that an important predictor of success is that offenders assessed as medium to high risk of recidivism should be selected for intensive treatment programmes. Effective risk assessment will allow accurate matching of the client group with the consequent delivery of the programme.

There are some problems attached to meta-analyses. Firstly, the 'apples and oranges' threat of mixing dissimilar studies into the analysis, resulting in meaningless findings; second, the 'file drawer' problem of selecting only published studies for analysis; third, 'garbage in garbage out', leading to the undue influence within the analysis of poorly designed and conducted original studies (Sharpe, 1997).

Static risk factors

Historically, risk assessments go wrong when there is too little attention to past records, poor information, poor assumptions and attending to the wrong things and other agendas. Risk assessment has also relied heavily on the use of static risk factors, but this reinforces the view that 'once a high-risk sex offender, always a high-risk sex offender', regardless of what treatment they have received and what personal attention the offender has given to addressing the originating areas of concern.

Hanson (1998; 1999) argued that risk assessments consider two distinct concepts: enduring propensities, or potentials to re-offend; and factors that indicate the onset of new offences. These offence triggers are not random, but can be expected to be organised into predictable patterns (offence cycles), some unique to the individual and some common to most sexual offenders.

Different evaluation questions require the consideration of different types of risk factors. Static, historical variables (e.g. prior offences, childhood maladjustment) can indicate deviant developmental trajectories and, as such, enduring propensities to sexually offend.

There are a variety of predictive methods, ranging from gut feeling (slightly better than chance), judgement after review, sexual precons or the range of emerging prediction scales. Table 11.1 below sets out some of the known static risk

predictors and some unvalidated predictors in common use.

Static risk factors cannot tell us when an offence will occur, nor whether any intervention has generated enough change to reduce an individual's probability of re-offending (Hudson et al., 2002).

In general terms, workers continue to struggle with how to make predictions regarding who is at risk of re-offending and under what conditions relapse may occur. To date, risk assessment instruments have primarily focused on static risk factors, but there are emerging materials relating to dynamic risk assessment. Whilst we can reliably identify groups of sex offenders who are at substantial risk of sexual recidivism, we know much less about how to reduce that risk (Hanson, 2002).

The advent of dynamic risk factors

Evaluating changes in risk levels (e.g. treatment outcome) requires the consideration of dynamic, changeable risk factors (e.g. co-operation with supervision, deviant sexual preferences). The relatively low recidivism rates of sexual offenders, makes it difficult to detect dynamic risk factors. Over a 4–5 year period, approximately 10–15% of sexual offenders will be detected committing a new sexual offence (Hanson and Bussiere, 1998). Although age is sometimes considered a dynamic factor, the most important dynamic factors are those that respond to treatment. Dynamic factors can further be classified as stable or acute. Stable factors have the potential to change, but typically endure for months or years (e.g. personality disorder) and, as such, represent ongoing risk potential. In contrast, acute factors (e.g. negative mood) may be present for a short duration (minutes, days) and can signal the timing of offending.

Table 11.1

Range of static predictors	Unvalidated predictors
• single, aged 18–24 • volume, diversity and early onset of sexual offending • unrelated or stranger victims • male victims • non-contact offences • general criminality • psychopathy • sexual preference	• employment difficulties • low job status • poor educational attainment • ethnic identity • anxiety/depression • poor social skills • denial • acquittal • judged motivation • judged empathy for victims

Stable dynamic risk factors are probably most useful for treatment providers and those responsible for release decisions, whilst acute factors are of more interest to those responsible for supervision (Hudson et al., 2002). Stable factors have potentially profound benefits, not least of which is rewarding the offender for the effort involved in modifying aspects of his behaviour and personality.

Dynamic variables are more subjective in nature than static risk factors and more difficult to measure in a consistent way across different workers. Reliance on the skills of the worker is not a bad thing as professional judgement is essential. What is needed, however, is a way of applying it in a more systematic and standardised manner.

Studies informing static and dynamic risk factor refinement

Most risk decisions require consideration of both static and dynamic risk factors.

Hanson and and Bussiere (1998) produced a meta-analysis of sexual offender recidivism studies in an attempt to predict relapse. This examined 61 different follow-up studies including a total of 28,972 sexual offenders. They found that the largest single predictor of sexual recidivism was the presence of deviant sexual preferences and they concluded that sex offender recidivism was closely related to sexual deviance. They suggested that this could be inferred in a number of ways, i.e. they had:

- Deviant sexual interests (PPG measurement).
- Committed a variety of sexual crimes.
- Begun offending at an early age, or had a lengthy history of sex offending.
- Targeted boys, strangers, or unrelated victims.

This suggests that a sexual offending history contributes most to the successful prediction of recidivism. For example, they found that under 10% of first offenders were re-convicted within five years of prison release, compared with a recidivism rate of over 30% for those with any previous sexual offence convictions.

Whilst they found that over 20 variables contributed to the successful prediction of sexual recidivism, for the most part the magnitude of the relationship was so small that it was of negligible practical use. In the end they were able to identify about 10 variables that made some, mostly small, contribution to

predictive accuracy, including being unmarried and failing to complete a treatment programme. They noted that risk scales that predicted general (i.e. non-sexual) recidivism well were related only weakly to sexual recidivism. Noticeably absent from the list of risk factors were any measures of subjective distress or general psychological symptoms (e.g. low self-esteem, depression).

Whilst dynamic risk factors are too important to ignore, there are no well-established dynamic risk factors for sexual offence recidivism. There are, however, some potential dynamic predictors of sexual assault recidivism:

- intimacy and attachment deficits
- negative peer influences
- attitudes tolerant of sexual abuse
- emotional/sexual self-regulation
- general self-regulation

Combining risk factors

Since no single factor is sufficient to determine whether offenders will or will not recidivate, practitioners need to consider a range of relevant risk factors. There are three plausible methods by which risk factors can be combined into overall evaluations of risk:

- Empirically guided clinical evaluations: which begin with the overall recidivism base rate, and then adjusts the risk level by considering factors that have been empirically associated with recidivism risk. The risk factors to be considered are explicit, but the method for weighting the importance of the risk factors is left to the judgement of the worker.
- Pure actuarial predictions: in contrast, explicitly state not only the variables to be considered, but also the precise procedure through which ratings of these variables will be translated into a risk level. In the pure actuarial sense, risk levels are estimated through mechanical, arithmetic procedures requiring a minimum of judgement.
- Clinically adjusted actuarial predictions: begin with a pure actuarial prediction, but then raises or lowers the risk level based on consideration of relevant factors that were not included in the actuarial method (see Quinsey et al., 1995). As research develops, actuarial methods can be expected to consistently outperform clinical predictions. With the current state of knowledge, however, both actuarial and guided clinical approaches can

be expected to provide risk assessments with moderate levels of accuracy.

In one of the few studies on dynamic risk factors, Hanson and Harris (2000) examined the records of 409 men, 208 of who had re-offended. Stable, dynamic predictors of sex offenders were, for men who offended against both boys and girls, the number of negative influences, attitudes supporting child sexual abuse, sexual entitlement, viewing oneself as minimal risk, and being manipulative or uncooperative with supervision. Victim access, viewing oneself as low risk and cooperation with supervision can be both stable and acute risk factors. Additional stable, dynamic risk factors that were correlated with re-offending in men who molested boys included substance abuse, positive influences, low remorse/victim blaming, rape attitudes, sexual preoccupation, failing to improve appearance, antisocial lifestyle, uncontrolled release environment and disengagement with the supervisory process.

Hudson et al. (2002) examined stable risk factors and recidivism. They found that what seem central are pro-social shifts in attitudes as the research found significant support for Hanson's (2000) attitudinal domain. Other variables measured did not map over well for Hanson's proposed list. They noted that we need to explore further issues concerning social context, self-perceptions of risk, and self-regulation – particularly around sex; the significant role of fantasy and the offence process.

In a special edition of *Sexual Abuse* (Volume 14(2), 2002) on dynamic risk assessment, clear evidence is cited that demonstrates that factors such as attitudes tolerant of sexual assault, emotional identification with children, and lifestyle instability provide unique information not captured by stable, historical factors. The challenge before us is to identify which of these needs are most important, how to integrate these factors into an overall risk assessment (Hanson, 2002), and the extent to which changes on the supposedly dynamic risk factors are associated with reductions in recidivism risk.

Dynamic risk assessment contains three elements:

1. How bad are his problems?
   - Long-term psychological factors that underlie risk.
   - Determines intensity of treatment required.
   - Refines static risk assessment.

2. Has he changed after treatment?.
   - Post-treatment functioning on psychological risk factors.
   - Has his long-term risk reduced?
3. When is he likely to re-offend?
   - Acute risk factors indicating immediate danger of re-offence.
   - Monthly monitoring by supervising officer.

Thornton (2002) outlines 5 basic dynamic factors. This is the basis of the dynamic part of his structured risk assessment (SRA). These factors include: (1) sexual interest (i.e. deviant arousal control, appropriate sexual interest, related issues); (2) socio-affective functioning (refers to emotional regulation skills, inadequacy or self-esteem, intimacy or quality of relationships); (3) distorted attitudes (i.e. cognitive distortions, restructuring distortions, pro-offending attitudes, etc.); (4) self management (i.e. lifestyle behaviours, impulse control and problem solving skills, etc.); and (5) criminogenic needs (behaviours reflecting antisocial, criminal behaviours, psychopathy, etc.).

What we know is that even high-risk offenders aren't offending all the time: they may go long periods without being known to re-offend: sometimes they are very risky and sometimes they are in an unusually safe state. The risk fluctuates over time and good risk management requires monitoring fluctuations in risk.

The 'panic now' checklist identifies three kinds of factors that indicate immediate risk of re-offending and any deterioration on any of these factors indicates a period of increased risk. The checklist identifies:

1. Victim access behaviours
   - hobbies that give access to victims
   - work that gives access to victims
   - domestic arrangements that give access to victims
   - grooming a specified individual
   - cruising without any good purpose
2. Rejection of supervision
   - missing appointments
   - lying to supervisor
   - trying to bully the supervisor
   - being excessively 'friendly' to the supervisor
   - asking to be seen less often as he is 'better now'
3. Lifestyle collapse
   - loses accommodation

- relationship breakdown
- loses job
- mood becomes more negative, especially angry

Actuarial risk scales for sexual offence recidivism

Note: Most of these are accessible on the Solicitor General Canada's website *http://www.sgc.gc.ca*

Rapid Risk Assessment for Sexual Offence Recidivism (RRASOR) (Hanson, 1997)

This brief actuarial tool is intended to be used for screening purposes. The RRASOR score for any individual is based on the number of past sex offence convictions or charges he has, his age at the time of assessment, his relationship to his victims, and the sex of his victims, with additional weight given to his sex offence history as Hanson does estimate sexual recidivism to be much higher given that many offences go undetected. It is possible to score from zero to six points on this scale. The scoring procedure is illustrated in Table 11.2 below.

Table 11.2: RRASOR

Items	Points
Past sex offences	
0	0
1 conviction or 1 to 2 charges	1
2 to 3 convictions or 3 to 5 charges	2
4 + convictions or 6 + charges	3
Age	
Less than 25	1
Victim gender	
Any male	1
Relationship to victim	
Any non-related	1

Nearly 2,600 sex offenders were rated with the RRASOR system and their re-conviction rates at five to ten years determined. Table 11.3 below illustrates that the system distinguished risk groups for sexual recidivism reasonably well, with a consistent increase in recidivism rates with higher scores. In addition, the majority of sex offenders were classified as low to moderate risk – 80% of the population scored between zero and two, and in this group five-year sexual recidivism was under 15%. Thus, if one relied on this system as a screening tool to identify a higher risk group for greater attention, it would be possible to focus on just 20% of the sample.

Although RRASOR was based on both rapists and child molesters, separating the two groups out did not have any great impact on the results. It was also interesting that although child molesters are generally older than rapists, the effect of age was similar in two groups – in other words, contrary to expectations, it was the younger child molester who was at highest risk of re-conviction.

It should be noted however that although the risk of reconviction is greatest in those who score three or higher, there are a much larger number of individuals who score zero to two. Therefore, in absolute terms, more of these latter individuals are re-convicted: at five years, 189 of the 2075 men scoring zero to two are re-convicted compared with 154 of the 517 who score three to five.

Thornton's Structured Anchored Clinical Judgement (SACJ-Min) (Grubin, 1998)

This risk calculation algorithm was developed by Dr David Thornton of HM Prison Service in the context of the national prison Sex Offender Treatment Programme (SOTP). It is designed so that the assessment of risk can change over time as more and different types of information about an offender become available. This is an

Table 11.3

Score	Number in group	% recidivism at 5 years	% recidivism at 10 years
0	527 (20%)	4%	7%
1	806 (31%)	8%	11%
2	742 (29%)	14%	21%
3	326 (13%)	25%	37%
4	139 (5%)	33%	49%
5	52 (2%)	50%	73%
Total	2592	13%	20%

example of a structured approach to combining actuarial risk scales with other empirically based risk factors. It too is based on variables described in the sex offender literature as being predictive of sexual re-offending, but unlike RRASOR is not dependent solely on archival data. The SACJ risk classification is a three-step process, with risk re-assessed at each step. Like RRASOR it is based on a simple point system with one point scored for each of the following:

- A current sexual offence.
- A past conviction for a sexual offence.
- A non-sexual violent offence in the current conviction.
- A past conviction for non-sexual violence.
- More than three past convictions of any sort.

The risk level is then determined as follows: If offenders have four or more of the initial factors, they are automatically considered high risk. If two or more factors are present, offenders are considered medium risk, and zero or one factor indicate low initial risk.

Step two relates to aggravating factors. If two or more of the following are present, the individual is moved up one risk category level:

- Male victim, any sexual offence.
- Stranger victim, any sex offence.
- Any non-contact sex offence.
- Substance abuse (not simply recreational).
- Ever been in care.
- Never married.
- Deviant sexual arousal.
- Score of 25+ on the Psychopathy Checklist (Hare, 1991).

Step three is based on information that is unlikely to be obtained except for sex offenders who enter treatment programmes, and in this sample involves progress in prison. The risk category is increased if the offender fails to complete an offending behaviour programme, shows a deterioration while in treatment, or has displayed 'sex offending relevant behaviour' in prison within the last five years. Conversely, the risk category is decreased one level if there is successful programme completion, there is significant improvement in risk factors associated with offending, and there is acceptable performance on these risk factors.

The SACJ risk classification was tested on a cohort of 533 sex offenders (of whom 80% had offended against children) released from prison

Table 11.4

Level	Number of offenders	Re-conviction
I	162 (30%)	15 (9%)
II	231 (43%)	53 (23%)
III	140 (26%)	64 (46%)
Total	533	132 (25%)

in 1979 and followed up for 16 years. The results based on information from step one and some from step two (victim gender, victim stranger, non-contact sexual offences, and marital status), a so-called 'low information' version of SACJ are illustrated in Table 11.4.

Thus, like RRASOR the SACJ risk assessment scale also appears to identify accurately three groups of sex offender:

- A lower risk group comprising about a third of the sample with a low rate of sexual re-conviction.
- A high-risk group comprising about a quarter of the sample of whom nearly half are re-convicted for sexual offences.
- A middle group of about half the sample amongst whom a quarter are re-convicted.

The SACJ has been adopted by many of the police forces in order to help them undertake their assessments as required under the requirements of The Sex Offenders Act (1997).

As screening tools, both the RRASOR and SACJ systems clearly have great potential, particularly if you accept that the average predictive accuracy of professional judgement to predict sex offence recidivism is only slightly better than chance (Hanson and Bussiere, 1998). There are some potential problems in the child protection arena given that:

1. There is likely to be an incongruence between re-conviction and re-offending rates.
2. The systems do not help us with those where there are allegations but no charges or convictions.
3. There is a need to look beyond frequency to severity of offending as the types of re-offences are not specified in their results.
4. They are unlikely to do well with respect to individuals who have committed their first sexual offence.
5. More refinement is needed if we are to identify the higher risk men in the middle group given they represent such high numbers of the population.

Table 11.5: STATIC-99

Risk factor	Codes		Score
	Charges	*Convictions*	
Prior sex offences (same rules as RRASOR)	None	None	0
	1–2	1	1
	3–5	2–3	2
	6+	4+	3
Prior sentencing dates (excluding index)	3 or less		0
	4 or more		1
Any convictions for non-contact sex offences	No	0	
	Yes	1	
Index non-sexual offence	No		0
	Yes		1
Prior non-sexual violence	No		0
	Yes		1
Any unrelated victims	No		0
	Yes		1
Any stranger victims	No		0
	Yes		1
Any male victims	No		0
	Yes		1
Young	Aged 25 or older		0
	Aged 18–24.99		1
Single	Ever lived with lover for at least two years?		
	Yes		0
	No		1
Total score	Add up scores from individual risk factors		

STATIC-99 (Hanson and Thornton, 1999; 2000)

This scale was developed by the authors of RRASOR and SACJ-Min by combining their items. Both these scales were intended to be relatively brief screening instruments for predicting sex offender recidivism. The scale is called Static-99 to indicate that it only includes static factors and that the version was completed in 1999 but remains work in progress. The actuarial risk scale will clearly benefit by including dynamic (changeable) risk factors as well as additional static variables (see Table 11.5).

The Static-99 is intended to be a measure of long-term risk potential. Given its lack of dynamic factors, it cannot be used to select treatment targets, measure change, evaluate whether offenders have benefited from treatment, or predict when (or under what circumstances) sex offenders are likely to recidivate.

Static-99 is intended for males aged at least 18 who are known to have committed at least one sex offence.

Translating scores into risk categories:

Predictive accuracy was tested using four diverse data sets from Canada and the UK (total n=1,301). The RRASOR and SACJ-Min showed roughly equivalent predictive accuracy and the combination of the two scales was more accurate than either original scale. Static-99 showed moderate predictive accuracy for both sexual recidivism and violent (including sexual) recidivism, but overall the incremental improvement over the two scales independently was small. It remains clearly more accurate, however, than unstructured clinical judgement.

Table 11.6

Score	Label for risk category
0, 1	Low
2, 3	Medium-low
4, 5	Medium-high
6+	High

MATRIX 2000

This is an updated and modified version of the SACJ outlined earlier in the chapter. It is intended for use with males aged at least 18 who have been convicted of at least one offence with a sexual element. It is not designed for use with alleged offenders. An offence with a 'sexual element' is one where underlying behaviour (rather than the formal charge) involves the sexual abuse of a child, illegal non-consenting sexual behaviour toward an adult, violence in response to sexual advance being turned down, or illegal behaviour motivated by an inappropriate sexual interest (e.g. sexual pleasure from violence; stealing women's underwear). This definition should be used when counting sexual appearances.

Static Risk Classification

The risk matrix 2000 is probably the best validated predictor for England and Wales and should form a useful starting point for assessment. The results summary for RM 2000 to the long-term sexual reconviction rates are set out in Table 11.8.

The Sex Offender Need Assessment Rating (SONAR) (Hanson and Harris, 2000)

There are no established scales that can be used to evaluate change in risk among sex offenders. SONAR was developed to fill this gap. The scale examines how well the dynamic risk factors identified in the Hanson and Harris (1998) study can be organised into a structured risk assessment. Evaluating change requires variables capable of changing, i.e. dynamic variables. It includes five relatively stable factors (intimacy deficits, negative social influences, attitudes tolerant of sex offending, sexual self-regulation, general self-regulation) and four acute factors (substance abuse; negative mood e.g. depression and anxiety; anger/hostility; opportunities for victim access). Acute risk factors are not necessarily related to long-term recidivism potential; instead, they are useful in identifying **when** sex offenders are most likely to re-offend.

Recovery assessments

Recovery assessments are an evaluation of a sex offender's capabilities, skills and progress in maintaining abstinence from sexual offending. They are based on the assumption that there is

Table 11.7 RISK MATRIX 2000.

Family name:

Forenames:

DOB:

Case ID:

Assessor:

Date of assessment:

Rm2000/S – Risk of Sexual Offending

Step One

(1) Age at commencement of risk	POINTS
Under 18	0
18 to 24	2
25 to 34	1
Older	0
(2) Sexual appearances	POINTS
• 1	0
• 2	1
• 3, 4	2
• 5 or more	3
(3) Criminal appearances	POINTS
• Less than 4	0
• 5 or more	1

Total points	**Category**
0	Low risk
1, 2	Medium risk
3, 4	High risk
5, 6	Very high risk

Step Two: Aggravating Factors

(A)	Any conviction for a contact sex offence against a male?	Yes/No
(B)	Any conviction for a contact sex offence against a stranger?	Yes/No*
(C)	'Single' (count as 'single' if never lived with an adult lover for at least two years.	Yes/No
(D)	Any conviction for a non-contact sex offence?	Yes/No

*Count as stranger if the victim did not know the offender 24 hours before the offence.

NB put up one risk category if two aggravating risk factors are present and up two categories if four aggravating risk factors are present.

Table 11.8

Low risk	1 in 10
Medium risk	2 in 10
High risk	4 in 10
Very high risk	6 in 10

no cure. Recovery is a lifelong process rather than something that develops overnight. This is grounded in the belief that sexual offending is a series of conscious and unconscious decisions that are likely to continue over a lifetime.

There are no recognised standards of evaluating recovery, with most professionals utilising their own programme criteria or goals to determine recovery. Kagnich (1997) conducted a survey on professionals' views of recovery, finding the following elements as very important in determining or evaluating recovery:

15 Common factors or elements used in evaluation recovery (Kagnich 1997)

- Motivation towards recovery
- Commitment towards treatment
- Personal responsibility
- Social interest
- Social (relationship) dimension
- Insight of offending cycle
- Lifestyle behaviours
- Insight into developmental/motivational dynamics
- Resolution of developmental/motivational dynamics
- Sexual identity issues
- Control of deviant arousal
- Type of psychopathology
- Level of disowning behaviours
- Relapse intervention skills
- Self structure

The concept of recovery is defined as a continuum of progress. Progress stems from the level of change in deviancy and related behaviours, including a reduction in deviant responses. It is assumed that the rate of recovery, at that time, can correlate to the risk of re-offending. Offenders with low levels of progress are more apt to re-offend. This concept of recovery doesn't infer a magical 'cure.' The term cure refers to a permanent abstinence or absence of the problem (i.e., deviant responses). Deviant behaviour is a choice and often involves a series of choices at both the conscious and unconscious levels. It is an ingrained voluntary/involuntary behaviour. Each choice is a decision, rather deliberate or automatic. The potential of relapse is always present. Thus, 'treatment' or some form of treatment is a lifelong process. It is also recognised that recovery is an ongoing lifelong process.

This concept of recovery is based on several assumptions. It is not a set of concepts edged in black or white. The recovery criteria in this chapter are based on the following assumptions:

- That there is no cure (or permanent abstinence).

- Sex offending is based on a series of choices, at both conscious and unconscious levels.
- Recovery is a lifelong process.
- An offender can lapse and relapse at any given time.
- Recovery is based on progress of maintaining abstinence. However, an offender can relapse at any time.
- It is proposed that sex offending is somewhat state dependent, involving state dependent memory learning behavioural processes. That is offending (relapse) is state dependent and evokes an offensive set of behaviours found in the cycle. Likewise, it is proposed that an offender's recovery is state dependently learned. In other words, an offender deep in recovery can defuse and rebound from lapses and/or minor relapses (i.e., lesser types of sexual offences).
- The recovery criteria listed below are based on common goals found in treatment plans.
- Relapse – offending occurs in patterns of behaviour referred to as the assault cycle (see Chapter 4 for further details). Recovery implies that the offender maintains abstinence from the assault cycle.

Criteria for recovery

Motivation towards recovery
Motivation is the internal drive to succeed or 'recover.' It is the offender's incentive, determination, and amount of energy aimed towards recovery. Quite often, offenders have external reasons to recover, for example to avoid incarceration, to retain their family unit together, etc. It is important in treatment that offenders shift from the external forms of motivation to internal. One of the internal sources of motivation is that they do not want to hurt any more individuals. The criteria of evaluation include:

- Internal motivation towards recovery versus release.
- Programme attendance.
- Programme participation.
- Complete task assignments.
- Type of participation in group therapy.

Commitment towards change/treatment
Commitment is the pledge, agreement, and compliance towards treatment with the goals of change. This definition includes an obligation in

which offenders are emotionally compelled to change through treatment. Quite often, some offenders simply go through the motion of treatment without making the necessary changes at deeper levels. This is considered superficial behaviour and a total lack of commitment towards treatment and recovery. Criteria include:

- Understanding that change requires a commitment towards managing one's behaviour.
- Programme attendance.
- Participation.
- Level of openness and honesty.
- Completion of task assignments.

Personal responsibility

Personal responsibility revolves around the locus of control one places on their behaviour. This applies to both admission and denial of offences and current behaviour in question. This includes accepting the consequences (victim impact) of sexually violating others, including the physical and emotional traumas. Evaluation criteria include:

- Placement of control or locus of control (self verses others).
- Admission vs. denial of offences and offence history.
- Defensive structures (minimising, justifying, rationalising, blaming, etc.).
- Taking responsibility for one's behaviour in general.
- Accepting the consequences (victim impact) of one's offending behaviour.

Social interest

Social interest is the care and concern for other individuals. This includes compassion and empathy. More specifically, sex offenders can be evaluated on the level and degree of empathy and remorse at both cognitive and emotional levels. Empathy is the compassion or understanding of the painful experiences of the victim at both intellectual and emotional levels. Remorse is the painful regret of violating the victim. Remorse implies guilt or conscience (distinction between right and wrong in regard to one's conduct).

Social interest can be indicated by reviewing: empathy, remorse, behavioural indicators, disowning behaviours and deviancy. Specific criteria include:

- Victim empathy (compassion, intellectual and emotional understanding of the victim's situation or victim impact).
- Sense of guilt (appropriate guilt).
- Remorse (painful regret of hurting others).
- Level of conscience (sense of right and wrong along with guilt).
- Care and concern for individuals in general.
- Victim empathy for one's own victims and for victims in general.

Social dimension or developing relationships including social skills and emotional regulation

The social dimension refers to the following: skills in developing and maintaining relationships, social skills, issues in relationships (possessiveness, power/control, exploitation, jealousy, dependency, enmeshed boundaries), and expression of feelings. Items to monitor:

- Emotional recognition, expression and regulation skills
- Level of social skills (i.e., active listening, empathy, respect, initiating/maintaining/ terminating conversation, assertion, giving/receiving, 'I' messages).
- Number of relationships.
- Quality of those relationships.
- Level of superficial behaviour within relationships.
- Relationship dynamics, i.e., possessiveness, jealousy, dependency, etc.
- Exploitation.
- Power and control issues.
- Intimacy without sexual connotations.
- Enmeshed relationship boundaries.
- Withdrawal, emotional/behavioural avoidance, and isolation of others.
- Appropriate expression of emotions/feelings.
- Sexual education.

Identifying one's offending cycle

The offending cycle consists of recurring patterns that are involved in the assault. Although there are general stages involved, the content of each cycle varies. These concepts are tools that help the offender interrupt his/her cycle. The offending cycle is the specific patterns of behaviour that the offender uses to offend. There are 36 deviant cycles (Carich, 1997). Items for the offender to look at would be:

- Insight into their offending cycle.
- Understanding the offending cycle dynamics.
- Applying the cycle to themselves.

The essence of any cycle consists of three parts (1) pre-assault, (2) assault, (3) post assault or aftermath. Offenders need to know their non-assault cycle or adaptive life cycle behaviours.

Change in lifestyle behaviours

Lifestyle behaviours refer to the specific and general tendencies or patterns of behaviour. These patterns of behaviour consist of: automatic thoughts, feelings, tendencies, belief systems, perceptual world views, actual behaviours and activities, etc. They have been formulated as personality disorders in accordance to psychiatric mental disorders. These include: antisocial, narcissistic, borderline, passive-aggressive and schizoidal. The degree and frequency or level that offenders have these behaviours varies. Not all offenders are antisocial and narcissistic or have the other characteristics listed below. The act of sexual assault implies antisocial and narcissistic behaviour. Some offenders have these characteristics only while offending while others have them ingrained in their lifestyle. Items to look at include:

- Antisocial behaviours (lacks empathy and remorse, tends to victimise, tends to exploit, violates rules, sadistic, phoniness, exploitive, lies, exhibits crooked thinking, tends to be controlling, defiantly manipulates) NOTE: Antisocial behaviour would be indicated by level of maintaining secrets, history of deviancy, history of victimology, history of lying, denying and overall crooked thinking and behaviour.
- Narcissistic (self-centred, unwarranted entitlement, egocentric, dramatic, grandiose, demanding, stuck on self, me only attitude, exaggerated self importance, out for self at other's expense).
- Borderline (poor impulse control, dependency, self-destructive behaviour, marked moodiness, unstable relationships, possessiveness, jealousy, unstable in general, over attachment towards others, enmeshed, idealisation).
- Schizoidal behaviours (flat affect, distant relationships, superficial relationships, lacks close relationships, alienated, isolated, lacks social skills, withdrawn).
- Passive-aggressive behaviours (expressing anger and hostility sideways or indirectly).
- Histrionic behaviours (over-dramatic).

Insight into one's developmental and motivational factors

Insight into developmental/motivational dynamics refers to one's specific and motivational/developmental dynamics that propel the decisions to offend. More specifically, it is those perceptions of specific developmental events that lead to key, essential or core issues that create the purposes of the offending. These are the specific emotional and psychological satisfactions gained from offending. Specific items include insight into one's developmental history encompasses both intellectual and emotional understanding of the various aetiological or developmental experiences that one has that feed the offending. This includes any type of psychosocial physiological experiences. These are fused with and transformed into various motivational factors. Motivational factors are the teleological factors of purposes of the offending behaviour. More specifically, this is what the individual gets out of the offending. This is 'why' he engages in sexual offending.

Resolution of developmental and motivational dynamics

Resolution of developmental problems and motivational dynamics to lesser degrees of intensity. Resolution to the point that those issues of traumas do not persist. The offender doesn't get the same type of gratification from offending as his motivations are changed. The problems are based upon perceptions of developmental events. The responses from these perceptions are changed. Specific items:

- Resolution to a lesser degree of intensity, various aetiological factors or significant developmental experiences, based upon perceptions.
- Resolution to a lesser degree of various motivational dynamics involved in offending.

Sexual identity issues

Sexual identity issues are any issues involving sexual role confusion and/or traumas associated with sexual preference and selection. By definition, sex offenders have sexual identity issues that can be determined by the selection and targets of their sexual attraction. Specific items include:

- By definition, sex offenders have sexual identity issues. These issues need to be identified, explored and resolved.

- Resolving sexual identity issues involves understanding one's sexual preference and feeling comfortable with it.

Arousal control

Control of deviant urges/arousal refers to the overall management of deviant responses. Thus, arousal control is the management of one's deviant cycles. These are explored in the learned techniques and the offender to control one's arousal. Specific items:

- Level of deviant fantasies.
- Level of violent fantasies.
- Level of normal fantasies.
- Sexual interests.
- Level of masturbation towards deviant fantasies.
- Level of masturbation towards normal fantasies.
- Level of masturbation towards sadistic fantasies.

Type of psychopathology

Psychopathology refers to the specific mental health problems and dysfunctions, including paraphilias. Specific items:

- Axis I – degree and type of pathology.
- Axis II – degree and type of pathology.
- Axis III – medical pathology.
- Orientation and alertness in time, person and place.
- Overall moodiness, affect or emotional states presented.
- Speech patterns and other indications of psychosis.
- Level of organicity.

Level of disowning behaviours

Level of disowning behaviours are the degree of and/or amount of irresponsibility in ways of distorted thinking and defences or other dysfunctional coping strategies. Disowning behaviours are any behaviours that enable one's offending and/or the offender to avoid responsibility. Specific items include:

- Defensive structures (i.e., denial, rationalising, displacements, etc.)
- Cognitive distortions (i.e., justification, entitlement, extremes, minimising, etc.)
- Dysfunctional coping strategies.

Relapse interventions skills

Relapse intervention skills are the specific coping strategies designated to help offenders identify offending cycles, triggers, cues,

disowning behaviours, and specific skills that are used to defuse cycles and/or deviant responses. Thus, these skills enable the offender to prevent lapses and ultimately relapses. They are able to defuse various risk factors and/or situations. Specific items may include:

- Understanding of the various developmental motivational dynamics as related to sex offending and relapse.
- Can identify specific deviant cycles and patterns of offending.
- Can identify triggers or those events that facilitate, initiate and stimulate offending behaviours.
- Identify relapse cues or indicators of offending responses.
- Identify and defuse various disowning behaviours.
- Develop relapse intervention skills that occur at a spontaneous and conscious level.
- Understands various risks, factors, and/or situations, along with a level of competence in order to evade and/or defuse offending situations.

Self structure in general

Self structure refers to the internal/external perceptions of one's self. This includes one's self-worth, self-concept, self-esteem, self-image, level of confidence, etc. This also encompasses both inferiority and superiority along with various compensation strategies. Other references are presented below:

- Internal core beliefs/feelings about self (self-concept, self-image).
- Self-esteem.
- Self-confidence.
- Areas of inferiority.

Characteristics of a recovering offender:

- More honest.
- Less frequency of deviant behaviour.
- Consistently appears less crooked.
- Consistently appears less entitled.
- Consistently appears less narcissistic.
- Takes responsibility in general.
- Takes responsibility for one's offending.
- Expresses/experiences victim empathy.
- Capable of explaining dynamics of offending.
- Motivating issues seem to be less.
- Know one's cycle.
- Know one's cues.
- Know one's triggers.
- Refutes cognitive distortions.

- Uses anger controls and interventions.
- Has a variety of coping strategies.
- Work on long term goals.
- Proud of accomplishments.
- Positive self esteem.
- Upkeep of personal hygiene.
- Admit they need treatment for life.
- Know they need structure.
- Consistency in behaviour.
- Stable support system.
- Sense of independence.
- Confront self and others.
- Empathy in general.
- Sense of spiritual.
- Doesn't keep secrets.

The formal establishment of criteria for the evaluation of recovery is quite new in the field and the majority of professionals continue to use the completion of programme goals or risk assessments as the baseline on offender management and progress. Based on the discussion earlier in this chapter around static and dynamic risk factors, it is useful to identify how these concepts relate to the recovery assessment process.

Historical risk factors considered in the recovery process would include:

- multiple victims
- history of offending
- repeated offending
- legal history
- multiple paraphilias
- multiple victim types
- gender of victim types
- violent/sadistic crimes
- murder/attempted murder
- substance misuse
- rage history
- victim vulnerability
- male victim type
- offender trauma
- self-destructive or suicidal
- anti-social behaviour history*

Historical risk factors are further categorised by the following:

---

*These 16 factors have been recently combined into 8 factors, since several were related: motivation/commitment, personal responsibility/disowning behaviours, social interest (victim empathy), social-affective dimension, cycle/RP skills, lifestyle behaviours and psychopathology, arousal control, and clinical core issues (i.e. developmental/motivational dynamics, sexual identity, self structure).

- victimology
- criminal behaviour
- paraphilias and psychopathology
- rage history
- offender trauma and resources

List of dynamic risk factors used for recovery risk assessment include:

- Personal responsibility (i.e., openness, honesty, denial, misses therapy sessions, etc.).
- Locus of control (i.e., blames, distorts, justifies, minimises).
- Level of cooperation (i.e., disruptive, holds back data, etc.).
- Current level of antisocial behaviours (i.e., phoniness, criminal activities, honesty/dishonesty, sneakiness, lying, etc.).
- Current level of narcissistic behaviours (i.e., self-centred, unwarranted entitlement, exaggerated self-importance, arrogance, demanding, etc.).
- Current level of schizoidal behaviours (i.e., alienate, isolate, flat affect, withdrawal, lacks relationships, etc.).
- Current relationship skills (i.e., social skills, possessiveness, over-controlling, dependency, peer group relationships, etc.).
- Current level of social interest (i.e., empathy, remorse, compassion in general, non-sexual victimisation).
- Current use of substances such as non-prescribed drugs and alcohol (i.e., cravings, actually using substances, associates with drug abusers, lives with drug abuser, etc.).
- Use relapse prevention or intervention skills (i.e., acknowledges lapses, cycles, knowledge of deviant cycle, appropriate coping skills, etc.).
- Manages deviancy/arousal control (i.e., levels of masturbation, deviant fantasies, urges, overindulgence in sex, etc.).
- Stability/instability in general (i.e., relocates residences, unstable relationships, self-destructive, controls impulsiveness, etc.)
- Current disinhibitors vs. inhibitors.
- Psychopathology (i.e., psychosis, suicidal, self-destructive behaviour, manic behaviour, depression, etc.).

(Carich, 1996, p114).

These can be further categorised as:

- compliance
- skills
- psychopathy/antisocial behaviour

- cycle behaviour
- interpersonal behaviour

Progress assessments

Progress assessments are based on assessing the offender's progress or levels of change in treatment. Treatment programmes vary on structure, components, processes and often treatment goals. However, a list of basic treatment goals would include the need to:

- Develop motivation and commitment towards recovery.
- Develop victim empathy at both emotional and intellectual levels.
- Develop remorse.
- Develop the general notion of social interest.
- Develop appropriate and healthy, functioning relationships without sexual connotations.
- Resolve various issues within relationships such as possessiveness, jealousy, over-attachment, etc.
- Develop social skills.
- Develop appropriate sense of power and control.
- Develop a number of functional relationships.
- Clarify one's sexual identity.
- Change various dysfunctional lifestyle behaviours.
- Resolve issues with emotional alienation and isolation from others.
- Accept total responsibility and hold one's self-accountable for one's deviant behaviour and behaviour in general.
- Develop an understanding at both intellectual and emotional levels of one's developmental history, and in particular to those events that are transformed into the various motivational factors.
- Develop understanding of the motivations involved in sexual offending, in other words, the emotional satisfaction gained in sexual aggression.
- Learn to reduce one's deviant arousal and the frequency of arousal.
- Develop skills to learn to manage one's deviant behaviour.
- Resolve various developmental motivational dynamics to a more intense level.
- Express appropriate affect.
- Develop stress management skills.
- Develop relapse intervention skills.
- Identify one's offending cycle or mode of offending.
- Develop an appropriate sense of self-worth.

- Identify and change cognitive distortions or dysfunctional thinking.
- Identify and change disowning behaviours.
- Develop conflict resolution skills.

Healing curves as a potential framework for core issue recovery resolution

It is assumed that offending involves much more, in terms of motivational factors, than sexual gratification. Types of motivating factors or purposes of offending that stem from life experience include:

1. Attention
2. Power and control
3. Inferiority
4. Revenge
5. Anger/resentments
6. Low self worth
7. Low self esteem
8. Abandonment
9. Fear of rejection
10. Acceptance
11. Distorted sense of love
12. Loneliness
13. Way of attaching
14. Insecurity
15. Dependency needs
16. Jealousy
17. Feel better about self
18. Ego booster
19. Validating self
20. Stress reduction
21. Coping with problems
22. Poor self concept and image
23. 'Rust' adrenalin
24. Penis inferiority

Such motivational factors can operate at both a conscious and unconscious level and are frequently ignored within the treatment process. Such issues are referred to here as 'core clinical issues'. We believe that it is important that we identify and seek appropriate resolution to such factors within treatment. Resolution refers to the reduction of the relevant issues to a lower degree of intensity: a re-organisation, re-association of behavioural patterns and a re-synthesis of one's inner experiential realms (Rossi, 1993). What we then need to do is to locate a framework that facilitates the identification of and resolution to the identified motivating issues.

Rossi has argued that sex offenders encode sexually deviant behaviour through the mind/body process. This is through a series of choices and learned behaviours. The underlining process involves both the mind and bio-physiological processes of the brain (Rossi, 1993). Although both are interrelated and affect each other; we specify that significant developmental experiences are encoded into the brain, based upon current templates or world views. The offender has an internal switch box that accommodates learning and behaviour as well as experiential (cognitive, affective, biological, perceptual etc.) and sensory (such as auditory, visual and olfactory) modalities (Carich and Parwatikar, 1992; 1995). The offender then possesses deviant states or resources within an inner template system. Ward and Hudson (2000) describe templates and scripts that are conscious and unconscious constructed of deep seated inner beliefs, cognitive schemes and themes. More specifically, they state that scripts as a set of rules for predicting, interpreting, responding to, and controlling a set of interpersonal meaningful scenes, for example, knowing how to respond appropriately during an argument with a partner in a restaurant; whereas social scripts provide a template with which to structure fundamental social interactions and help individuals locate values, beliefs, and goals within a cultural context. For example, participating in a wedding ceremony situated in the restaurant.

Recently script to the area of sexuality has been applied. Sexual scripts are involved in learning the meaning of internal states, organising the sequences of specifically sexual acts, decoding novel situations, setting the limits on sexual responses and linking meanings from non-sexual aspects of life to specifically sexual experience. Sexual scripts are comprised of three levels spanning the internal, interpersonal, and cultural contexts. The latter level involves the incorporation in coherent knowledge of norms, values, rules, and beliefs. The integration of these elements into scripts enables individuals to interpret sexually relevant behaviours and functions as a guide in sexual encounters. A sexual script spells out when sex is to take place, with whom, what to do, and how to interpret the cues or signals associated with different phases in a sexual encounter. These cues can be internal to the individual, interpersonal, or broadly cultural in nature. Related to sexual offending, one can connect a core issue with at least one core belief or theme,

whether conscious or unconscious. Regressed offenders encounter 'stressful' situations and appear to access deeply 'buried' offending states; whilst serial/chronic offenders formulate their lives or lifestyles based on well engrained deviant conscious/unconscious templates. Their offending decisions seem to be automatic. The automatic decisions are based on continuous assessing of offending templates.

Henderson-Odum (2001) developed a useful healing curve for considering offender whether an offender has satisfactorily resolved their identified core issues (see Figures 11.1 to 11.3).

Figure 11.1 illustrates the treatment change process curve and how the offender needs to move through a process of problem identification, through disorganisation to reorganisation. Figure 11.2 sets out the healing curve itself. The healing curve is a way to construct or view basic core/clinical issue resolution. The curve is based on a series of personal choices at all levels of awareness. The offender's issues may or may not involve trauma. The curve begins with trauma or developmental events and the resulting issues. Next follows defences and topic shame. It is pointed out that highly psychopathic offenders do not experience shame or empathy following the curve, offenders typically have poor self-concepts and low self esteem fuelled by unhealthy anger and resentments. They may blame others, from various inadequacies and inferiorities. They typically feel powerless, hopeless and helpless which results in victim stances. Many develop mini victim perpetrator cycles, taking a victim stancing role and then striking out. The other side of the curve involves healthy coping patterns, issue resolution, responsibility and positive self-concept and self-acceptance.

The curve does not derive from research but from intensive clinical experience.

The resolution process (Figure 11.3)

The essence of resolution involves the transformation of anger/bitterness into positive action. This includes letting go of anger and resentments through either forgiveness or giving them up. This requires a shift of the core belief/theme attached to the need/issue at an emotional level. At some point the offender balances a healthy level of victim empathy and remorse with positive self-esteem. The offender holds himself accountable and responsible for his choices and behaviour.

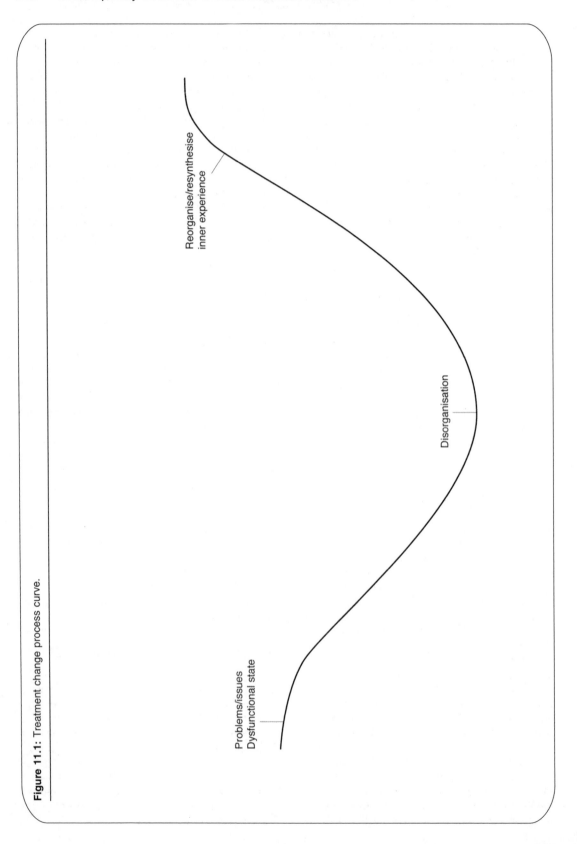

Figure 11.1: Treatment change process curve.

Figure 11.2: Healing curve.

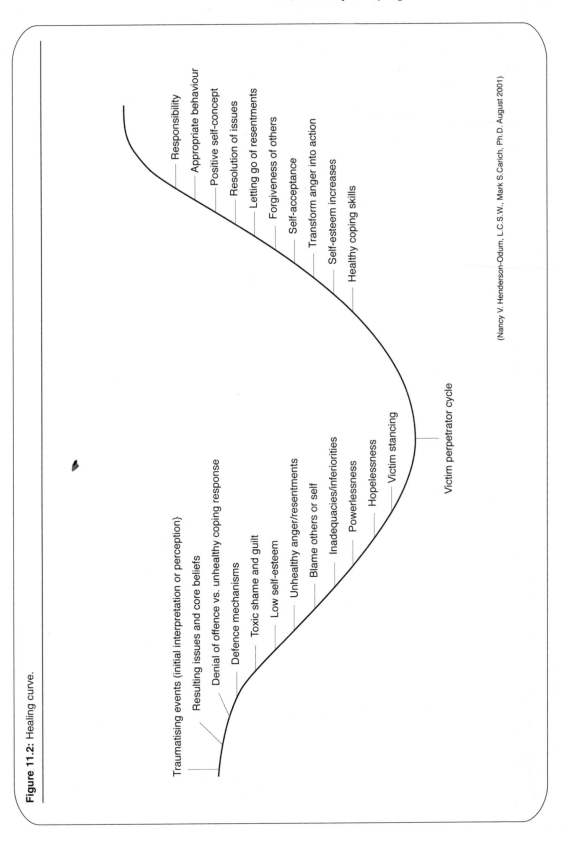

Traumatising events (initial interpretation or perception)

Resulting issues and core beliefs

Denial of offence vs. unhealthy coping response

Defence mechanisms

Toxic shame and guilt

Low self-esteem

Unhealthy anger/resentments

Blame others or self

Inadequacies/inferiorities

Powerlessness

Hopelessness

Victim stancing

Victim perpetrator cycle

Responsibility

Appropriate behaviour

Positive self-concept

Resolution of issues

Letting go of resentments

Forgiveness of others

Self-acceptance

Transform anger into action

Self-esteem increases

Healthy coping skills

(Nancy V. Henderson-Odum, L.C.S.W., Mark S.Carich, Ph.D. August 2001)

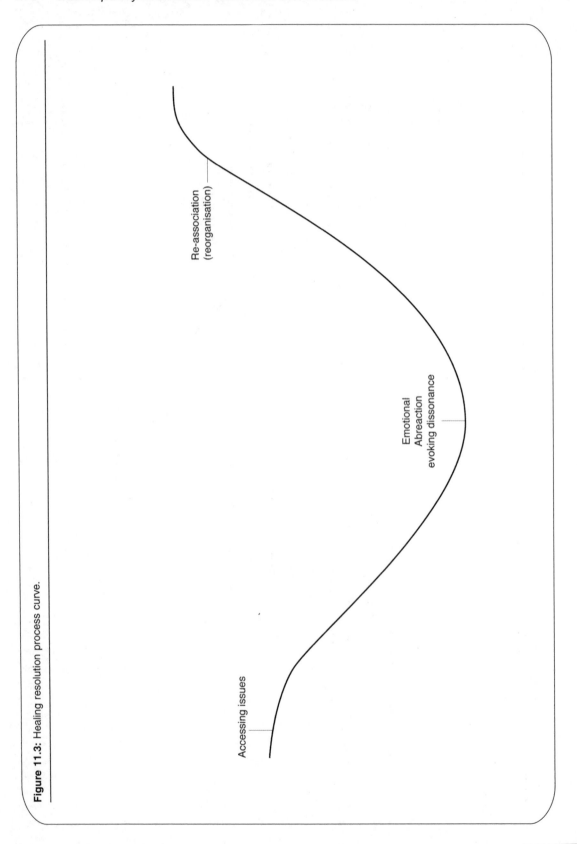

Figure 11.3: Healing resolution process curve.

The resolution process involves accessing issues with a fairly high level of emotional intensity and pattern reorganisation of the offender's inner experience. This involves restructuring the core beliefs/themes/schemata involved in the issues aimed towards resolution.

The treatment change process curve involves accessing problem states followed by disorganisation via dissociation and reorganisation of their inner experiences. Thus, the offender reorganises with new experiences. The process of reorganisation usually involves accessing inner emotional processes concerning the issue via some type of 'abreaction'. A similar process occurs concerning decoding deviant arousal and encoding appropriate arousal with borderline and/or chronic serial offenders. Most are comfortable with offending. Thus, while adding appropriate arousal and decreasing deviant arousal, the offender often feels like they are insecure or in transition while experiencing something quite meaningful. The new behaviours do not feel as comfortable. This requires an adjustment process. At this time, the change process is volatile and vulnerable, especially when dealing with highly pathological (borderline characteristically oriented) offenders.

Facilitating resolution

In order to facilitate resolution, the offender has to be encouraged to access his issues at deep emotional levels. Upon accessing issues, then the offender's underlining core beliefs or schematics need shifting. This is when the offender is most ready or vulnerable to change. Resolution involves 'letting go' of the issue. For some offenders, this involves learning (and applying) patterns of forgiveness. For others, it may involve breaking rigid patterns. Resolution of issues are best addressed when the offender is receptive, ready to change (to that particular issue) and emotionally vulnerable. The process entails processes of dissociating patterns and re-associating patterns. Accessing patterns typically involve abreactions. Watkins and Watkins (2000) describe abreactions as being '. . . a re-living, a re-experiencing, of an emotionally traumatic event which appears to have become fixated in an intra-psychic conflict resulting in painful and incapacitating symptoms. The patient is bound up in this event, unconsciously if not consciously and is not able to extricate himself from it and gain closure. The traumatic event, even though it may have occurred some

time in the past (perhaps many years ago), continues to exist within the patient's psyche. To be resolved it must be re-experienced and mastered. That word "mastered" is the key concept. A mere re-living of a horrible event does not mean that it has been mastered, and in fact it may have simply been reinforced. If we conceptualise an abreaction as merely an emotional re-living or a draining of the affect and stop at that point, then indeed a negative effect may result.'

Through resolution the offender regains mastery of the issue. The issue is reframed in such a manner that the offender re-experiences the issue differently. The release of the emotional energy reduces the power of the trauma or issue, making possible the interpretation and reframing of the understanding. They emphasise resolution: 'recovery' comes from within.

The process consists of the following basic steps:

1. Identifying issues and roles in the cycle.
2. Accessing issues.
3. Resolution or the processes of dissociating and re-associating behavioural patterns.
4. Future projection.

Within this process, the therapeutic message (of change the problems – as the content voices) is packaged in a way that addresses both the offender's systemic, cybernetic patterns of stability (maintaining sameness) and change (creating a difference). In therapy, the offender's system needs to be tapped through patterns of stability and change or supporting the offender while inducing change. This occurs through a meaningful psychotherapeutic relationship or rapport.

Conclusion

Risk is a complex and multi-dimensional concept, with everyone having their own definition and understanding of risk. Risk measurement has evolved considerably over time. This is important as accurate risk assessment is an essential precursor to effective case management, although it does not necessarily follow. Although the clinical method is often considered less reliable than the actuarial method, it can provide important information on:

- Individual risky behaviours.
- Stresses related to environmental factors.

- Assist in establishing appropriate treatment.
- Risk management plans.

Actuarial risk tools should be seen as a good way to augment the decisions made by workers. It also offers them a degree of protection by offering a systematic and more accountable method of defending decisions and eliminating perceptions of arbitrariness in decision-making (Lauen, 1997). Although actuarial methods have a greater track record for accuracy, they do have a number of limitations and can be used inappropriately:

- There are limitations to a technique that uses information generalised from a population to an individual under assessment.
- The use of meta-analyses to develop risk predictors can result in overly simplistic outcomes which fail to capture the complexity of the process involved.
- Prediction of risk where there is a low incidence of risky behaviours in the population as a whole.

(Kemshall, 2001).

Although empirically supported factors are the most easily defended, some plausible risk factors lack documented empirical support. As such, we have to extend the factors as new research becomes available. For example, anger received only tentative support in Hanson and Bussiere's (1998) meta-analysis, but prudent evaluators may want to include it on their lists given that chronic hostility predicted recidivism in subsequent research (Quinsey et al,. 1998). We also need to move beyond risk factors grounded only in the characteristics to their environment. Helpful environmental factors include a supportive family, and a stable and appropriate job and residence: all of which reduce the likelihood of recidivism (Witts et al., 1996). Those individuals who are impulsive, antisocial and lack social competence are more likely to create for themselves environments in which they are unmarried, do not hold a job for long and have no stable residence. Hanson and Harris (1998) identified clearly that sex offenders are more likely to recidivate given uncontrolled release environments and ready access to victims. It is thus prudent of us to explore the features of an offender's environment that inhibit or disinhibit sex offending (Hanson, 2000).

The advent of dynamic risk factors is undoubtedly helpful in measuring changes in risk levels of sex offenders. This has been championed by researchers. However, much of the prediction involves informal, intuitive clinical criteria developed by seasoned experts in practice as associated with increased relapse (Witt et al., 1996).

We would see that most good risk assessments are likely to use both static and dynamic risk factors as well as employing clinical and actuarial risk tools.

Although recovery assessments differ from initial and risk assessments, recovery assessment outcomes should correlate with risk assessment outcomes. The concept of recovery assessments is an embryonic one in need of development whilst the long-standing concept of risk assessments is evolving rapidly. One area that requires considerable development still is in relation to the integration of assets and strengths into the risk balancing exercise (Calder, 2002b and c).

The resolution process discussed above could be the essential key change process involved in more stable sex offender recoveries. This involves shifting the offenders' templates from deviant to nondeviant at both conscious and unconscious levels of awareness.

References

Andrews D A And Bonta J (1994) *The Psychology of Criminal Conduct*. Cincinnati, OH: Anderson Publishing Co.

Calder M C (1997) *Juveniles and Children Who Sexually Abuse: A Guide to Risk Assessment*. Dorset: Russell House Publishing.

Calder M C (1999) *Assessing Risk in Adult Males Who Sexually Abuse Children: A Practitioner's Guide*. Lyme Regis, Dorset: Russell House Publishing.

Calder M C (1999b) A Conceptual Framework for Managing Young People Who Sexually Abuse: Towards a Consortium Approach. In Calder M C (Ed.) *Working With Young People Who Sexually Abuse: New Pieces of the Jigsaw Puzzle*. Dorset: Russell House Publishing, 109–50.

Calder M C (2000) *Complete Guide to Sexual Abuse Assessments*. Lyme Regis, Dorset: Russell House Publishing.

Calder M C (2001) *Juveniles and Children Who Sexually Abuse: Frameworks for Assessment* (2nd edn.) Lyme Regis, Dorset: Russell House Publishing.

Calder M C (Ed.) (2002) *Young People Who Sexually Abuse: Building the Evidence Base for*

Your Practice. Dorset: Russell House Publishing.

Calder M C (2002b) A Framework for Conducting Risk Assessments. *Child Care in Practice.* 8: 1, 1–18.

Calder M C (2002c) The Assessment Framework: A Critique and Reformulation. In Calder M C and Hackett S (Eds.) *Assessment in Child Care: Using and Developing Frameworks for Practice.* Dorset: Russell House Publishing.

Calder M C (2003) Actuarial Risk Tools and Work with Sex Offenders: Potential Problems and Pathways to Practice Application. Keynote presentation to NOTA North Wales, 30 May 2003.

Carich M S (1991) The Sex Offender Recovery Inventory. *INMAS Newsletter.* 4: 4, 13–7.

Carich M S (1996) *15-Factor Sex Offender Recovery Scale.* Unpublished Manuscript.

Carich M S (1997) *Evaluating Sex Offender Recovery: A Booklet for Professionals.* Unpublished Manuscript.

Carich M S (1997b) Towards a Concept of Recovery in Sex Offenders. *The Forum.* 9: 2, 10–1.

Carich M S, Fischer S and Cambell T D (1994) *Recovery Risk Assessment Scale for Sex Offenders.* Unpublished Paper.

Carich M S and Harper J J (2002) Sexual Offending: Toward a Continuum View and Definition of Sexual Aggression. *The Forensic Therapist.* 1: 21–3.

Carich M S and Metzger C (1997) *Treatment Plan: Goals and Objectives.* Unpublished Paper.

Carich M S and Parwitakar S D (1992) A Mind-Body Connection a Sex Offender Switch Box: A Brief Review. *INMAS Newsletter.* 5: 3 2–4.

Carich M S and Parwatikar S D (1995) Mind-Body Interaction: Theory and Its Applications to Sex Offenders. *Journal of Correctional Research.* 1.

Carich M and Spilman K (2002) Can Guilty Committed Sex Offenders Recover Part I: Criteria to Evaluate Recovery. *The Forensic Therapist.* 1 (1): 2–8.

Carson D (1994) Dangerous People: Through a Broader Concept of 'Risk' and 'Danger' to Better Decisions. *Expert Evidence.* 3: 2 21–69.

English D and Pecora P (1994) Risk Assessment as a Practice Method in Child Protective Services. *Child Welfare.* LXX111: 451–73.

Gagon J H (1990) The Explicit and Implicit use of the Scripting Perspective in Sex Research. *Annual Review of Sex Research* 1: 1–43.

Grubin D (1998) *Sex Offending Against Children: Understanding the Risk.* London: Home Office Research, Development and Statistics Directorate.

Hanson R K (1997) *The Development of a Brief Actuarial Risk Scale for Sexual Offence Recidivism.* Ottawa: Department of The Solicitor General of Canada.

Hanson R K (2000) *Risk Assessment.* Beaverton, Oregon: ATSA.

Hanson R K (2002) Introduction to the Special Section on Dynamic Risk Assessment With Sex Offenders. *Sexual Abuse: A Journal of Research and Treatment.* 14: 2 99–101.

Hanson R K and Bussiere M T (1998) Predicting Relapse: A Meta-Analysis of Sexual Offender Recidivism Studies. *Journal of Consulting and Clinical Psychology.* 66: 348–62.

Hanson R K and Harris A J R (1998) Dynamic Predictors of Sexual Recidivism. Ottawa: Department of The Solicitor General of Canada.

Hanson R K and Harris A J R (2000) *The Sex Offender Need Assessment Rating (SONAR): A Method for Measuring Change in Risk Levels.* Ottawa: Department of The Solicitor General of Canada.

Hanson R K and Harris A J R (2002b) Where Should We Intervene? Dynamic Predictors of Sexual Offence Recidivism. *Criminal Justice and Behaviour.* 27: 6–35.

Hanson K and Harris A (2001) A Structured Approach to Evaluating Change among Sexual Offenders. *Sexual Abuse: A Journal of Research and Treatment.* 13: 105–22.

Hanson R K and Thornton D (1999) *Static 99: Improving Actuarial Risk Assessments for Sex Offenders.* Ottawa: Department of The Solicitor General of Canada.

Hanson R K and Thornton D (2000) Improving Risk Assessments for Sex Offenders: A Comparison of Three Actuarial Scales. *Law and Human Behaviour.* 24: 1 119–36.

Henderson-Odum N (2001) Personal Communication.

Hudson S M, Wales D S, Bakker L and Ward T (2002) Dynamic Risk Factors: The Kia Marama Evaluation. *Sexual Abuse: A Journal Of Research and Treatment.* 14: 2 103–19.

Izzo R L and Ross R R (1990) Meta-Analysis of Rehabilitation Programs for Juvenile Delinquents: A Brief Report. *Criminal Justice and Behaviour.* 17: 134–42.

Kemshall H (2001) *Risk Assessment and Management of Known Sexual and Violent*

Offenders: A Review of Current Issues. Police Research Series Paper 140. London: Policing and Reducing Crime Unit.

Lauen R J (1997) *Positive Approaches to Corrections: Research, Policy and Practice.* Maryland: American Correctional Association.

Longo R E (2002) A Holistic/integrated approach to Treating Sexual Offenders. In Schwartz B K (Ed.) *The Sex Offender: Current Treatment Modalities and System Issues* Volume IV. Kingston, NJ: Civic Research Institute.

McEwan S and Sullivan J (1996) Sex Offender Risk Assessment. In Kemshall H and Pritchard J (Eds.) *Good Practice in Risk Assessment and Risk Management.* London: Jessica Kingsley, 146–58.

Quinsey V L, Harris G T, Rice M E and Cormier C A (1998) *Violent Offenders: Appraising and Managing Risk.* Washington, DC: American Psychological Association.

Rossi E L (1993) *The Psychobiology of Mind-Body Healing: New Concepts of Therapeutic Hypnosis.* (2nd edn.).New York: WW Norton.

Schwartz B K and Canfield G M S (1998) Treating the Sexually Dangerous Person: The Massachusetts Treatment Center. In Marshall W L, Fernandez Y M, Hudson S M and Ward T (Eds.) *Sourcebook of Treatment Programs for Sexual Offenders.* 235–45.

Sharpe D (1997) Of Apples and Oranges, File Drawers and Garbage: Why Validity Issues in Meta-Analyses Will not go Away. *Clinical Psychology Review.* 17: 881–901.

Stafford W and Hardy C (1996) *Risk Assessment and Guardian Ad Litem.* Presentation to The 7th AGM And Spring Conference of The National Association of Guardian Ad Litem and Reporting Officers. St William's College, York, 18 March, 1996.

Thornton D (2002) Constructing and Testing a Framework for Dynamic Risk Assessment. *Sexual Abuse: A Journal of Research and Treatment.* 14(2): 137–51.

Wald M and Woolverton M (1990) Risk Assessment: The Emperor's New Clothes. *Child Welfare.* LX1X: 483–511.

Ward T and Hudson S (2000) Sexual Offenders' Implicit Planing: A Conceptual Model. *Sexual Abuse: A Journal of Research and Treatment* 12(3): 189–202.

Witt P H, Delrusso J D, Oppenheim J and Ferguson G (1996) Sex Offender Risk Assessment and the Law. *The Journal Of Psychiatry and Law.* Fall 1996: 343–77.

Conditions of Community Supervision for Sex Offenders on Probation and Post Incarceration

NAME _____ NUMBER _____ DATE _____

AGENCY _____

ADULT OFFENDER VICTIM TYPE

☐ Adult Victim

	Number of victims	*Number of victims*
____ Peeper	____ male–age range ____	____ female–age range ____
____ Exhibitionist	____ male–age range ____	____ female–age range ____
____ Obscene phone calling	____ male–age range ____	____ female–age range ____
____ Rape	____ male–age range ____	____ female–age range ____
____ Murder	____ male–age range ____	____ female–age range ____
____ Other	____ male–age range ____	____ female–age range ____

☐ Adolescent Victim
(puberty–18 yrs)

	Number of victims	*Number of victims*
____ Peeper	____ male–age range ____	____ female–age range ____
____ Exhibitionist	____ male–age range ____	____ female–age range ____
____ Obscene phone calling	____ male–age range ____	____ female–age range ____
____ Rape	____ male–age range ____	____ female–age range ____
____ Murder	____ male–age range ____	____ female–age range ____
____ Other	____ male–age range ____	____ female–age range ____

☐ Child Victim

	Number of victims	*Number of victims*
____ Peeper	____ male–age range ____	____ female–age range ____
____ Exhibitionist	____ male–age range ____	____ female–age range ____
____ Obscene phone calling	____ male–age range ____	____ female–age range ____
____ Rape	____ male–age range ____	____ female–age range ____
____ Murder	____ male–age range ____	____ female–age range ____
____ Other	____ male–age range ____	____ female–age range ____

*Place an '×' if applicable. Some of the items require further approval after release.

GENERAL AND SPECIFIC RULES, REGULATIONS AND OBLIGATIONS:

____ 1. Some type of supervised residential placement (i.e., independent living, halfway house, etc.

____ 2. Sex offender-specific treatment (Agency _____)

____ 3. Attend other types of treatment (_____)

____ 4. Probation/Parole rules:

      ____ (a) No weapons of any type (including knives, guns, bow and arrow, etc.).

      ____ (b) Check in with probation/parole agents.

      ____ (c) Submit to alcohol and/or other substance abuse tests as required.

____ 5. No contact with children unless otherwise approved or authorised by treatment personnel, parole, and if applicable residential placement supervision. If approved, supervised contact with children.

____ 6. No type of pornography (i.e., tapes, films, magazines, books, etc.).

____ 7. No use of alcohol and/or drugs including any medications that are not prescribed.

____ 8. Maintain approved employment with minimal contact with victim types and assault situations, unless otherwise approved.

____ 9. Do not pick up hitchhikers.

____ 10. For rapists, do not drive alone with females (unless pre-arranged date and approved).

____ 11. Do not associate with drug and alcohol abusers and/or users.

____ 12. Do not frequent areas where children may be (i.e., parks, schools, etc.) unless otherwise supervised, authorised, or approved by appropriate individuals.

____ 13. Do not drive alone at night.

____ 14. Maintain full-time school (_____).

____ 15. No involvement with women who have children.

____ 16. Do not associate with ex-felons unless otherwise approved.

____ 17. Assume responsibility for treatment cost (in conjunction with various agreements by treatment providers).

____ 18. Assume responsibility for treatment of victim's cost (in conjunction with orders by court and other appropriate sources).

____ 19. Submit to polygraph exams as requested or required.

____ 20. If required, pay for the cost of the polygraph exam.

RESIDENTIAL PLACEMENT

____ 1. In-house residential placement (i.e., halfway house)
  (a) No-leave policy unless under strict staff supervision or otherwise specified.
  (b) Must obey all rules and regulations of the halfway house.
  (c) Must pay any fees assigned.
  (d) Will volunteer services for the halfway house as needed or as requested in terms of restitution.

____ 2. Specific House Rules include:
  (a) Curfew
  (b) Privileges given under graduated fashion:
  1. restricted phone use unless otherwise approved (date _____ by _____)
  2. independent travel (approved by _____ date _____)
  3. house restrictions lifted (date _____ approved by _____)
  (c) Approved employment (date _____ location _____)
  (d) Check in and out system
  (e) Supervised movement
  (f) Unrestricted movement (approved by _____ date _____)

____ 3. Independent Living Status Approved (date _____)
  (a) Independent living with supervision (date _____)
  (b) Independent Living Status without supervision (date _____)

____ 4. Approved Employment (date _____ location _____)

____ 5. Submit to substance abuse test.

____ 6. Will not use alcohol and/or drugs unless medically prescribed.

MONITORING/SUPERVISION

____ 1. Surveillance
  ____ (a) electronic monitoring
  ____ (b) hidden observation
  ____ (c) interview by phone/personal contact
  ____ (d) collateral interviews

____ 2. Supervised travel
  ____ (a) check in and out system
  ____ (b) travel log (date, time, destination/place, miles, etc.)
  ____ (c) supervised travel with responsible individual

____ 3. Initially House Restriction for a _____ period of time.

____ 4. Curfew (_____)

____ 5. Maintain a daily journal as a form of self-monitoring.

TREATMENT PROGRAMME
____ 1. Sex Offender-Specific Treatment (Provider _____)
    ____ (a) group
    ____ (b) individual
    ____ (c) behavioural treatment
    ____ (d) medication treatment
____ 2. Sex Offender-Specific Assessment
    ____ (a) polygraph assessment
    ____ (b) plethysmograph assessment
    ____ (c) testing/inventories
    ____ (d) clinical interview
    ____ (e) record review
____ 3. Couple/Marital and Family Therapy
____ 4. Supportive Treatment
    ____ (a) Anabuse – unless medically contraindicated
    ____ (b) SA (Sex Anonymous) – (not recommended for chronic offenders)
    ____ (c) AA (Alcoholics Anonymous)
    ____ (d) NA (Narcotics Anonymous)
    ____ (e) other anonymous-based support _____
    ____ (f) substance abuse-specific treatment
    ____ (g) serotonin reuptake inhibitors
    ____ (h) other psychotropic medications
    ____ (i) Depo-Provera or other hormonal medications
____ 5. Sex Offender-Specific Treatment Requirements
    ____ (a) daily journal
    ____ (b) victimology
    ____ (c) autobiography or life history
    ____ (d) RP skills (i.e., identify cycle, triggers/risk factors, cues, interventions, etc.)
    ____ (e) future autobiography (projecting self into the future)
    ____ (f) cognitive/social restructuring
    ____ (g) behavioural treatment/covert techniques to reduce and control arousal
    ____ (h) psycho-educational modules _____
    ____ (l) Depo-Provera or other related medication _____
    ____ (j) psychotropic medications
    ____ (k) arousal control/psychotropic medications (serotonin reuptake inhibitors) _____
____ 6. Treatment Goals
    ____ (a) re-integrate offender back into society
    ____ (b) learn or enhance coping skills
    ____ (c) maintain victim empathy
    ____ (d) reduce deviant arousal and develop appropriate arousals
    ____ (e) enhance arousal control skills
    ____ (f) enhance interpersonal relationship skills
    ____ (g) enhance relapse intervention skills
    ____ (h) work on any type of core issues that emerge (but do not get sidetracked)
    ____ (i) further enhance responsibility levels
    ____ (j) further identify and change any type of cognitive distortions or dysfunctional thinking styles
    ____ (k) further enhance the identification of the deviant cycle along with interventions
    ____ (l) enhance stress management skills

Treatment Plan – Goals and Objectives

1. Goal: Attitude, responsibility, and motivational level toward recovery. (Recovery factors 1, 2, 3 and 13)

Objectives

A. Group attendance.
B. To actively participate in group.
C. To develop internal motivation toward recovery.
D. To develop a commitment toward treatment.
E. Complete task assignments (compliance).
F. Initiate and maintain journal or log.
G. Outline life history and/or autobiography.
H. Complete life history and/or autobiography.
I. Identify offence specific cognitive distortions.
J. To accept responsibility for offences.
K. Restructure offence distortions.
L. Identify global distortions.
M. Restructure global distortions.
N. To develop responsibility in general for one's behaviour.

2. Goal: Offender shows social interest in general care, concern, victim empathy and remorse. (Recovery factor 4)

Objectives

A. To develop a general care and concern for others, by consistently expressing concern for others.
B. To develop global empathy in general by consistently expressing understanding of others.
C. To develop empathy at intellectual levels for victims, i.e., can cognitively express understanding for victims.
D. To develop victim empathy for one's specific victims at an intellectual level.
E. To develop victim empathy for one's specific victims at an emotional level as defined by:
   1. Emotional Recognition
   2. Victim Harm Recognition
   3. Assuming Responsibility
   4. Perspective Taking
   5. Emotional Expression
F. To develop remorse (consistently expresses guilt or painful regret for violating victims).
G. To express empathy (consistently uses perspective taking skills).

3. Goal: Offender develops appropriate social relationships and skills. (Recovery factor 5)

Objectives

A. Learn specific social skills:
   1. Respect (doesn't discount)
   2. 'I' messages
   3. Eye contact
   4. Active listening skills
   5. Confrontation skills
   6. Initiating conversations
   7. Maintaining conversations

        8. Terminating conversations
        9. Conflict resolution/compromising skills
     10. Paraphrasing skills
     11. Summarising skills
     12. Other: _____
- B. To identify and resolve specific interpersonal issues:
      1. Power/control
      2. Possessiveness
      3. Jealousy
      4. Enmeshed boundaries
      5. Isolation/alienation
      6. Rejection
      7. Dependency
      8. Unstable relationships
      9. Other: _____
- C. Affective expression skills:
      1. Identify feelings
      2. Access and express feelings
- D. To develop appropriate close intimate relationships or attachments without sexual connotations:
      1. Engage in interpersonal relationships
      2. Develop appropriate relationships

4. Goal: Offender understands assault cycle concept and identifies his assault cycle. (Recovery factor 6)

Objectives
- A. Offender understands the assault cycle.
- B. Offender applies the assault cycle concept.
- C. Offender identifies his assault cycle:
      1. Offender identifies basic 3-stage cycle
      2. Offender identifies 4-stage cycle
      3. Offender identifies 6-stage cycle

5. Goal: Offender displays target specific lifestyle characteristics. (Recovery factor 7)

- A. Antisocial behavioural characteristics/patterns.
      1. Exploitation (takes advantage of others)
      2. Lies (purposefully and wholly untruthful statements) or distorts information (through omission, adding facts, or embellishments)
      3. Deceives others (deliberate concealing/hiding the truth: intentionally misleading; secrecy)
      4. Current display of destructive and sadistic behaviour or cruelty
- B. Narcissistic behavioural characteristics/patterns that need changing:
      1. Attitude of superiority
      2. Brags, exaggerates, and exhibits grandiose behaviours
      3. Exaggerated sense of self-importance
      4. Distorted sense of entitlement, unrealistic expectations/demands
      5. Self-centred (out for self)
- C. Borderline behavioural characteristics/patterns that need changing.
      1. Seeks immediate gratification and/or poor impulse control (especially in sexual behaviour and substance abuse)
      2. Repeated suicidal ideation/threats/gestures/attempts
      3. Emotionally unstable (marked intense moodiness with mood shifts)

6. Goal: Offender displays insight into development/motivational dynamics and including sexual identity issues. (Recovery factors 8, 9, 10)

Objectives

A. Identify key developmental events (perceptions) that contribute to sex offending dynamics and increase autonomy/independence lifestyle.
B. Identify key motivational factors.
C. Resolve key changing one's perceptions of those developmental events and/or traumas.
D. Identify sexual identity issues.
E. Resolve any key motivational dynamics or core issues that feed the offending process. Specifics include:
    1. Insecurity
    2. Rejection/acceptance
    3. Abandonment
    4. Manhood issues
    5. Inferiority
    6. Low self-worth
    7. Other: _____

7. Goal: Offender will control his deviant behaviour. (Recovery factor 11)

Objectives

A. Assess and identify deviant arousal patterns:
    ____ child (m/f) _____ adol. (m/f)
    ____ adult (m/f) _____ other
B. Track deviant urges/fantasies (self-report).
C. Reduce deviant arousal patterns.
D. Develop self-management arousal control skills.
E. Develop appropriate arousal/fantasies.
F. Reduce excessive masturbation.
G. Eliminate self-abusive sexual behaviour.

8. Goal: Reduce and manage offender's psycho-pathology. (Recovery factor 12)

Objectives

A. Identify any psychopathologies.
B. Resolve any/or reduce specified pathologies of: _____

9. Goal: Offender will develop and understand relapse intervention model, process and skills. (Recovery factor 14)

Objectives

A. Understand relapse prevention/intervention models and related concepts.
B. Identify assault cycle/relapse process.
C. Identify triggers/risk factors (high/low).
D. Identify relapse cues.
E. Identifying dysfunctional coping patterns (maladaptive coping response) and/or automatic relapse intervention responses.
F. Develop functional coping (adaptive coping response).
G. Identify lapse behaviours.

10. Goal: Offender will develop appropriate self-structure, self-esteem, self-image, self-confidence, self-worth, and self-control based on non-deviant/victimising behaviours. (Recovery factor 15)

Objectives

- A. Identify patterns of dynamics ('old me' identities) involving poor self-concept constructs including: worth, image, inferiority, esteem, confidence, security, etc., that leads to compensation via offending.
- B. Identify underlying perceptions and related key core beliefs of 'old me' pattern.
- C. Defuse dysfunctional patterns of 'old me' via cognitive restructuring and cognitive behavioural experiential approaches.
- D. Develop an appropriate worth and self-concept or self-structure.

Recovery factors

1. Motivation toward recovery
2. Commitment toward recovery
3. Personal responsibility
4. Social interest (victim empathy)
5. Social dimensions
6. Assault cycle
7. Lifestyle behaviour
8. Insight into developmental/motivational dynamics
9. Resolution of developmental/motivational dynamics
10. Sexual identity
11. Arousal control
12. Psychopathology
13. Disowning behaviours
14. RP/Relapse intervention skills
15. Self structure

References

Carich M S and Lampley M C (1999) Recovery Assessments with Young People who Sexually Abuse. In Calder M (Ed.) *Working with Young People Who Sexually Abuse: New Pieces of the Jigsaw Puzzle.* Lyme Regis, Dorset: Russell House Publishing.

Carich M S (1999) Evaluation of Recovery: 15 Common Factors or Elements In Calder M (Ed.) *Assessing Risk in Adult Males Who Sexually Abuse Children.* Lyme Regis, Dorset: Russell House Publishing.

Carich M S (1997) Toward the Concept of Recovery in Sex Offenders. *The Forum.* 9: 2, 10–11.

Metzger C and Carich M S (1999) An Overview of the Eleven Point Treatment Plan. In Calder M (Ed.) *Assessing Risk in Adult Males Who Sexually Abuse Children.* Lyme Regis, Dorset: Russell House Publishing.

Metzger C and Carich M S (1999) Eleven Point Comprehensive Sex Offender Treatment Plan. In Calder M (Ed.) *Assessing Risk in Adult Males Who Sexually Abuse Children.* Lyme Regis, Dorset: Russell House Publishing.